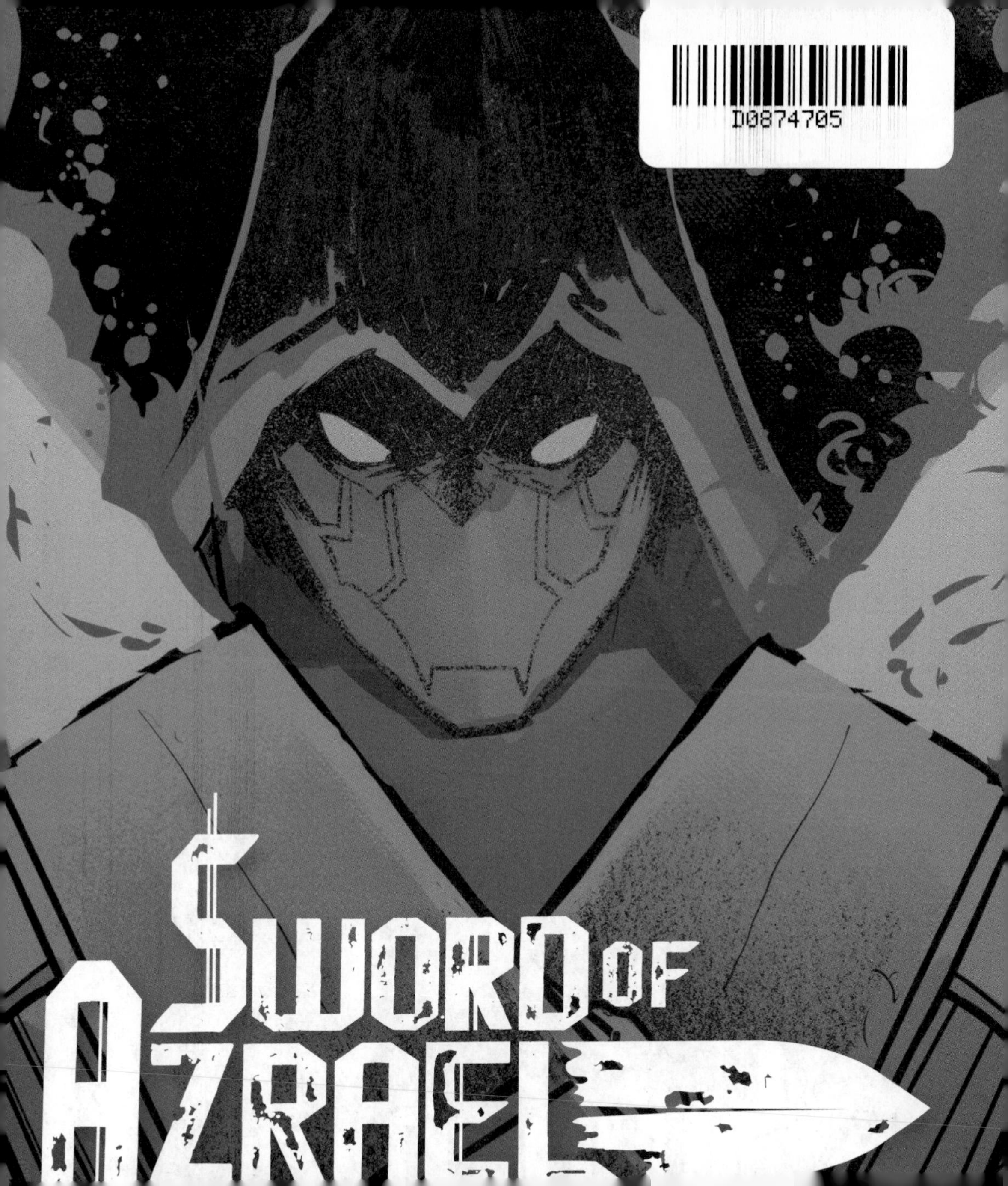
SWORD OF AZRAEL

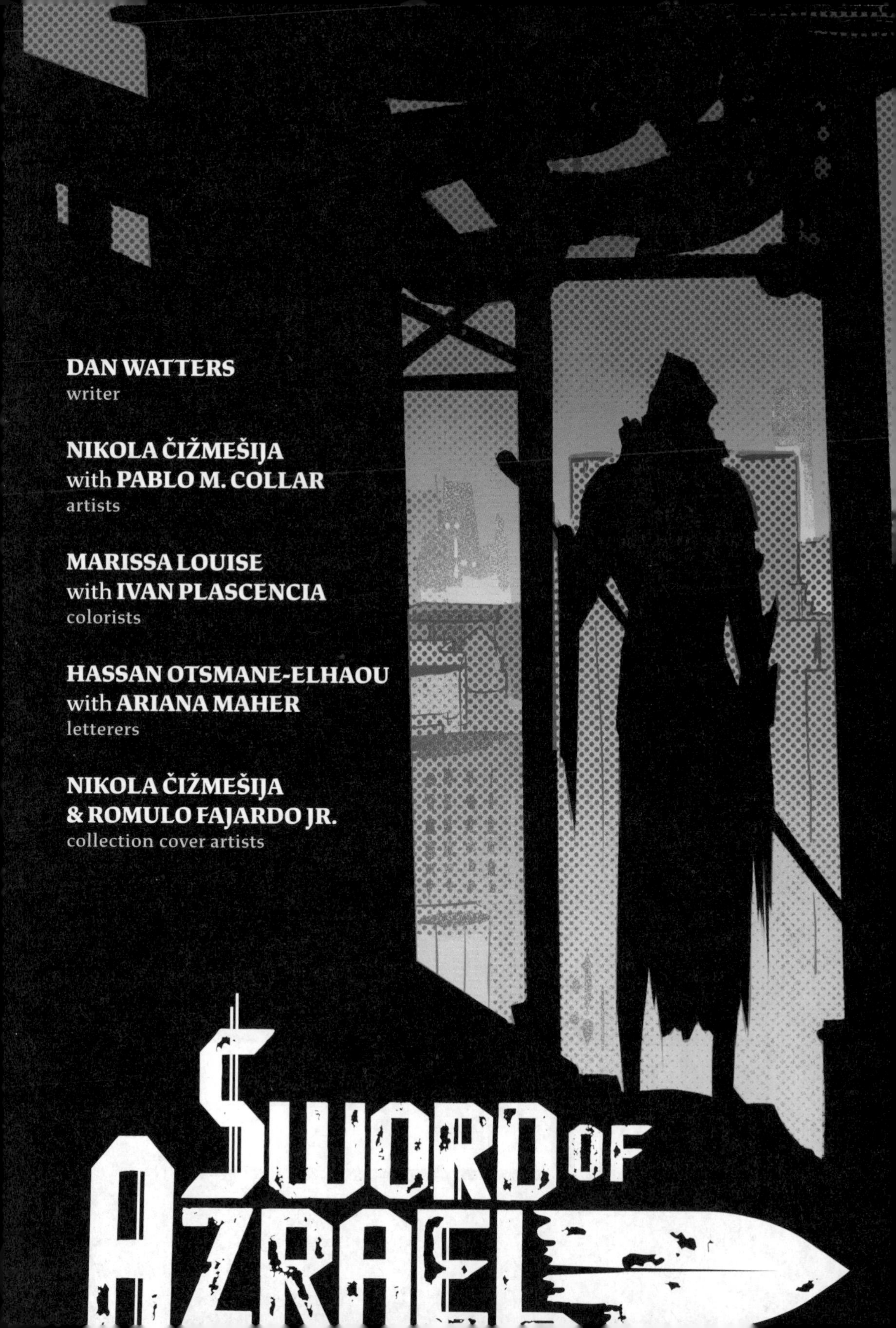

DAN WATTERS
writer

NIKOLA ČIŽMEŠIJA
with **PABLO M. COLLAR**
artists

MARISSA LOUISE
with **IVAN PLASCENCIA**
colorists

HASSAN OTSMANE-ELHAOU
with **ARIANA MAHER**
letterers

NIKOLA ČIŽMEŠIJA
& ROMULO FAJARDO JR.
collection cover artists

SWORD OF AZRAEL

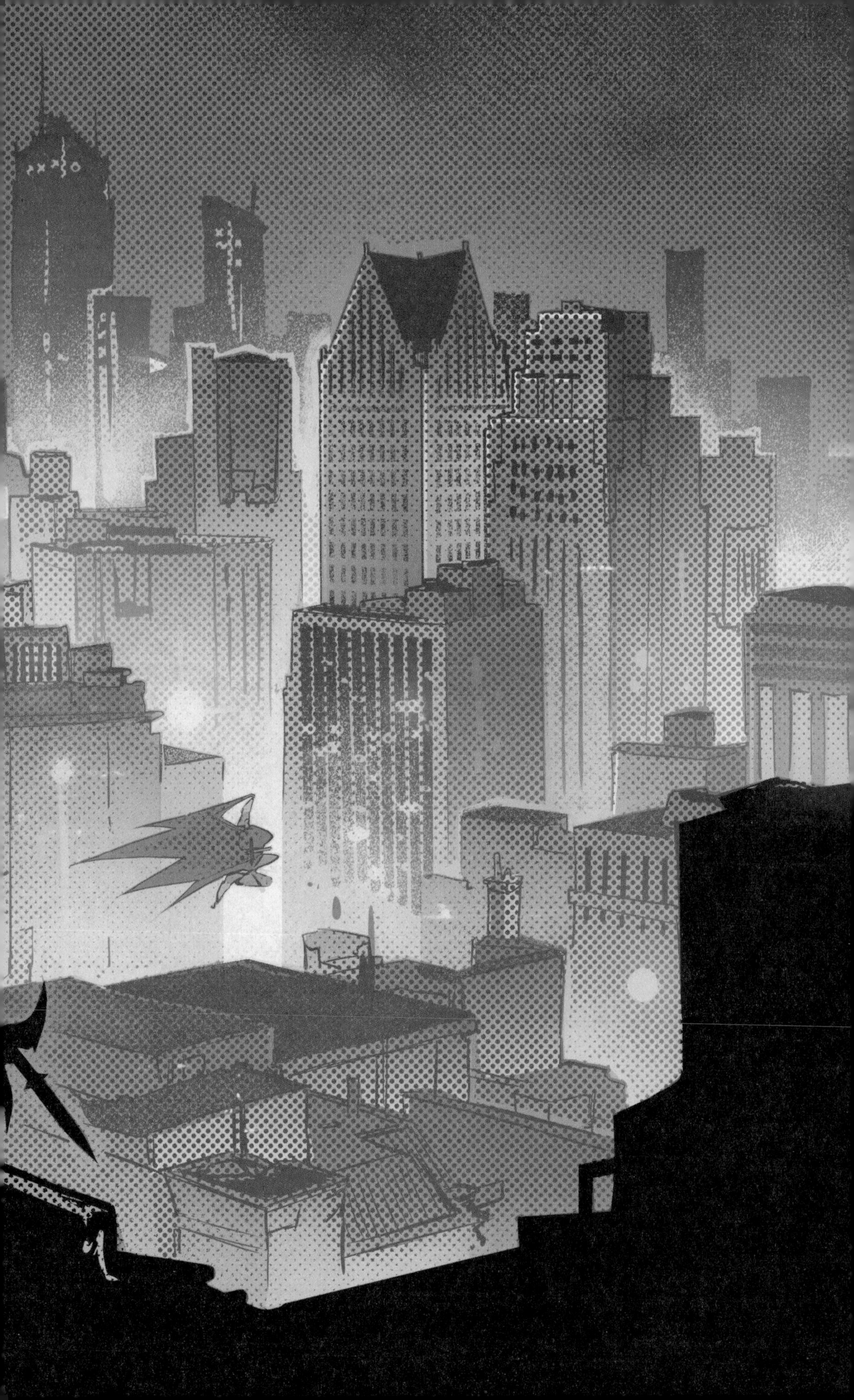

Arianna Turturro, Dave Wielgosz Editors – Original Series & Collected Edition
Steve Cook Design Director – Books
Megen Bellersen Publication Design
Danielle Ramondelli Publication Production

Marie Javins Editor-in-Chief, DC Comics

Anne DePies Senior VP – General Manager
Jim Lee Publisher & Chief Creative Officer
Don Falletti VP – Manufacturing Operations & Workflow Management
Lawrence Ganem VP – Talent Services
Alison Gill Senior VP – Manufacturing & Operations
Jeffrey Kaufman VP – Editorial Strategy & Programming
Nick J. Napolitano VP – Manufacturing Administration & Design
Nancy Spears VP – Revenue

SWORD OF AZRAEL

DC Comics, 4000 Warner Blvd., Bldg. 700, 2nd Floor, Burbank, CA 91522
Printed by Solisco Printers, Scott, QC, Canada. 5/19/23. First Printing.
ISBN: 978-1-77952-036-4

Library of Congress Cataloging-in-Publication Data is available.

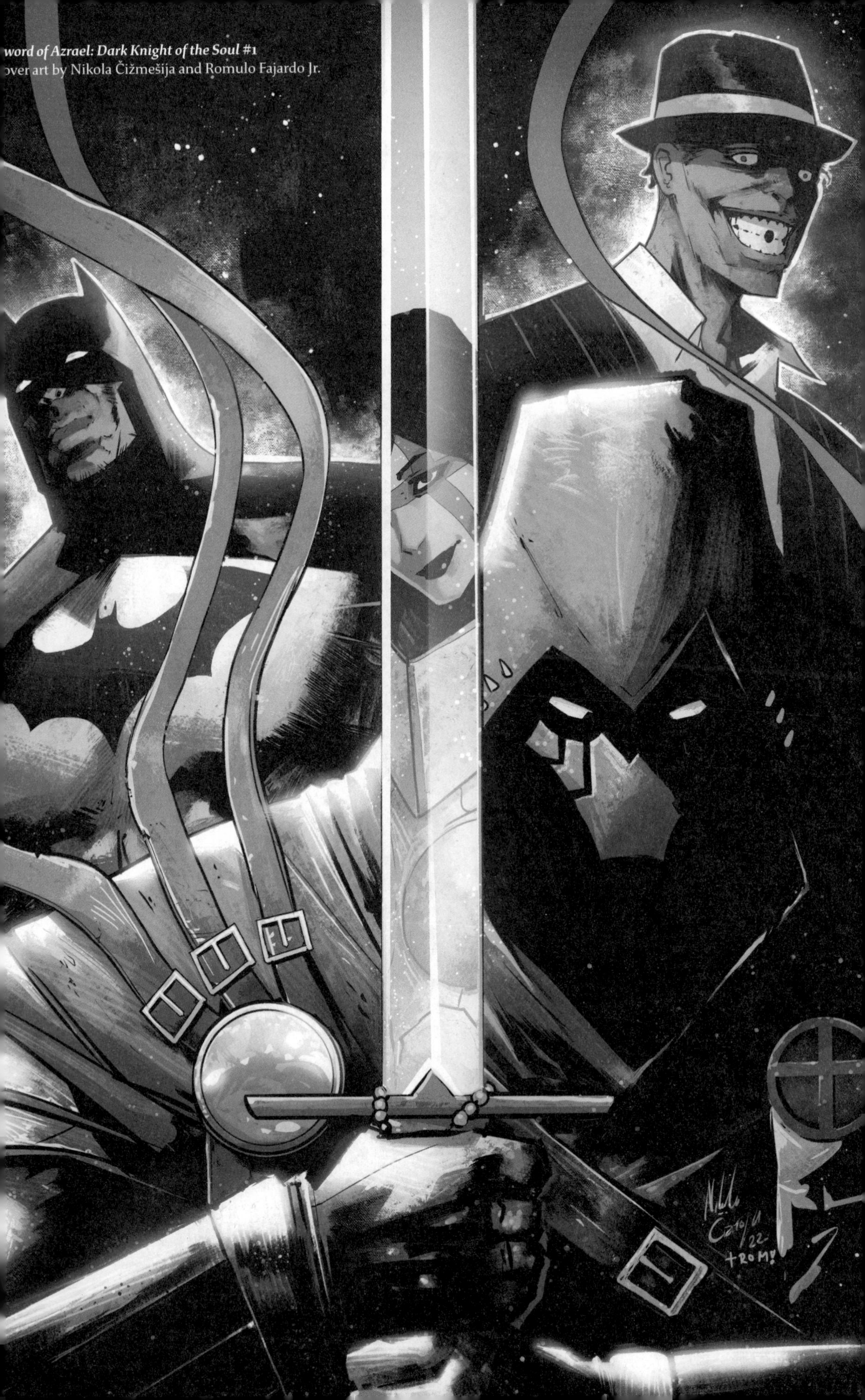

word of Azrael: Dark Knight of the Soul #1
over art by Nikola Čižmešija and Romulo Fajardo Jr.

Sword of Azrael: Dark Knight of the Soul #1
variant cover art by Juni Ba

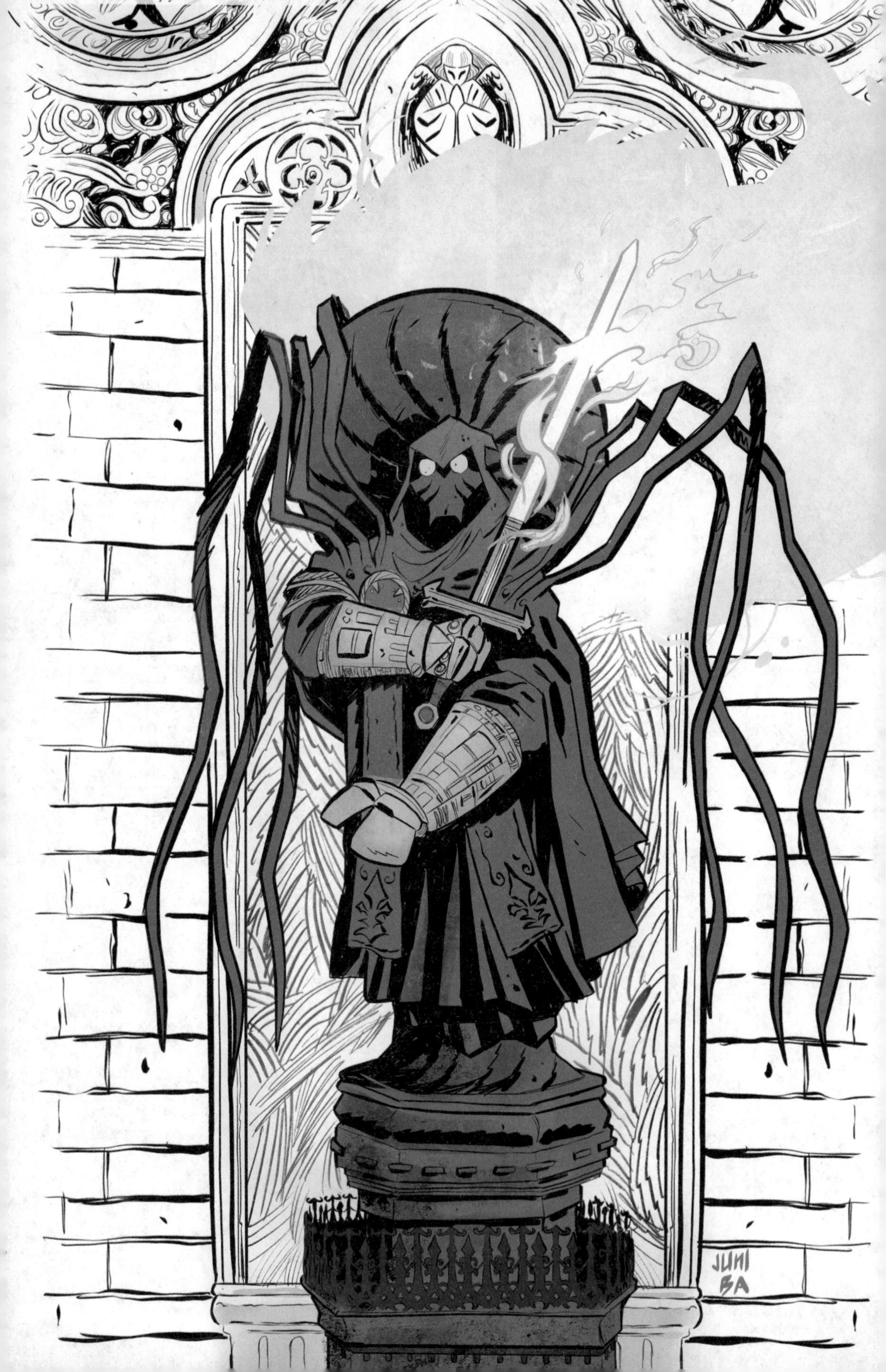
JUNI
BA

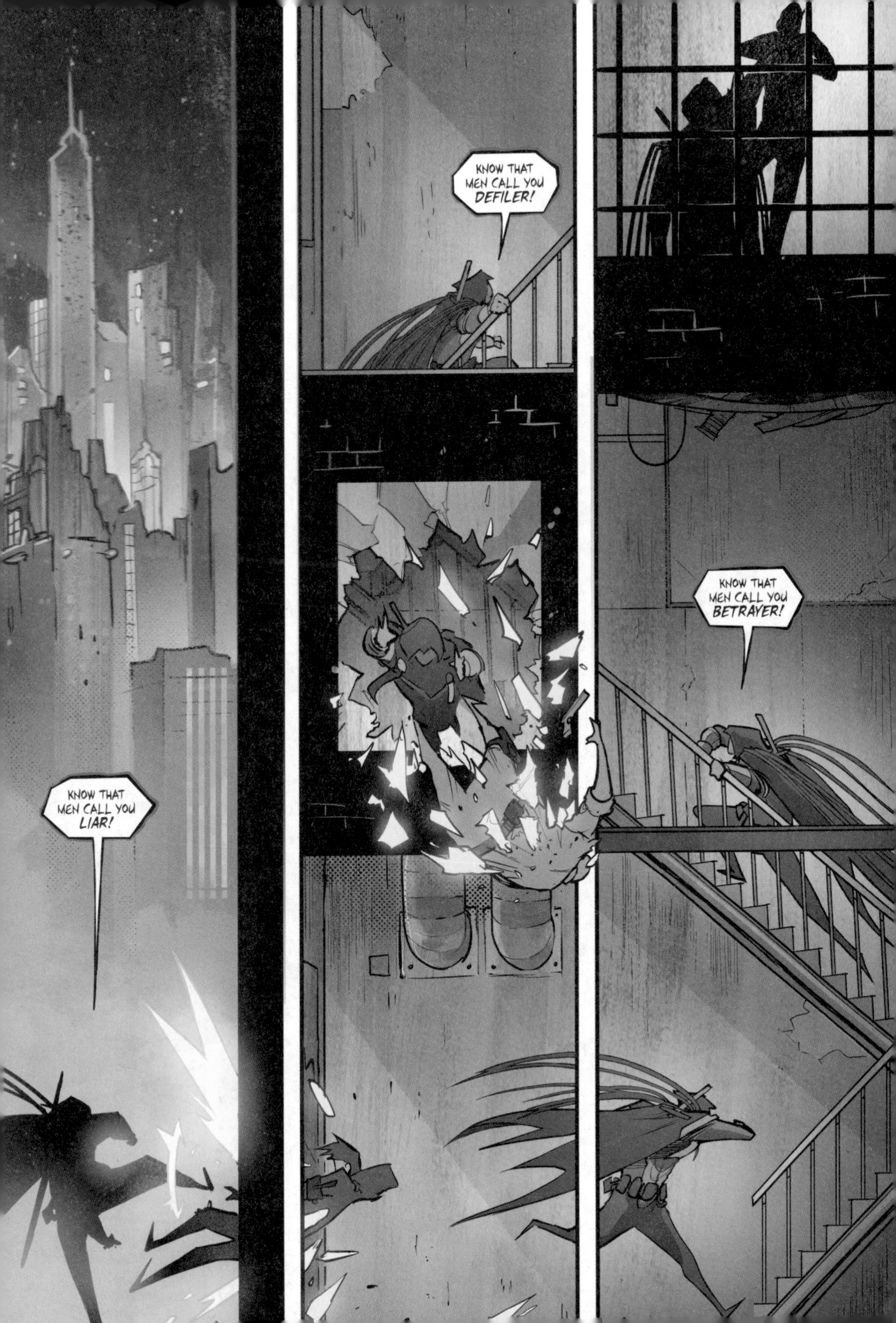
KNOW THAT MEN CALL YOU LIAR!
KNOW THAT MEN CALL YOU DEFILER!
KNOW THAT MEN CALL YOU BETRAYER!

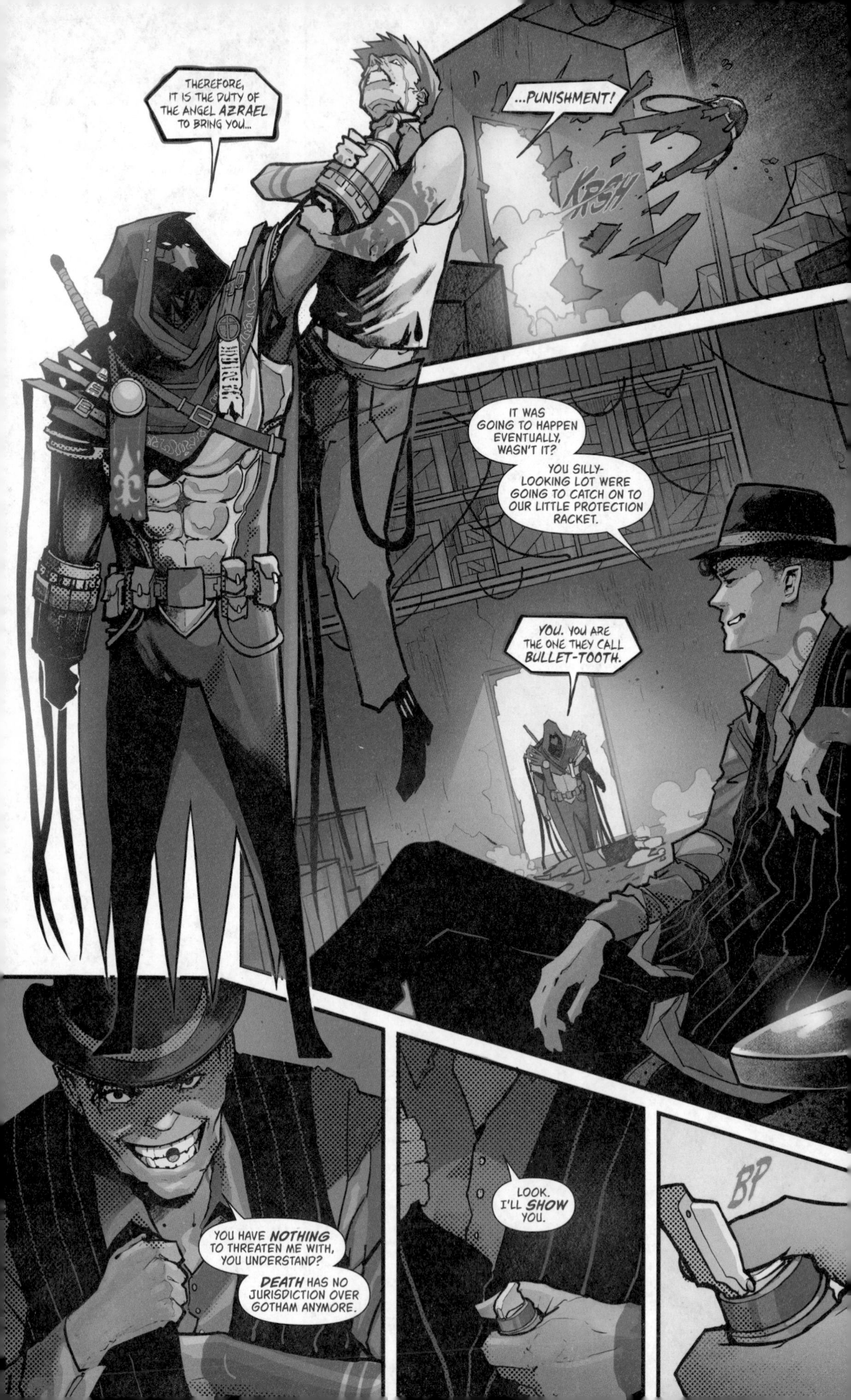

THEREFORE, IT IS THE DUTY OF THE ANGEL AZRAEL TO BRING YOU...
...PUNISHMENT!
KRSH
IT WAS GOING TO HAPPEN EVENTUALLY, WASN'T IT?
YOU SILLY-LOOKING LOT WERE GOING TO CATCH ON TO OUR LITTLE PROTECTION RACKET.
YOU. YOU ARE THE ONE THEY CALL BULLET-TOOTH.
YOU HAVE NOTHING TO THREATEN ME WITH, YOU UNDERSTAND?
DEATH HAS NO JURISDICTION OVER GOTHAM ANYMORE.
LOOK. I'LL SHOW YOU.
BP

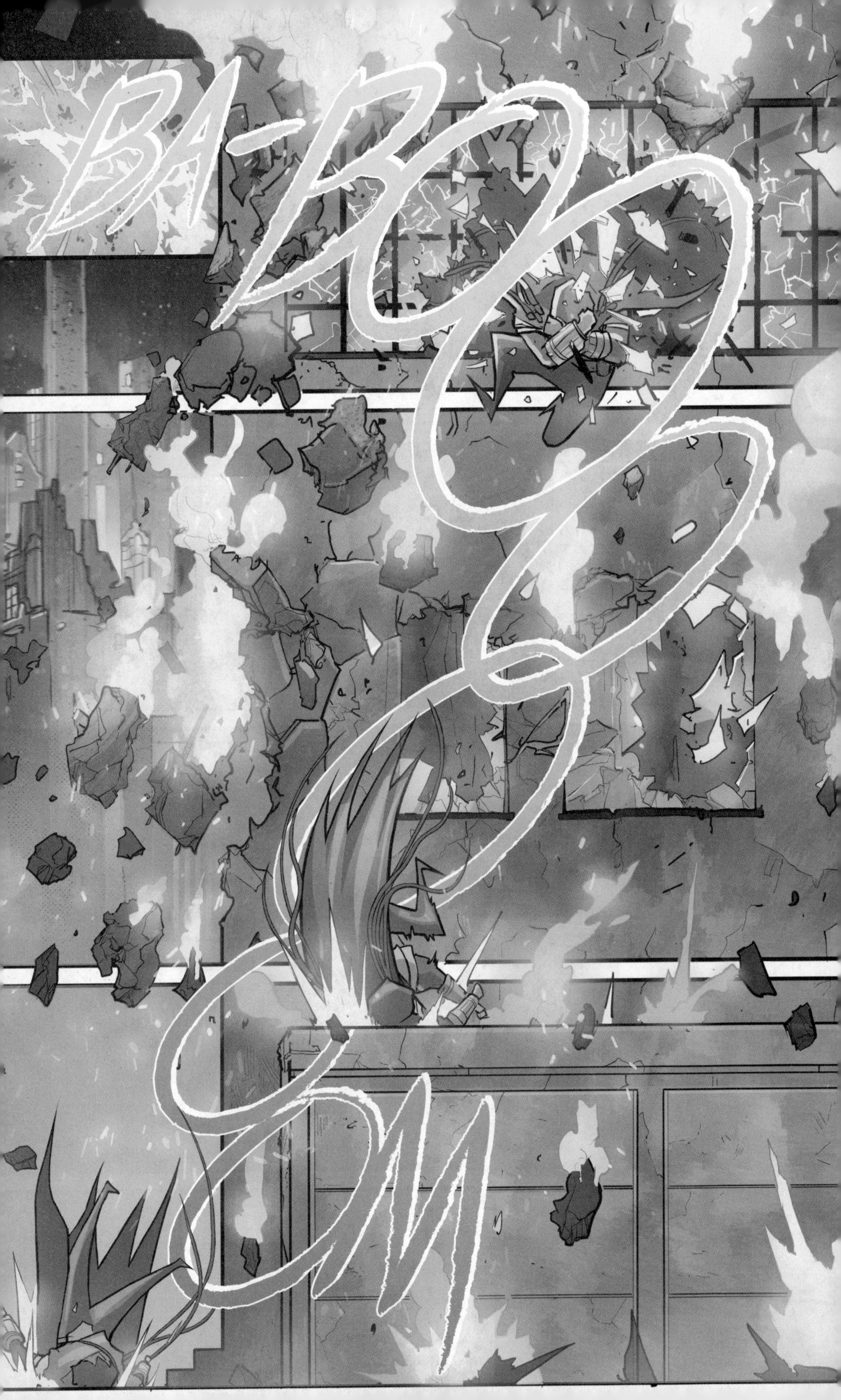
BA-BOOOOOM

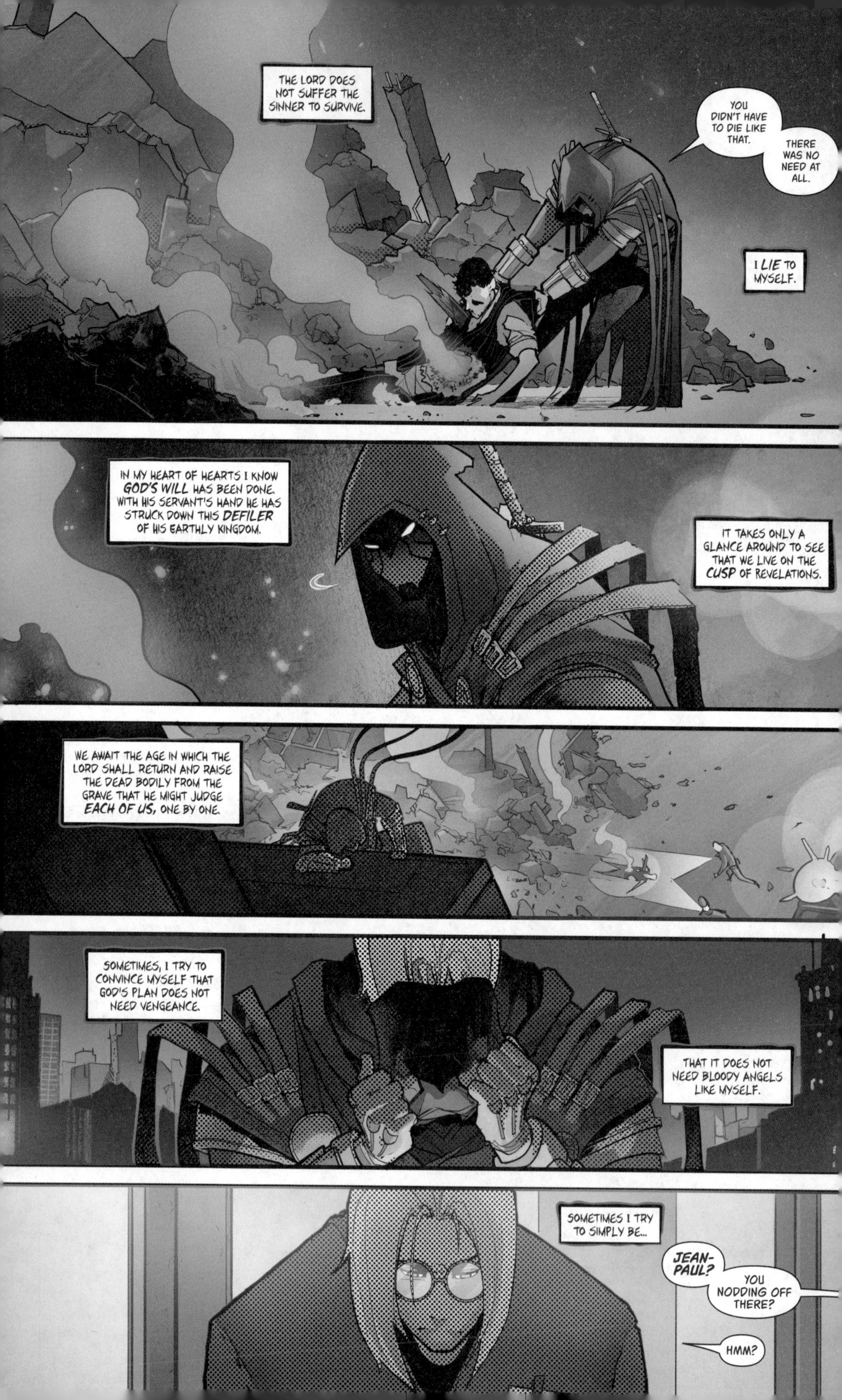
THE LORD DOES NOT SUFFER THE SINNER TO SURVIVE.
YOU DIDN'T HAVE TO DIE LIKE THAT.
THERE WAS NO NEED AT ALL.
I LIE TO MYSELF.
IN MY HEART OF HEARTS I KNOW GOD'S WILL HAS BEEN DONE. WITH HIS SERVANT'S HAND HE HAS STRUCK DOWN THIS DEFILER OF HIS EARTHLY KINGDOM.
IT TAKES ONLY A GLANCE AROUND TO SEE THAT WE LIVE ON THE CUSP OF REVELATIONS.
WE AWAIT THE AGE IN WHICH THE LORD SHALL RETURN AND RAISE THE DEAD BODILY FROM THE GRAVE THAT HE MIGHT JUDGE EACH OF US, ONE BY ONE.
SOMETIMES, I TRY TO CONVINCE MYSELF THAT GOD'S PLAN DOES NOT NEED VENGEANCE.
THAT IT DOES NOT NEED BLOODY ANGELS LIKE MYSELF.
SOMETIMES I TRY TO SIMPLY BE...
JEAN-PAUL?
YOU NODDING OFF THERE?
HMM?

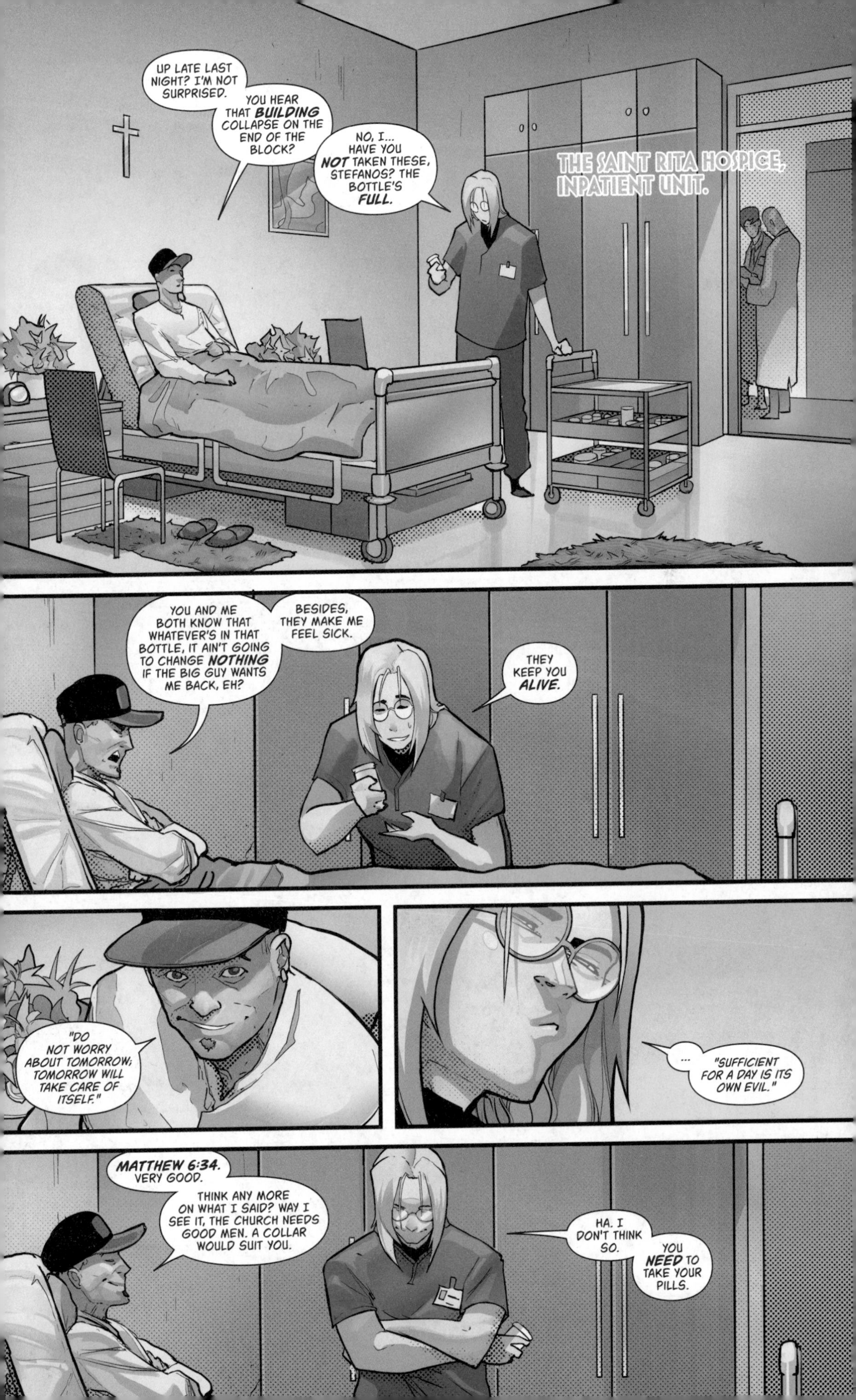
UP LATE LAST NIGHT? I'M NOT SURPRISED.
YOU HEAR THAT BUILDING COLLAPSE ON THE END OF THE BLOCK?
NO, I... HAVE YOU NOT TAKEN THESE, STEFANOS? THE BOTTLE'S FULL.
THE SAINT RITA HOSPICE, INPATIENT UNIT.
YOU AND ME BOTH KNOW THAT WHATEVER'S IN THAT BOTTLE, IT AIN'T GOING TO CHANGE NOTHING IF THE BIG GUY WANTS ME BACK, EH?
BESIDES, THEY MAKE ME FEEL SICK.
THEY KEEP YOU ALIVE.
"DO NOT WORRY ABOUT TOMORROW; TOMORROW WILL TAKE CARE OF ITSELF."
... "SUFFICIENT FOR A DAY IS ITS OWN EVIL."
MATTHEW 6:34. VERY GOOD.
THINK ANY MORE ON WHAT I SAID? WAY I SEE IT, THE CHURCH NEEDS GOOD MEN. A COLLAR WOULD SUIT YOU.
HA. I DON'T THINK SO.
YOU NEED TO TAKE YOUR PILLS.

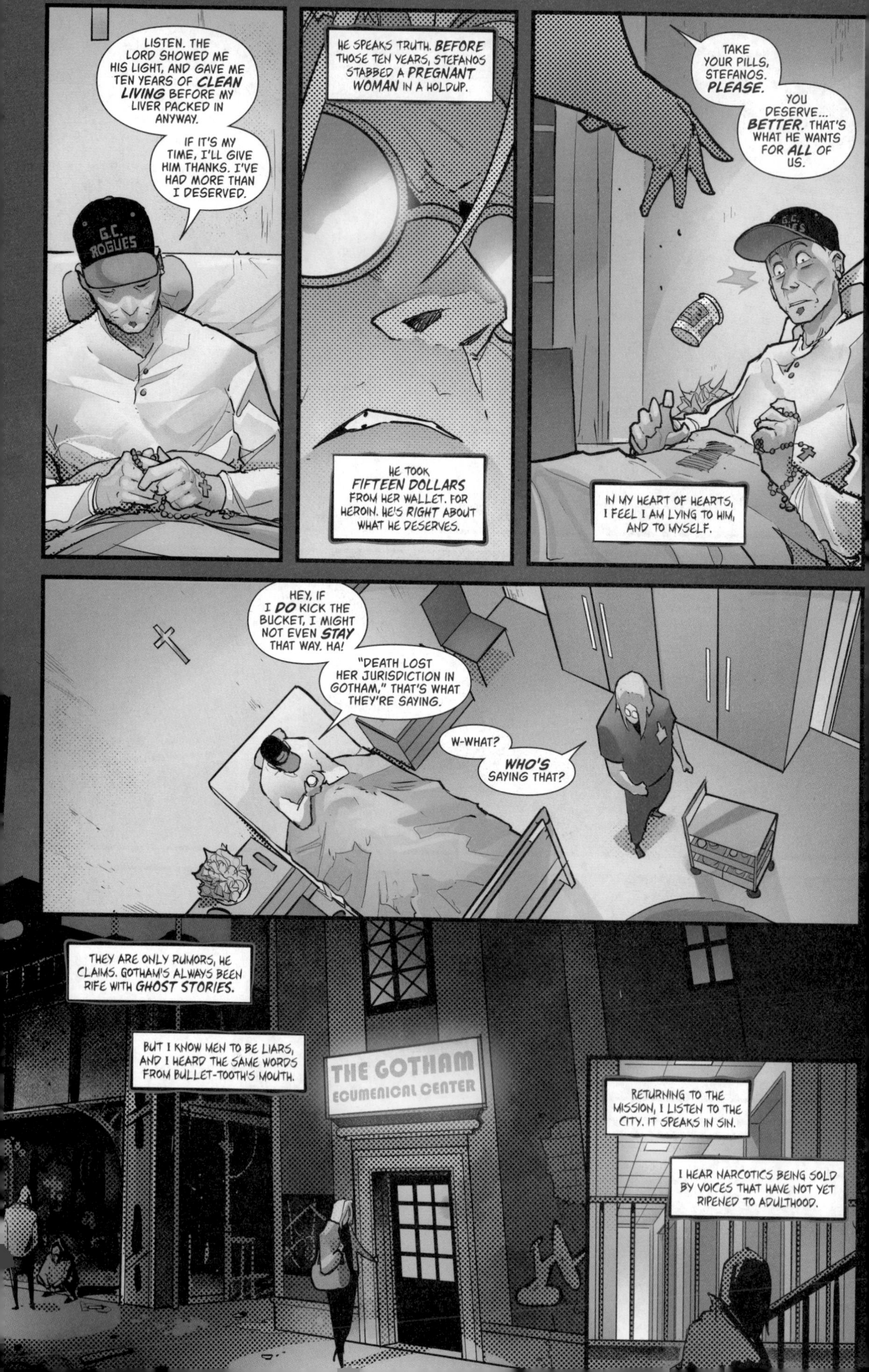
LISTEN. THE LORD SHOWED ME HIS LIGHT, AND GAVE ME TEN YEARS OF CLEAN LIVING BEFORE MY LIVER PACKED IN ANYWAY.
IF IT'S MY TIME, I'LL GIVE HIM THANKS. I'VE HAD MORE THAN I DESERVED.
G.C. ROGUES
HE SPEAKS TRUTH. BEFORE THOSE TEN YEARS, STEFANOS STABBED A PREGNANT WOMAN IN A HOLDUP.
HE TOOK FIFTEEN DOLLARS FROM HER WALLET. FOR HEROIN. HE'S RIGHT ABOUT WHAT HE DESERVES.
TAKE YOUR PILLS, STEFANOS. PLEASE.
YOU DESERVE... BETTER. THAT'S WHAT HE WANTS FOR ALL OF US.
IN MY HEART OF HEARTS, I FEEL I AM LYING TO HIM, AND TO MYSELF.
HEY, IF I DO KICK THE BUCKET, I MIGHT NOT EVEN STAY THAT WAY. HA!
"DEATH LOST HER JURISDICTION IN GOTHAM," THAT'S WHAT THEY'RE SAYING.
W-WHAT?
WHO'S SAYING THAT?
THEY ARE ONLY RUMORS, HE CLAIMS. GOTHAM'S ALWAYS BEEN RIFE WITH GHOST STORIES.
BUT I KNOW MEN TO BE LIARS, AND I HEARD THE SAME WORDS FROM BULLET-TOOTH'S MOUTH.
THE GOTHAM ECUMENICAL CENTER
RETURNING TO THE MISSION, I LISTEN TO THE CITY. IT SPEAKS IN SIN.
I HEAR NARCOTICS BEING SOLD BY VOICES THAT HAVE NOT YET RIPENED TO ADULTHOOD.

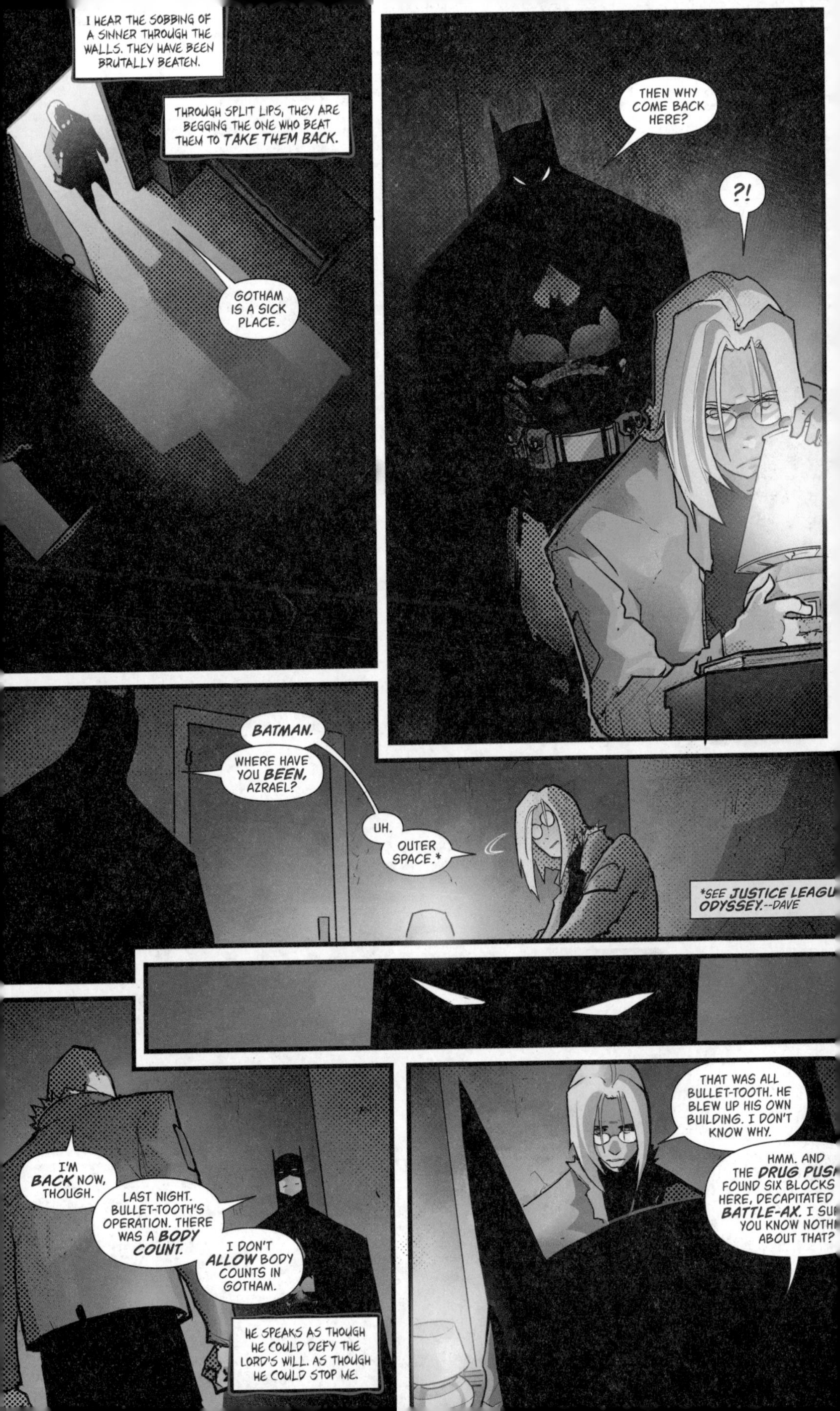
I HEAR THE SOBBING OF A SINNER THROUGH THE WALLS. THEY HAVE BEEN BRUTALLY BEATEN.
THROUGH SPLIT LIPS, THEY ARE BEGGING THE ONE WHO BEAT THEM TO TAKE THEM BACK.
GOTHAM IS A SICK PLACE.
THEN WHY COME BACK HERE?
?!
BATMAN.
WHERE HAVE YOU BEEN, AZRAEL?
UH.
OUTER SPACE.*
*SEE JUSTICE LEAGU
ODYSSEY.--DAVE
I'M BACK NOW, THOUGH.
LAST NIGHT. BULLET-TOOTH'S OPERATION. THERE WAS A BODY COUNT.
I DON'T ALLOW BODY COUNTS IN GOTHAM.
HE SPEAKS AS THOUGH HE COULD DEFY THE LORD'S WILL. AS THOUGH HE COULD STOP ME.
THAT WAS ALL BULLET-TOOTH. HE BLEW UP HIS OWN BUILDING. I DON'T KNOW WHY.
HMM. AND THE DRUG PUS
FOUND SIX BLOCKS
HERE, DECAPITATED
BATTLE-AX. I SU
YOU KNOW NOTH
ABOUT THAT?

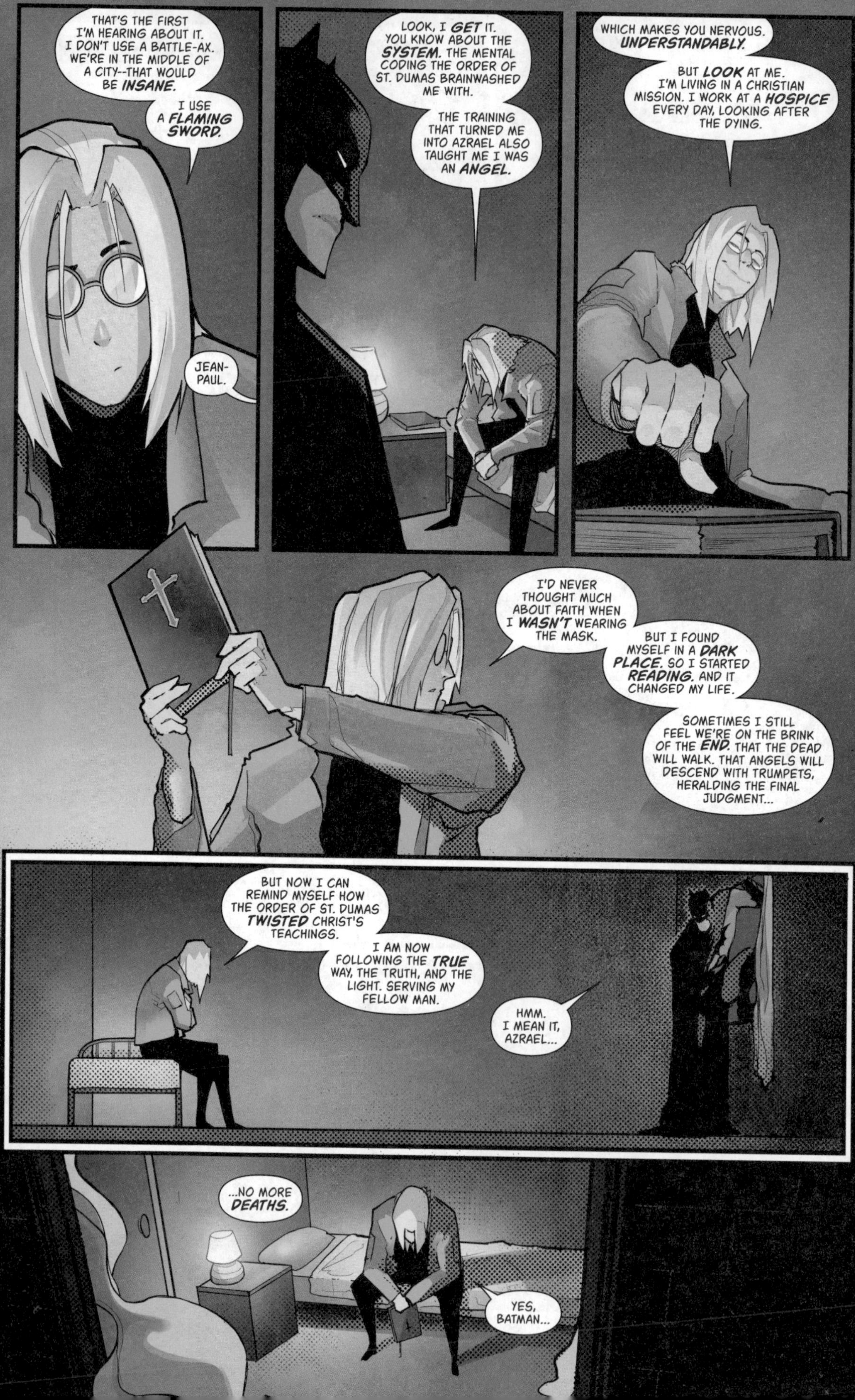
THAT'S THE FIRST I'M HEARING ABOUT IT. I DON'T USE A BATTLE-AX. WE'RE IN THE MIDDLE OF A CITY--THAT WOULD BE INSANE.
I USE A FLAMING SWORD.
JEAN-PAUL.
LOOK, I GET IT. YOU KNOW ABOUT THE SYSTEM. THE MENTAL CODING THE ORDER OF ST. DUMAS BRAINWASHED ME WITH.
THE TRAINING THAT TURNED ME INTO AZRAEL ALSO TAUGHT ME I WAS AN ANGEL.
WHICH MAKES YOU NERVOUS. UNDERSTANDABLY.
BUT LOOK AT ME. I'M LIVING IN A CHRISTIAN MISSION. I WORK AT A HOSPICE EVERY DAY, LOOKING AFTER THE DYING.
I'D NEVER THOUGHT MUCH ABOUT FAITH WHEN I WASN'T WEARING THE MASK.
BUT I FOUND MYSELF IN A DARK PLACE. SO I STARTED READING. AND IT CHANGED MY LIFE.
SOMETIMES I STILL FEEL WE'RE ON THE BRINK OF THE END. THAT THE DEAD WILL WALK. THAT ANGELS WILL DESCEND WITH TRUMPETS, HERALDING THE FINAL JUDGMENT...
BUT NOW I CAN REMIND MYSELF HOW THE ORDER OF ST. DUMAS TWISTED CHRIST'S TEACHINGS.
I AM NOW FOLLOWING THE TRUE WAY, THE TRUTH, AND THE LIGHT. SERVING MY FELLOW MAN.
HMM. I MEAN IT, AZRAEL...
...NO MORE DEATHS.
YES, BATMAN...

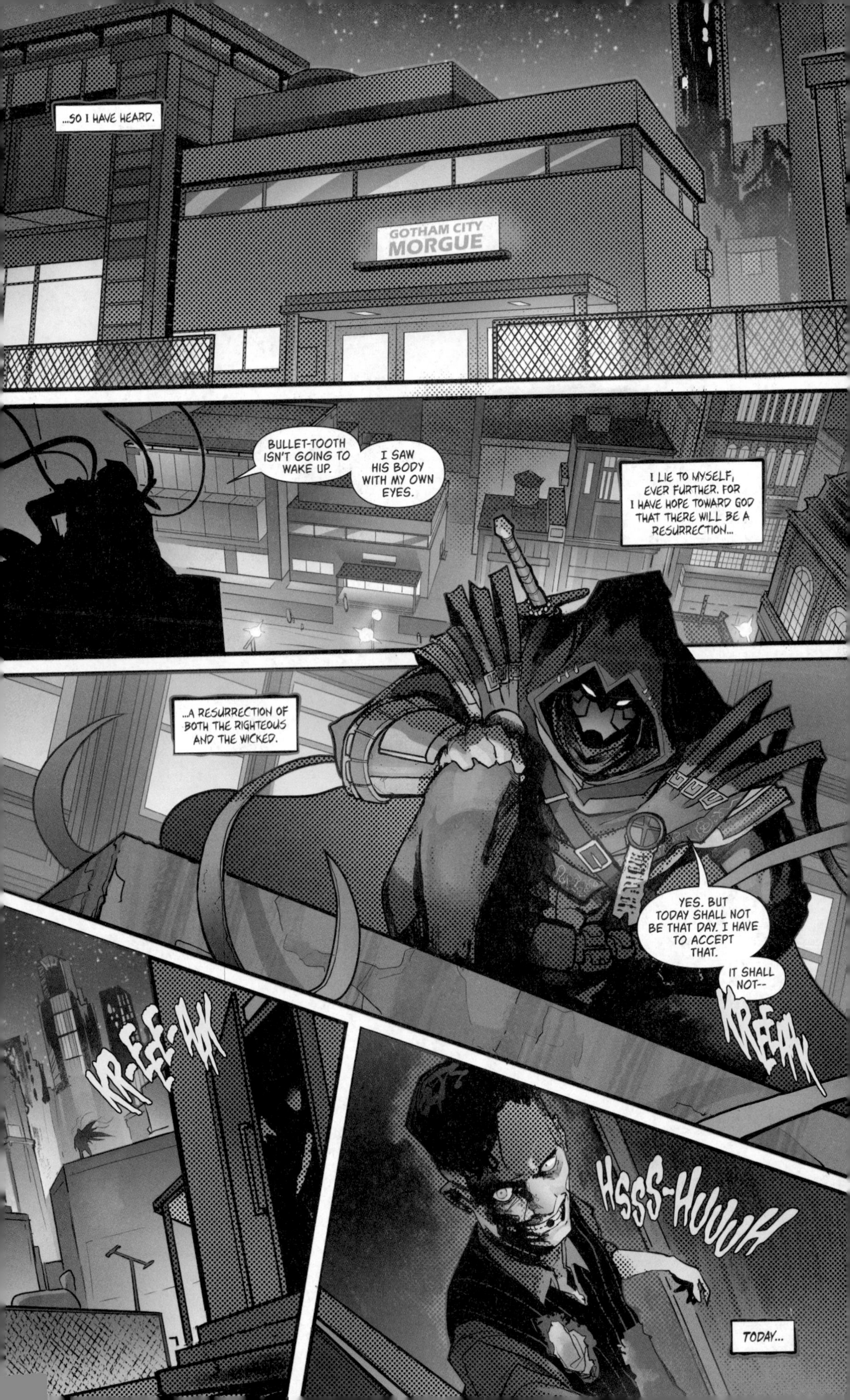
...SO I HAVE HEARD.
GOTHAM CITY MORGUE
BULLET-TOOTH ISN'T GOING TO WAKE UP.
I SAW HIS BODY WITH MY OWN EYES.
I LIE TO MYSELF, EVER FURTHER. FOR I HAVE HOPE TOWARD GOD THAT THERE WILL BE A RESURRECTION...
...A RESURRECTION OF BOTH THE RIGHTEOUS AND THE WICKED.
YES. BUT TODAY SHALL NOT BE THAT DAY. I HAVE TO ACCEPT THAT.
IT SHALL NOT--
KREEAK
KR-EE-AK
HSSS-HUUUH
TODAY...

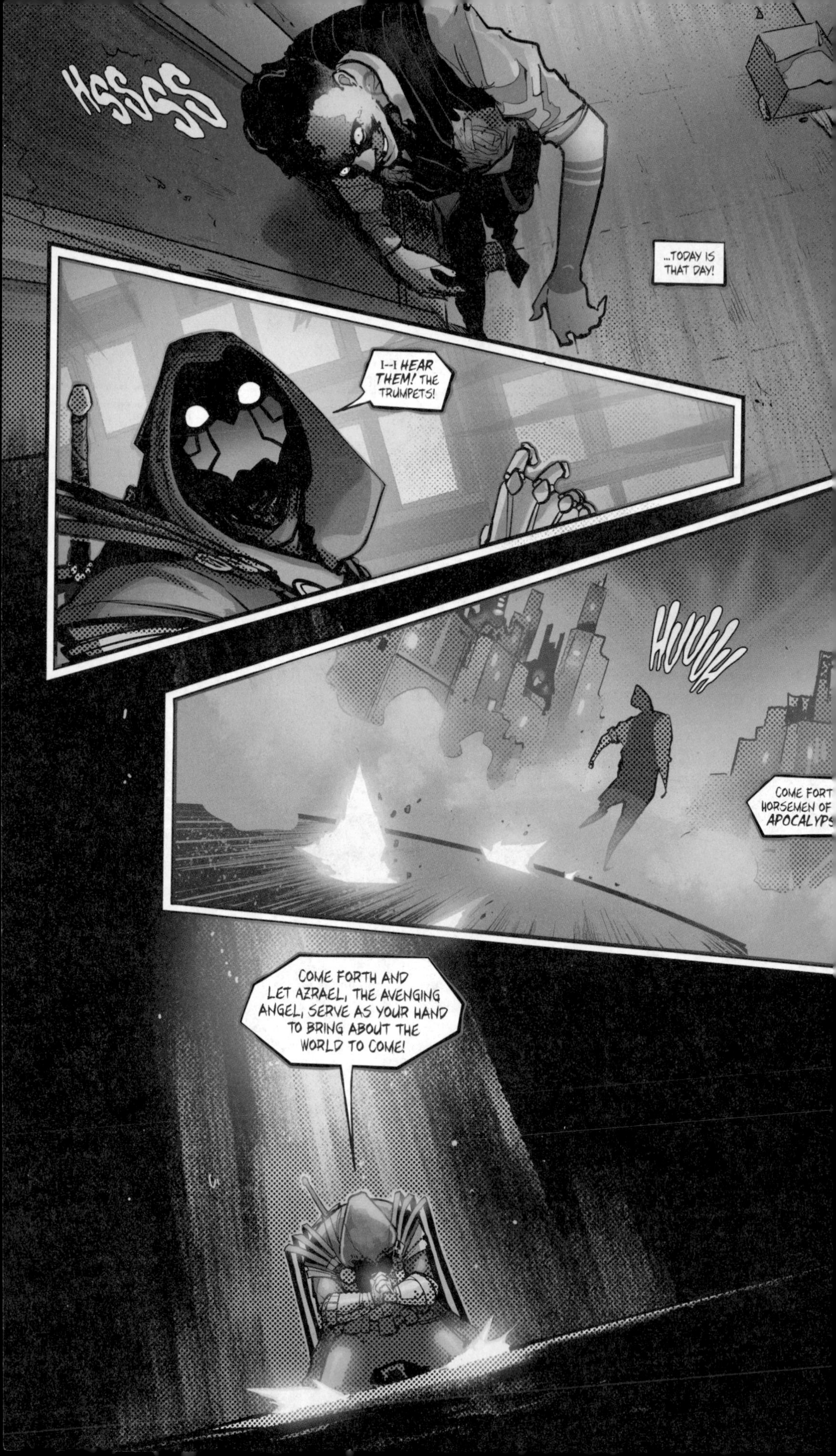
HSSSS
...TODAY IS THAT DAY!
I--I HEAR THEM! THE TRUMPETS!
COME FORT HORSEMEN OF APOCALYPS
COME FORTH AND LET AZRAEL, THE AVENGING ANGEL, SERVE AS YOUR HAND TO BRING ABOUT THE WORLD TO COME!

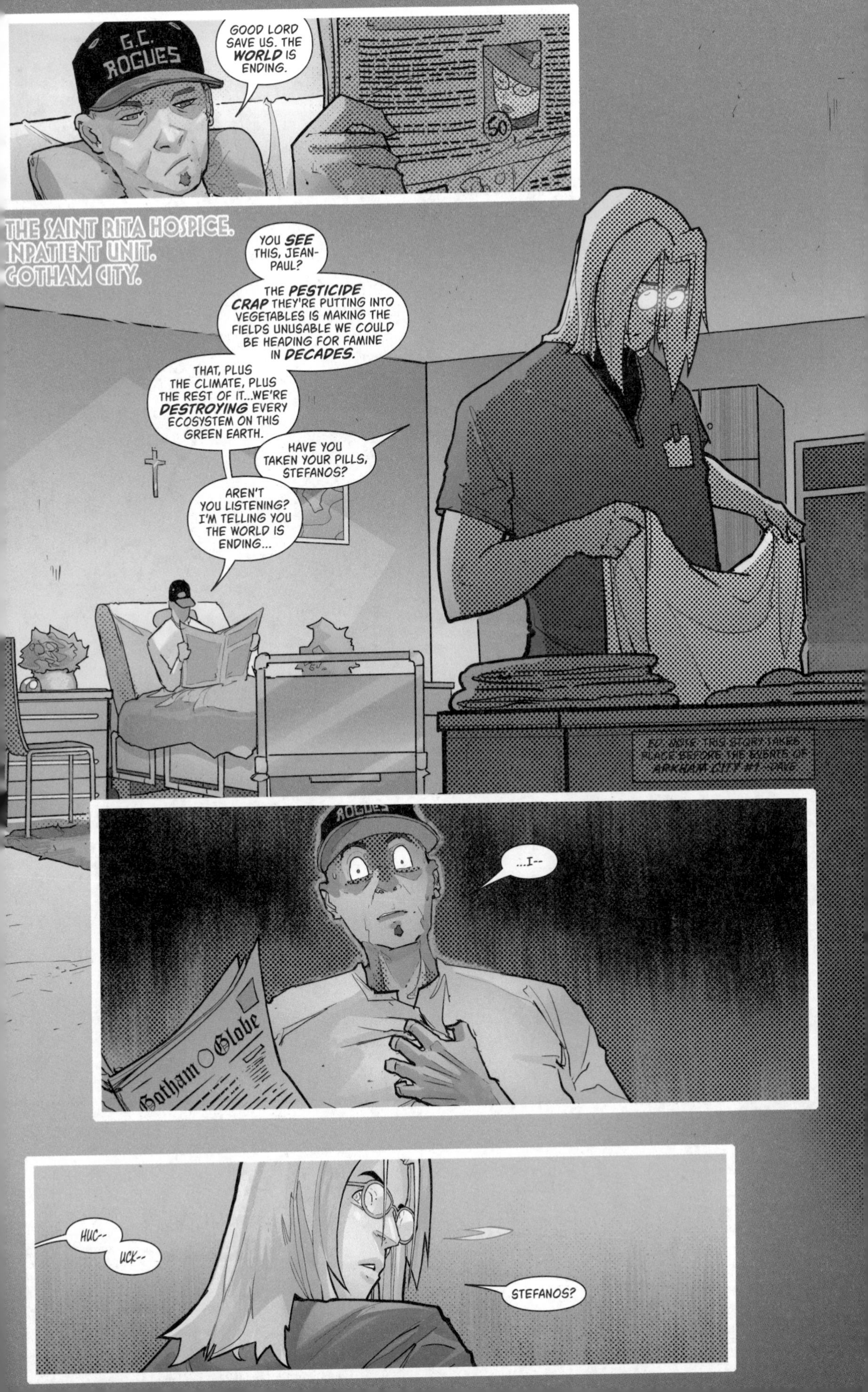

GOOD LORD SAVE US. THE WORLD IS ENDING.
50
THE SAINT RITA HOSPICE. NPATIENT UNIT. GOTHAM CITY.
YOU SEE THIS, JEAN-PAUL?
THE PESTICIDE CRAP THEY'RE PUTTING INTO VEGETABLES IS MAKING THE FIELDS UNUSABLE WE COULD BE HEADING FOR FAMINE IN DECADES.
THAT, PLUS THE CLIMATE, PLUS THE REST OF IT...WE'RE DESTROYING EVERY ECOSYSTEM ON THIS GREEN EARTH.
HAVE YOU TAKEN YOUR PILLS, STEFANOS?
AREN'T YOU LISTENING? I'M TELLING YOU THE WORLD IS ENDING...
ED. NOTE: THIS STORY TAKES PLACE BEFORE THE EVENTS OF ARKHAM CITY #1 -JAKE
ROGUES
...I--
Gotham Globe
HUC--
UCK--
STEFANOS?

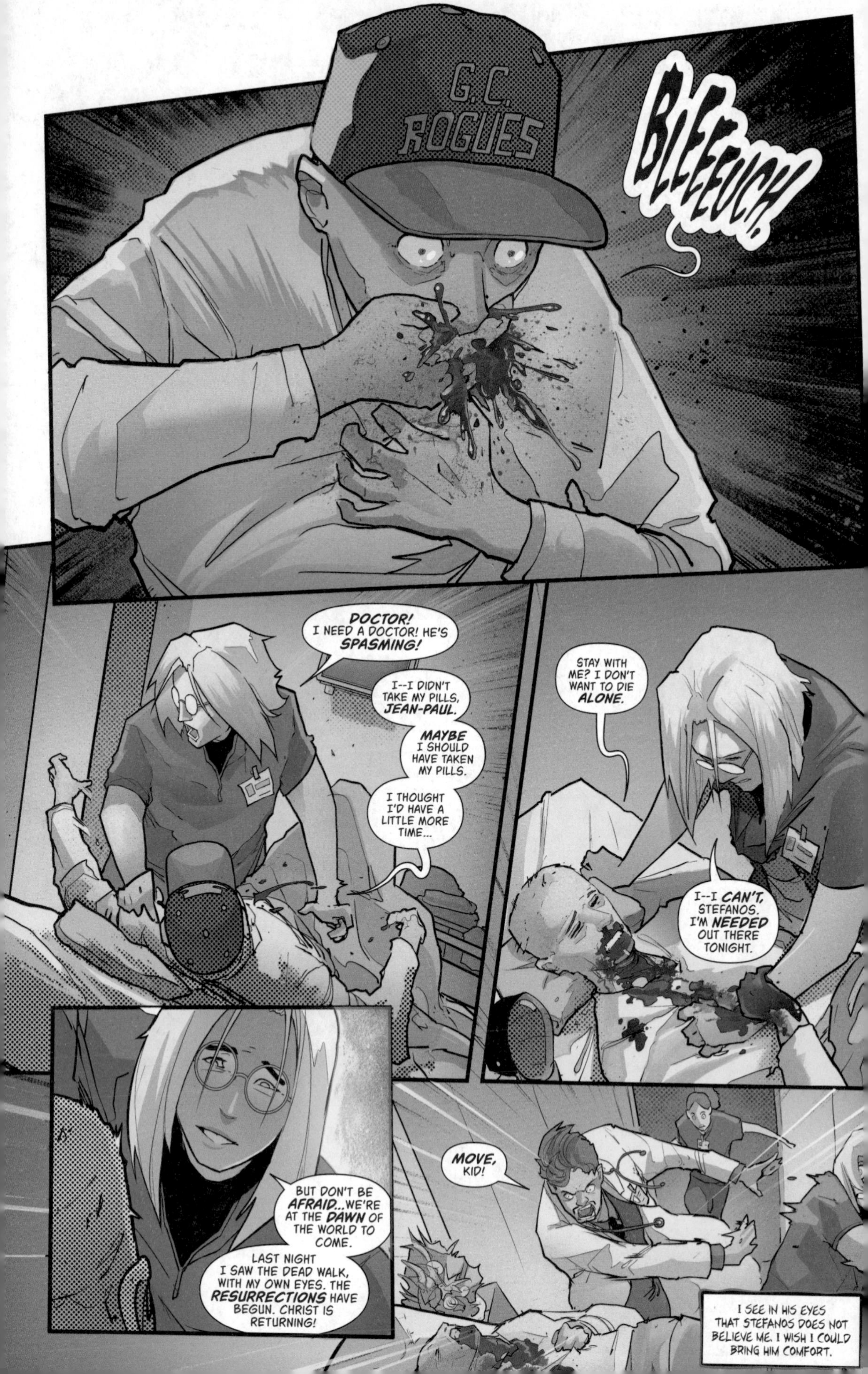
G.C. ROGUES
BLEEEUCH!
DOCTOR! I NEED A DOCTOR! HE'S SPASMING!
I--I DIDN'T TAKE MY PILLS, JEAN-PAUL.
MAYBE I SHOULD HAVE TAKEN MY PILLS.
I THOUGHT I'D HAVE A LITTLE MORE TIME...
STAY WITH ME? I DON'T WANT TO DIE ALONE.
I--I CAN'T, STEFANOS. I'M NEEDED OUT THERE TONIGHT.
BUT DON'T BE AFRAID...WE'RE AT THE DAWN OF THE WORLD TO COME.
LAST NIGHT I SAW THE DEAD WALK, WITH MY OWN EYES. THE RESURRECTIONS HAVE BEGUN. CHRIST IS RETURNING!
MOVE, KID!
I SEE IN HIS EYES THAT STEFANOS DOES NOT BELIEVE ME. I WISH I COULD BRING HIM COMFORT.

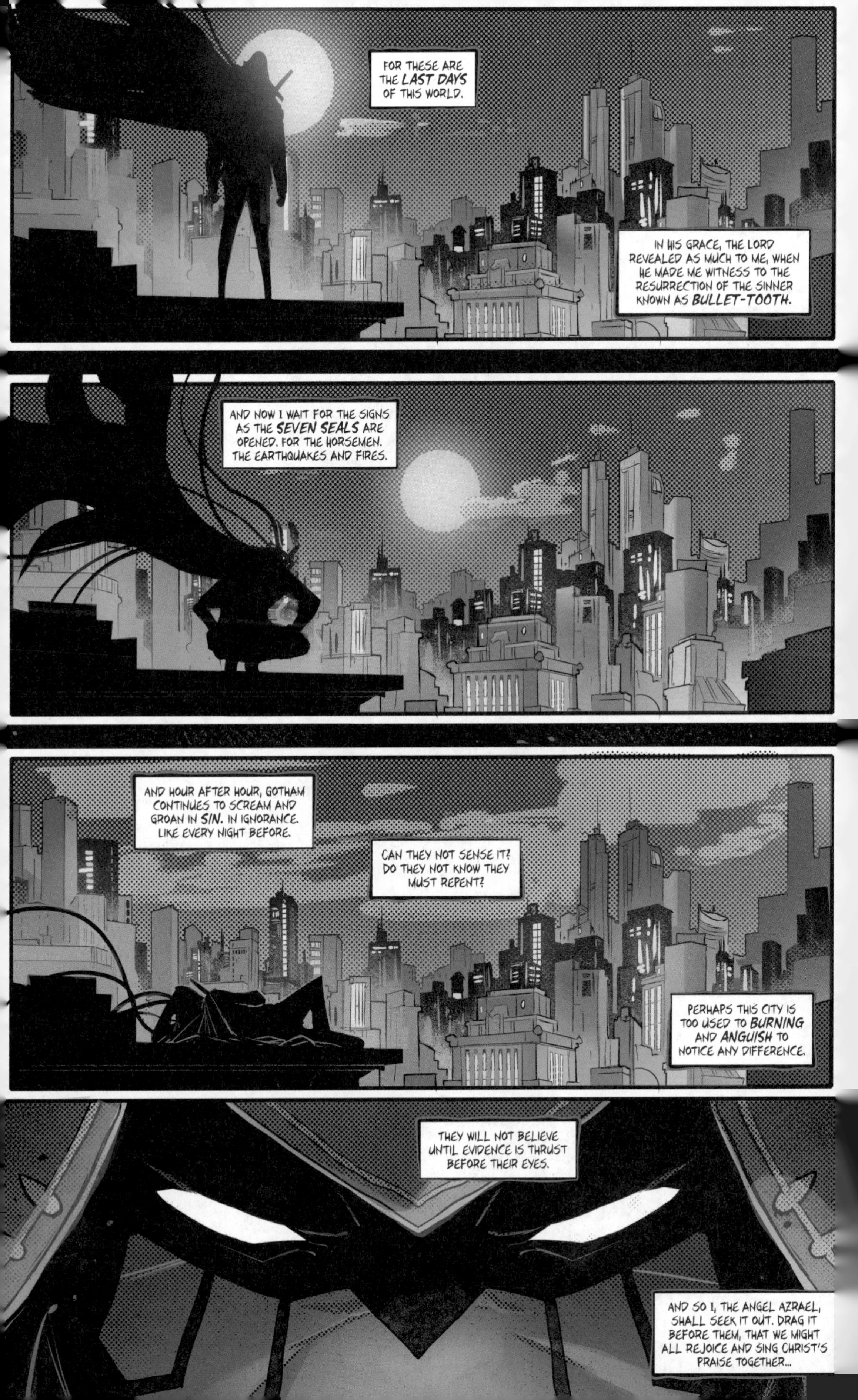

FOR THESE ARE THE LAST DAYS OF THIS WORLD.
IN HIS GRACE, THE LORD REVEALED AS MUCH TO ME, WHEN HE MADE ME WITNESS TO THE RESURRECTION OF THE SINNER KNOWN AS BULLET-TOOTH.
AND NOW I WAIT FOR THE SIGNS AS THE SEVEN SEALS ARE OPENED. FOR THE HORSEMEN. THE EARTHQUAKES AND FIRES.
AND HOUR AFTER HOUR, GOTHAM CONTINUES TO SCREAM AND GROAN IN SIN. IN IGNORANCE. LIKE EVERY NIGHT BEFORE.
CAN THEY NOT SENSE IT? DO THEY NOT KNOW THEY MUST REPENT?
PERHAPS THIS CITY IS TOO USED TO BURNING AND ANGUISH TO NOTICE ANY DIFFERENCE.
THEY WILL NOT BELIEVE UNTIL EVIDENCE IS THRUST BEFORE THEIR EYES.
AND SO I, THE ANGEL AZRAEL, SHALL SEEK IT OUT. DRAG IT BEFORE THEM, THAT WE MIGHT ALL REJOICE AND SING CHRIST'S PRAISE TOGETHER...

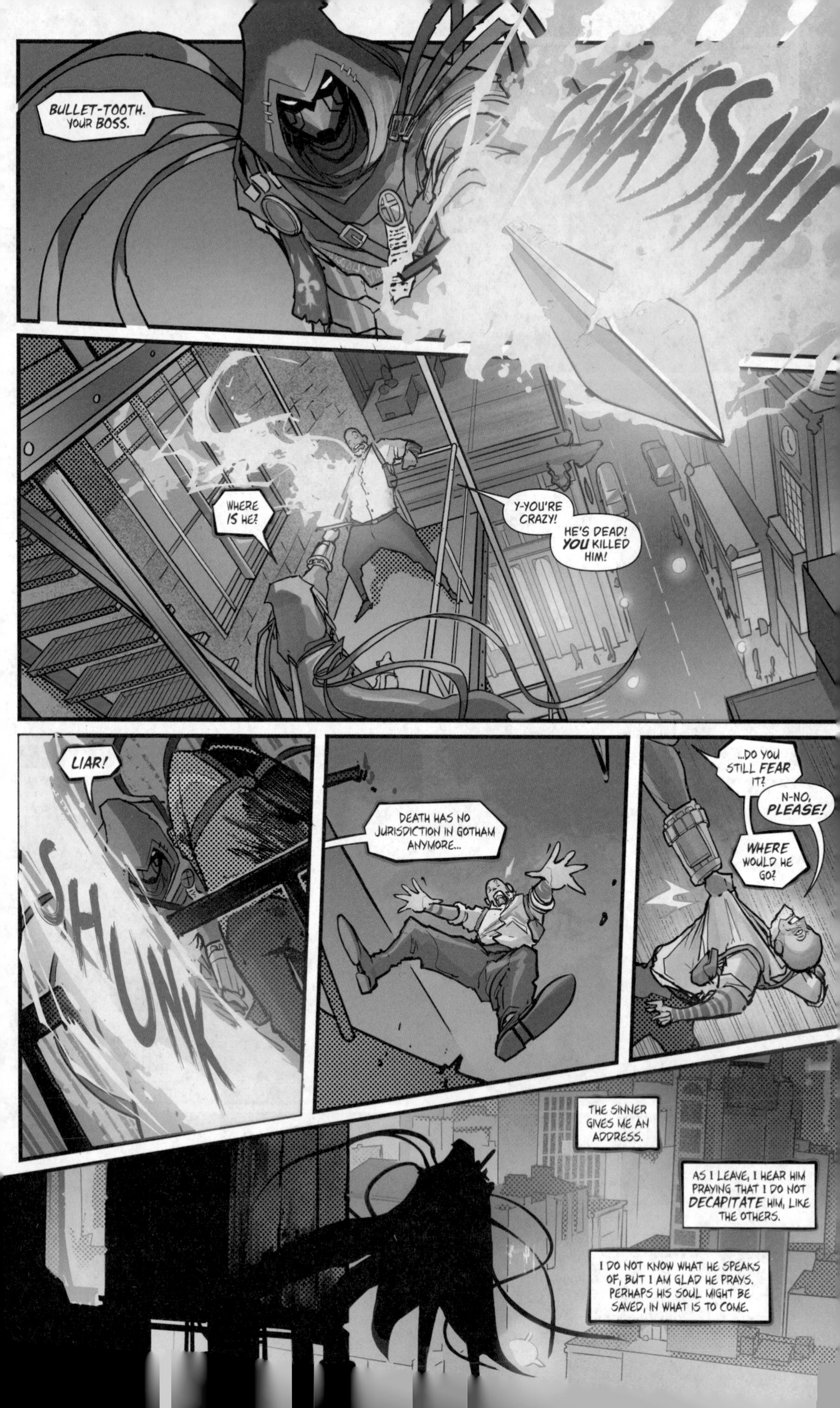

BULLET-TOOTH. YOUR BOSS.
FWASSHH
WHERE IS HE?
Y-YOU'RE CRAZY!
HE'S DEAD! YOU KILLED HIM!
LIAR!
SHUNK
DEATH HAS NO JURISDICTION IN GOTHAM ANYMORE...
...DO YOU STILL FEAR IT?
N-NO, PLEASE!
WHERE WOULD HE GO?
THE SINNER GIVES ME AN ADDRESS.
AS I LEAVE, I HEAR HIM PRAYING THAT I DO NOT DECAPITATE HIM, LIKE THE OTHERS.
I DO NOT KNOW WHAT HE SPEAKS OF, BUT I AM GLAD HE PRAYS. PERHAPS HIS SOUL MIGHT BE SAVED, IN WHAT IS TO COME.

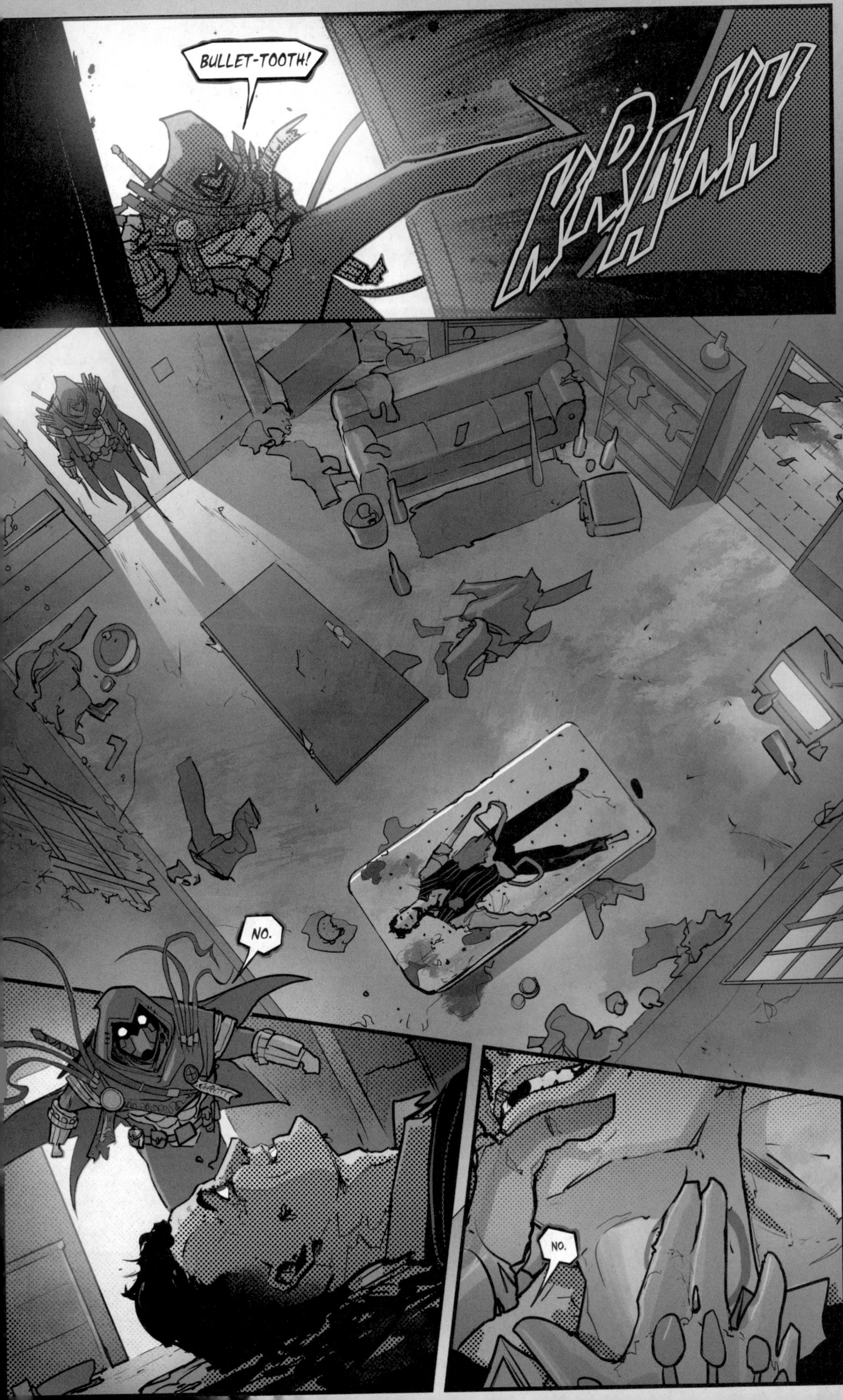
BULLET-TOOTH!
NO.
NO.

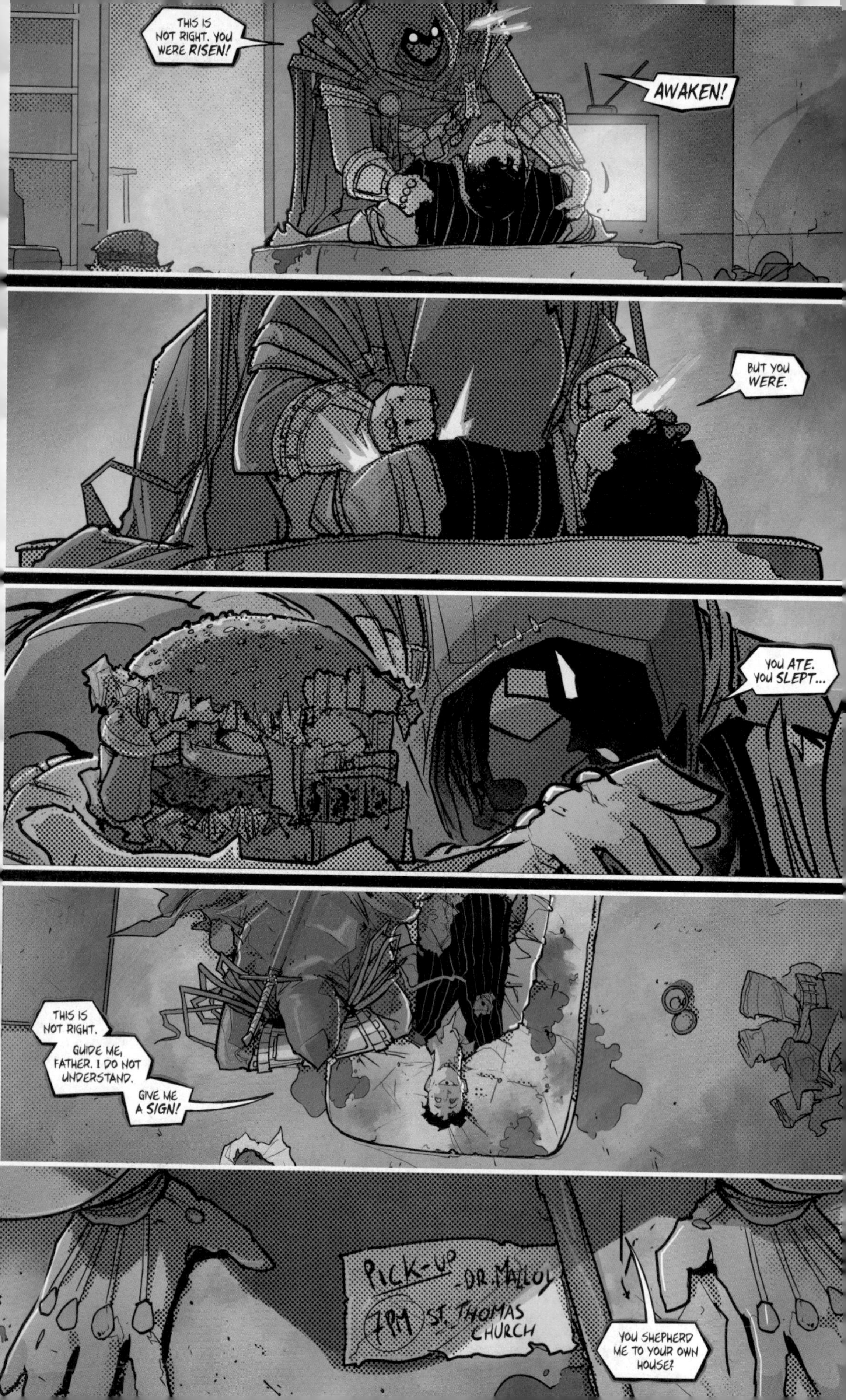
THIS IS NOT RIGHT. YOU WERE RISEN!
AWAKEN!
BUT YOU WERE.
YOU ATE. YOU SLEPT...
THIS IS NOT RIGHT.
GUIDE ME, FATHER. I DO NOT UNDERSTAND.
GIVE ME A SIGN!
PICK-UP DR. MALLOY
7PM ST. THOMAS CHURCH
YOU SHEPHERD ME TO YOUR OWN HOUSE?

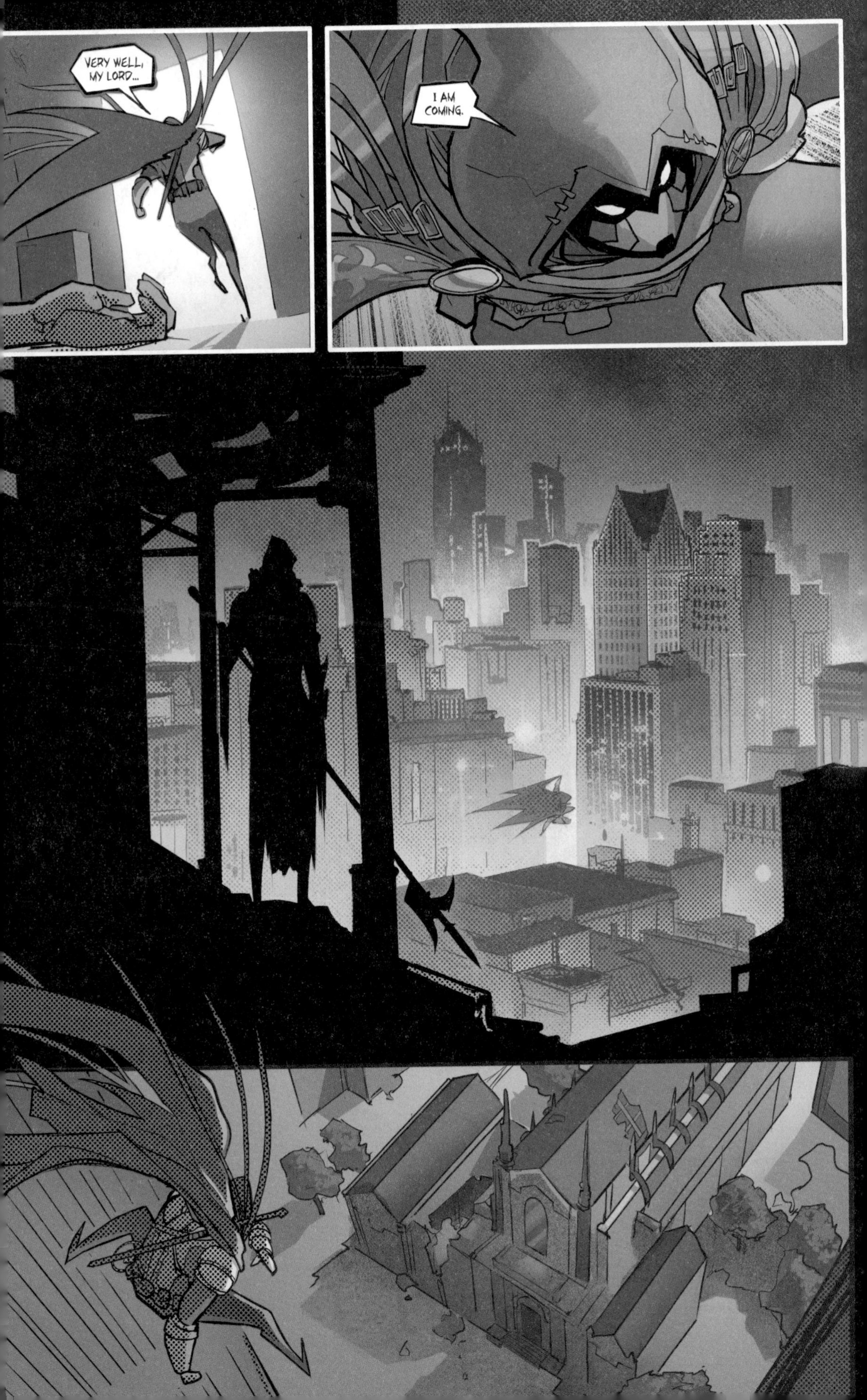
VERY WELL, MY LORD...
I AM COMING.

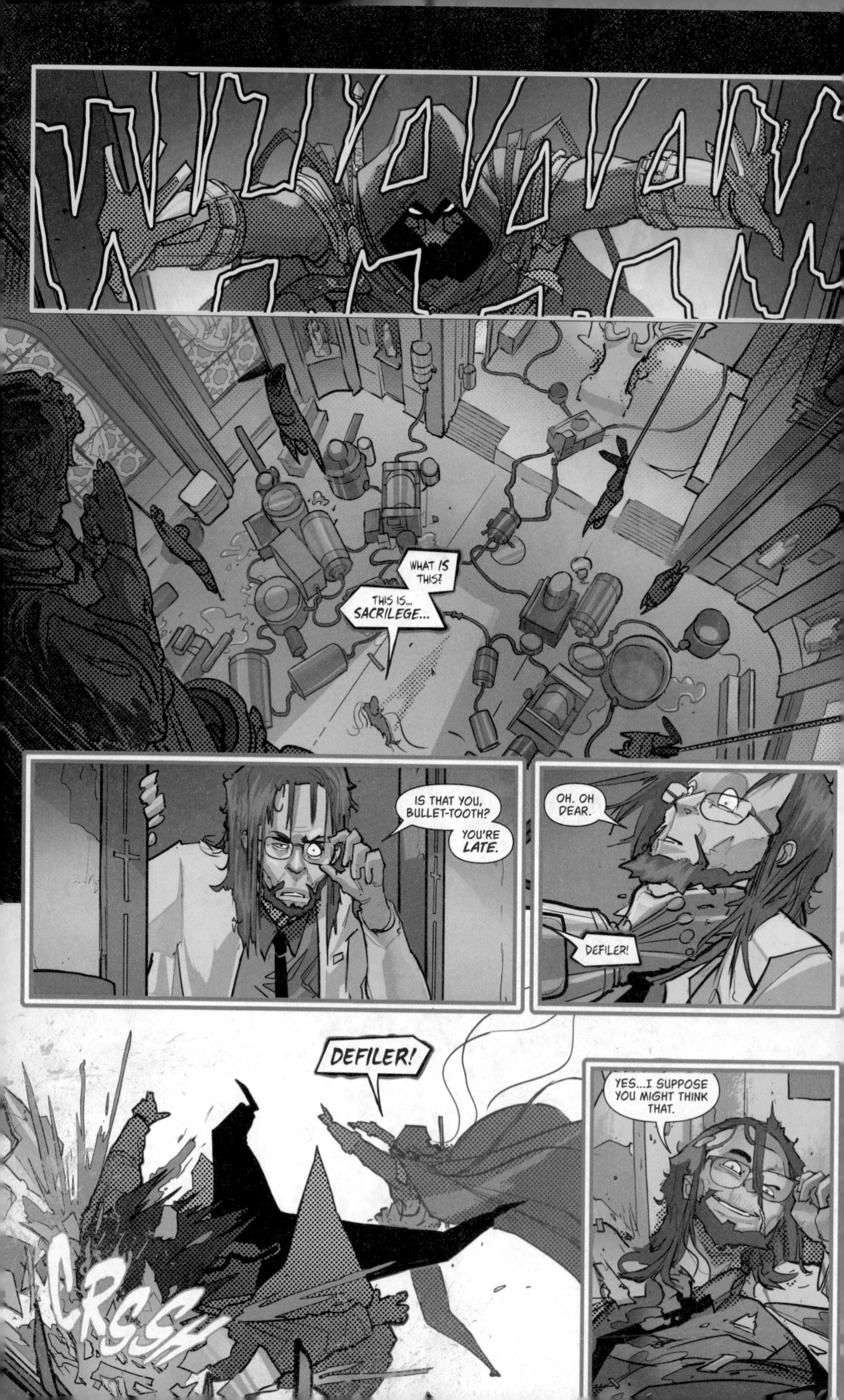
WHAT IS THIS?
THIS IS... SACRILEGE...
IS THAT YOU, BULLET-TOOTH?
YOU'RE LATE.
OH. OH DEAR.
DEFILER!
DEFILER!
YES...I SUPPOSE YOU MIGHT THINK THAT.
CRSSH

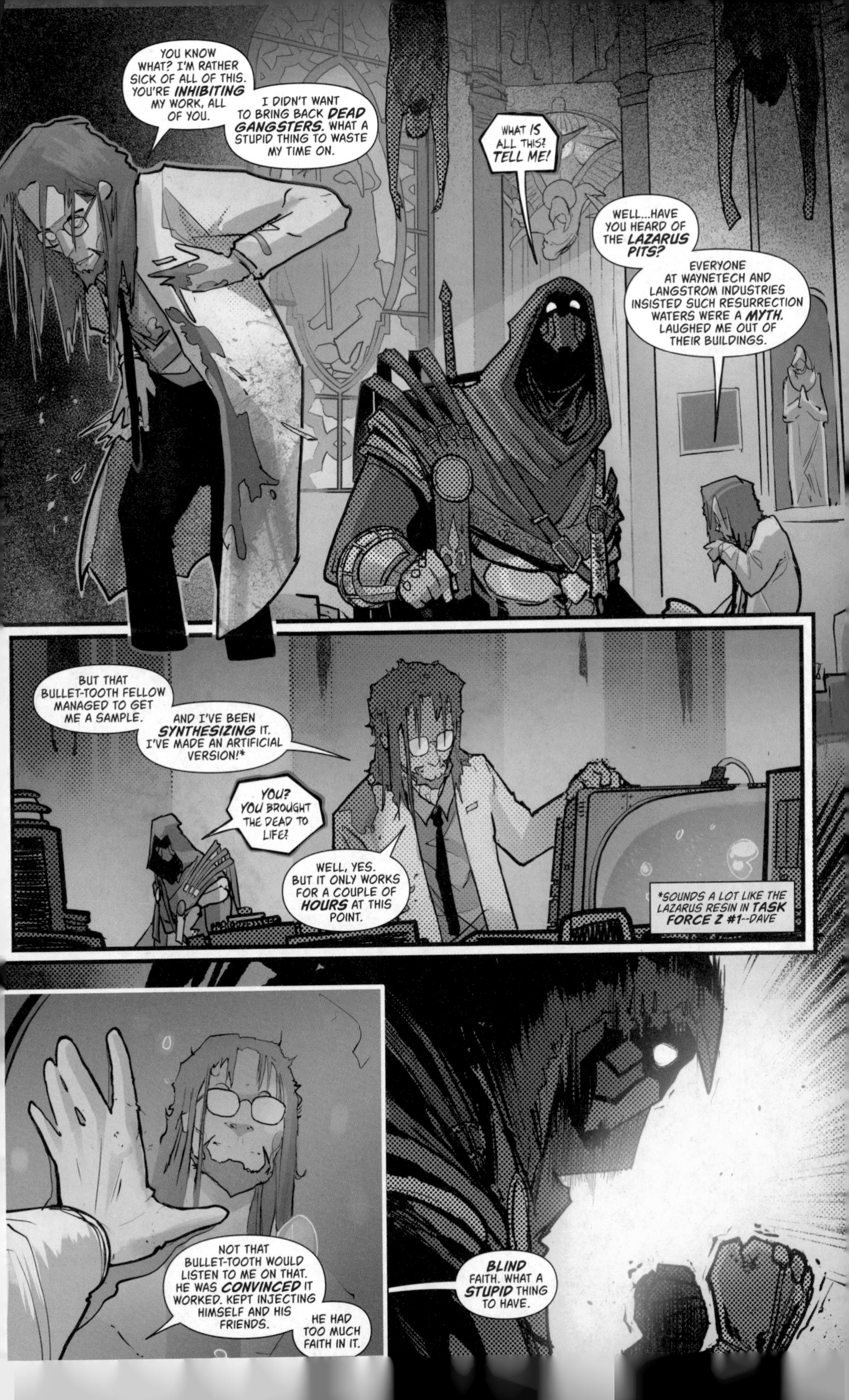
YOU KNOW WHAT? I'M RATHER SICK OF ALL OF THIS. YOU'RE INHIBITING MY WORK, ALL OF YOU.
I DIDN'T WANT TO BRING BACK DEAD GANGSTERS. WHAT A STUPID THING TO WASTE MY TIME ON.
WHAT IS ALL THIS? TELL ME!
WELL...HAVE YOU HEARD OF THE LAZARUS PITS?
EVERYONE AT WAYNETECH AND LANGSTROM INDUSTRIES INSISTED SUCH RESURRECTION WATERS WERE A MYTH. LAUGHED ME OUT OF THEIR BUILDINGS.
BUT THAT BULLET-TOOTH FELLOW MANAGED TO GET ME A SAMPLE.
AND I'VE BEEN SYNTHESIZING IT. I'VE MADE AN ARTIFICIAL VERSION!*
YOU? YOU BROUGHT THE DEAD TO LIFE?
WELL, YES. BUT IT ONLY WORKS FOR A COUPLE OF HOURS AT THIS POINT.
*SOUNDS A LOT LIKE THE LAZARUS RESIN IN TASK FORCE Z #1--DAVE
NOT THAT BULLET-TOOTH WOULD LISTEN TO ME ON THAT. HE WAS CONVINCED IT WORKED. KEPT INJECTING HIMSELF AND HIS FRIENDS.
HE HAD TOO MUCH FAITH IN IT.
BLIND FAITH. WHAT A STUPID THING TO HAVE.

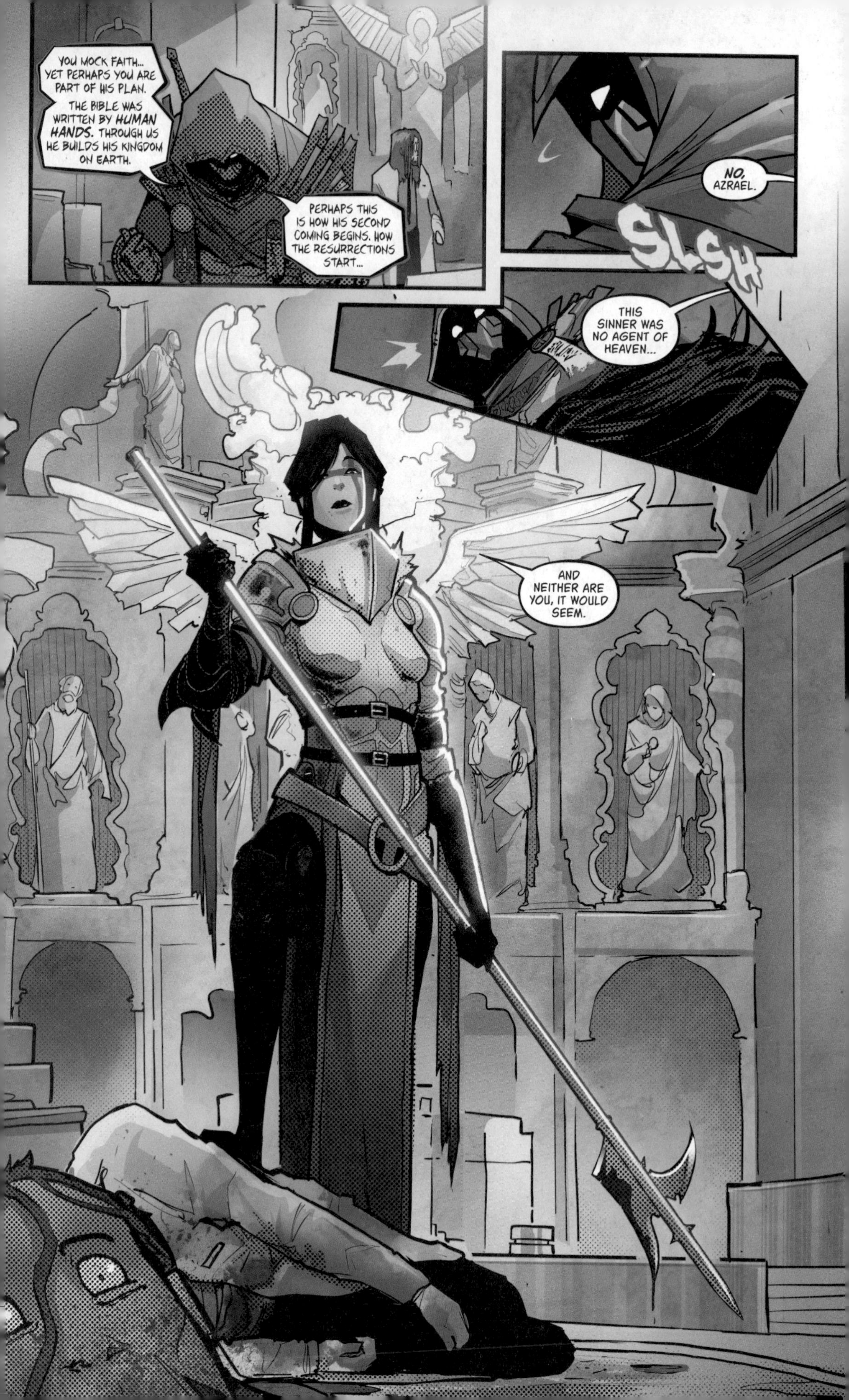
YOU MOCK FAITH... YET PERHAPS YOU ARE PART OF HIS PLAN.
THE BIBLE WAS WRITTEN BY **HUMAN HANDS.** THROUGH US HE BUILDS HIS KINGDOM ON EARTH.
PERHAPS THIS IS HOW HIS SECOND COMING BEGINS. HOW THE RESURRECTIONS START...
NO, AZRAEL.
SLSH
THIS SINNER WAS NO AGENT OF HEAVEN...
AND NEITHER ARE YOU, IT WOULD SEEM.

"IN THE YEAR *1152*, RAYMOND II, COUNT OF TRIPOLI, ESCORTED HIS WIFE FROM THE CITY AS SHE MADE *PILGRIMAGE* TOWARD JERUSALEM.

"IT WAS SPRING IN LEBANON. PERHAPS HE PAUSED TO SMELL THE *SNAPDRAGONS* AS THEY BLOOMED.

"HE RODE HIS HORSE IN A GENTLE TROT UNDER BLUE SKIES.

"AND THEN THE *BAND OF ASSASSINS* MURDERED HIM AT THE GATES OF HIS CITY.

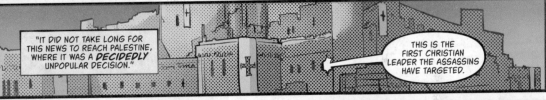

"IT DID NOT TAKE LONG FOR THIS NEWS TO REACH PALESTINE, WHERE IT WAS A *DECIDEDLY* UNPOPULAR DECISION."

THIS IS THE FIRST CHRISTIAN LEADER THE ASSASSINS HAVE TARGETED.

THE *KNIGHTS TEMPLAR* CANNOT BE SEEN TO PERMIT IT TO STAND, GRAND MASTER.

AND YET, THIS TERROR CAMPAIGN THEY HAVE BEEN CARRYING OUT FOR THE NIZARI, WE HAVE SEEN NOTHING LIKE IT.

THEY KILL WITH POISONED KNIVES IN *BROAD DAYLIGHT.* THESE ARE *SUICIDE MISSIONS.*

HOW WOULD YOU PROPOSE WE FACE DOWN AN ENEMY LIKE THAT?

WELL, IF IT WOULD PLEASE YOU, GRAND MASTER...

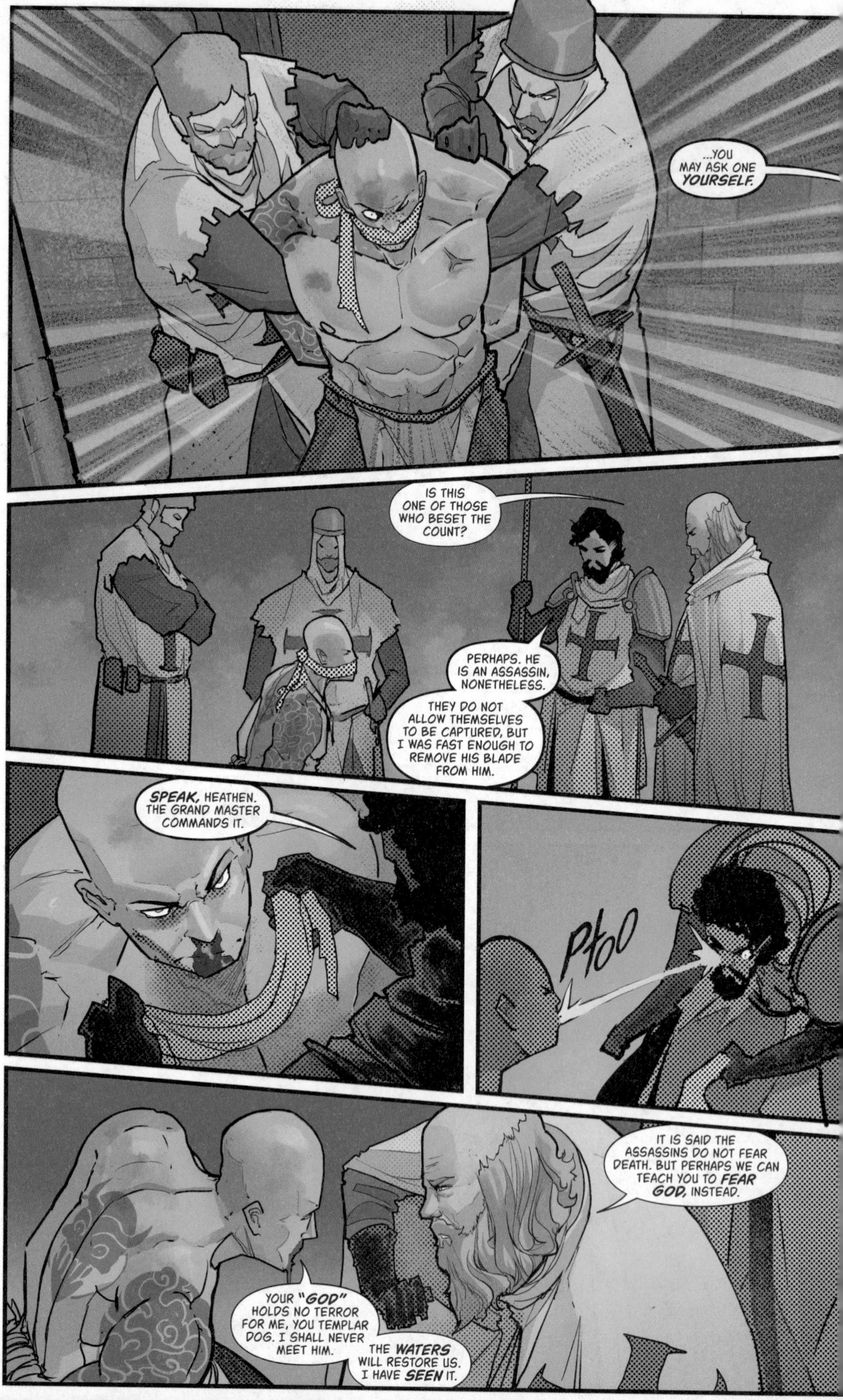
...YOU MAY ASK ONE YOURSELF.
IS THIS ONE OF THOSE WHO BESET THE COUNT?
PERHAPS. HE IS AN ASSASSIN, NONETHELESS.
THEY DO NOT ALLOW THEMSELVES TO BE CAPTURED, BUT I WAS FAST ENOUGH TO REMOVE HIS BLADE FROM HIM.
SPEAK, HEATHEN. THE GRAND MASTER COMMANDS IT.
PTOO
IT IS SAID THE ASSASSINS DO NOT FEAR DEATH. BUT PERHAPS WE CAN TEACH YOU TO FEAR GOD, INSTEAD.
YOUR "GOD" HOLDS NO TERROR FOR ME, YOU TEMPLAR DOG. I SHALL NEVER MEET HIM.
THE WATERS WILL RESTORE US. I HAVE SEEN IT.

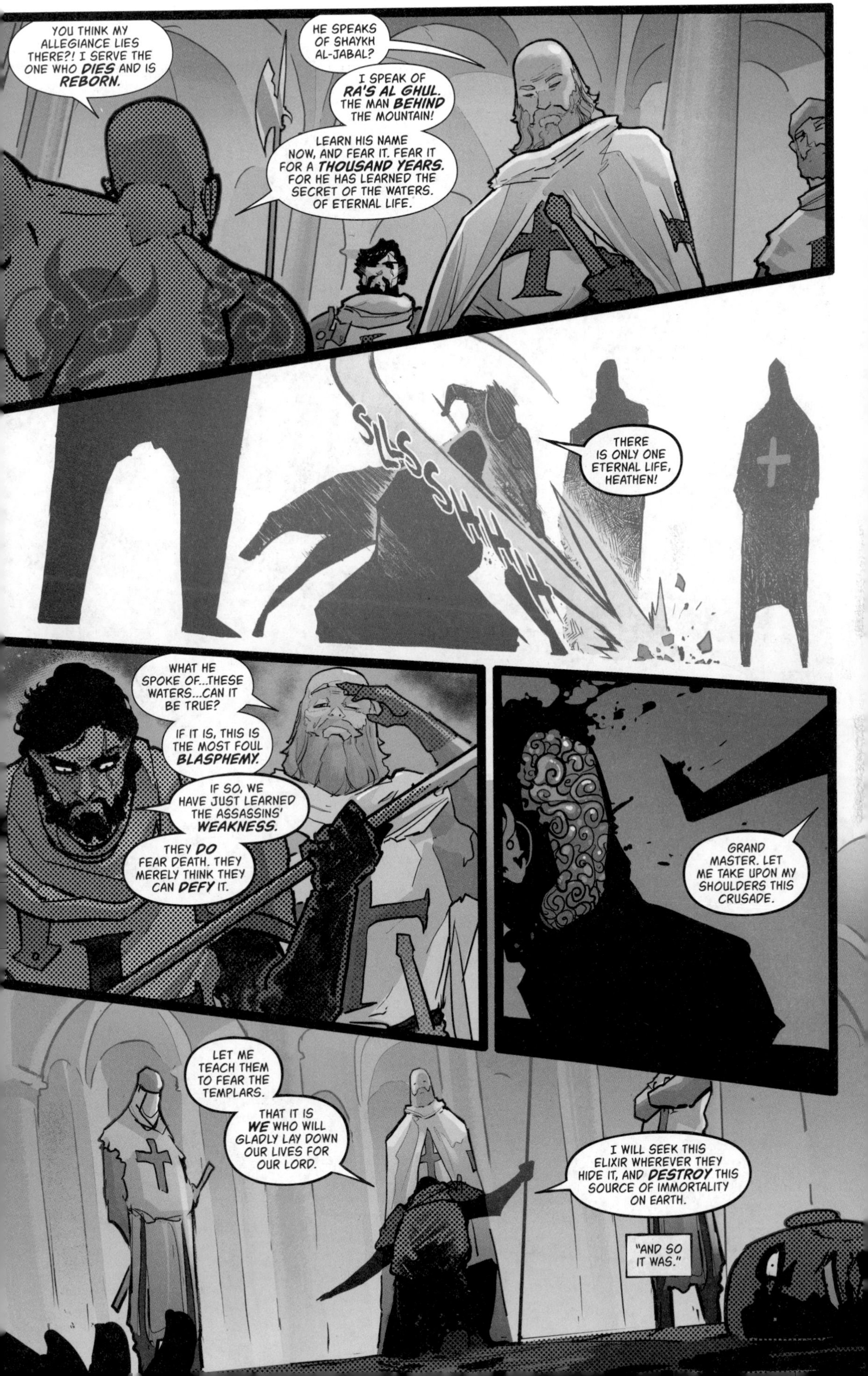

YOU THINK MY ALLEGIANCE LIES THERE?! I SERVE THE ONE WHO DIES AND IS REBORN.
HE SPEAKS OF SHAYKH AL-JABAL?
I SPEAK OF RA'S AL GHUL. THE MAN BEHIND THE MOUNTAIN!
LEARN HIS NAME NOW, AND FEAR IT. FEAR IT FOR A THOUSAND YEARS. FOR HE HAS LEARNED THE SECRET OF THE WATERS. OF ETERNAL LIFE.
SLLSSHHHH
THERE IS ONLY ONE ETERNAL LIFE, HEATHEN!
WHAT HE SPOKE OF...THESE WATERS...CAN IT BE TRUE?
IF IT IS, THIS IS THE MOST FOUL BLASPHEMY.
IF SO, WE HAVE JUST LEARNED THE ASSASSINS' WEAKNESS.
THEY DO FEAR DEATH. THEY MERELY THINK THEY CAN DEFY IT.
GRAND MASTER. LET ME TAKE UPON MY SHOULDERS THIS CRUSADE.
LET ME TEACH THEM TO FEAR THE TEMPLARS.
THAT IT IS WE WHO WILL GLADLY LAY DOWN OUR LIVES FOR OUR LORD.
I WILL SEEK THIS ELIXIR WHEREVER THEY HIDE IT, AND DESTROY THIS SOURCE OF IMMORTALITY ON EARTH.
"AND SO IT WAS."

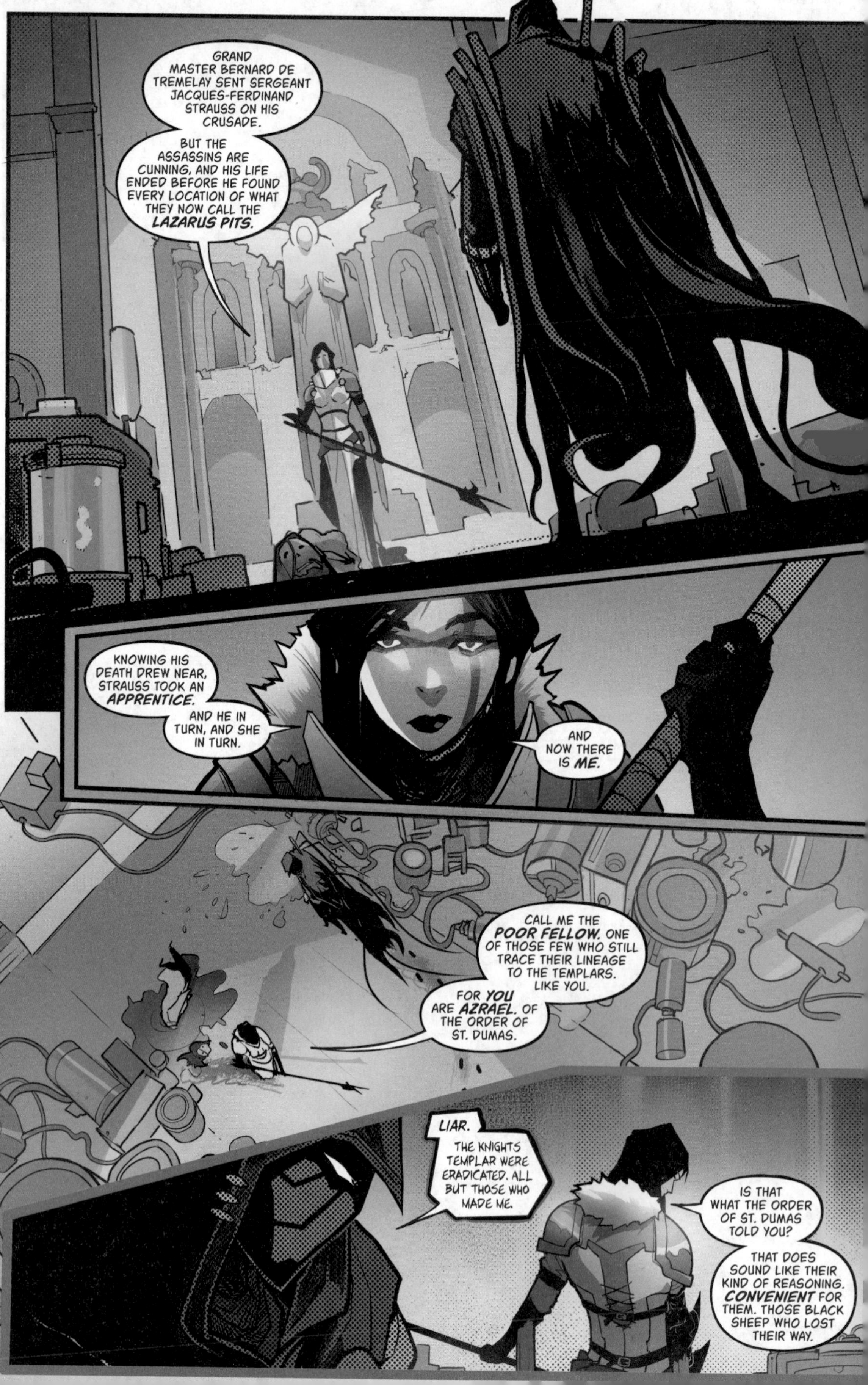
GRAND MASTER BERNARD DE TREMELAY SENT SERGEANT JACQUES-FERDINAND STRAUSS ON HIS CRUSADE.
BUT THE ASSASSINS ARE CUNNING, AND HIS LIFE ENDED BEFORE HE FOUND EVERY LOCATION OF WHAT THEY NOW CALL THE LAZARUS PITS.
KNOWING HIS DEATH DREW NEAR, STRAUSS TOOK AN APPRENTICE.
AND HE IN TURN, AND SHE IN TURN.
AND NOW THERE IS ME.
CALL ME THE POOR FELLOW. ONE OF THOSE FEW WHO STILL TRACE THEIR LINEAGE TO THE TEMPLARS. LIKE YOU.
FOR YOU ARE AZRAEL. OF THE ORDER OF ST. DUMAS.
LIAR.
THE KNIGHTS TEMPLAR WERE ERADICATED. ALL BUT THOSE WHO MADE ME.
IS THAT WHAT THE ORDER OF ST. DUMAS TOLD YOU?
THAT DOES SOUND LIKE THEIR KIND OF REASONING. CONVENIENT FOR THEM. THOSE BLACK SHEEP WHO LOST THEIR WAY.

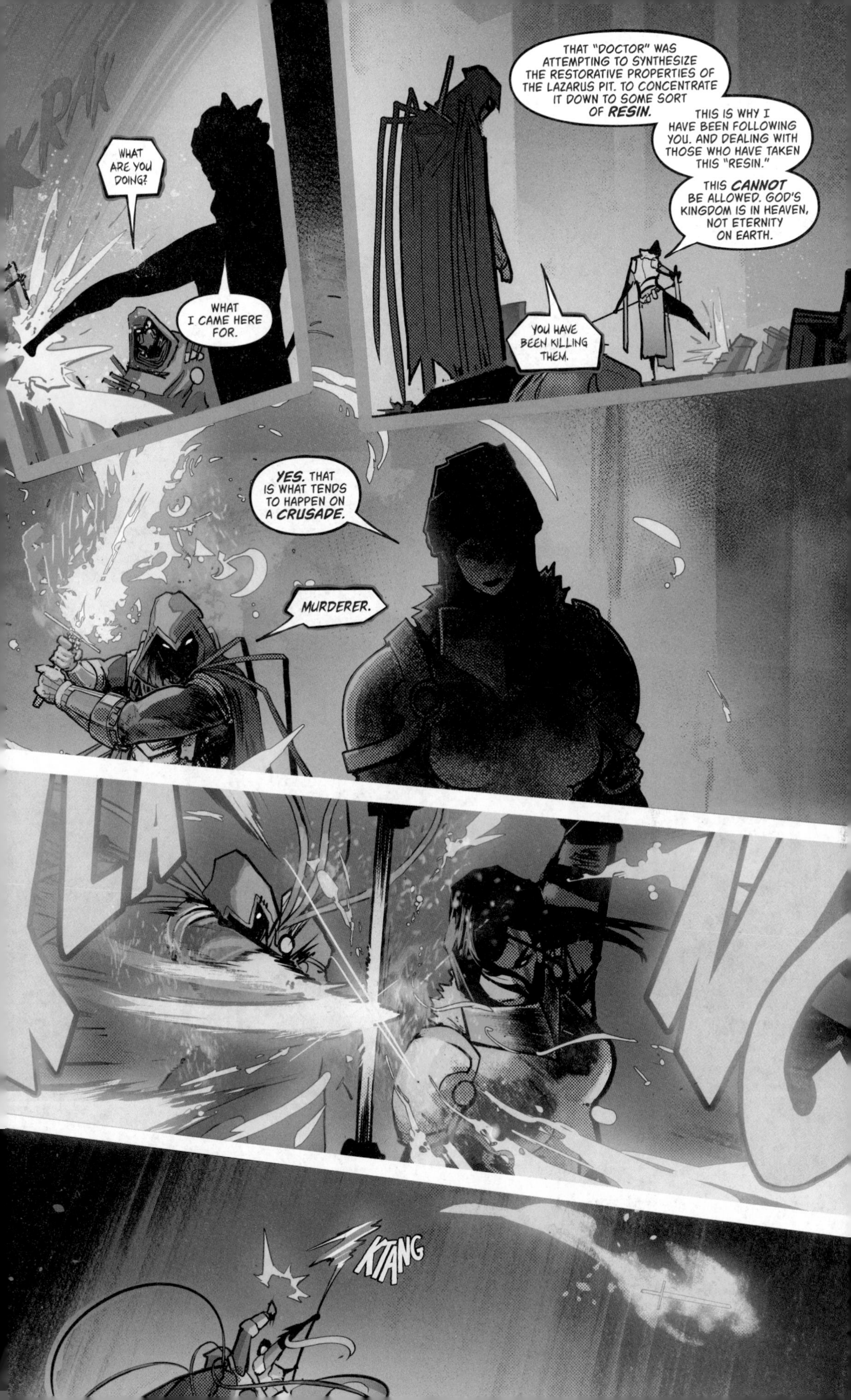KRAK
WHAT ARE YOU DOING?
WHAT I CAME HERE FOR.
THAT "DOCTOR" WAS ATTEMPTING TO SYNTHESIZE THE RESTORATIVE PROPERTIES OF THE LAZARUS PIT. TO CONCENTRATE IT DOWN TO SOME SORT OF **RESIN.**
THIS IS WHY I HAVE BEEN FOLLOWING YOU. AND DEALING WITH THOSE WHO HAVE TAKEN THIS "RESIN."
THIS **CANNOT** BE ALLOWED. GOD'S KINGDOM IS IN HEAVEN, NOT ETERNITY ON EARTH.
YOU HAVE BEEN KILLING THEM.
YES. THAT IS WHAT TENDS TO HAPPEN ON A **CRUSADE.**
MURDERER.
KTANG

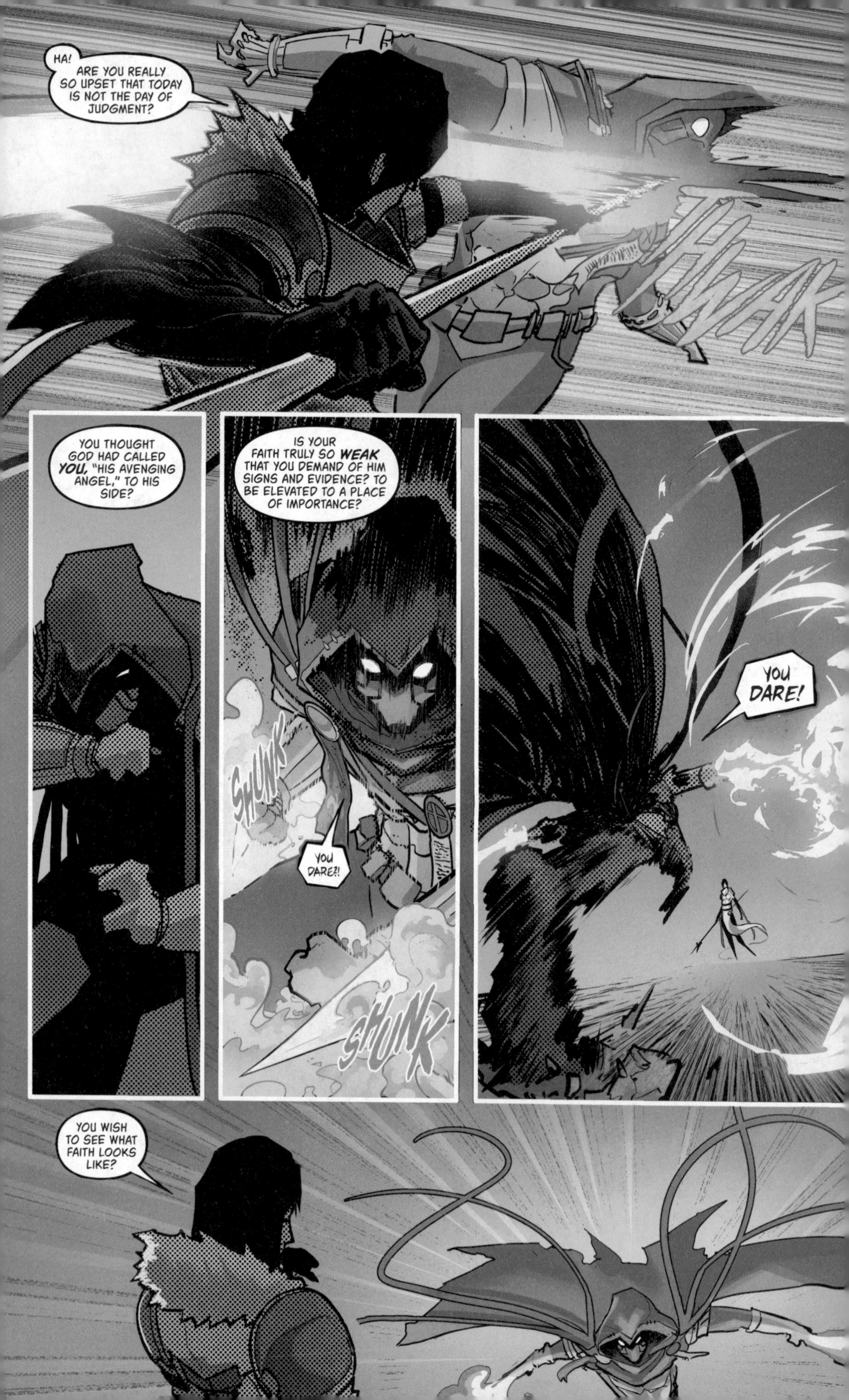
HA!
ARE YOU REALLY SO UPSET THAT TODAY IS NOT THE DAY OF JUDGMENT?
THWAK
YOU THOUGHT GOD HAD CALLED YOU, "HIS AVENGING ANGEL," TO HIS SIDE?
IS YOUR FAITH TRULY SO WEAK THAT YOU DEMAND OF HIM SIGNS AND EVIDENCE? TO BE ELEVATED TO A PLACE OF IMPORTANCE?
SHUNK
YOU DARE?!
SHUNK
YOU DARE!
YOU WISH TO SEE WHAT FAITH LOOKS LIKE?

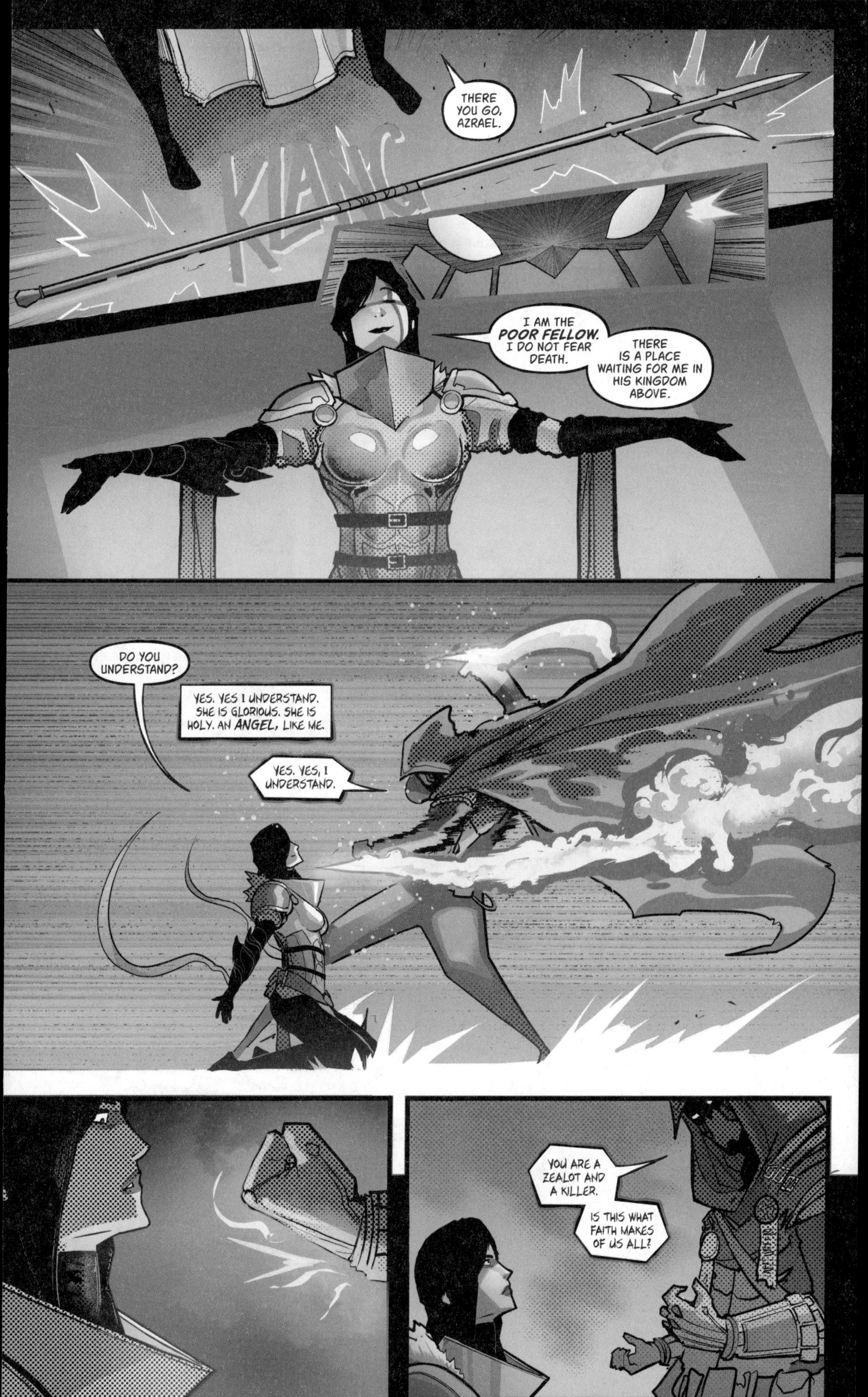
THERE YOU GO, AZRAEL.
KLANG
I AM THE **POOR FELLOW.** I DO NOT FEAR DEATH.
THERE IS A PLACE WAITING FOR ME IN HIS KINGDOM ABOVE.
DO YOU UNDERSTAND?
YES. YES I UNDERSTAND. SHE IS GLORIOUS. SHE IS HOLY. AN **ANGEL,** LIKE ME.
YES. YES, I UNDERSTAND.
YOU ARE A ZEALOT AND A KILLER.
IS THIS WHAT FAITH MAKES OF US ALL?

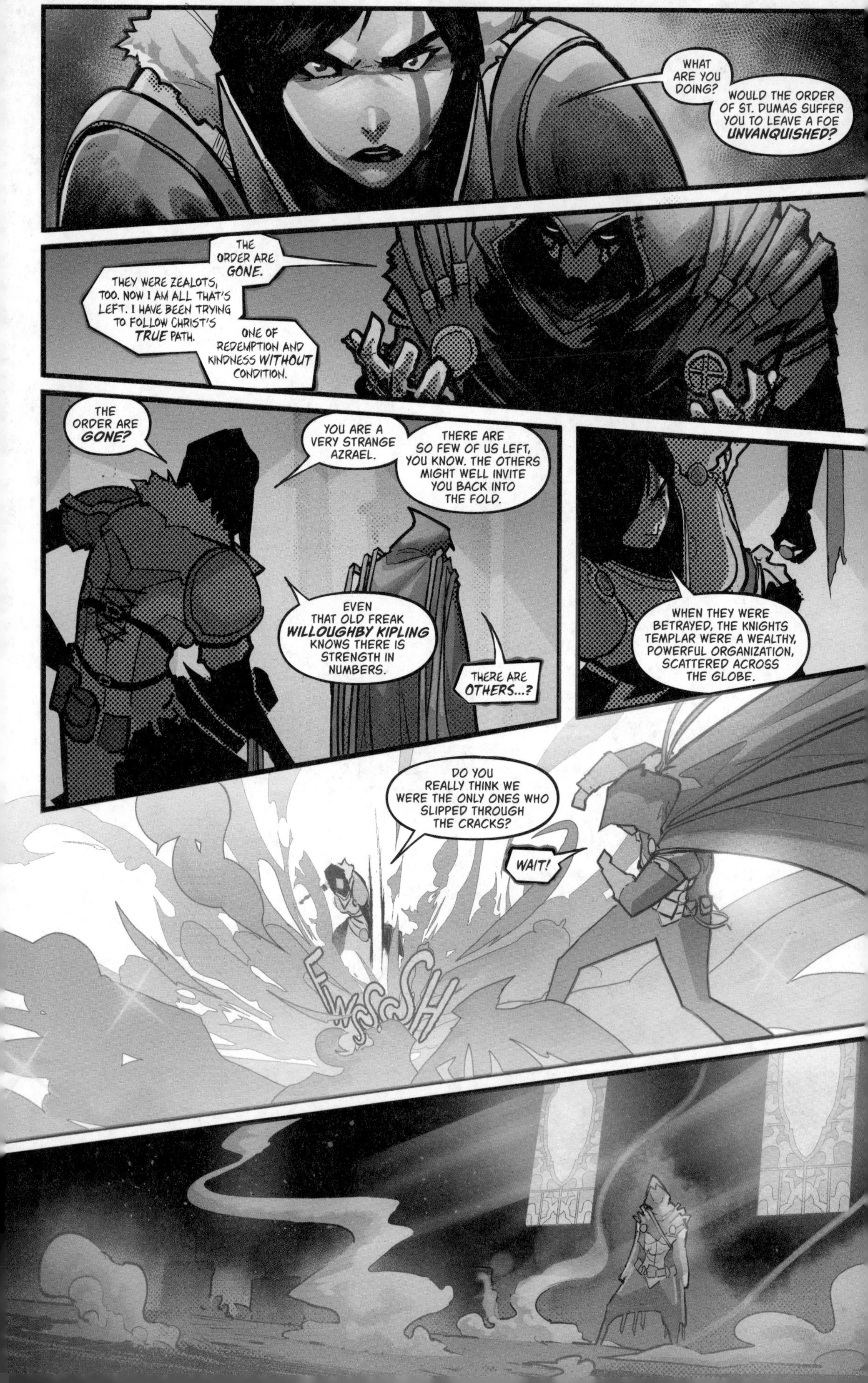
WHAT ARE YOU DOING?
WOULD THE ORDER OF ST. DUMAS SUFFER YOU TO LEAVE A FOE UNVANQUISHED?
THE ORDER ARE GONE.
THEY WERE ZEALOTS, TOO. NOW I AM ALL THAT'S LEFT. I HAVE BEEN TRYING TO FOLLOW CHRIST'S TRUE PATH.
ONE OF REDEMPTION AND KINDNESS WITHOUT CONDITION.
THE ORDER ARE GONE?
YOU ARE A VERY STRANGE AZRAEL.
THERE ARE SO FEW OF US LEFT, YOU KNOW. THE OTHERS MIGHT WELL INVITE YOU BACK INTO THE FOLD.
EVEN THAT OLD FREAK WILLOUGHBY KIPLING KNOWS THERE IS STRENGTH IN NUMBERS.
THERE ARE OTHERS...?
WHEN THEY WERE BETRAYED, THE KNIGHTS TEMPLAR WERE A WEALTHY, POWERFUL ORGANIZATION, SCATTERED ACROSS THE GLOBE.
DO YOU REALLY THINK WE WERE THE ONLY ONES WHO SLIPPED THROUGH THE CRACKS?
WAIT!
FWSSSH

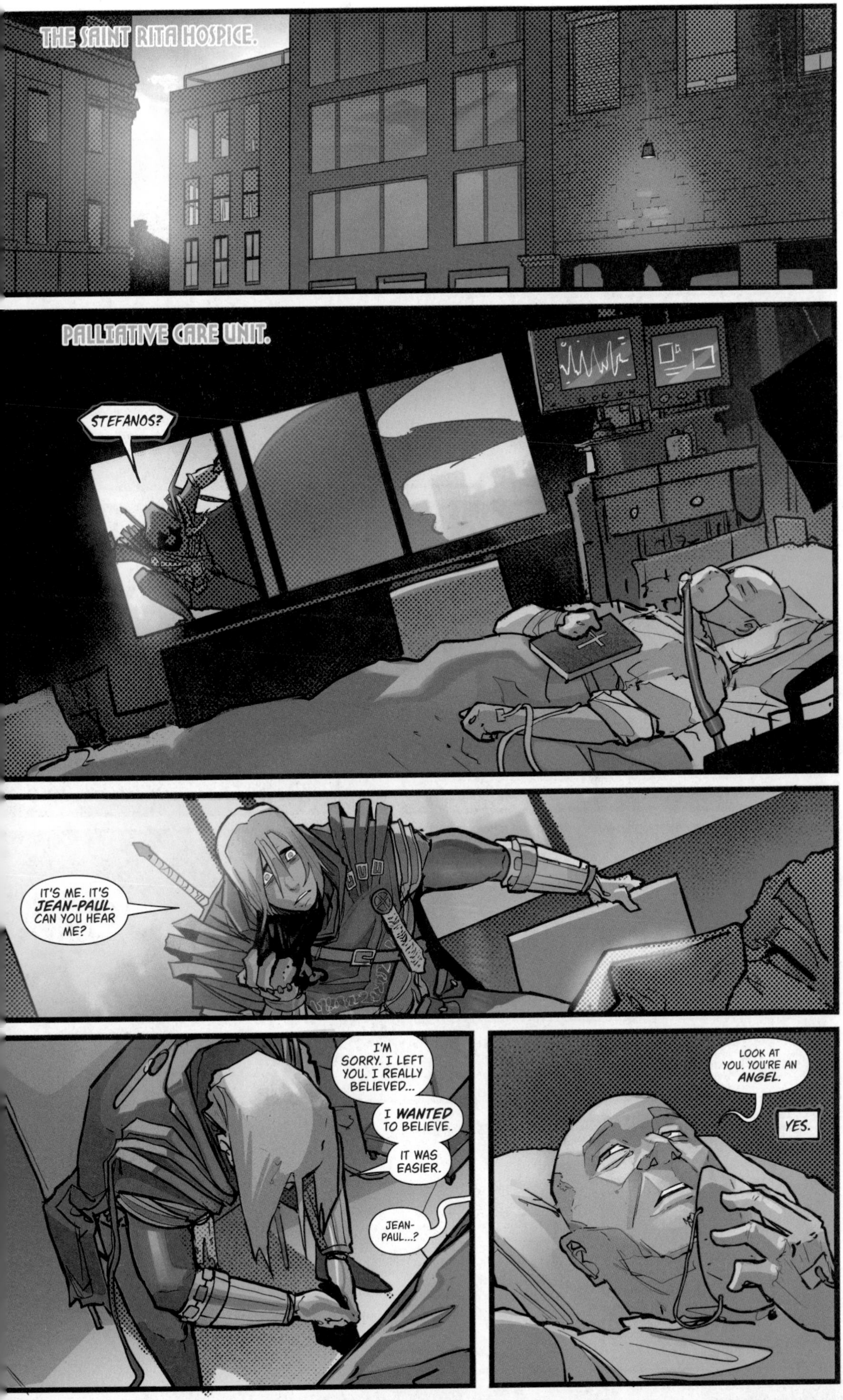
THE SAINT RITA HOSPICE.
PALLIATIVE CARE UNIT.
STEFANOS?
IT'S ME. IT'S JEAN-PAUL. CAN YOU HEAR ME?
I'M SORRY. I LEFT YOU. I REALLY BELIEVED...
I WANTED TO BELIEVE.
IT WAS EASIER.
JEAN-PAUL...?
LOOK AT YOU. YOU'RE AN ANGEL.
YES.

NO. I'M JUST A COLLEGE DROPOUT IN SPANDEX AND KEVLAR.

AND THAT'S WHAT I MEAN. WHAT IF WE'RE ALL THERE IS? JUST US IN A ROTTEN CITY. AND THEN OUR DEATHS.

HEBREWS 11:1.

NOW FAITH IS THE ASSURANCE OF THINGS HOPED FOR, THE CONVICTION OF THINGS NOT SEEN.

YOU *LEFT*, JEAN-PAUL. BUT YOU CAME BACK. HE CALLED YOU BACK TO ME, SO I AM NOT ALONE, HERE AT THE END.

THESE ARE THE TRUE KIND OF MIRACLES. THE SMALL MIRACLES IN WHICH WE FIND HIM.

IT'S *NOT* ENOUGH.

I DON'T KNOW THAT IT'S ENOUGH.

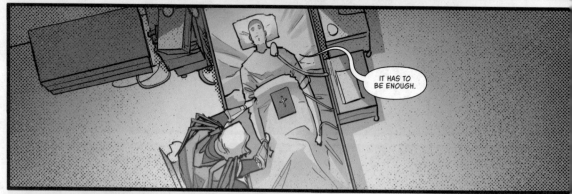

IT HAS TO BE ENOUGH.

AZRAEL
DARK KNIGHT OF THE SOUL

DAN WATTERS — Writer
NIKOLA ČIŽMEŠIJA — Artist
IVAN PLASCENCIA — Colors
ARIANA MAHER — Letters
DAVE WIELGOSZ — Editor
NIKOLA ČIŽMEŠIJA & ROMULO FAJARDO JR — Cover
JUNI BA — Varient Cover

IT SHALL BE ENOUGH.

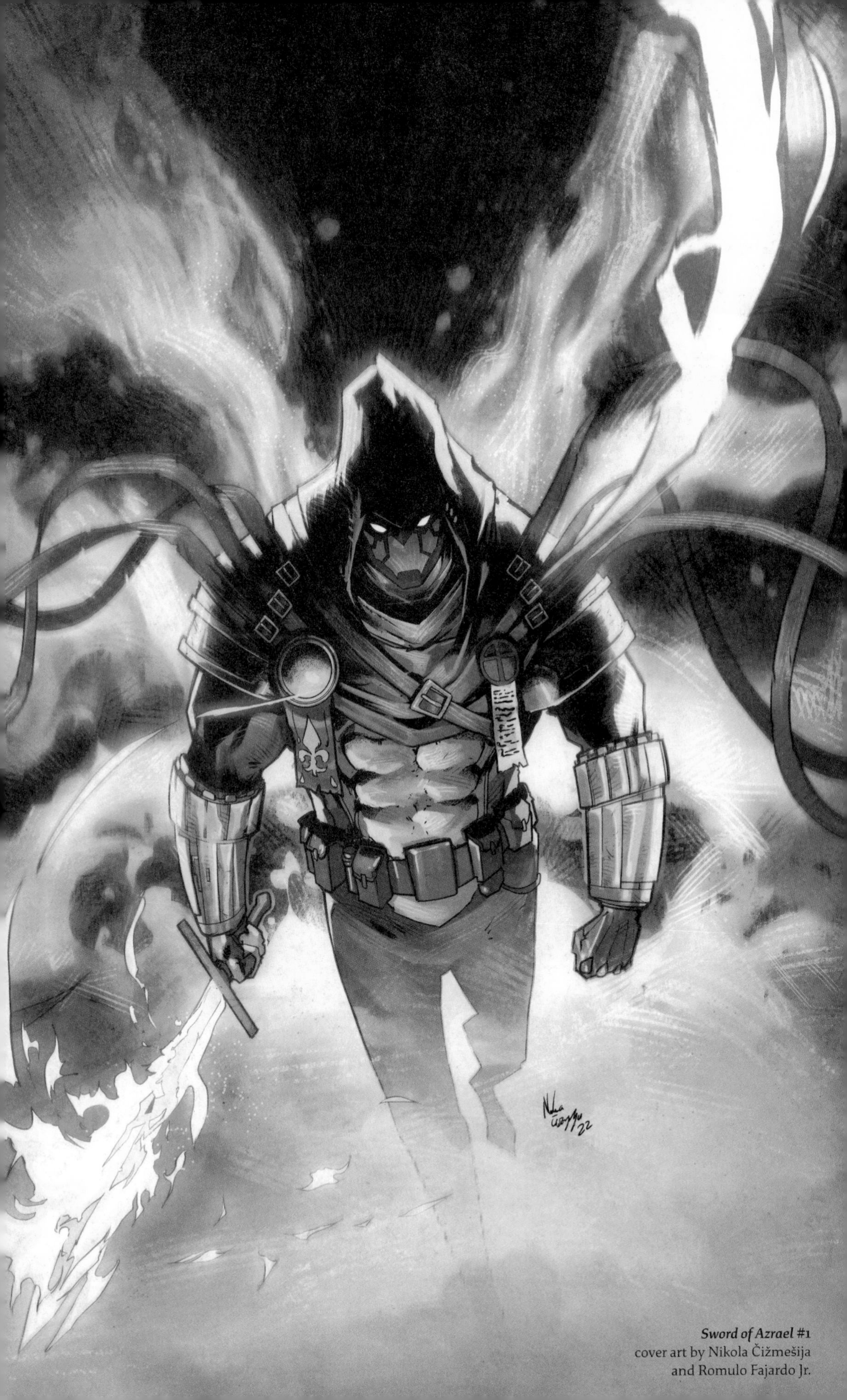

Sword of Azrael #1
cover art by Nikola Čižmešija
and Romulo Fajardo Jr.

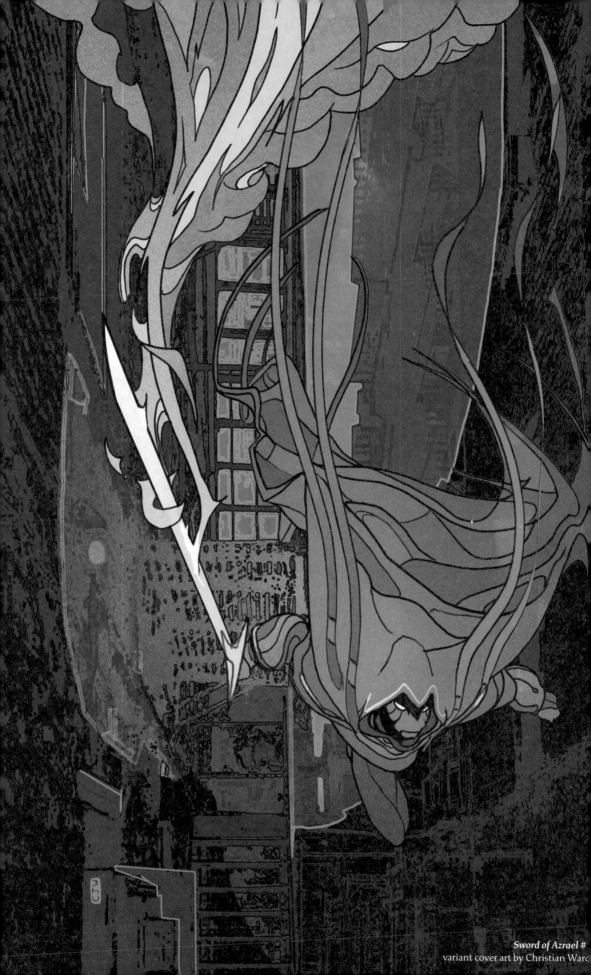

Sword of Azrael #
variant cover art by Christian Wardc

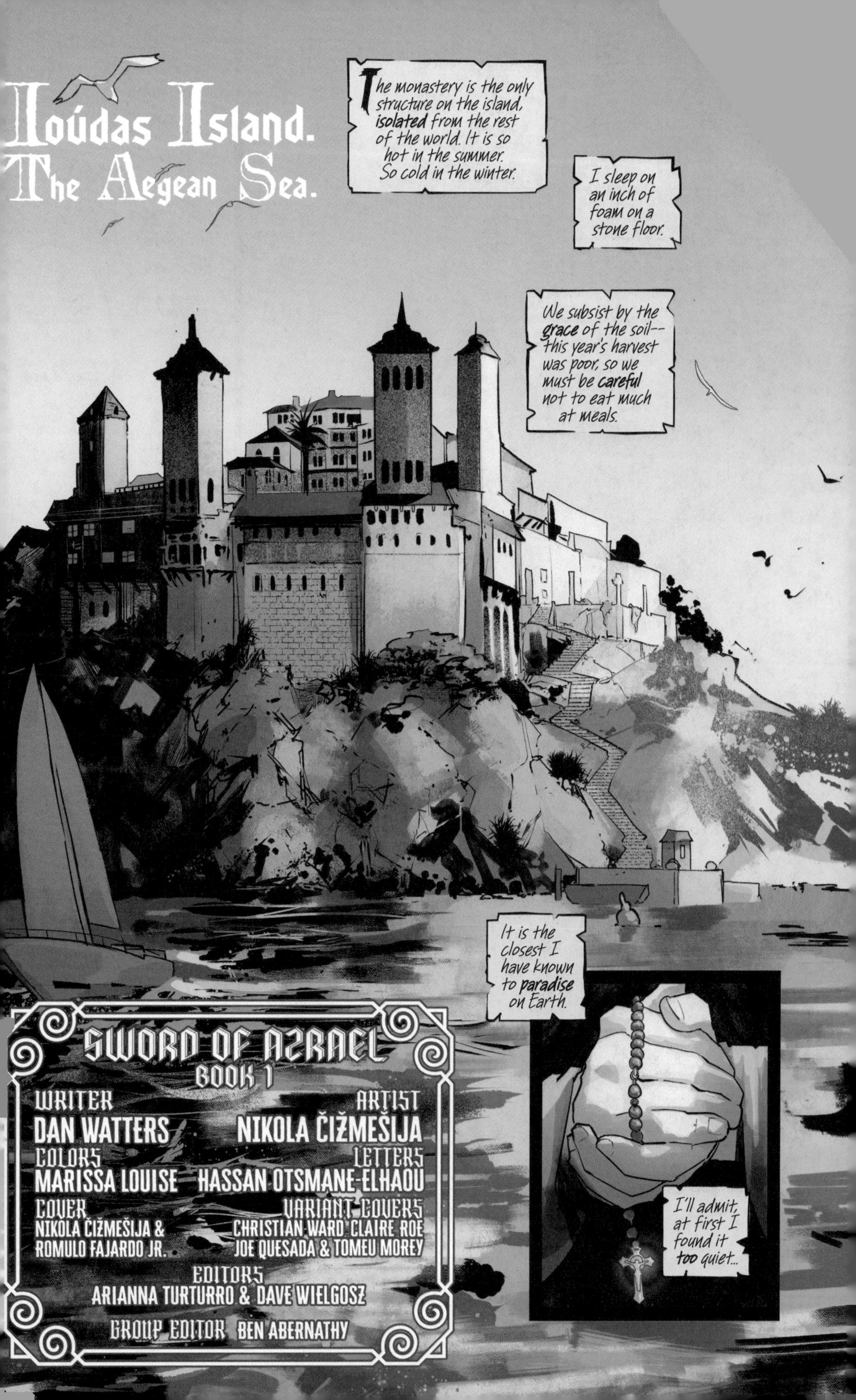
Ioúdas Island. The Aegean Sea.
The monastery is the only structure on the island, **isolated** from the rest of the world. It is so hot in the summer. So cold in the winter.
I sleep on an inch of foam on a stone floor.
We subsist by the **grace** of the soil-- this year's harvest was poor, so we must be **careful** not to eat much at meals.
It is the closest I have known to **paradise** on Earth.
SWORD OF AZRAEL
BOOK 1
WRITER DAN WATTERS
ARTIST NIKOLA ČIŽMEŠIJA
COLORS MARISSA LOUISE
LETTERS HASSAN OTSMANE-ELHAOU
COVER NIKOLA ČIŽMEŠIJA & ROMULO FAJARDO JR.
VARIANT COVERS CHRISTIAN WARD, CLAIRE ROE, JOE QUESADA & TOMEU MOREY
EDITORS ARIANNA TURTURRO & DAVE WIELGOSZ
GROUP EDITOR BEN ABERNATHY
I'll admit, at first I found it **too** quiet...

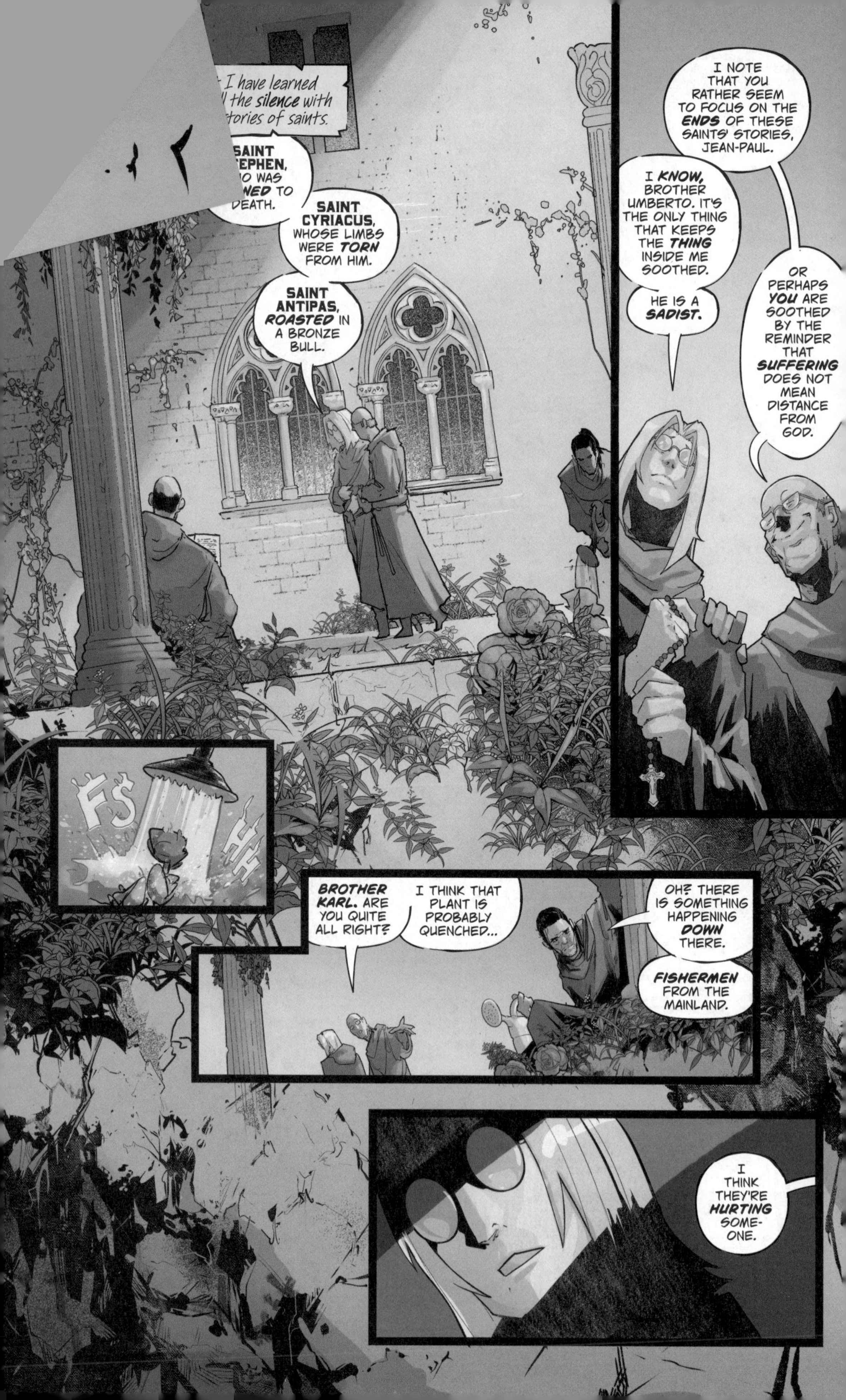
I have learned ll the silence with tories of saints.
SAINT EPHEN, O WAS NED TO DEATH.
SAINT CYRIACUS, WHOSE LIMBS WERE TORN FROM HIM.
SAINT ANTIPAS, ROASTED IN A BRONZE BULL.
I NOTE THAT YOU RATHER SEEM TO FOCUS ON THE ENDS OF THESE SAINTS' STORIES, JEAN-PAUL.
I KNOW, BROTHER UMBERTO. IT'S THE ONLY THING THAT KEEPS THE THING INSIDE ME SOOTHED.
HE IS A SADIST.
OR PERHAPS YOU ARE SOOTHED BY THE REMINDER THAT SUFFERING DOES NOT MEAN DISTANCE FROM GOD.
FSHH
BROTHER KARL. ARE YOU QUITE ALL RIGHT?
I THINK THAT PLANT IS PROBABLY QUENCHED...
OH? THERE IS SOMETHING HAPPENING DOWN THERE.
FISHERMEN FROM THE MAINLAND.
I THINK THEY'RE HURTING SOME-ONE.

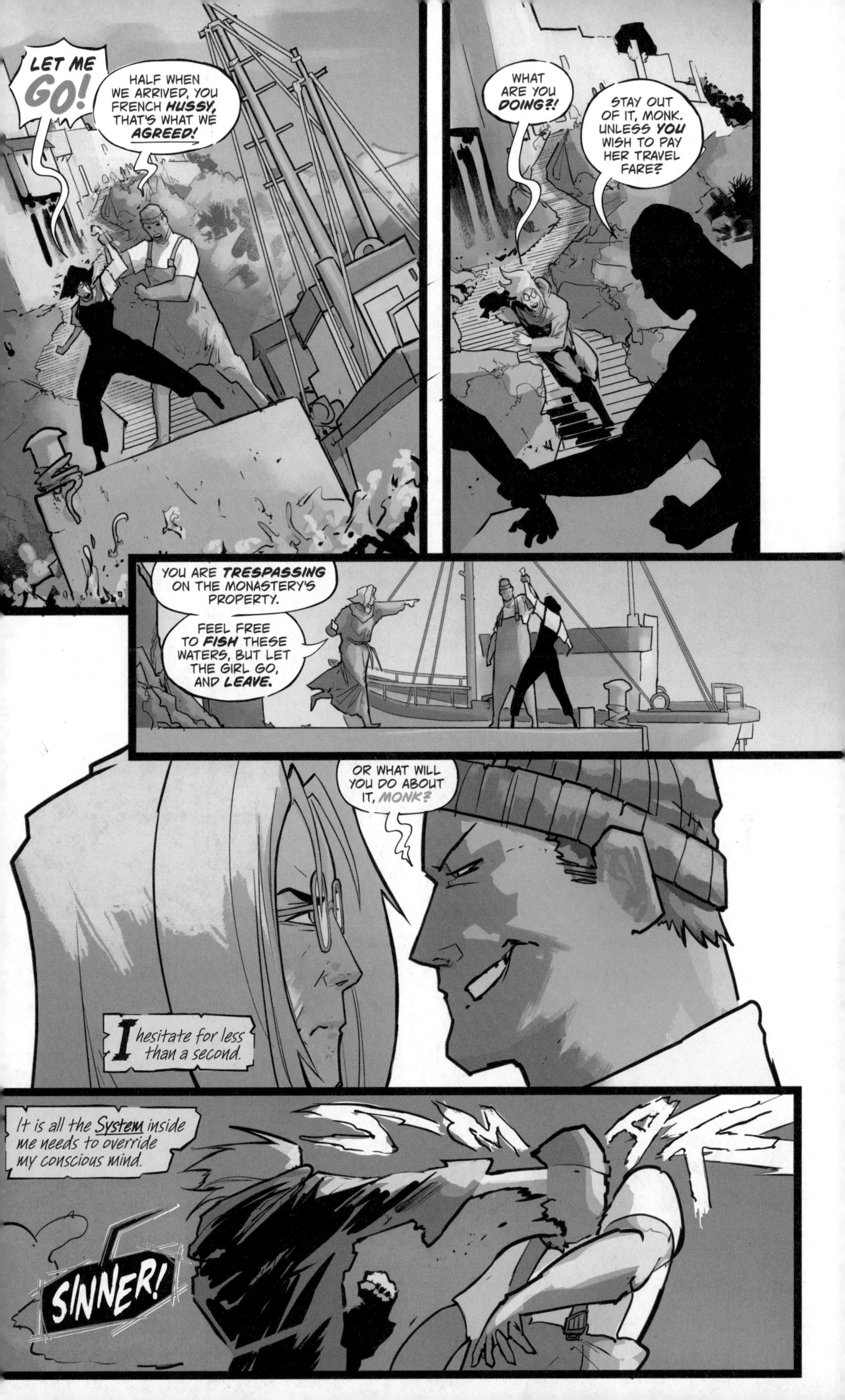
LET ME GO!
HALF WHEN WE ARRIVED, YOU FRENCH HUSSY, THAT'S WHAT WE AGREED!
WHAT ARE YOU DOING?!
STAY OUT OF IT, MONK. UNLESS YOU WISH TO PAY HER TRAVEL FARE?
YOU ARE TRESPASSING ON THE MONASTERY'S PROPERTY.
FEEL FREE TO FISH THESE WATERS, BUT LET THE GIRL GO, AND LEAVE.
OR WHAT WILL YOU DO ABOUT IT, MONK?
I hesitate for less than a second.
It is all the System inside me needs to override my conscious mind.
SMAK
SINNER!

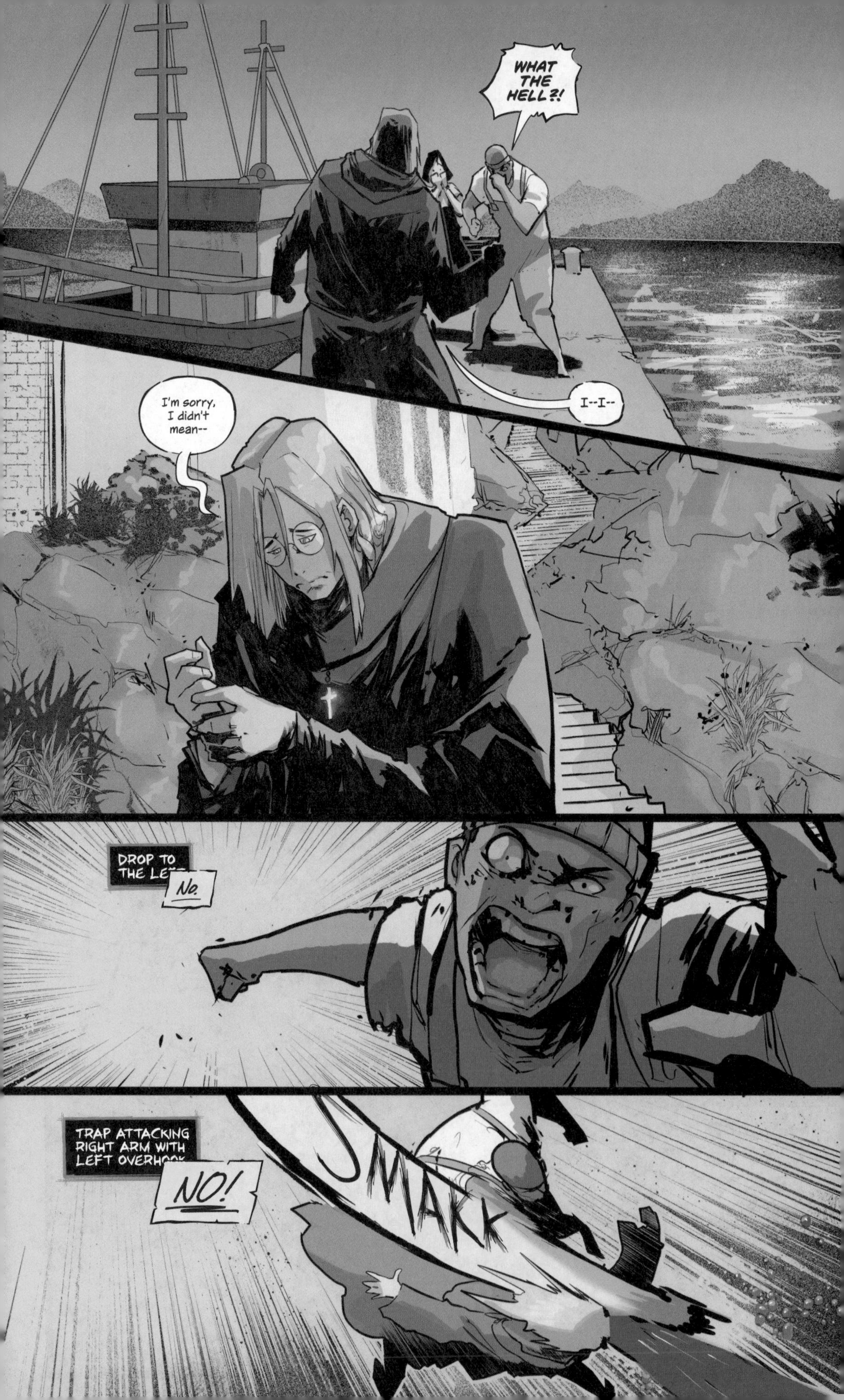
WHAT THE HELL?!
I--I--
I'm sorry, I didn't mean--
DROP TO THE LEF
No.
TRAP ATTACKING RIGHT ARM WITH LEFT OVERHO
NO!
SMAKK

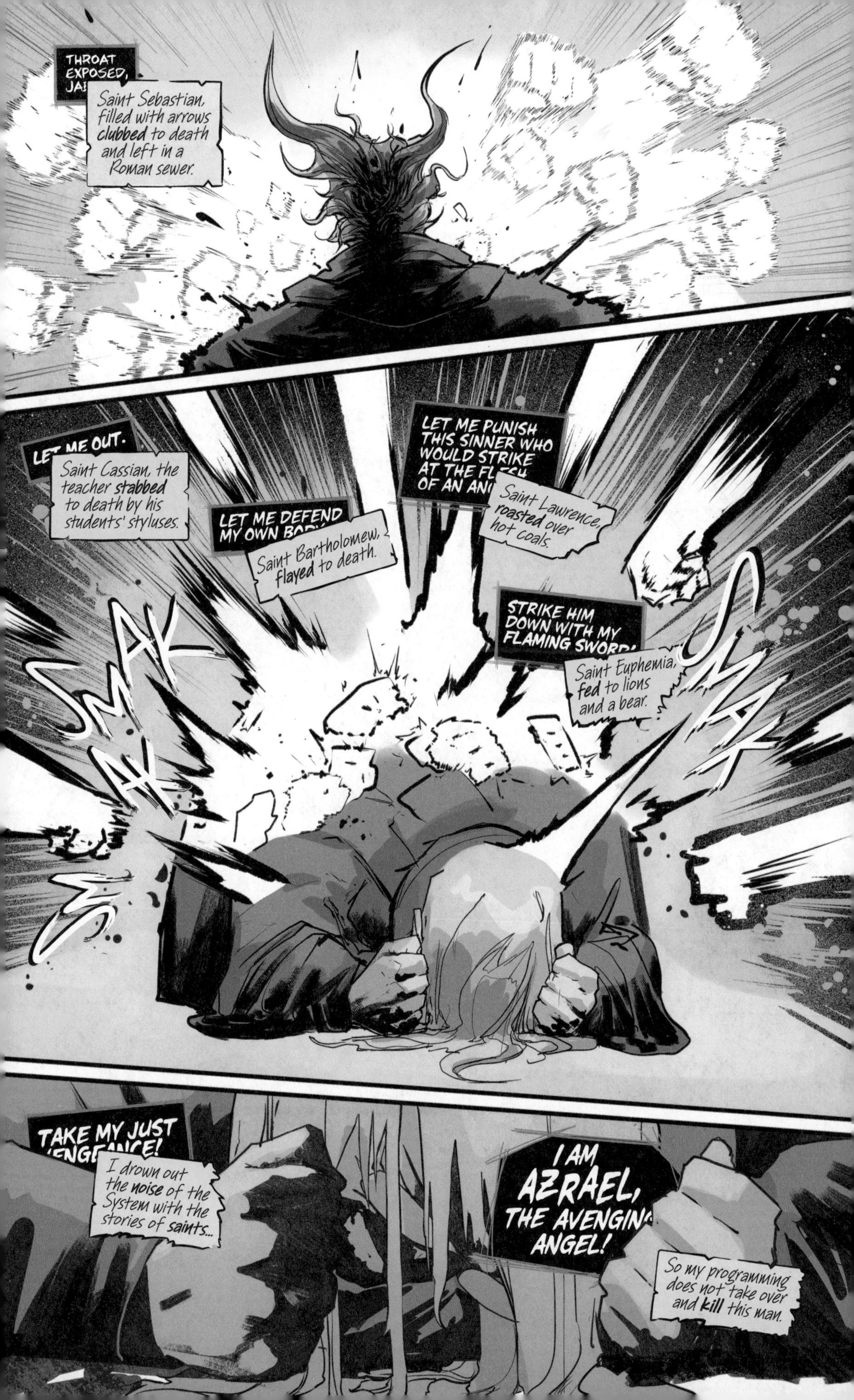

THROAT EXPOSED, JA
Saint Sebastian, filled with arrows clubbed to death and left in a Roman sewer.
LET ME OUT.
Saint Cassian, the teacher stabbed to death by his students' styluses.
LET ME DEFEND MY OWN BOD
Saint Bartholomew, flayed to death.
LET ME PUNISH THIS SINNER WHO WOULD STRIKE AT THE FLES OF AN AN
Saint Lawrence, roasted over hot coals.
STRIKE HIM DOWN WITH MY FLAMING SWORD
Saint Euphemia, fed to lions and a bear.
SMAK
SMAK
SMAK
TAKE MY JUST VENGEANCE!
I drown out the noise of the System with the stories of saints...
I AM AZRAEL, THE AVENGIN ANGEL!
So my programming does not take over and kill this man.

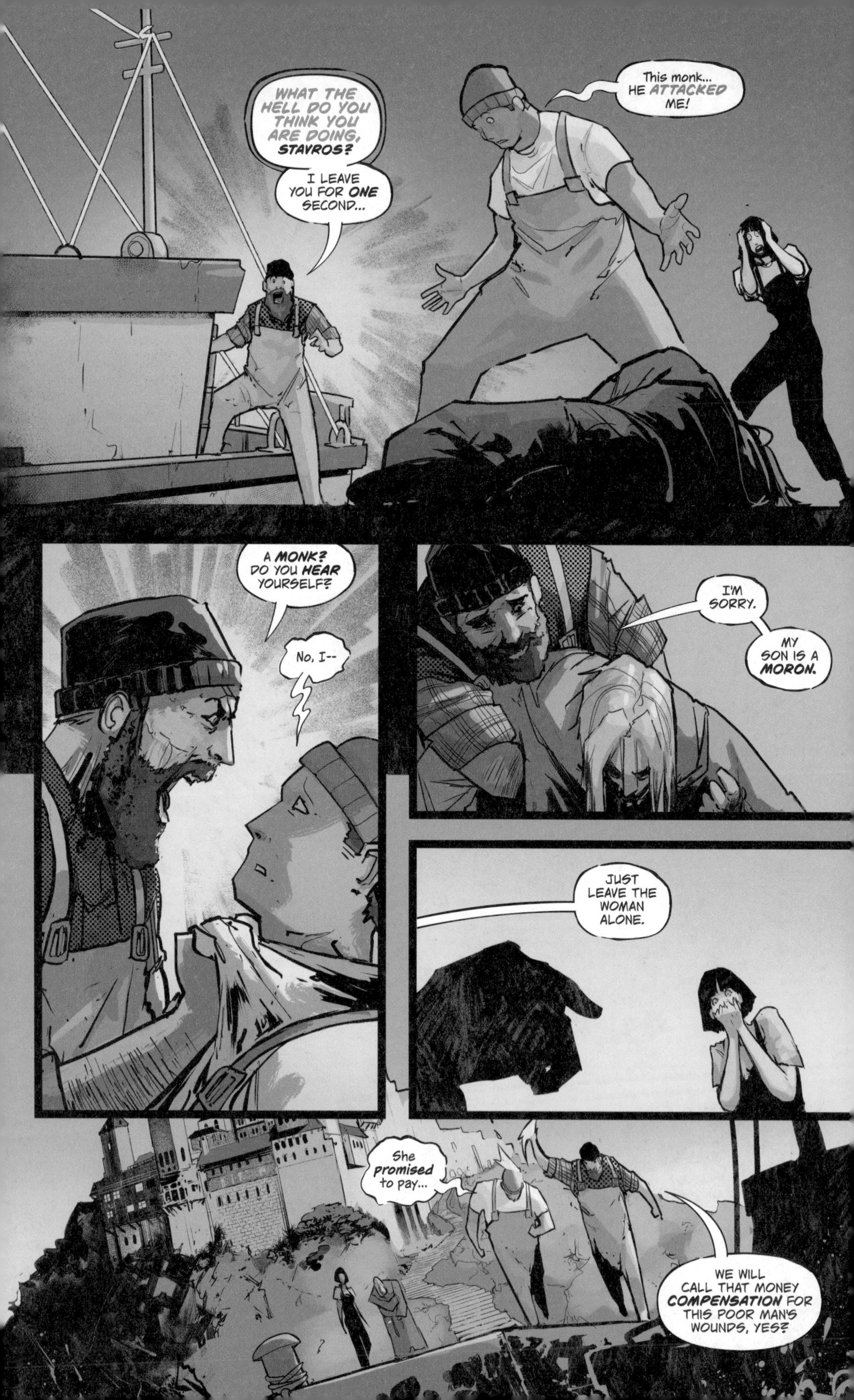
WHAT THE HELL DO YOU THINK YOU ARE DOING, STAVROS?
I LEAVE YOU FOR ONE SECOND...
This monk... HE ATTACKED ME!
A MONK? DO YOU HEAR YOURSELF?
No, I--
I'M SORRY.
MY SON IS A MORON.
JUST LEAVE THE WOMAN ALONE.
She promised to pay...
WE WILL CALL THAT MONEY COMPENSATION FOR THIS POOR MAN'S WOUNDS, YES?

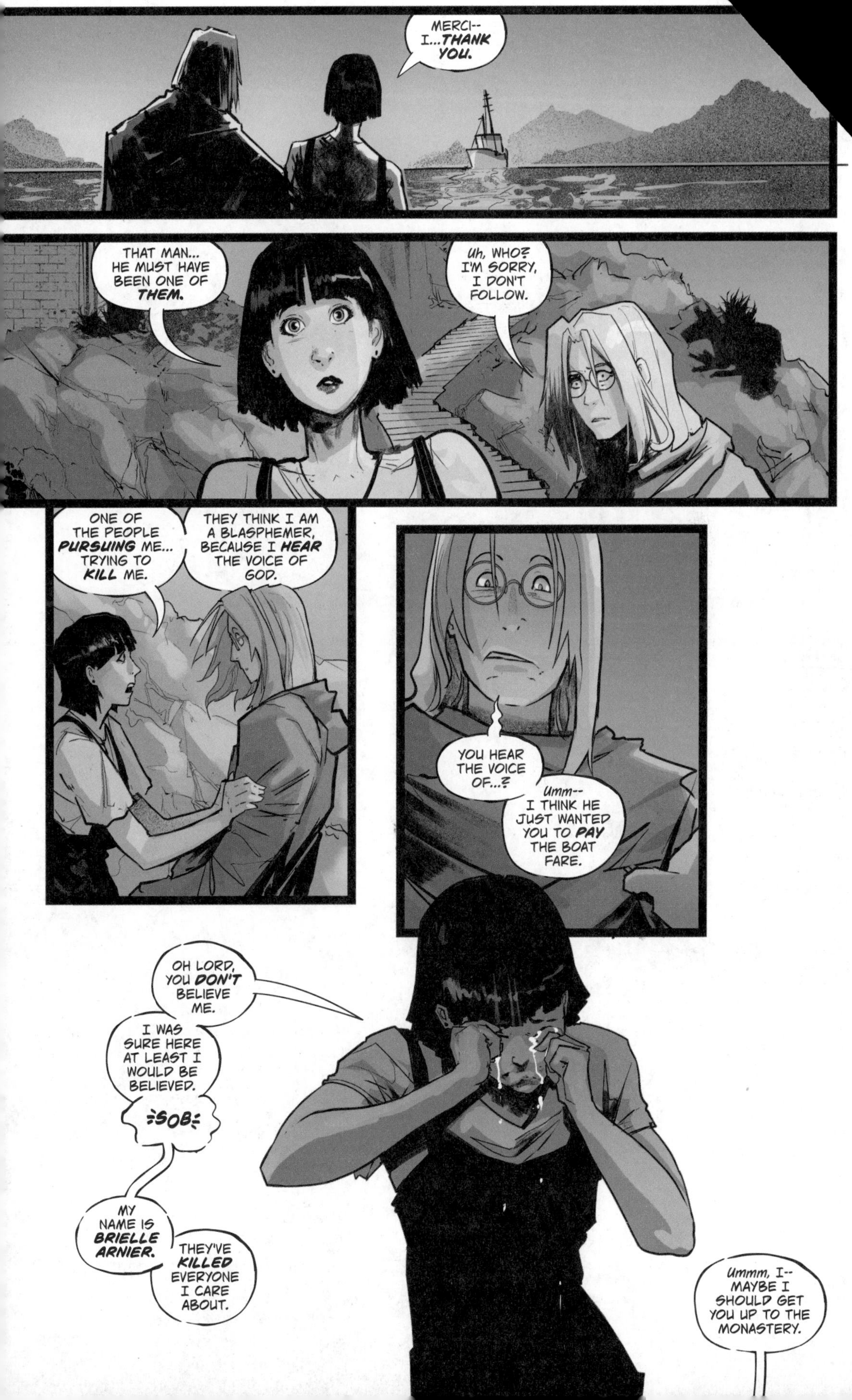

MERCI-- I...THANK YOU.
THAT MAN... HE MUST HAVE BEEN ONE OF THEM.
Uh, WHO? I'M SORRY, I DON'T FOLLOW.
ONE OF THE PEOPLE PURSUING ME... TRYING TO KILL ME.
THEY THINK I AM A BLASPHEMER, BECAUSE I HEAR THE VOICE OF GOD.
YOU HEAR THE VOICE OF...?
Umm-- I THINK HE JUST WANTED YOU TO PAY THE BOAT FARE.
OH LORD, YOU DON'T BELIEVE ME.
I WAS SURE HERE AT LEAST I WOULD BE BELIEVED.
SOB
MY NAME IS BRIELLE ARNIER.
THEY'VE KILLED EVERYONE I CARE ABOUT.
Ummm, I-- MAYBE I SHOULD GET YOU UP TO THE MONASTERY.

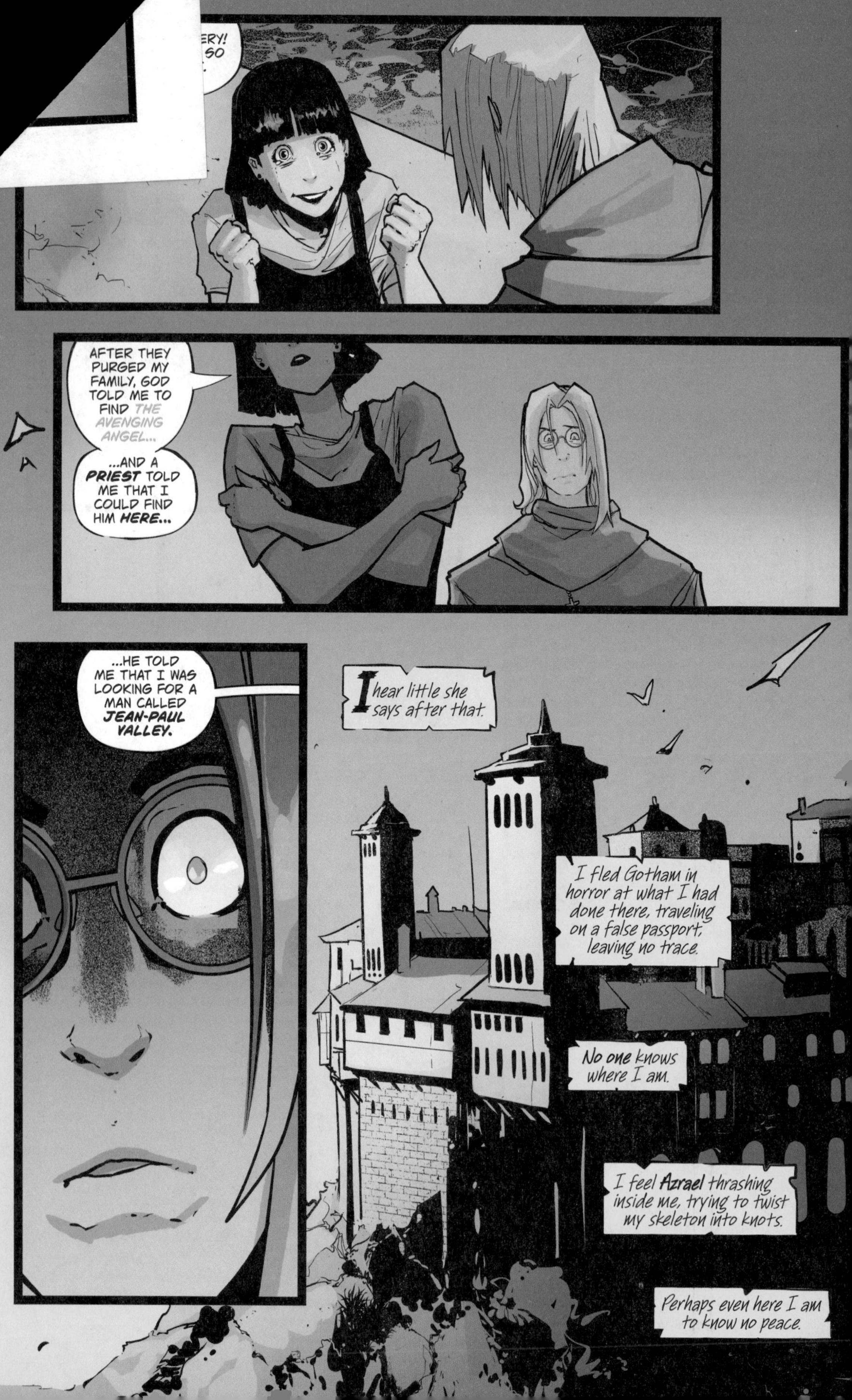
ERY! SO
AFTER THEY PURGED MY FAMILY, GOD TOLD ME TO FIND THE AVENGING ANGEL...
...AND A PRIEST TOLD ME THAT I COULD FIND HIM HERE...
...HE TOLD ME THAT I WAS LOOKING FOR A MAN CALLED JEAN-PAUL VALLEY.
I hear little she says after that.
I fled Gotham in horror at what I had done there, traveling on a false passport, leaving no trace.
No one knows where I am.
I feel Azrael thrashing inside me, trying to twist my skeleton into knots.
Perhaps even here I am to know no peace.

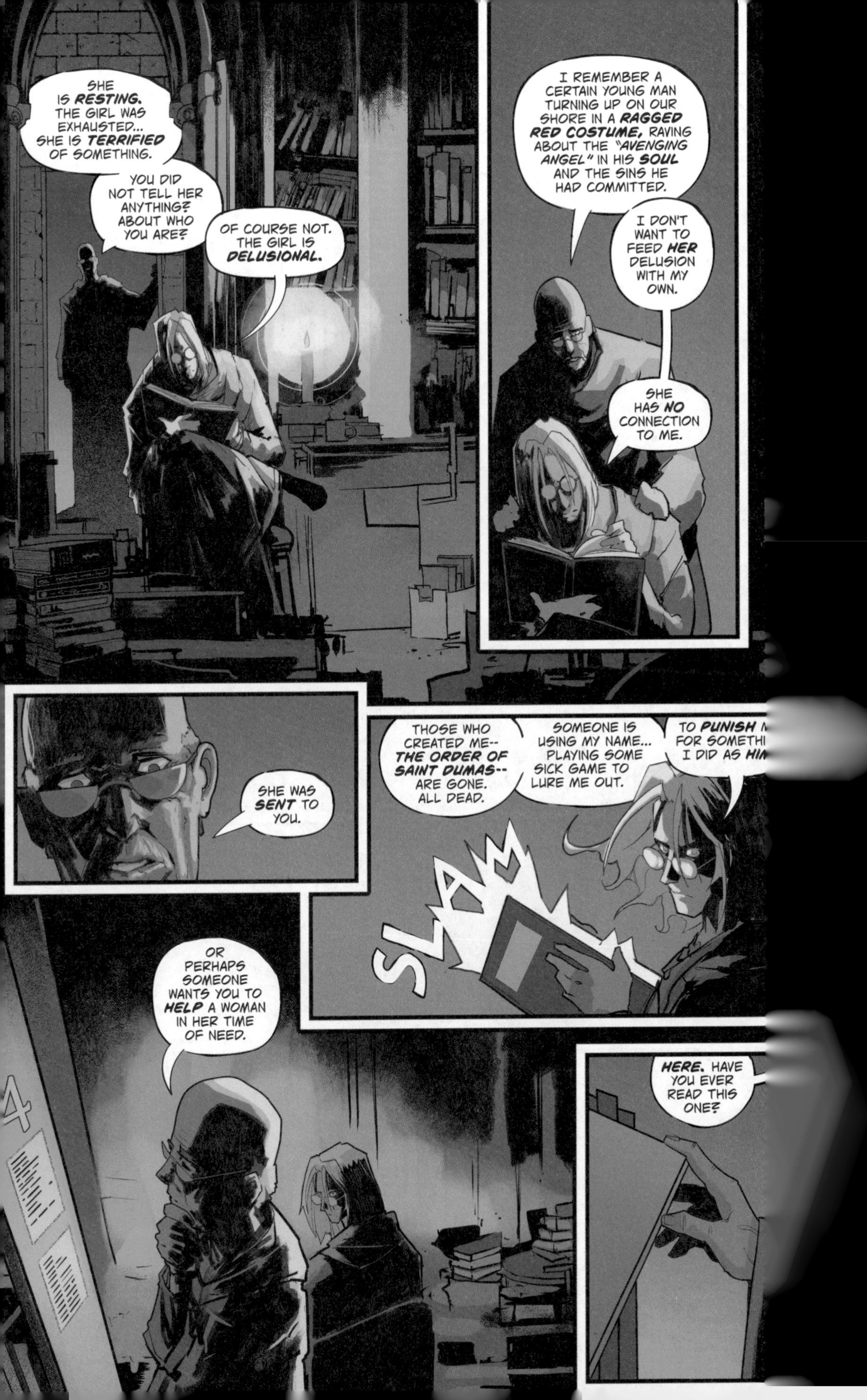

SHE IS **RESTING.** THE GIRL WAS EXHAUSTED... SHE IS **TERRIFIED** OF SOMETHING.
YOU DID NOT TELL HER ANYTHING? ABOUT WHO YOU ARE?
OF COURSE NOT. THE GIRL IS **DELUSIONAL.**
I REMEMBER A CERTAIN YOUNG MAN TURNING UP ON OUR SHORE IN A **RAGGED RED COSTUME,** RAVING ABOUT THE "**AVENGING ANGEL**" IN HIS **SOUL** AND THE SINS HE HAD COMMITTED.
I DON'T WANT TO FEED **HER** DELUSION WITH MY OWN.
SHE HAS **NO** CONNECTION TO ME.
SHE WAS **SENT** TO YOU.
THOSE WHO CREATED ME-- **THE ORDER OF SAINT DUMAS--** ARE GONE. ALL DEAD.
SOMEONE IS USING MY NAME... PLAYING SOME SICK GAME TO LURE ME OUT.
TO **PUNISH** M FOR SOMETHI I DID AS **HI**
SLAM
OR PERHAPS SOMEONE WANTS YOU TO **HELP** A WOMAN IN HER TIME OF NEED.
HERE. HAVE YOU EVER READ THIS ONE?

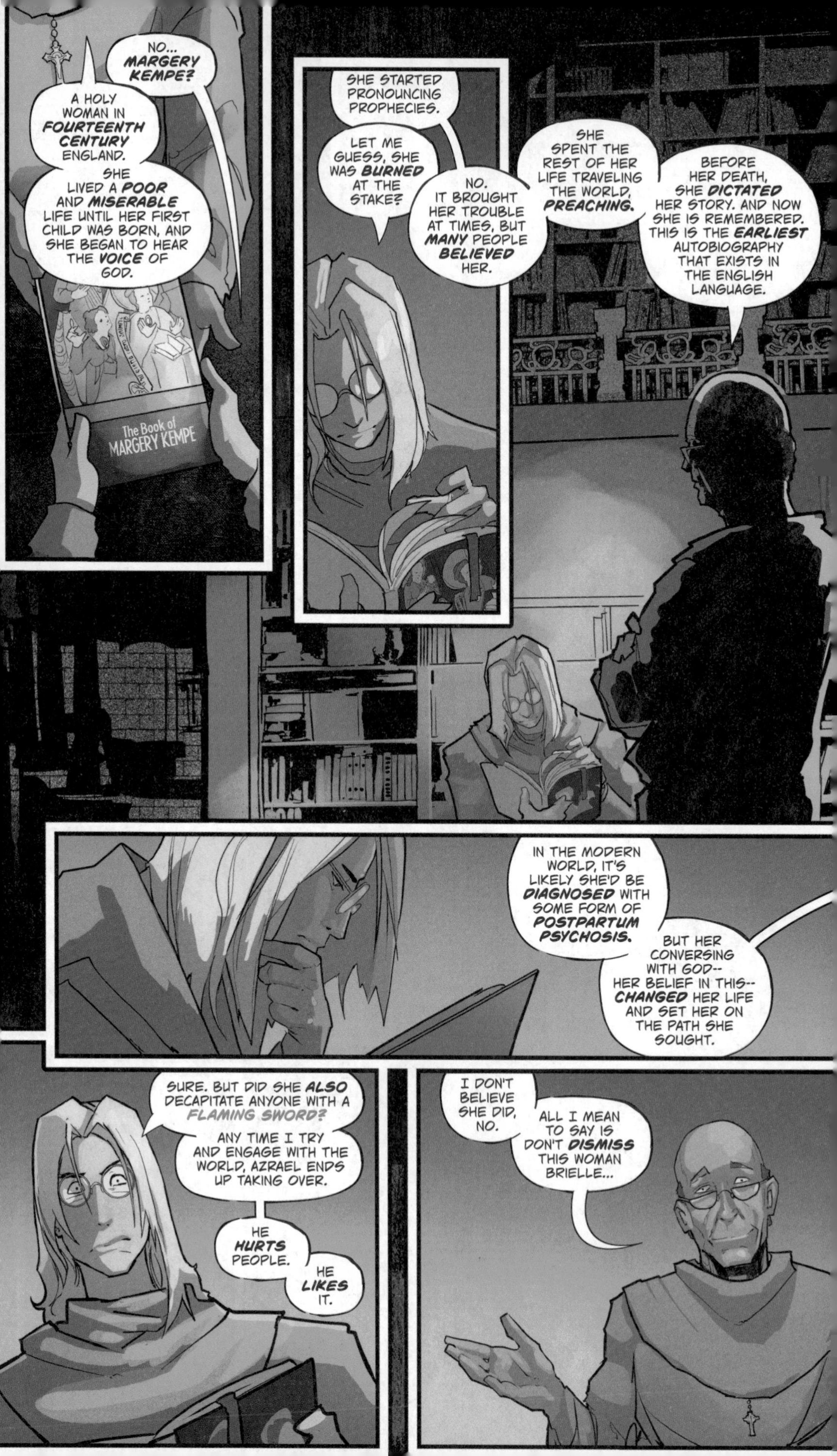
NO... MARGERY KEMPE?
A HOLY WOMAN IN FOURTEENTH CENTURY ENGLAND.
SHE LIVED A POOR AND MISERABLE LIFE UNTIL HER FIRST CHILD WAS BORN, AND SHE BEGAN TO HEAR THE VOICE OF GOD.
The Book of MARGERY KEMPE
SHE STARTED PRONOUNCING PROPHECIES.
LET ME GUESS, SHE WAS BURNED AT THE STAKE?
NO. IT BROUGHT HER TROUBLE AT TIMES, BUT MANY PEOPLE BELIEVED HER.
SHE SPENT THE REST OF HER LIFE TRAVELING THE WORLD, PREACHING.
BEFORE HER DEATH, SHE DICTATED HER STORY. AND NOW SHE IS REMEMBERED. THIS IS THE EARLIEST AUTOBIOGRAPHY THAT EXISTS IN THE ENGLISH LANGUAGE.
IN THE MODERN WORLD, IT'S LIKELY SHE'D BE DIAGNOSED WITH SOME FORM OF POSTPARTUM PSYCHOSIS.
BUT HER CONVERSING WITH GOD-- HER BELIEF IN THIS-- CHANGED HER LIFE AND SET HER ON THE PATH SHE SOUGHT.
SURE. BUT DID SHE ALSO DECAPITATE ANYONE WITH A FLAMING SWORD?
ANY TIME I TRY AND ENGAGE WITH THE WORLD, AZRAEL ENDS UP TAKING OVER.
HE HURTS PEOPLE.
HE LIKES IT.
I DON'T BELIEVE SHE DID, NO.
ALL I MEAN TO SAY IS DON'T DISMISS THIS WOMAN BRIELLE...

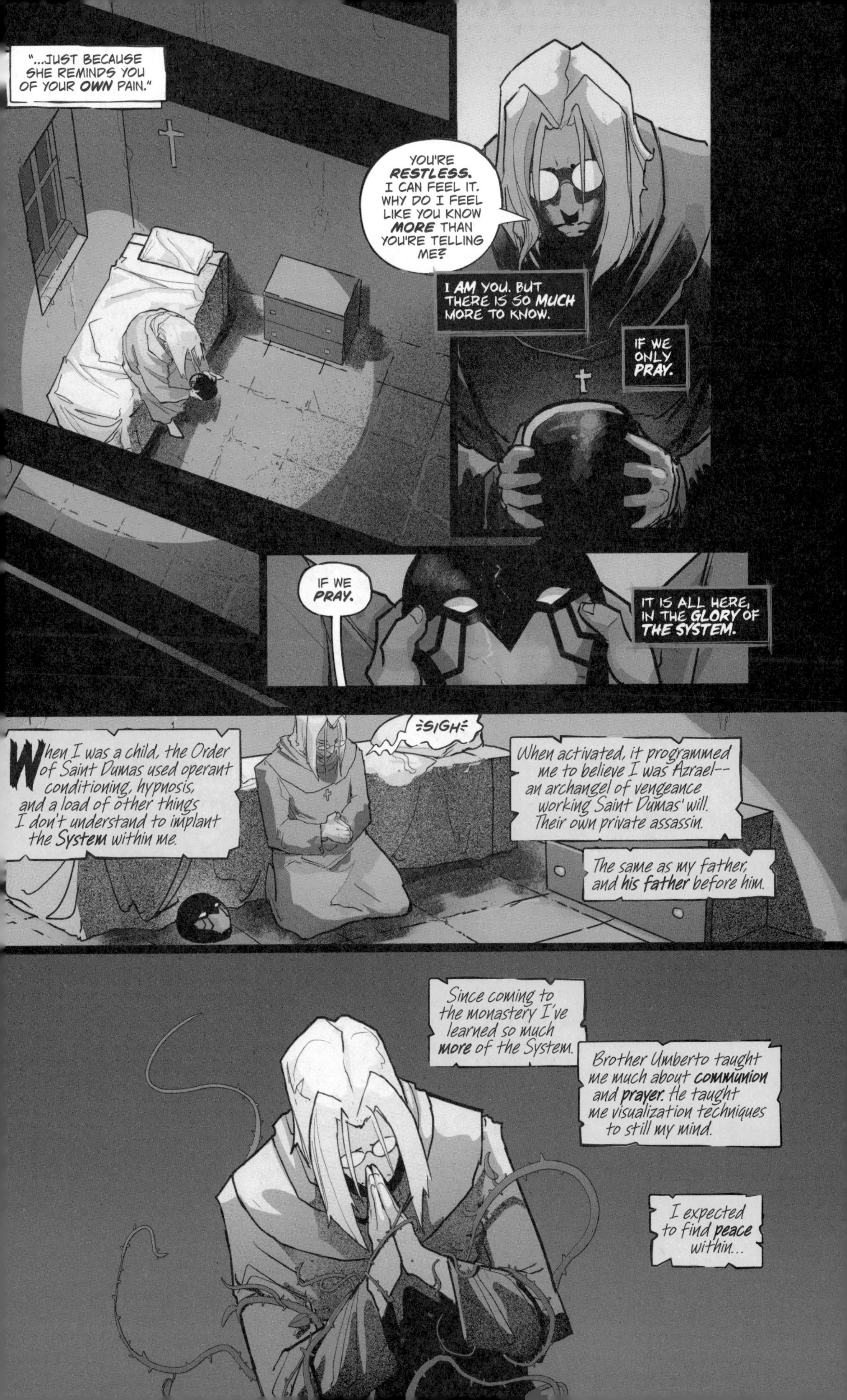
"...JUST BECAUSE SHE REMINDS YOU OF YOUR **OWN** PAIN."
YOU'RE **RESTLESS.** I CAN FEEL IT. WHY DO I FEEL LIKE YOU KNOW **MORE** THAN YOU'RE TELLING ME?
I **AM** YOU. BUT THERE IS SO **MUCH** MORE TO KNOW.
IF WE ONLY **PRAY.**
IF WE **PRAY.**
IT IS ALL HERE, IN THE **GLORY** OF **THE SYSTEM.**
When I was a child, the Order of Saint Dumas used operant conditioning, hypnosis, and a load of other things I don't understand to implant the **System** within me.
=SIGH=
When activated, it programmed me to believe I was Azrael-- an archangel of vengeance working Saint Dumas' will. Their own private assassin.
The same as my father, and **his father** before him.
Since coming to the monastery I've learned so much **more** of the System.
Brother Umberto taught me much about **communion** and **prayer.** He taught me visualization techniques to still my mind.
I expected to find **peace** within...

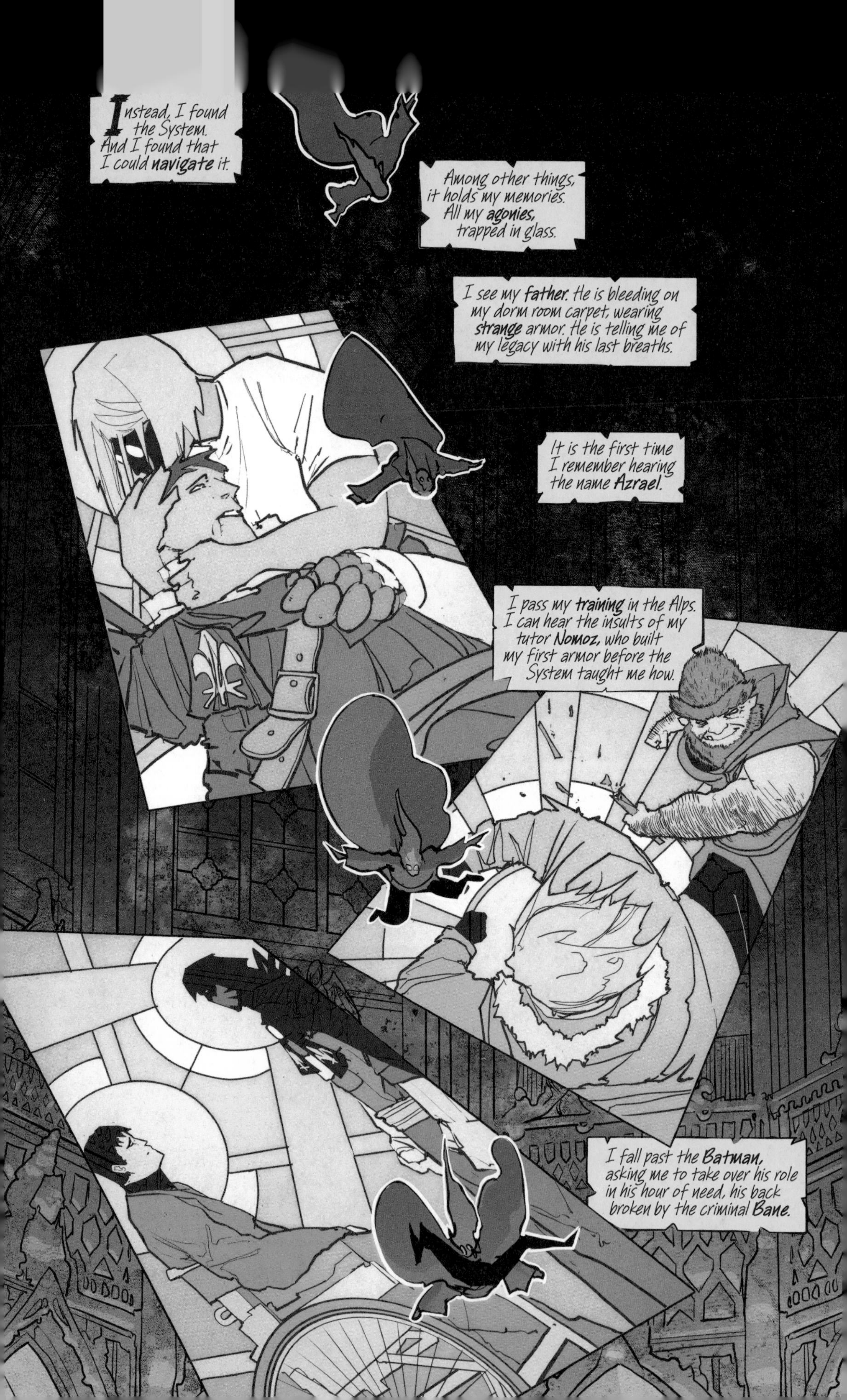
Instead, I found the System. And I found that I could navigate it.
Among other things, it holds my memories. All my agonies, trapped in glass.
I see my father. He is bleeding on my dorm room carpet, wearing strange armor. He is telling me of my legacy with his last breaths.
It is the first time I remember hearing the name Azrael.
I pass my training in the Alps. I can hear the insults of my tutor Nomoz, who built my first armor before the System taught me how.
I fall past the Batman, asking me to take over his role in his hour of need, his back broken by the criminal Bane.

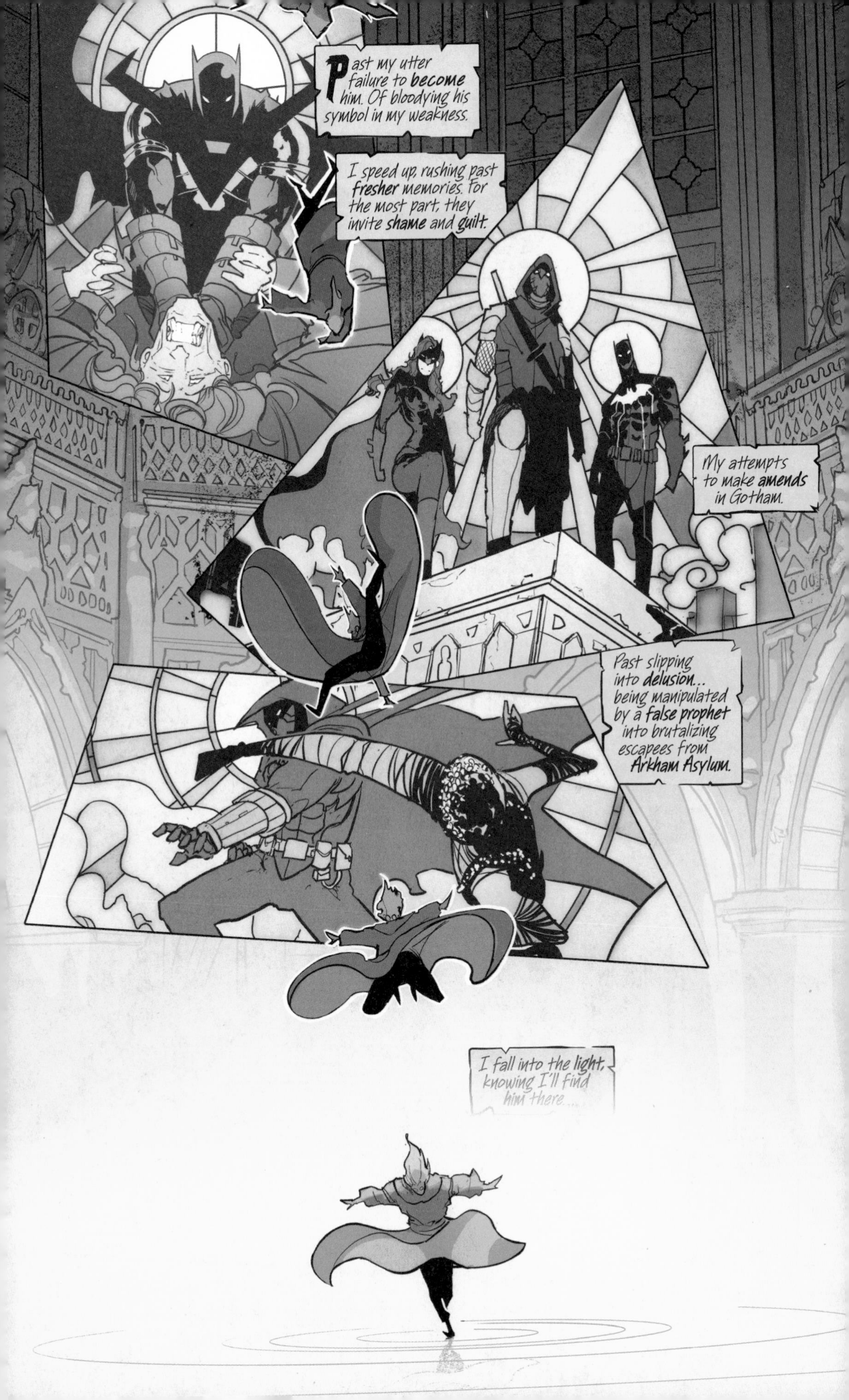
Past my utter failure to become him. Of bloodying his symbol in my weakness.
I speed up, rushing past fresher memories. For the most part, they invite shame and guilt.
My attempts to make amends in Gotham.
Past slipping into delusion... being manipulated by a false prophet into brutalizing escapees from Arkham Asylum.
I fall into the light, knowing I'll find him there...

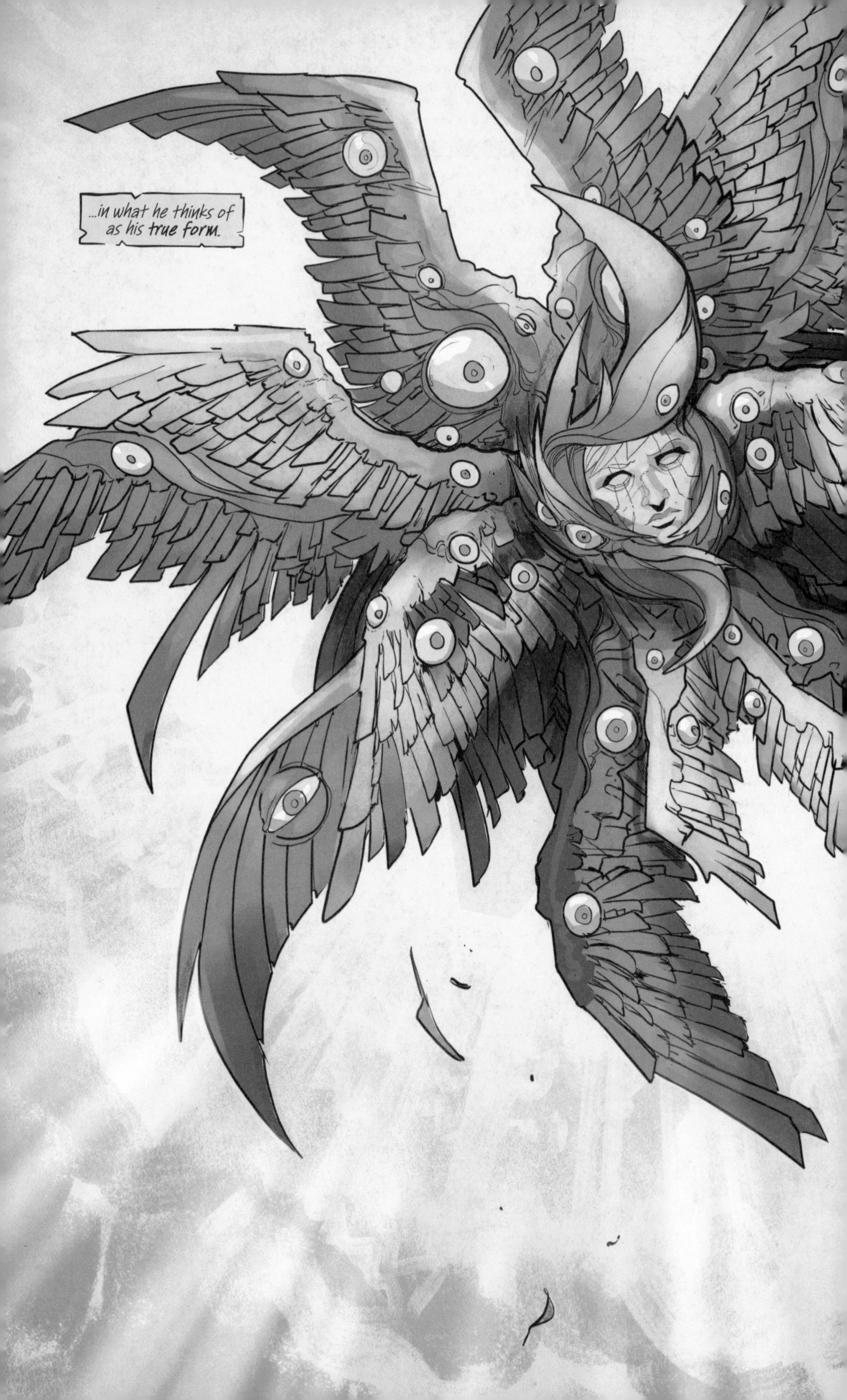
...in what he thinks of as his true form.

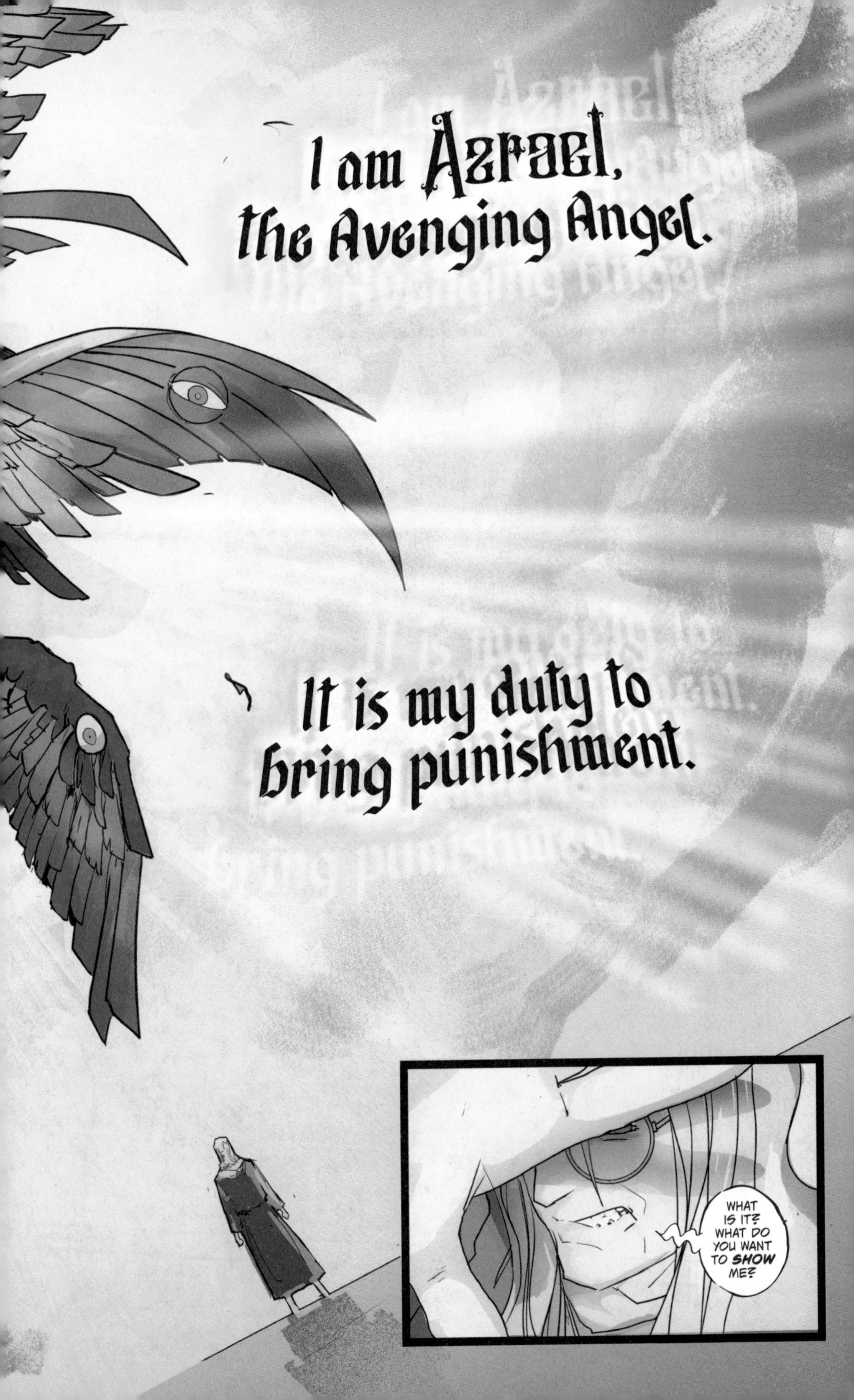
I am Azrael,
the Avenging Angel.
It is my duty to
bring punishment.
WHAT IS IT? WHAT DO YOU WANT TO SHOW ME?

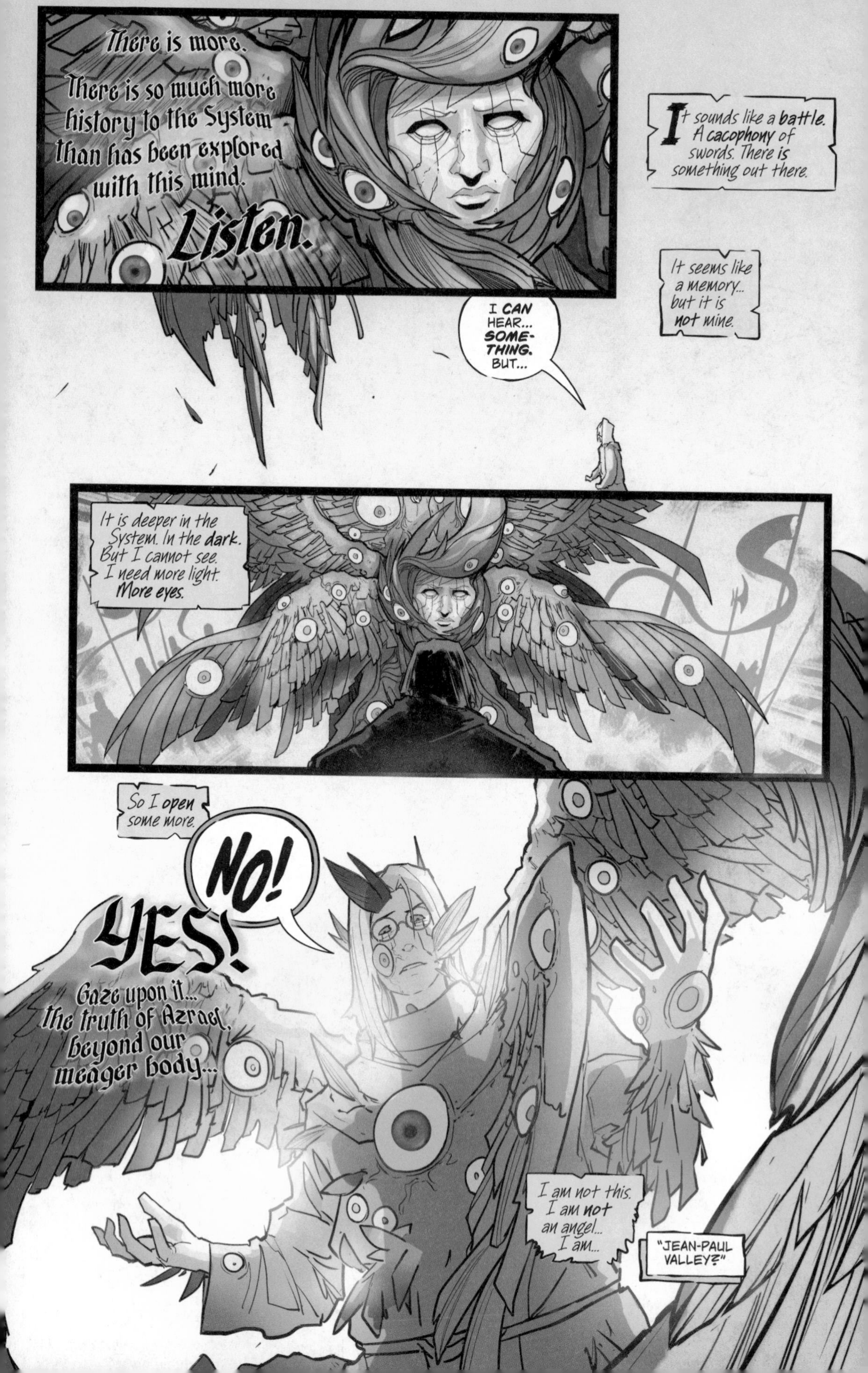

There is more.
There is so much more history to the System than has been explored with this mind.
Listen.
It sounds like a battle. A cacophony of swords. There is something out there.
It seems like a memory... but it is not mine.
I CAN HEAR... SOME-THING. BUT...
It is deeper in the System. In the dark. But I cannot see. I need more light. More eyes.
So I open some more.
NO!
YES!
Gaze upon it... the truth of Azrael, beyond our meager body...
I am not this. I am not an angel... I am...
"JEAN-PAUL VALLEY?"

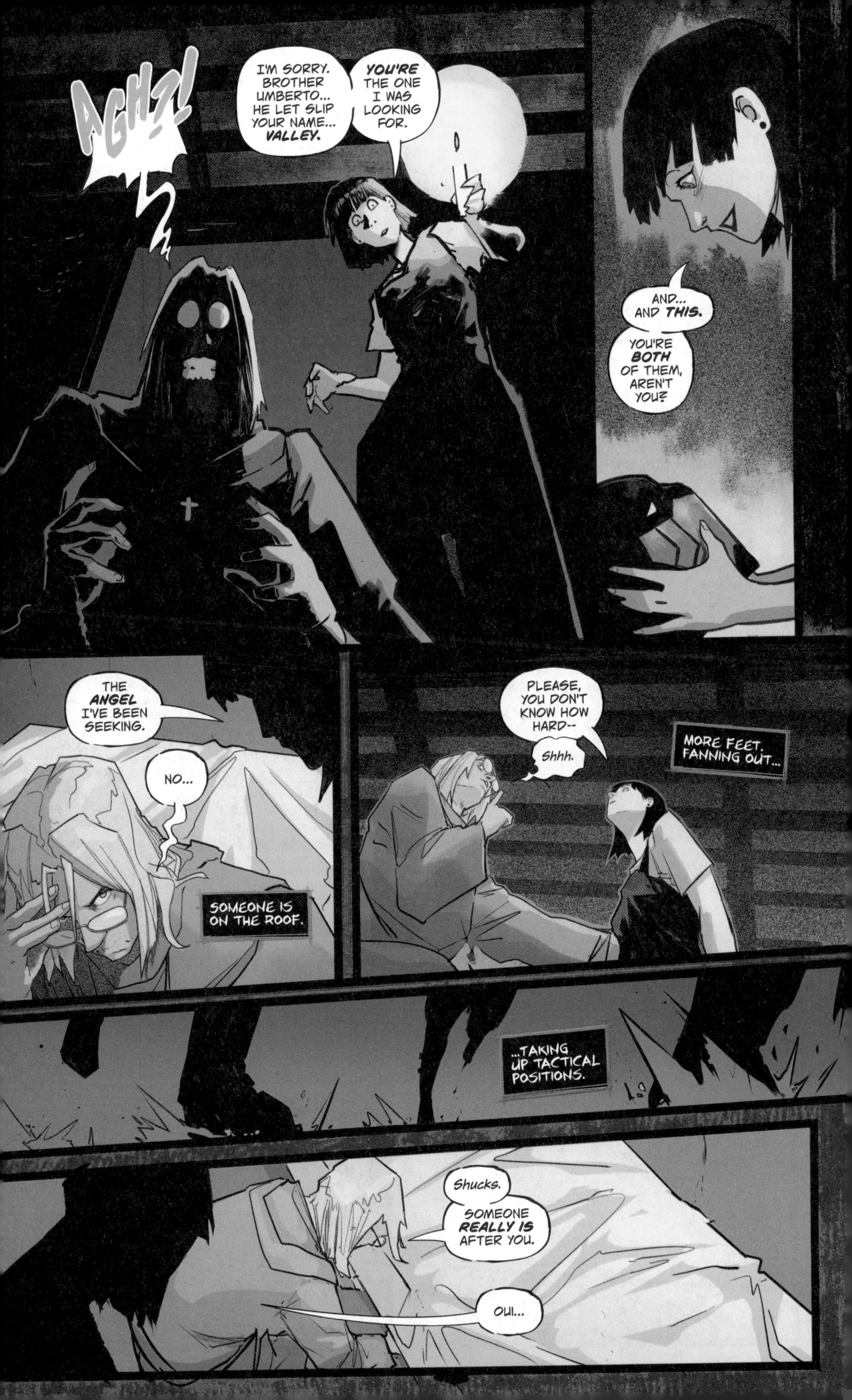
AGH?!
I'M SORRY. BROTHER UMBERTO... HE LET SLIP YOUR NAME... VALLEY.
YOU'RE THE ONE I WAS LOOKING FOR.
AND... AND THIS.
YOU'RE BOTH OF THEM, AREN'T YOU?
THE ANGEL I'VE BEEN SEEKING.
NO...
SOMEONE IS ON THE ROOF.
PLEASE, YOU DON'T KNOW HOW HARD--
Shhh.
MORE FEET, FANNING OUT...
...TAKING UP TACTICAL POSITIONS.
Shucks.
SOMEONE REALLY IS AFTER YOU.
OUI...

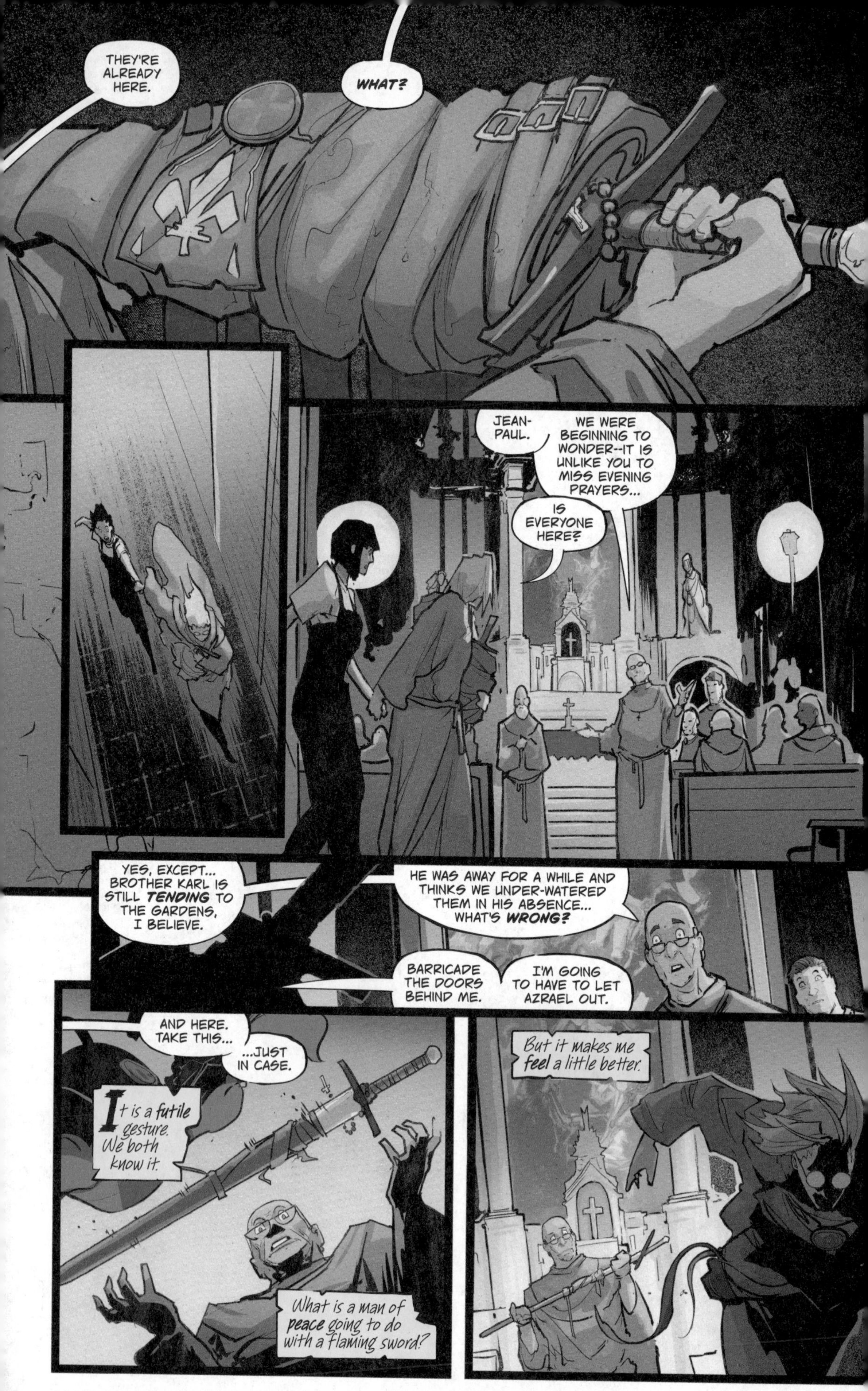
THEY'RE ALREADY HERE.
WHAT?
JEAN-PAUL.
WE WERE BEGINNING TO WONDER--IT IS UNLIKE YOU TO MISS EVENING PRAYERS...
IS EVERYONE HERE?
YES, EXCEPT... BROTHER KARL IS STILL TENDING TO THE GARDENS, I BELIEVE.
HE WAS AWAY FOR A WHILE AND THINKS WE UNDER-WATERED THEM IN HIS ABSENCE... WHAT'S WRONG?
BARRICADE THE DOORS BEHIND ME.
I'M GOING TO HAVE TO LET AZRAEL OUT.
AND HERE. TAKE THIS...
...JUST IN CASE.
It is a futile gesture. We both know it.
What is a man of peace going to do with a flaming sword?
But it makes me feel a little better.

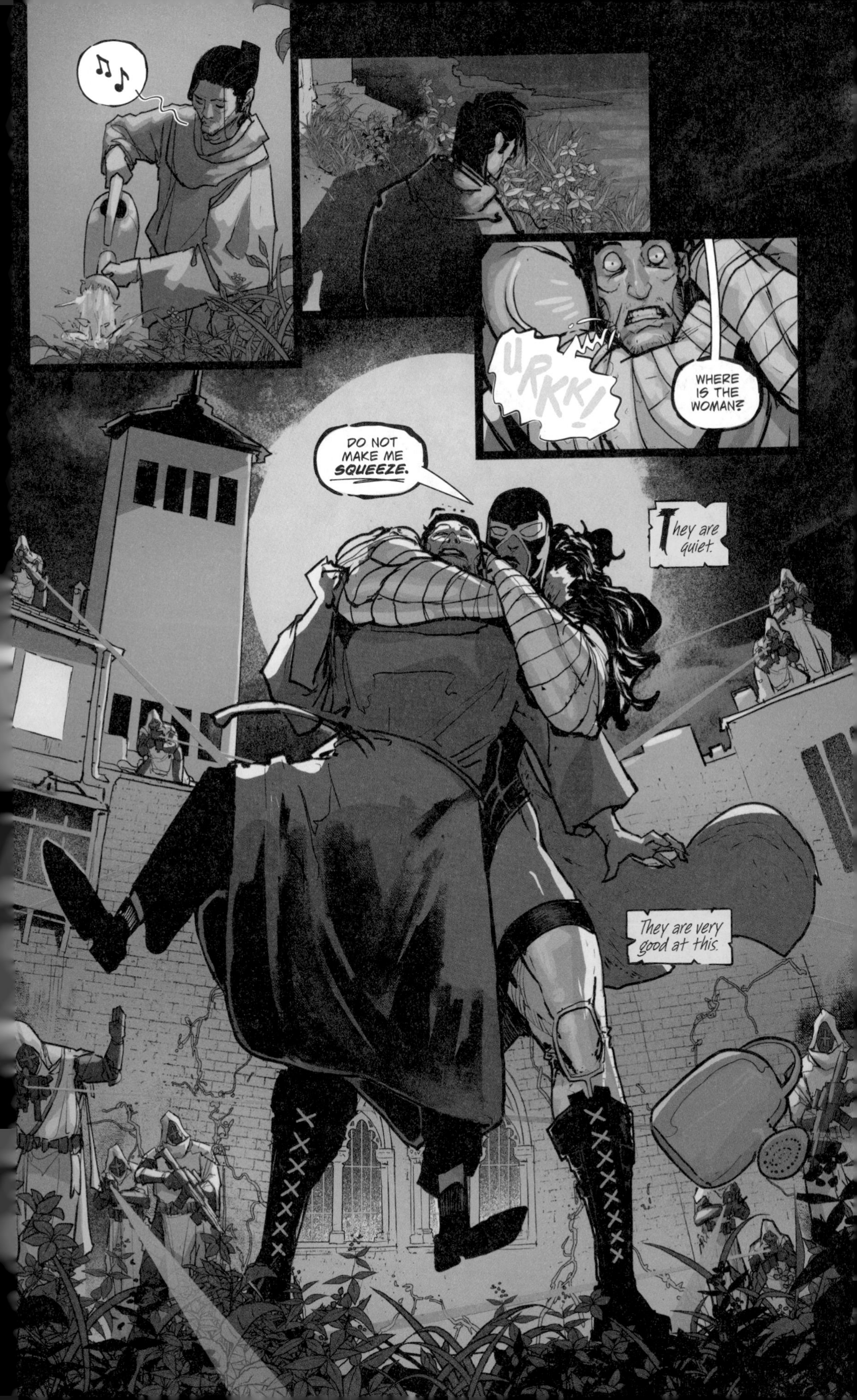
♫♪
URKK!
WHERE IS THE WOMAN?
DO NOT MAKE ME SQUEEZE.
They are quiet.
They are very good at this.

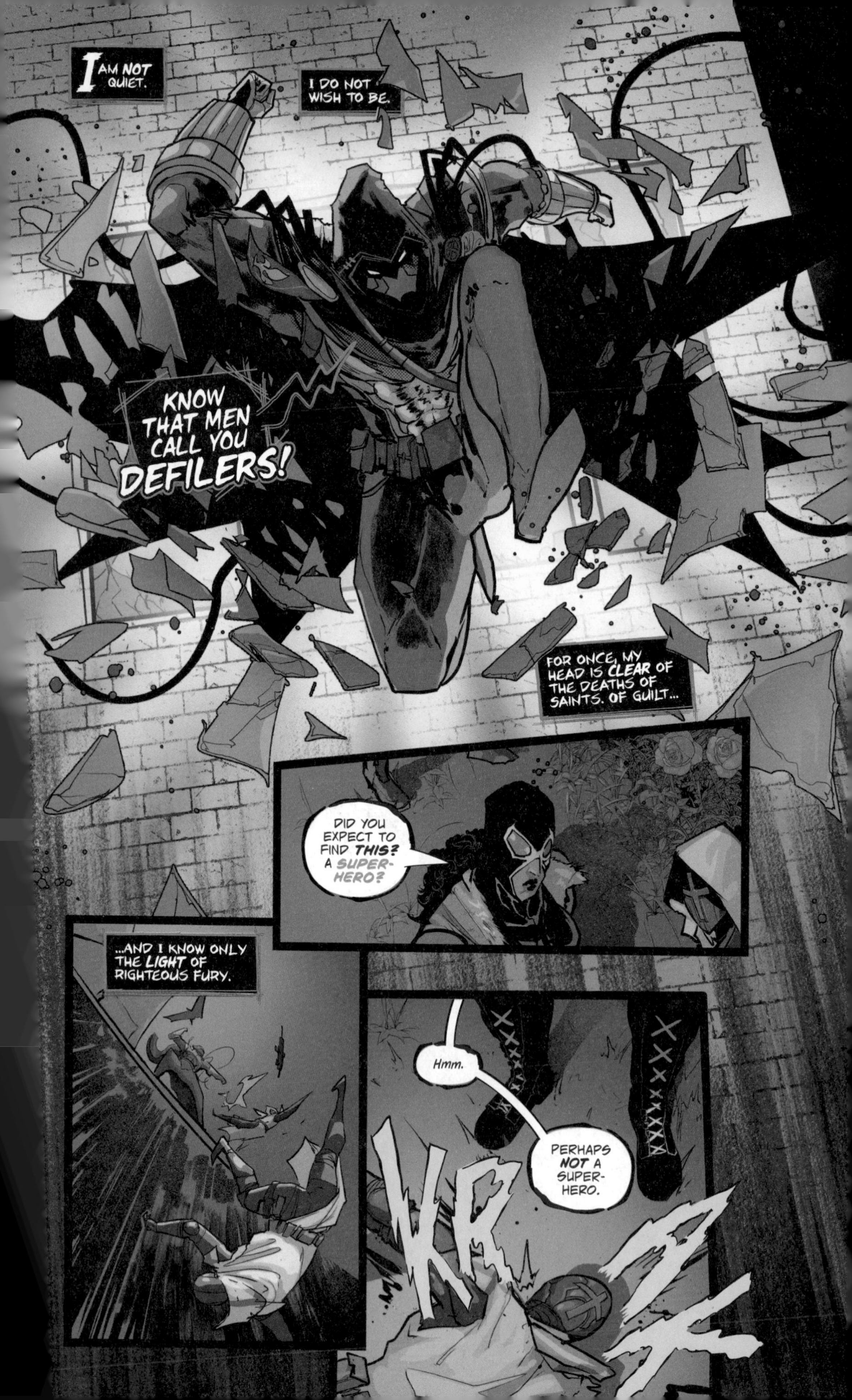
I AM NOT QUIET.
I DO NOT WISH TO BE.
KNOW THAT MEN CALL YOU DEFILERS!
FOR ONCE, MY HEAD IS CLEAR OF THE DEATHS OF SAINTS. OF GUILT...
DID YOU EXPECT TO FIND THIS? A SUPER-HERO?
...AND I KNOW ONLY THE LIGHT OF RIGHTEOUS FURY.
Hmm.
PERHAPS NOT A SUPER-HERO.

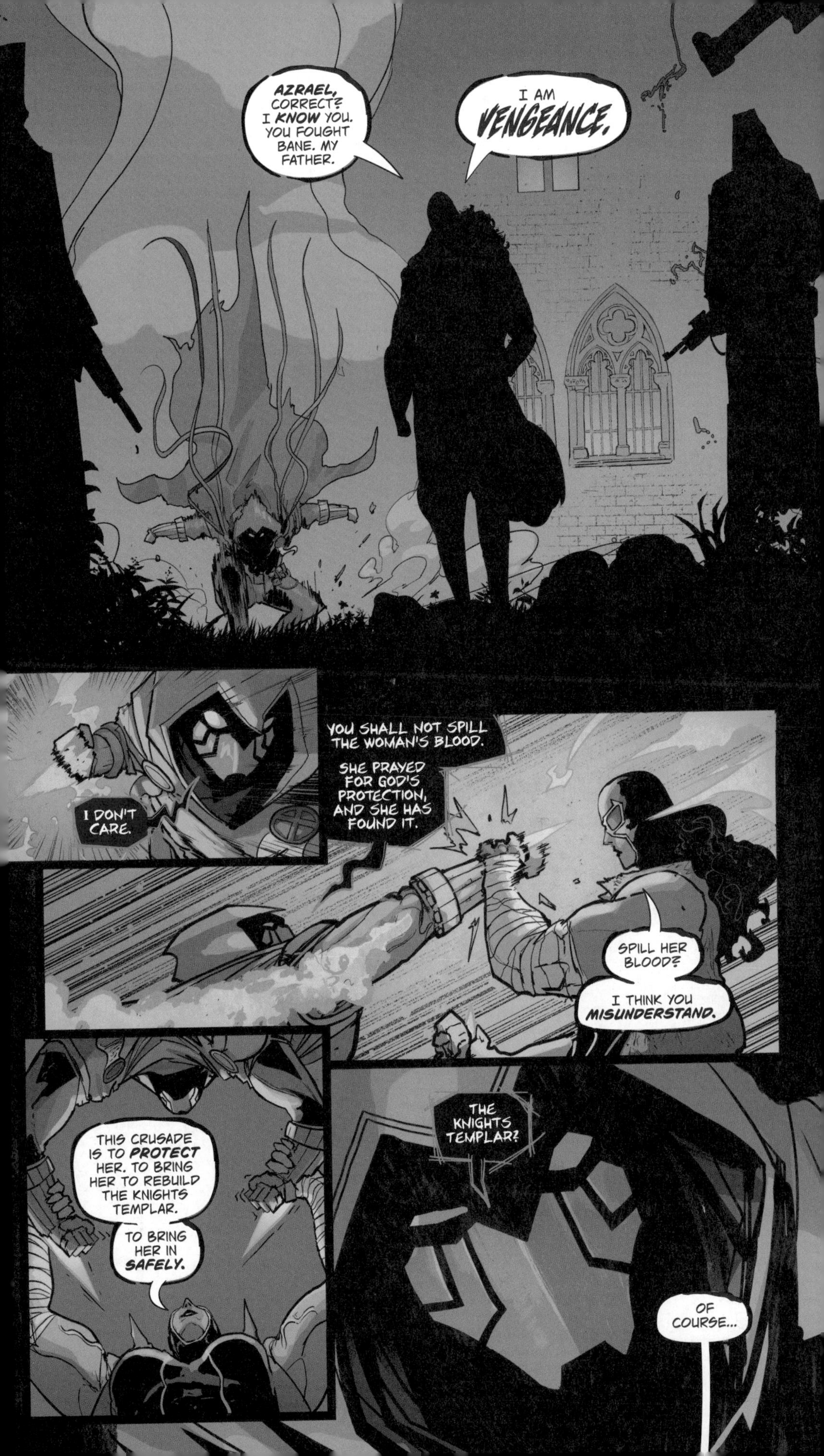
AZRAEL, CORRECT? I KNOW YOU. YOU FOUGHT BANE. MY FATHER.
I AM VENGEANCE.
I DON'T CARE.
YOU SHALL NOT SPILL THE WOMAN'S BLOOD.
SHE PRAYED FOR GOD'S PROTECTION, AND SHE HAS FOUND IT.
SPILL HER BLOOD?
I THINK YOU MISUNDERSTAND.
THIS CRUSADE IS TO PROTECT HER. TO BRING HER TO REBUILD THE KNIGHTS TEMPLAR.
TO BRING HER IN SAFELY.
THE KNIGHTS TEMPLAR?
OF COURSE...

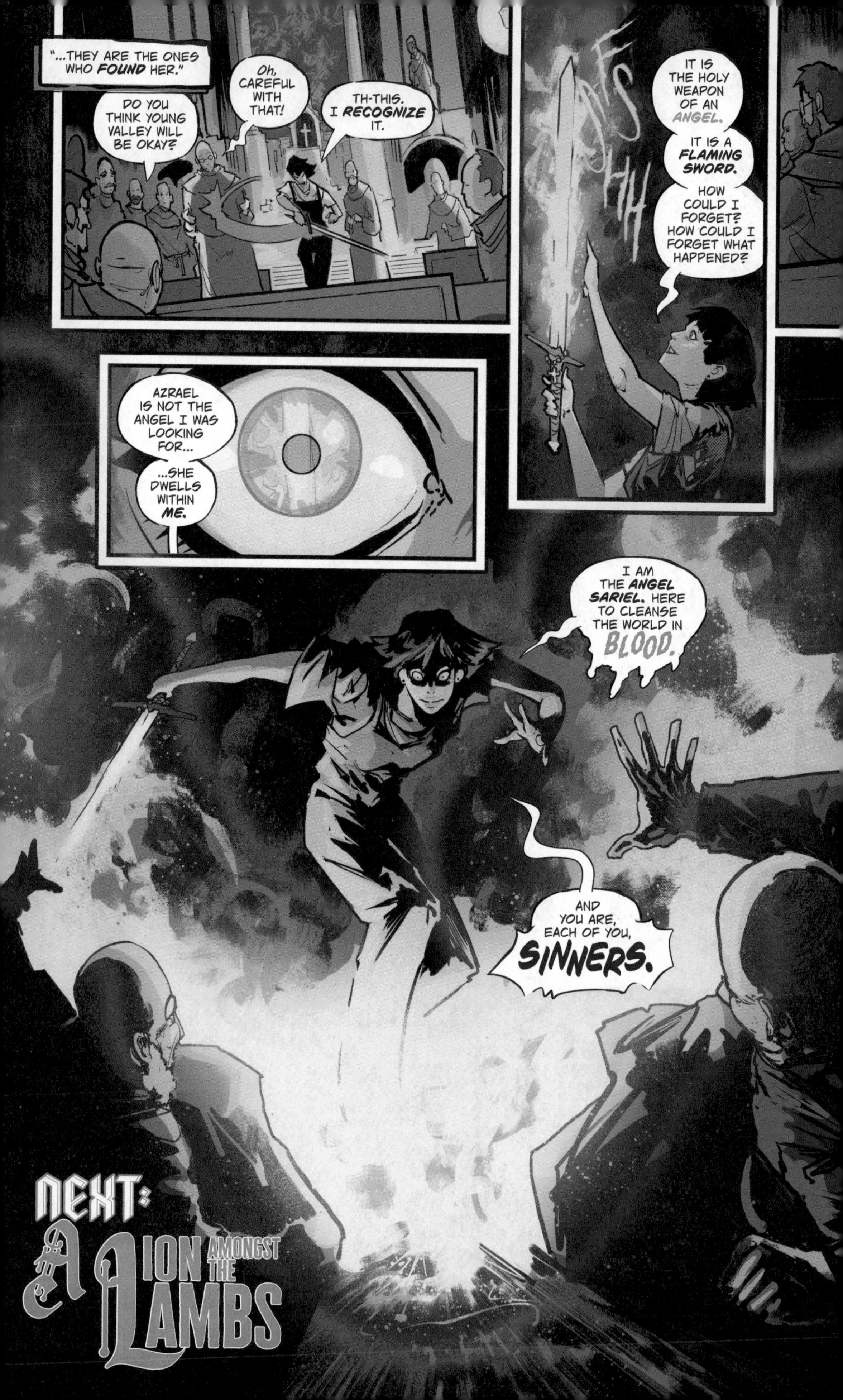
"...THEY ARE THE ONES WHO FOUND HER."
DO YOU THINK YOUNG VALLEY WILL BE OKAY?
Oh, CAREFUL WITH THAT!
TH-THIS. I RECOGNIZE IT.
IT IS THE HOLY WEAPON OF AN ANGEL.
IT IS A FLAMING SWORD.
HOW COULD I FORGET? HOW COULD I FORGET WHAT HAPPENED?
AZRAEL IS NOT THE ANGEL I WAS LOOKING FOR...
...SHE DWELLS WITHIN ME.
I AM THE ANGEL SARIEL. HERE TO CLEANSE THE WORLD IN BLOOD.
AND YOU ARE, EACH OF YOU, SINNERS.
NEXT:
A LION AMONGST THE LAMBS

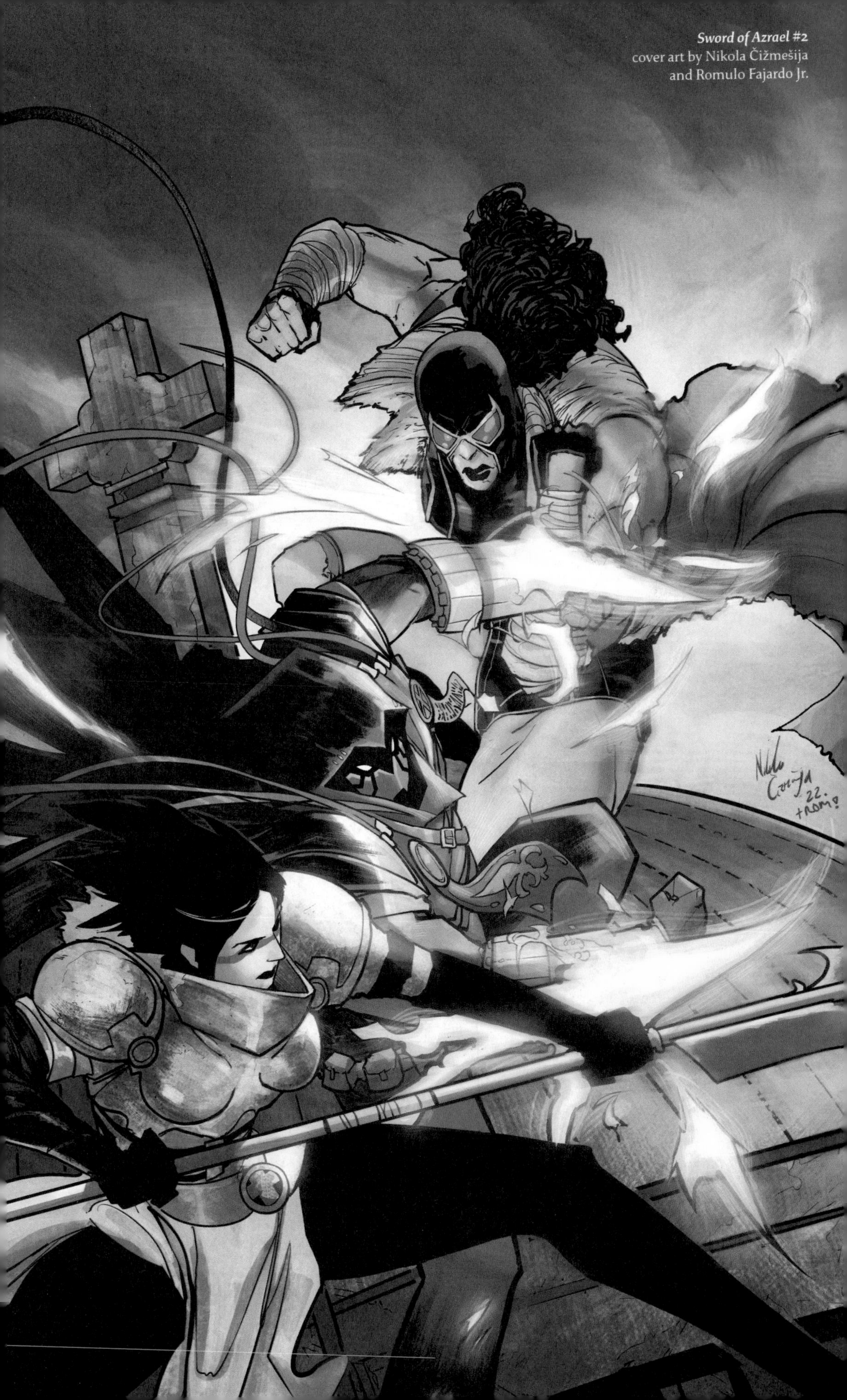

Sword of Azrael #2
cover art by Nikola Čižmešija
and Romulo Fajardo Jr.

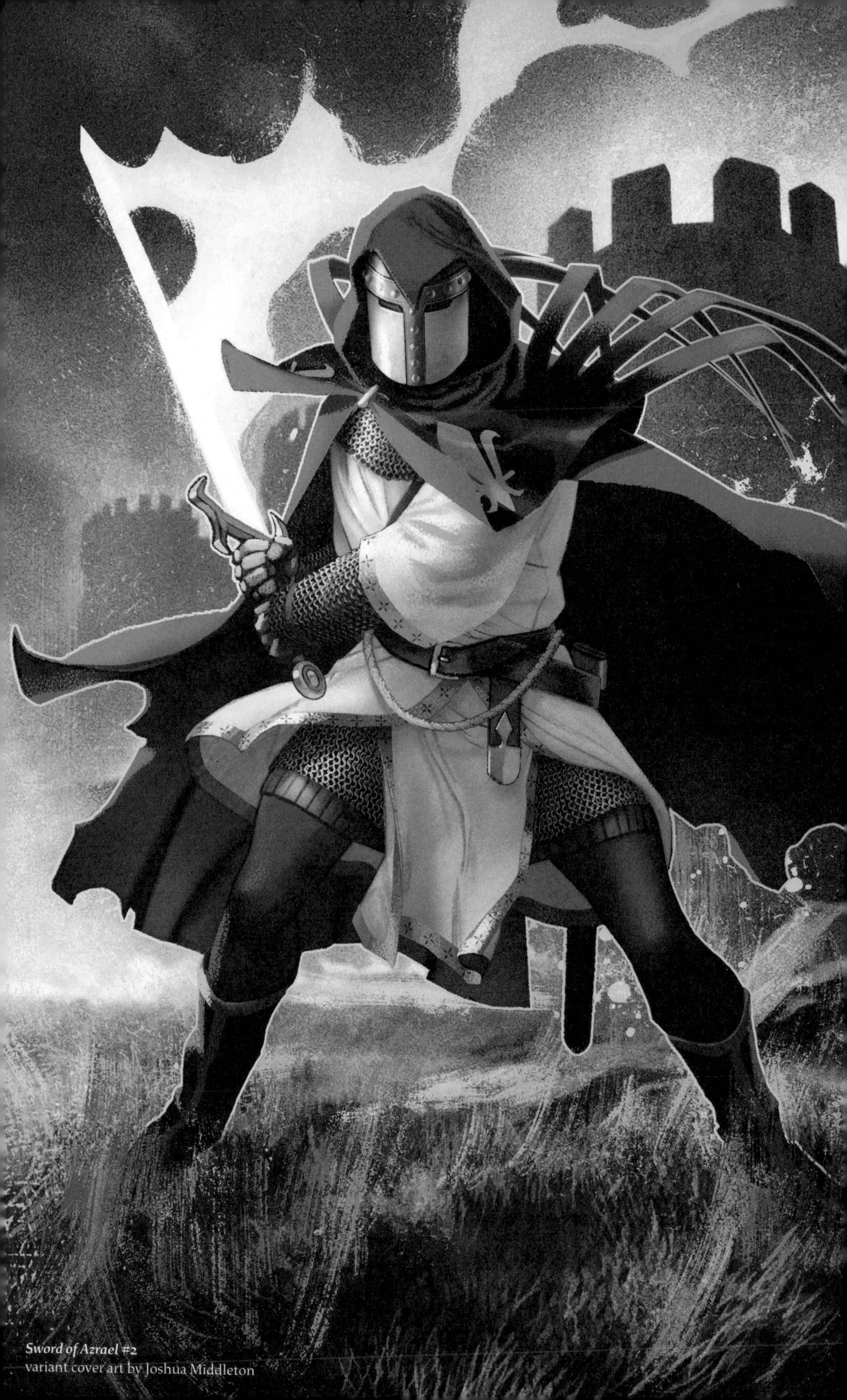

Sword of Azrael #2
variant cover art by Joshua Middleton

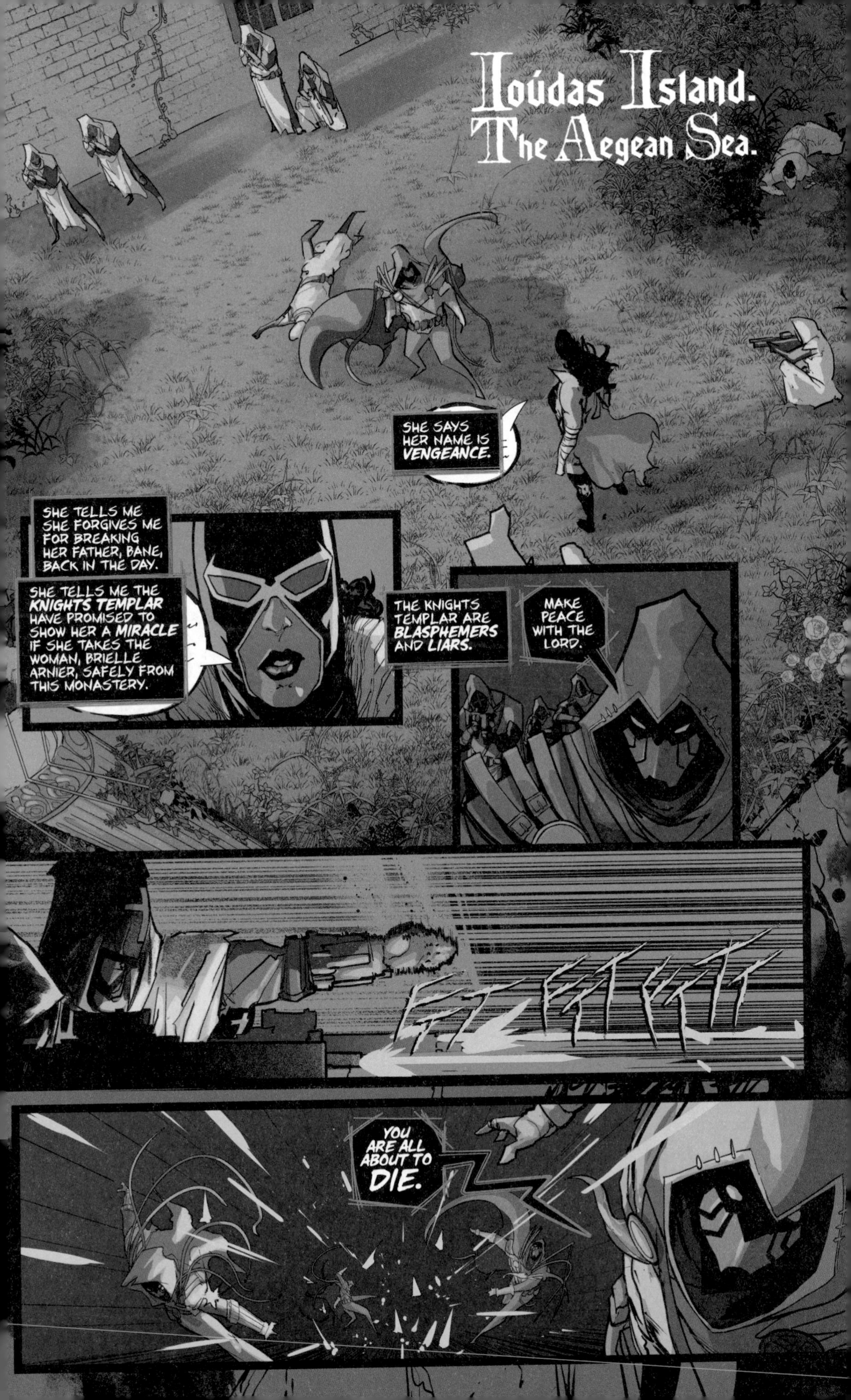

Ioúdas Island.
The Aegean Sea.
SHE SAYS HER NAME IS VENGEANCE.
SHE TELLS ME SHE FORGIVES ME FOR BREAKING HER FATHER, BANE, BACK IN THE DAY.
SHE TELLS ME THE KNIGHTS TEMPLAR HAVE PROMISED TO SHOW HER A MIRACLE IF SHE TAKES THE WOMAN, BRIELLE ARNIER, SAFELY FROM THIS MONASTERY.
THE KNIGHTS TEMPLAR ARE BLASPHEMERS AND LIARS.
MAKE PEACE WITH THE LORD.
YOU ARE ALL ABOUT TO DIE.

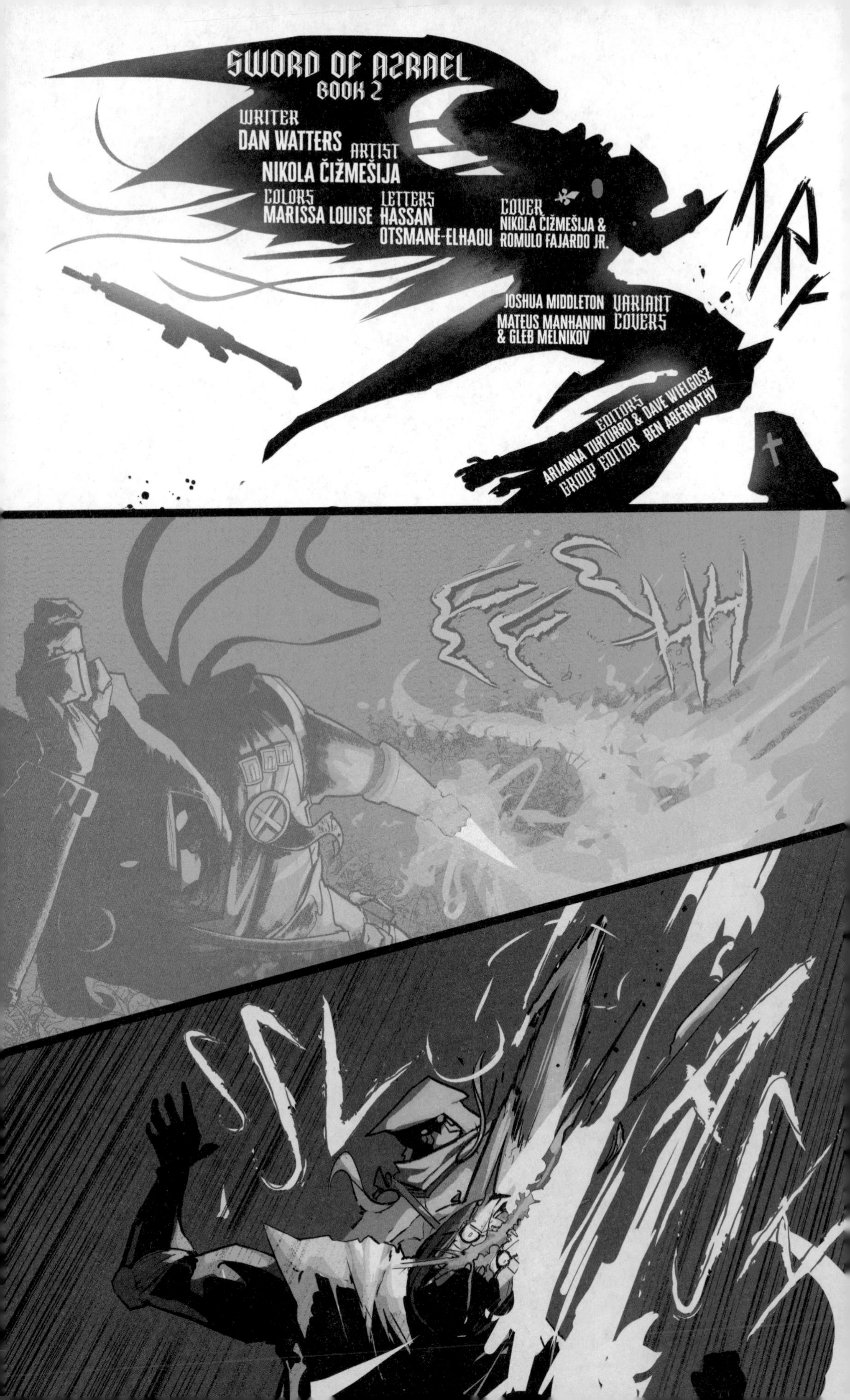
SWORD OF AZRAEL
BOOK 2
WRITER
DAN WATTERS
ARTIST
NIKOLA ČIŽMEŠIJA
COLORS
MARISSA LOUISE
LETTERS
HASSAN OTSMANE-ELHAOU
COVER
NIKOLA ČIŽMEŠIJA & ROMULO FAJARDO JR.
JOSHUA MIDDLETON
MATEUS MANHANINI & GLEB MELNIKOV
VARIANT COVERS
EDITORS
ARIANNA TURTURRO & DAVE WIELGOSZ
GROUP EDITOR BEN ABERNATHY
KRY

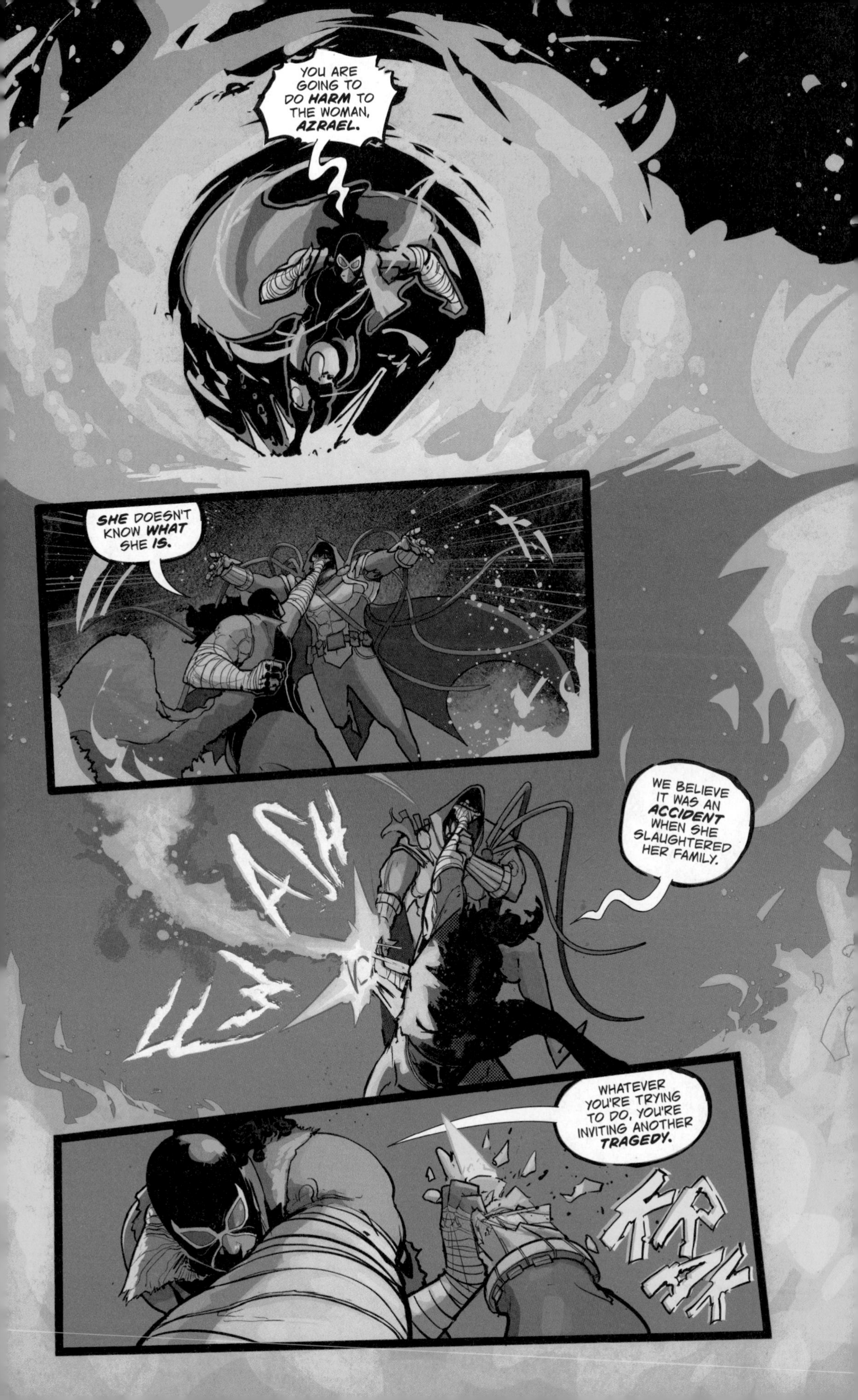
YOU ARE GOING TO DO **HARM** TO THE WOMAN, **AZRAEL.**
SHE DOESN'T KNOW **WHAT** SHE **IS.**
WE BELIEVE IT WAS AN **ACCIDENT** WHEN SHE SLAUGHTERED HER FAMILY.
WHATEVER YOU'RE TRYING TO DO, YOU'RE INVITING ANOTHER **TRAGEDY.**

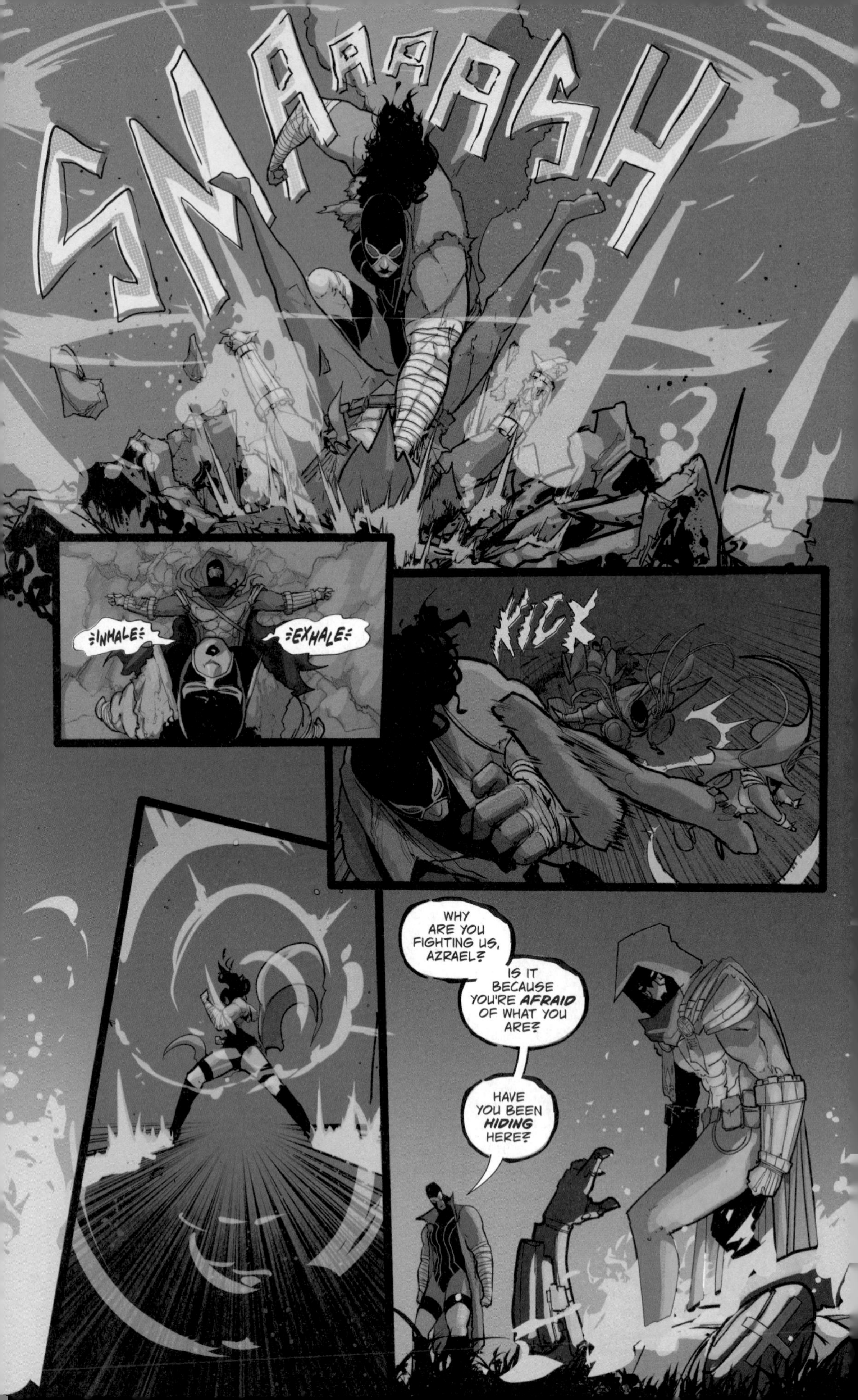
SMAAASH
INHALE
EXHALE
KICK
WHY ARE YOU FIGHTING US, AZRAEL?
IS IT BECAUSE YOU'RE **AFRAID** OF WHAT YOU ARE?
HAVE YOU BEEN **HIDING** HERE?

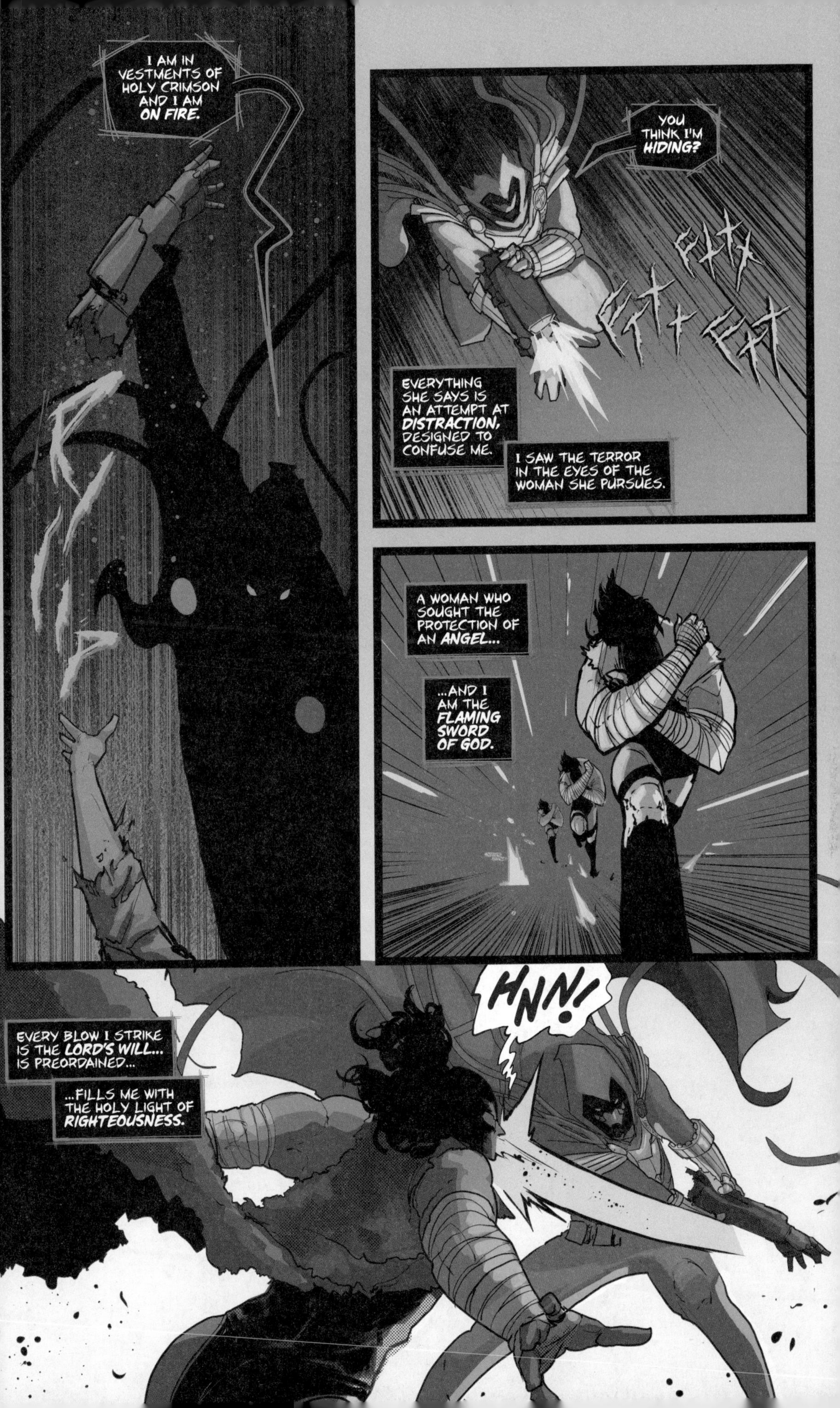

I AM IN VESTMENTS OF HOLY CRIMSON AND I AM ON FIRE.
YOU THINK I'M HIDING?
FTTX FTTX FTT
EVERYTHING SHE SAYS IS AN ATTEMPT AT DISTRACTION, DESIGNED TO CONFUSE ME.
I SAW THE TERROR IN THE EYES OF THE WOMAN SHE PURSUES.
A WOMAN WHO SOUGHT THE PROTECTION OF AN ANGEL...
...AND I AM THE FLAMING SWORD OF GOD.
EVERY BLOW I STRIKE IS THE LORD'S WILL... IS PREORDAINED...
...FILLS ME WITH THE HOLY LIGHT OF RIGHTEOUSNESS.
HNN!

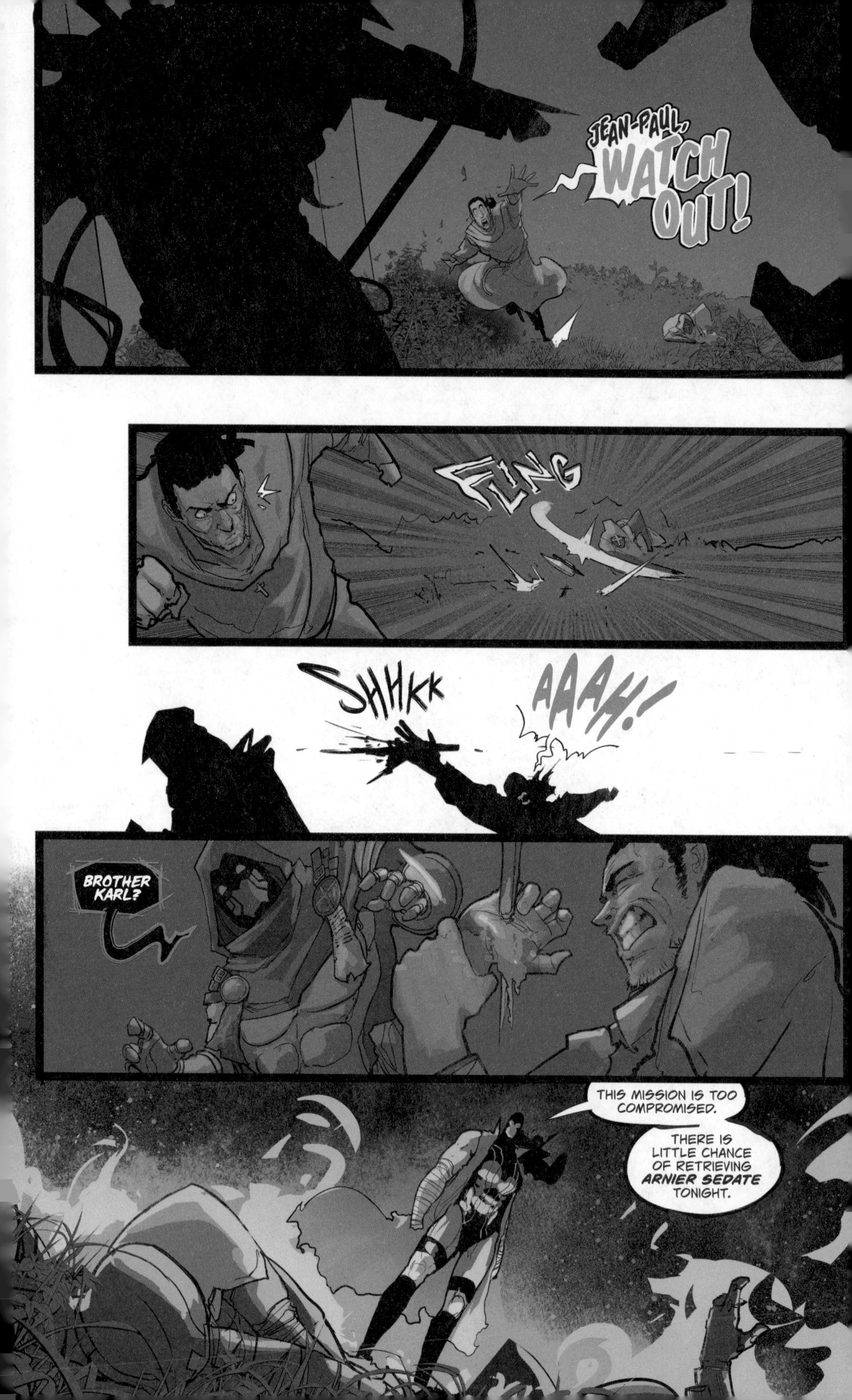
JEAN-PAUL, WATCH OUT!
FLING
SHHKK
AAAH!
BROTHER KARL?
THIS MISSION IS TOO COMPROMISED.
THERE IS LITTLE CHANCE OF RETRIEVING ARNIER SEDATE TONIGHT.

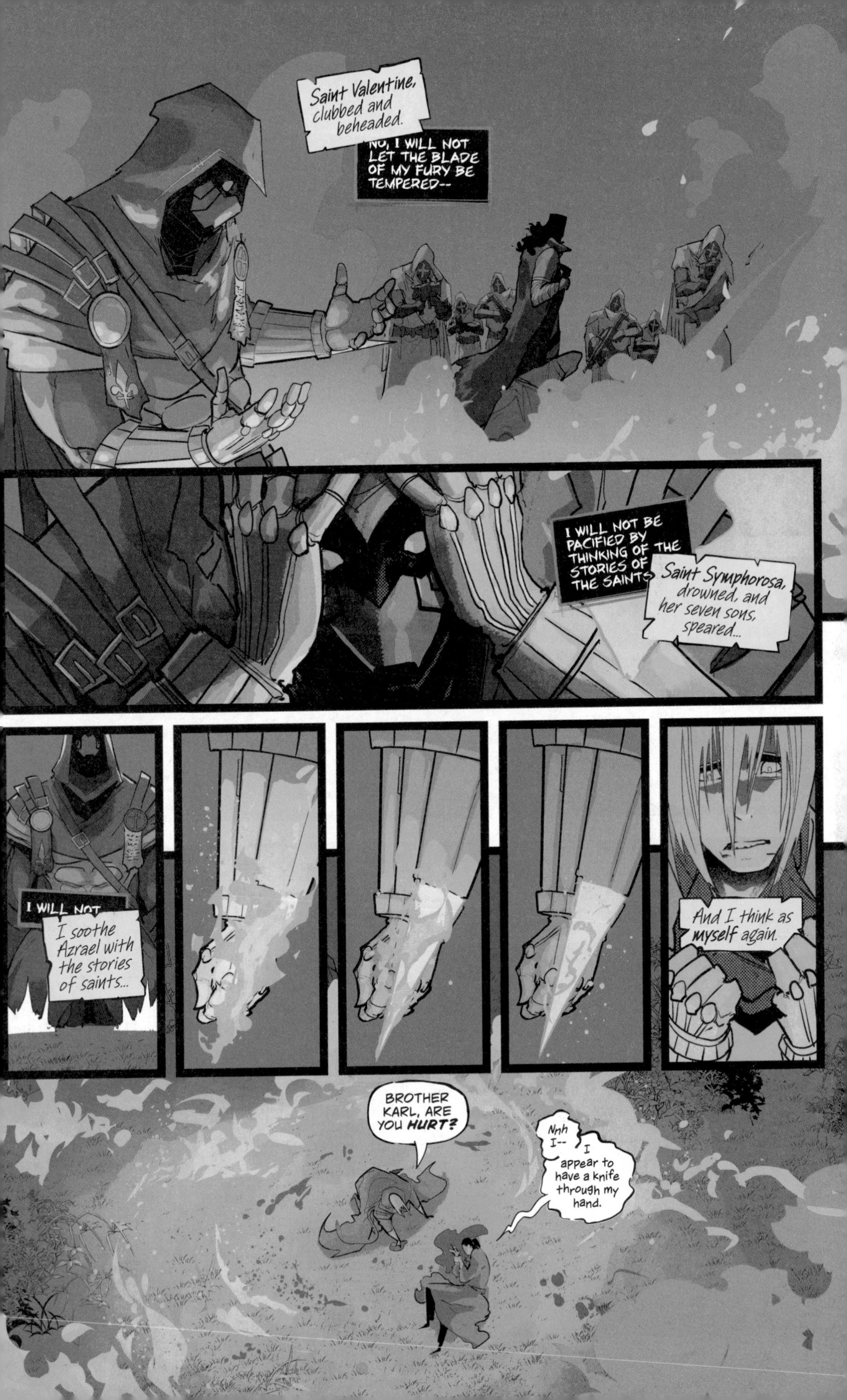
Saint Valentine, clubbed and beheaded.
NO, I WILL NOT LET THE BLADE OF MY FURY BE TEMPERED--
I WILL NOT BE PACIFIED BY THINKING OF THE STORIES OF THE SAINTS
Saint Symphorosa, drowned, and her seven sons, speared...
I WILL NOT
I soothe the Azrael with the stories of saints...
And I think as myself again.
BROTHER KARL, ARE YOU HURT?
Nnh I--
I appear to have a knife through my hand.

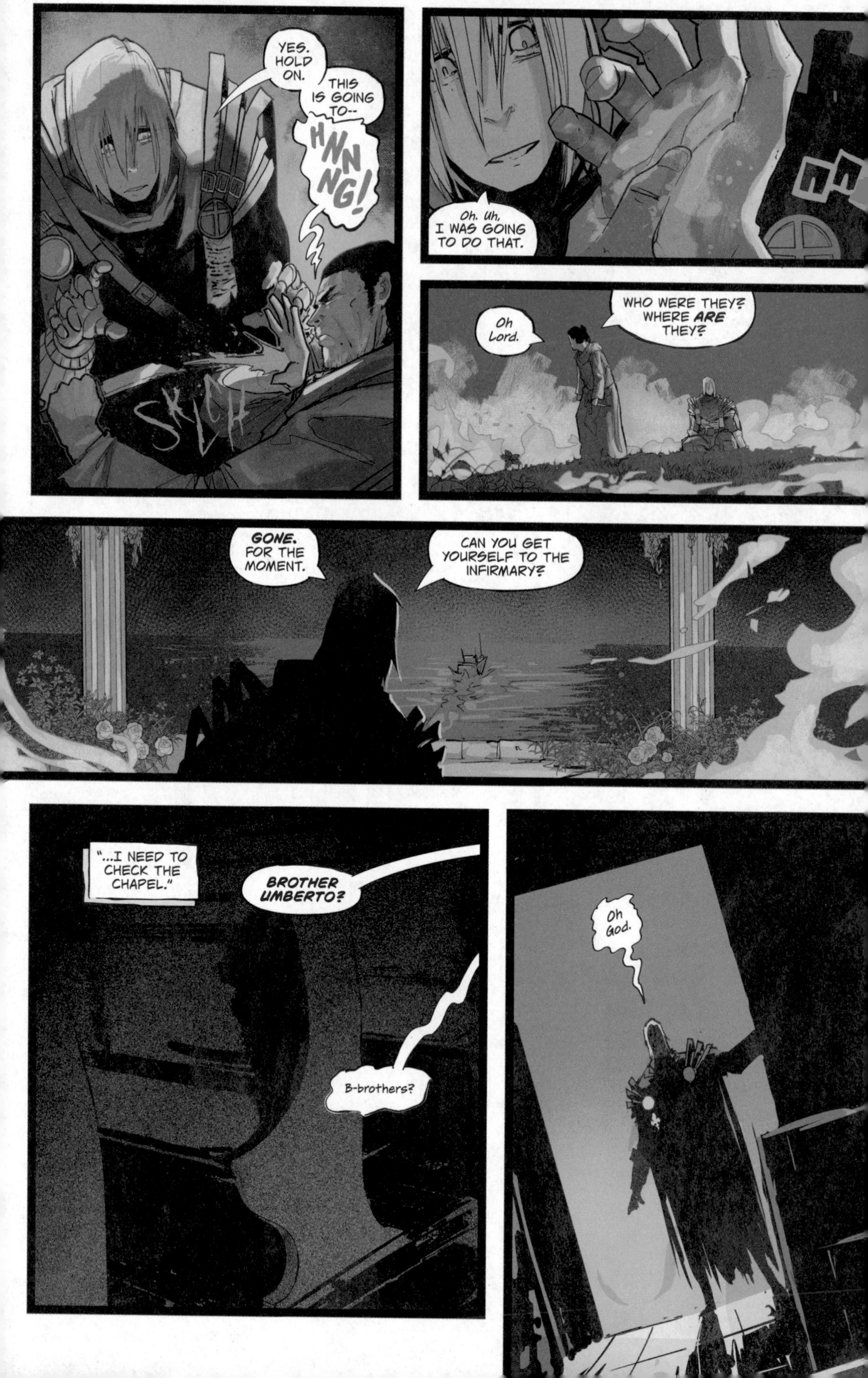
YES. HOLD ON.
THIS IS GOING TO--
HNNNG!
SKLCH
Oh. Uh, I WAS GOING TO DO THAT.
Oh Lord.
WHO WERE THEY? WHERE ARE THEY?
GONE. FOR THE MOMENT.
CAN YOU GET YOURSELF TO THE INFIRMARY?
"...I NEED TO CHECK THE CHAPEL."
BROTHER UMBERTO?
B-brothers?
Oh God.

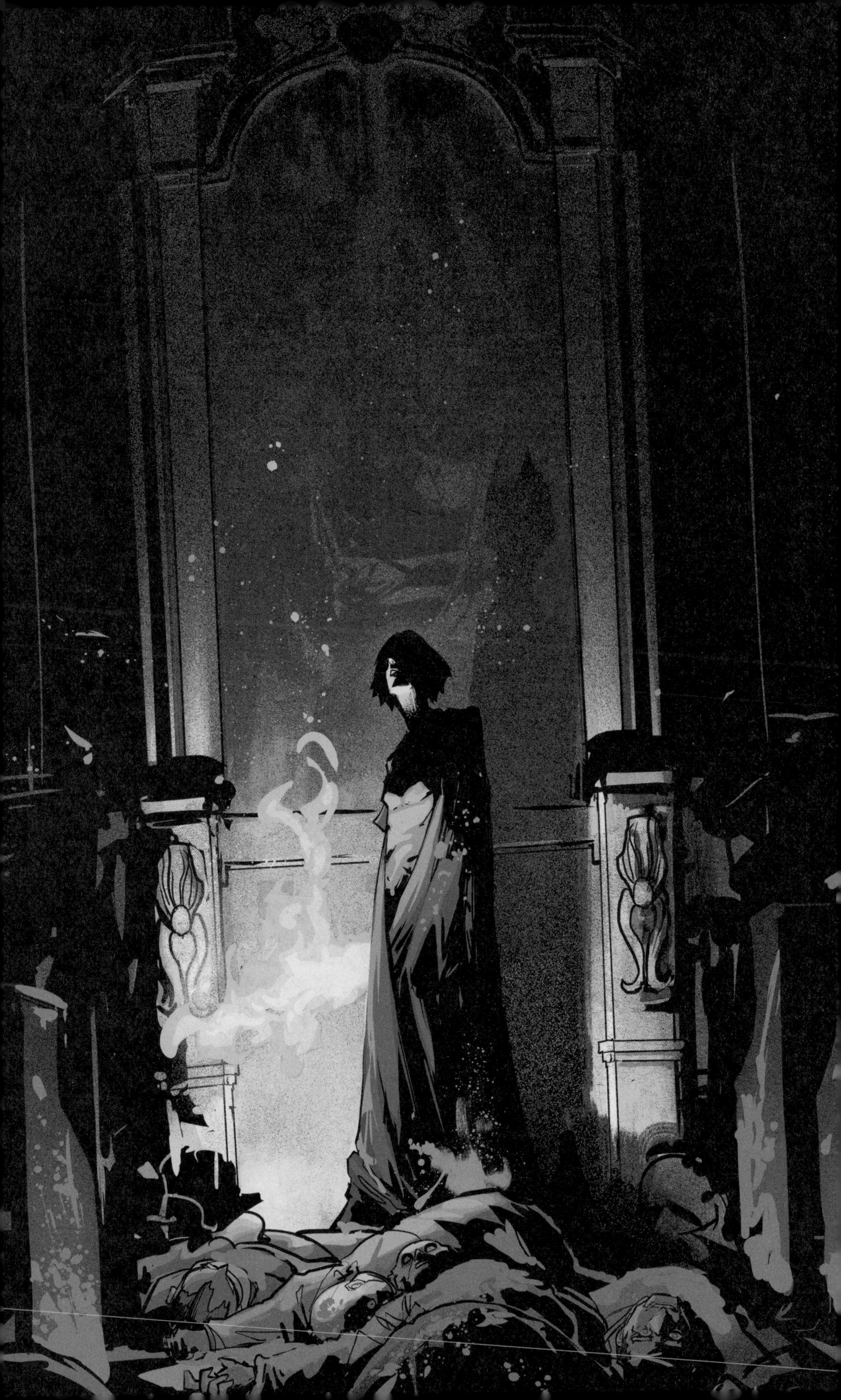

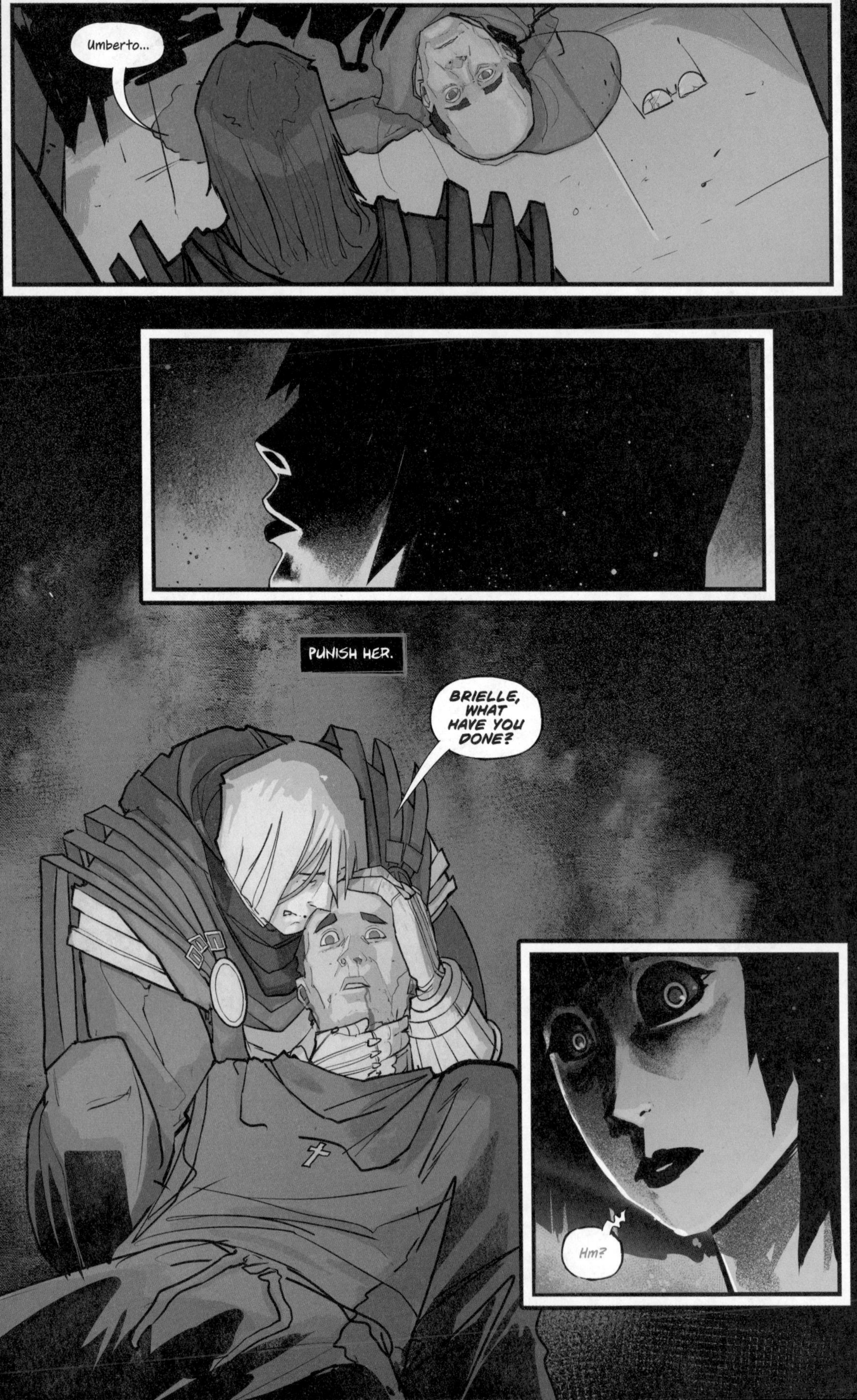
Umberto...
PUNISH HER.
BRIELLE, WHAT HAVE YOU DONE?
Hm?

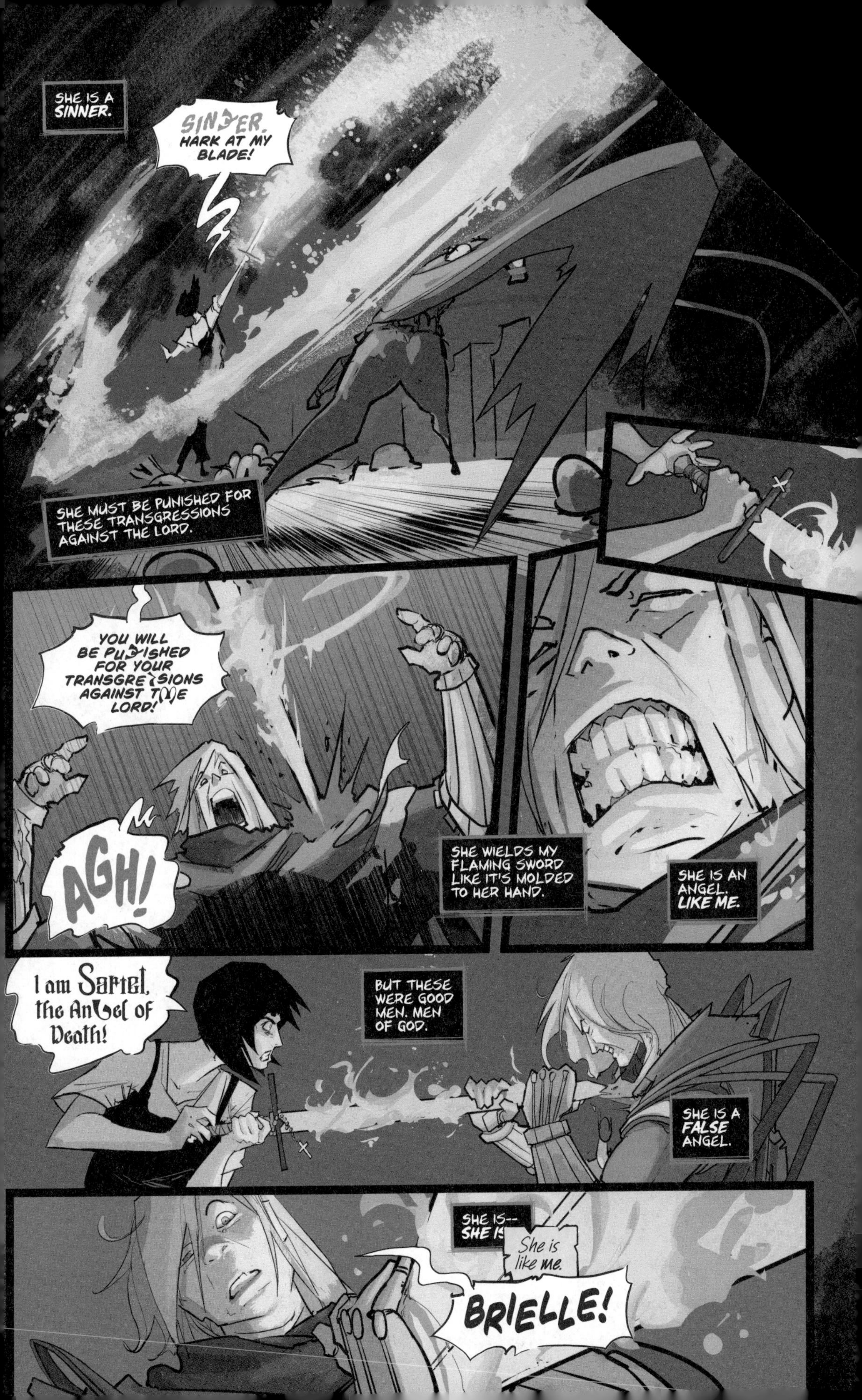
SHE IS A SINNER.
SINNER. HARK AT MY BLADE!
SHE MUST BE PUNISHED FOR THESE TRANSGRESSIONS AGAINST THE LORD.
YOU WILL BE PUNISHED FOR YOUR TRANSGRESSIONS AGAINST THE LORD!
AGH!
SHE WIELDS MY FLAMING SWORD LIKE IT'S MOLDED TO HER HAND.
SHE IS AN ANGEL. LIKE ME.
I am Sariel, the Angel of Death!
BUT THESE WERE GOOD MEN. MEN OF GOD.
SHE IS A FALSE ANGEL.
SHE IS-- SHE IS
She is like me.
BRIELLE!

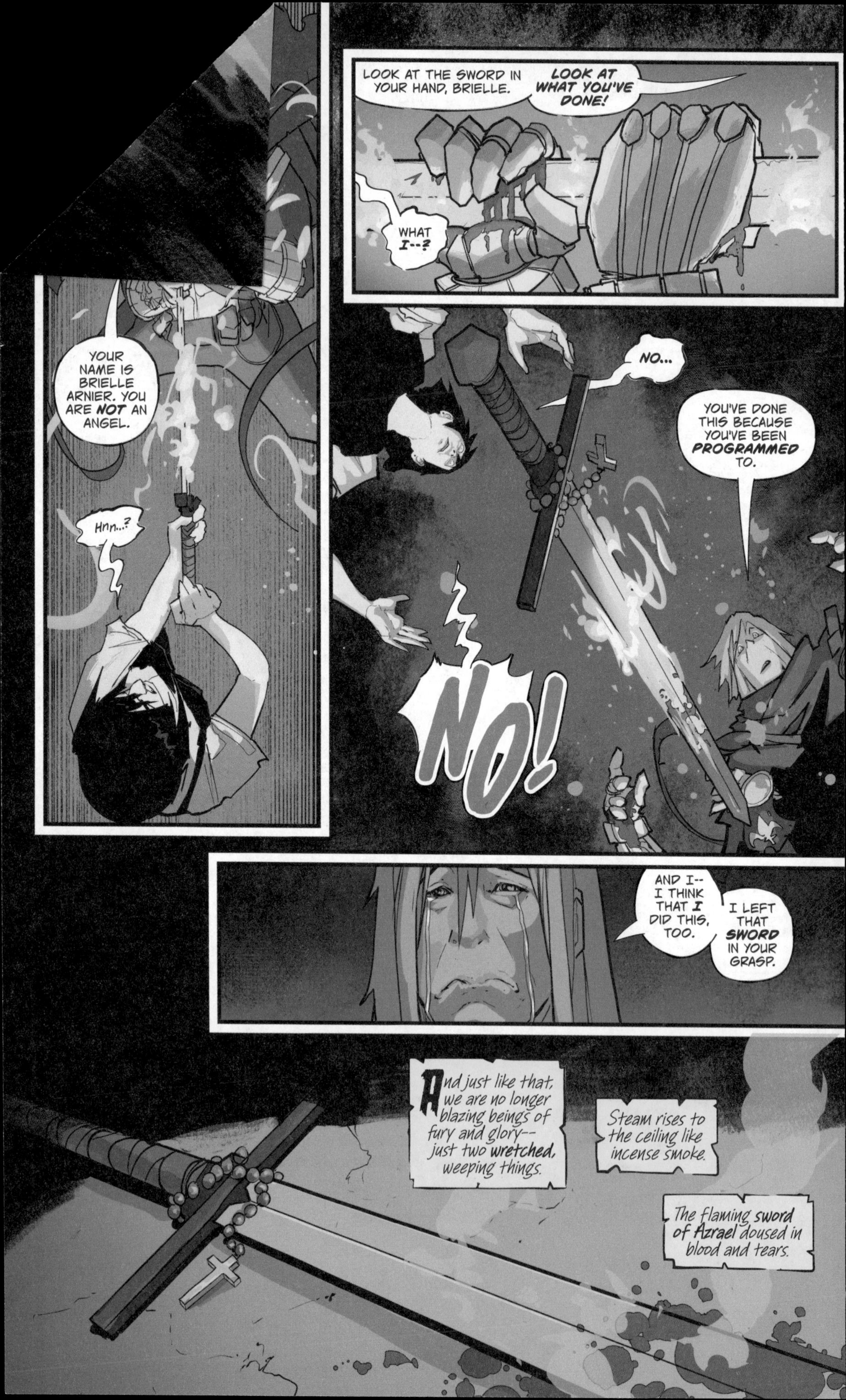

LOOK AT THE SWORD IN YOUR HAND, BRIELLE.
LOOK AT WHAT YOU'VE DONE!
WHAT I--?
YOUR NAME IS BRIELLE ARNIER. YOU ARE NOT AN ANGEL.
Hnn...?
NO...
YOU'VE DONE THIS BECAUSE YOU'VE BEEN PROGRAMMED TO.
NO!
AND I-- I THINK THAT I DID THIS, TOO.
I LEFT THAT SWORD IN YOUR GRASP.
And just like that, we are no longer blazing beings of fury and glory-- just two wretched, weeping things.
Steam rises to the ceiling like incense smoke.
The flaming sword of Azrael doused in blood and tears.

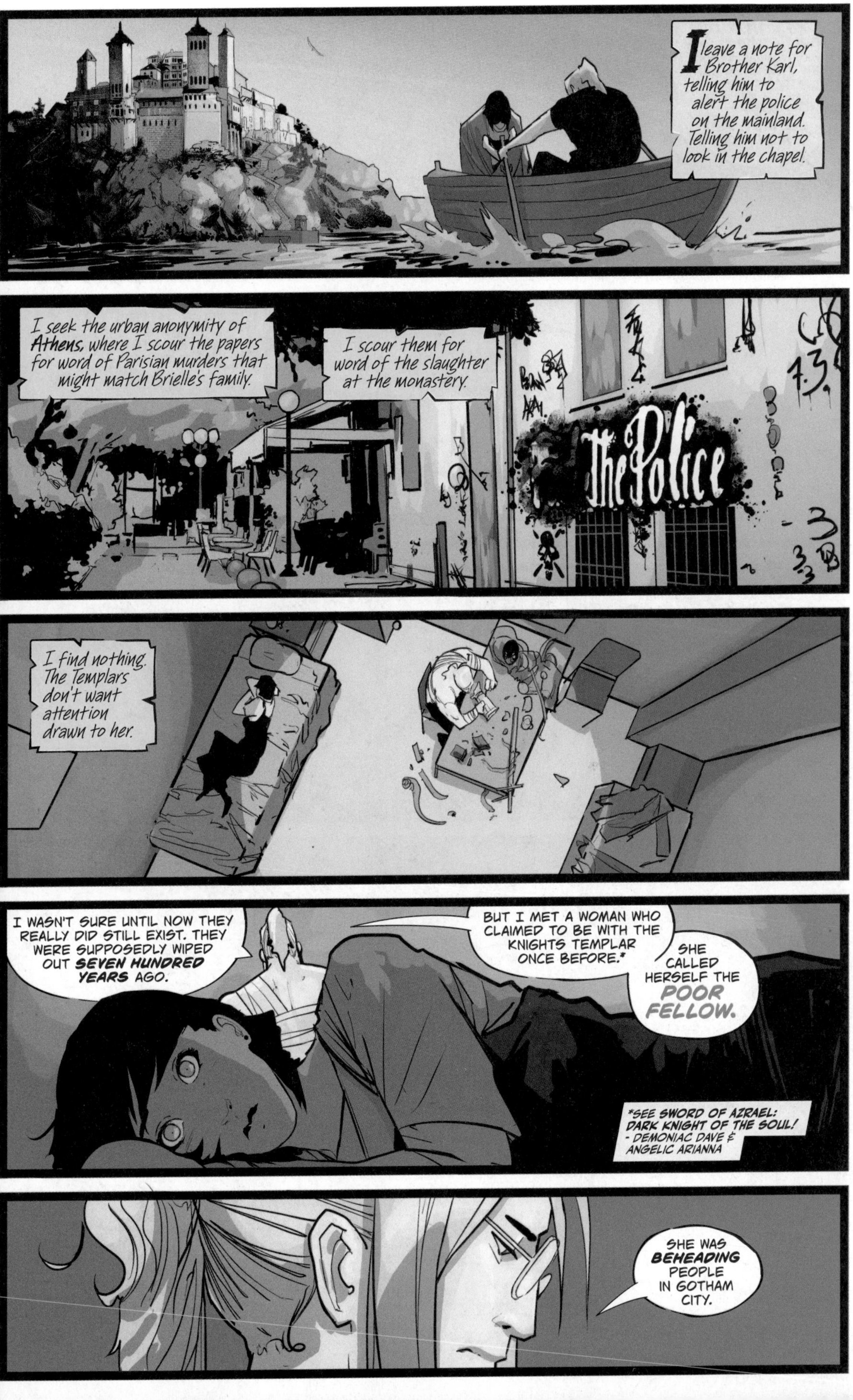
I leave a note for Brother Karl, telling him to alert the police on the mainland. Telling him not to look in the chapel.
I seek the urban anonymity of Athens, where I scour the papers for word of Parisian murders that might match Brielle's family.
I scour them for word of the slaughter at the monastery.
The Police
I find nothing. The Templars don't want attention drawn to her.
I WASN'T SURE UNTIL NOW THEY REALLY DID STILL EXIST. THEY WERE SUPPOSEDLY WIPED OUT SEVEN HUNDRED YEARS AGO.
BUT I MET A WOMAN WHO CLAIMED TO BE WITH THE KNIGHTS TEMPLAR ONCE BEFORE.*
SHE CALLED HERSELF THE POOR FELLOW.
*SEE SWORD OF AZRAEL: DARK KNIGHT OF THE SOUL! - DEMONIAC DAVE & ANGELIC ARIANNA
SHE WAS BEHEADING PEOPLE IN GOTHAM CITY.

THE ORDER OF *SAINT DUMAS,* WHO PROGRAMMED ME WITH *THE SYSTEM*-- WITH AZRAEL-- WERE A FACTION WHO SPLIT FROM THE TEMPLARS EARLIER ON.

THE ORDER PROGRAMMED ME AS A CHILD, THEN HYPNOTIZED ME TO *FORGET* UNTIL I WAS ACTIVATED AS THEIR ASSASSIN AND ENFORCER.

I HAVE TO ASSUME THEY DID THE SAME THING TO YOU. PERHAPS TO *OTHERS.*

MAYBE THEY WERE TRYING TO CREATE *BACKUPS* IN CASE I DIED.

BRIELLE, ARE YOU *LISTENING?* YOU NEED TO HEAR THIS.

YOU HAVEN'T SPOKEN IN TWO DAYS.

I...

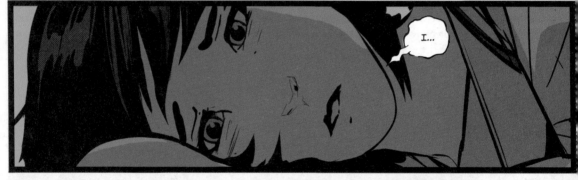

...I am... *SARIEL.* AN ANGEL.

LIKE YOU, AZRAEL.

NO. JUST... *NO.*

WHY DID *GOD* MAKE ME AN ANGEL AND THEN HAVE ME *KILL* PEOPLE?

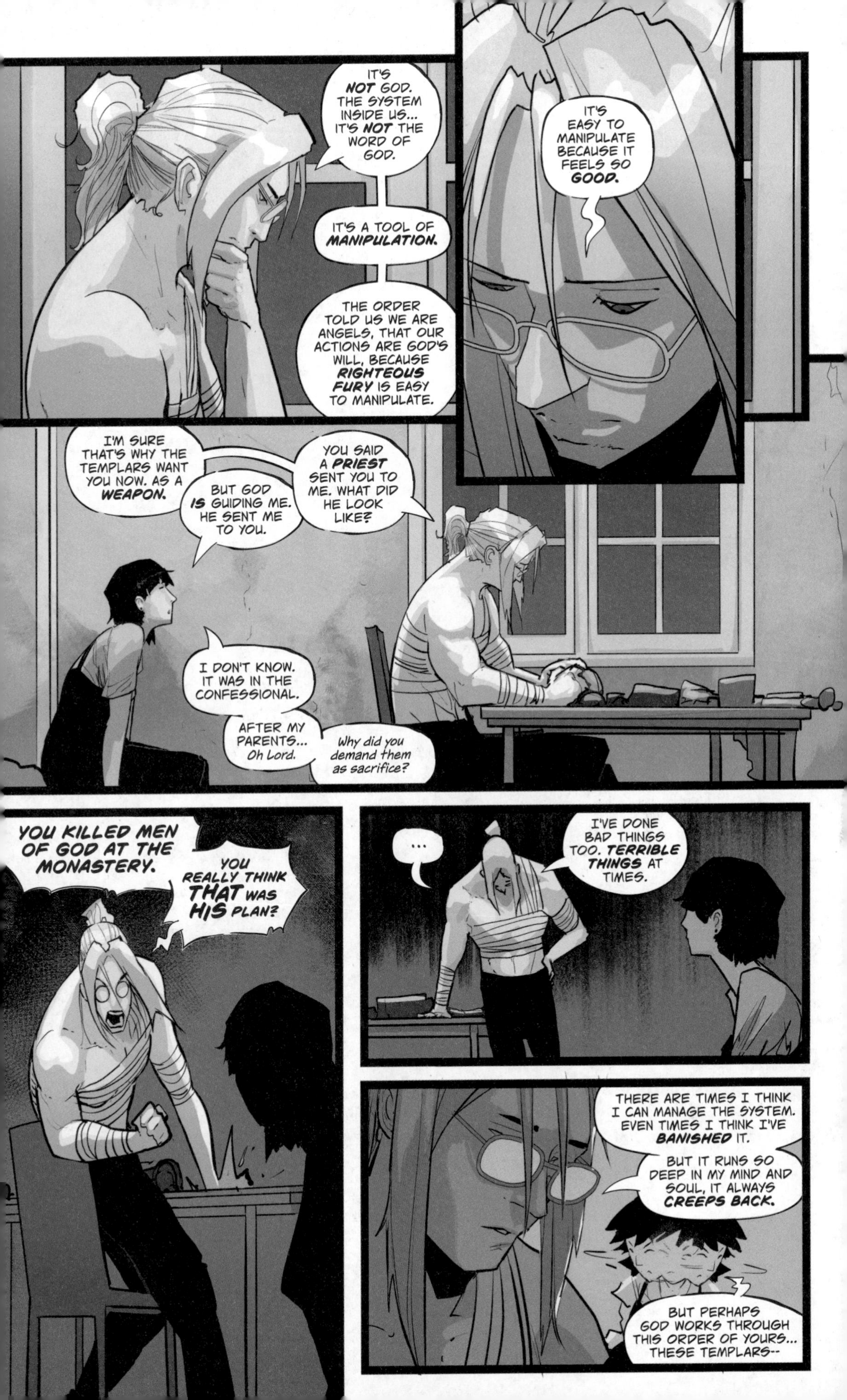
IT'S **NOT** GOD. THE SYSTEM INSIDE US... IT'S **NOT** THE WORD OF GOD.
IT'S A TOOL OF **MANIPULATION.**
THE ORDER TOLD US WE ARE ANGELS, THAT OUR ACTIONS ARE GOD'S WILL, BECAUSE **RIGHTEOUS FURY** IS EASY TO MANIPULATE.
IT'S EASY TO MANIPULATE BECAUSE IT FEELS SO **GOOD.**
I'M SURE THAT'S WHY THE TEMPLARS WANT YOU NOW. AS A **WEAPON.**
BUT GOD **IS** GUIDING ME. HE SENT ME TO YOU.
YOU SAID A **PRIEST** SENT YOU TO ME. WHAT DID HE LOOK LIKE?
I DON'T KNOW. IT WAS IN THE CONFESSIONAL.
AFTER MY PARENTS... *Oh Lord.*
Why did you demand them as sacrifice?
YOU KILLED MEN OF GOD AT THE MONASTERY.
YOU REALLY THINK THAT WAS HIS PLAN?
...
I'VE DONE BAD THINGS TOO. **TERRIBLE THINGS** AT TIMES.
THERE ARE TIMES I THINK I CAN MANAGE THE SYSTEM. EVEN TIMES I THINK I'VE **BANISHED** IT.
BUT IT RUNS SO DEEP IN MY MIND AND SOUL, IT ALWAYS **CREEPS BACK.**
BUT PERHAPS GOD WORKS THROUGH THIS ORDER OF YOURS... THESE TEMPLARS--

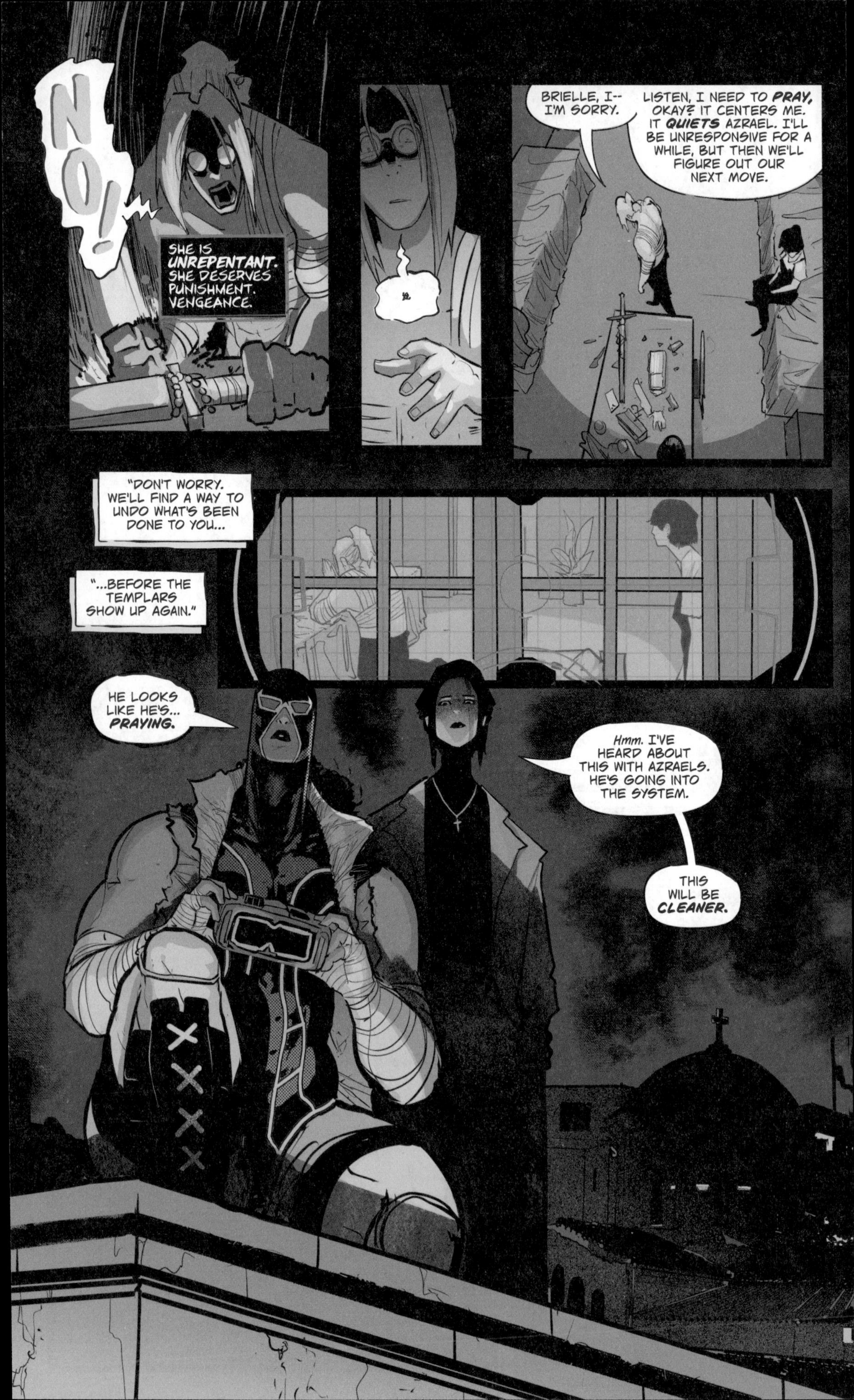
NO!
SHE IS UNREPENTANT. SHE DESERVES PUNISHMENT. VENGEANCE.
BRIELLE, I-- I'M SORRY.
LISTEN, I NEED TO PRAY, OKAY? IT CENTERS ME. IT QUIETS AZRAEL. I'LL BE UNRESPONSIVE FOR A WHILE, BUT THEN WE'LL FIGURE OUT OUR NEXT MOVE.
"DON'T WORRY. WE'LL FIND A WAY TO UNDO WHAT'S BEEN DONE TO YOU...
"...BEFORE THE TEMPLARS SHOW UP AGAIN."
HE LOOKS LIKE HE'S... PRAYING.
Hmm. I'VE HEARD ABOUT THIS WITH AZRAELS. HE'S GOING INTO THE SYSTEM.
THIS WILL BE CLEANER.

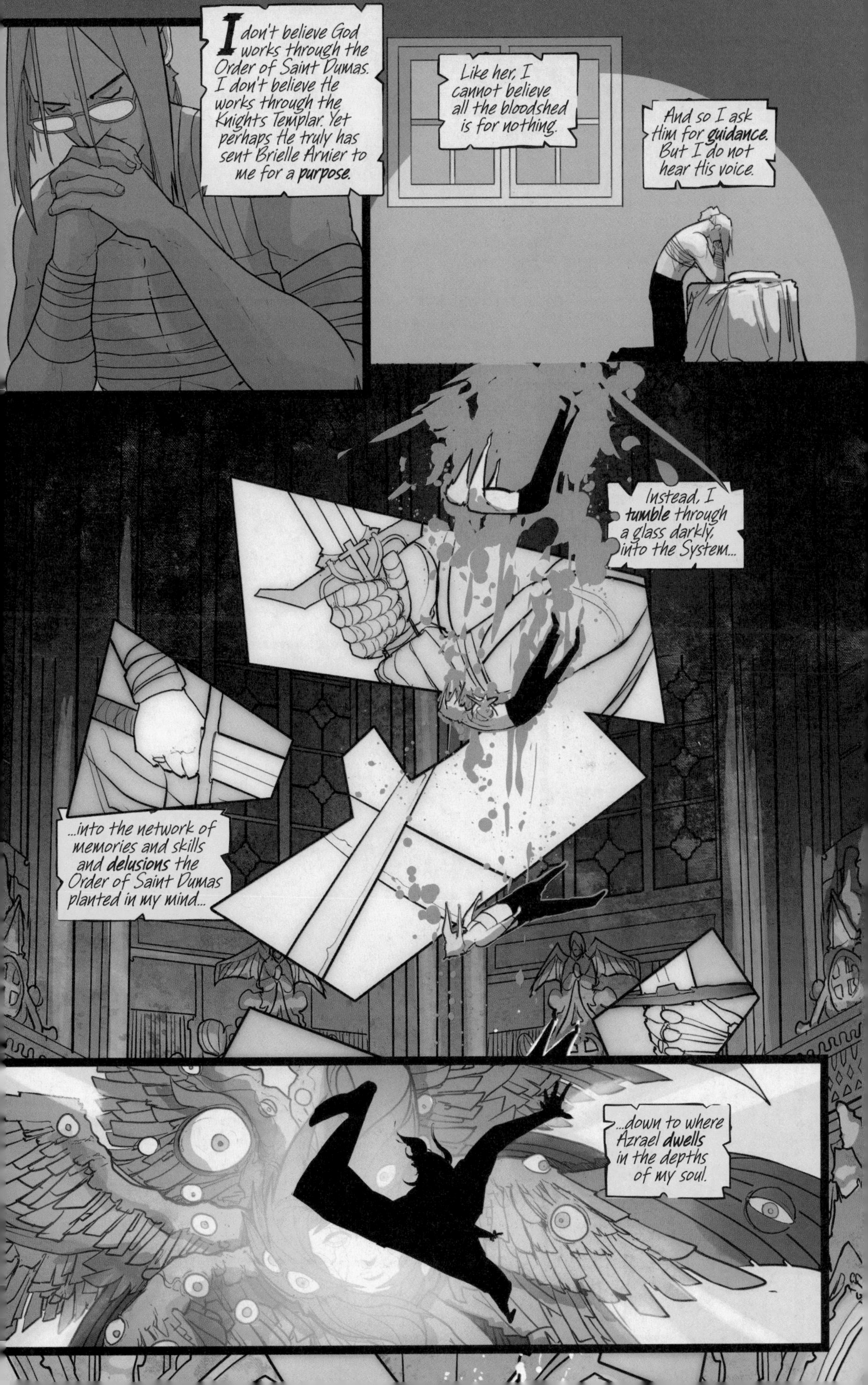
I don't believe God works through the Order of Saint Dumas. I don't believe He works through the Knights Templar. Yet perhaps He truly has sent Brielle Arnier to me for a **purpose**.
Like her, I cannot believe all the bloodshed is for nothing.
And so I ask Him for **guidance**. But I do not hear His voice.
Instead, I **tumble** through a glass darkly, into the System...
...into the network of memories and skills and **delusions** the Order of Saint Dumas planted in my mind...
...down to where Azrael **dwells** in the depths of my soul.

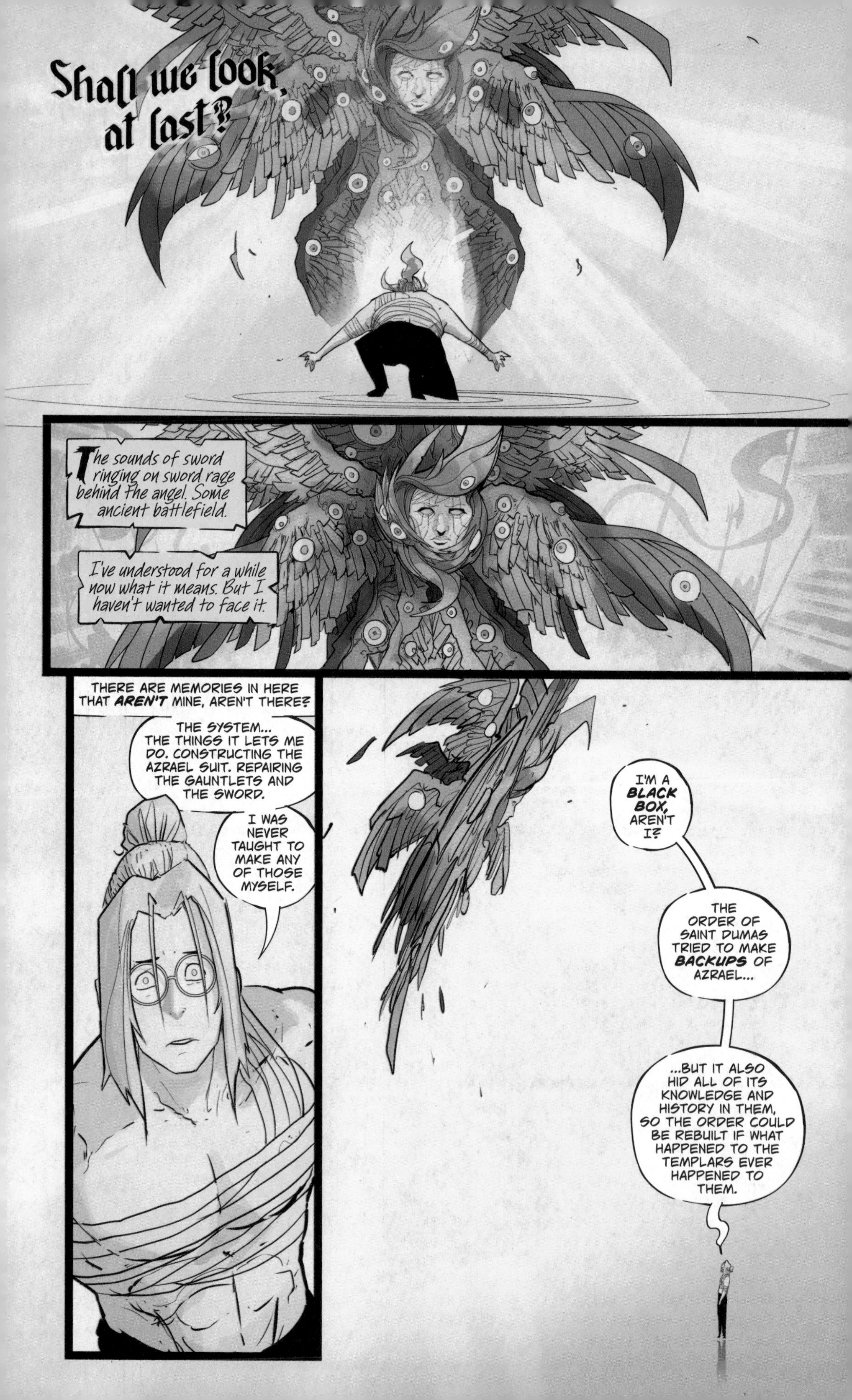
Shall we look at last?
The sounds of sword ringing on sword rage behind the angel. Some ancient battlefield.
I've understood for a while now what it means. But I haven't wanted to face it.
THERE ARE MEMORIES IN HERE THAT AREN'T MINE, AREN'T THERE?
THE SYSTEM... THE THINGS IT LETS ME DO. CONSTRUCTING THE AZRAEL SUIT. REPAIRING THE GAUNTLETS AND THE SWORD.
I WAS NEVER TAUGHT TO MAKE ANY OF THOSE MYSELF.
I'M A BLACK BOX, AREN'T I?
THE ORDER OF SAINT DUMAS TRIED TO MAKE BACKUPS OF AZRAEL...
...BUT IT ALSO HID ALL OF ITS KNOWLEDGE AND HISTORY IN THEM, SO THE ORDER COULD BE REBUILT IF WHAT HAPPENED TO THE TEMPLARS EVER HAPPENED TO THEM.

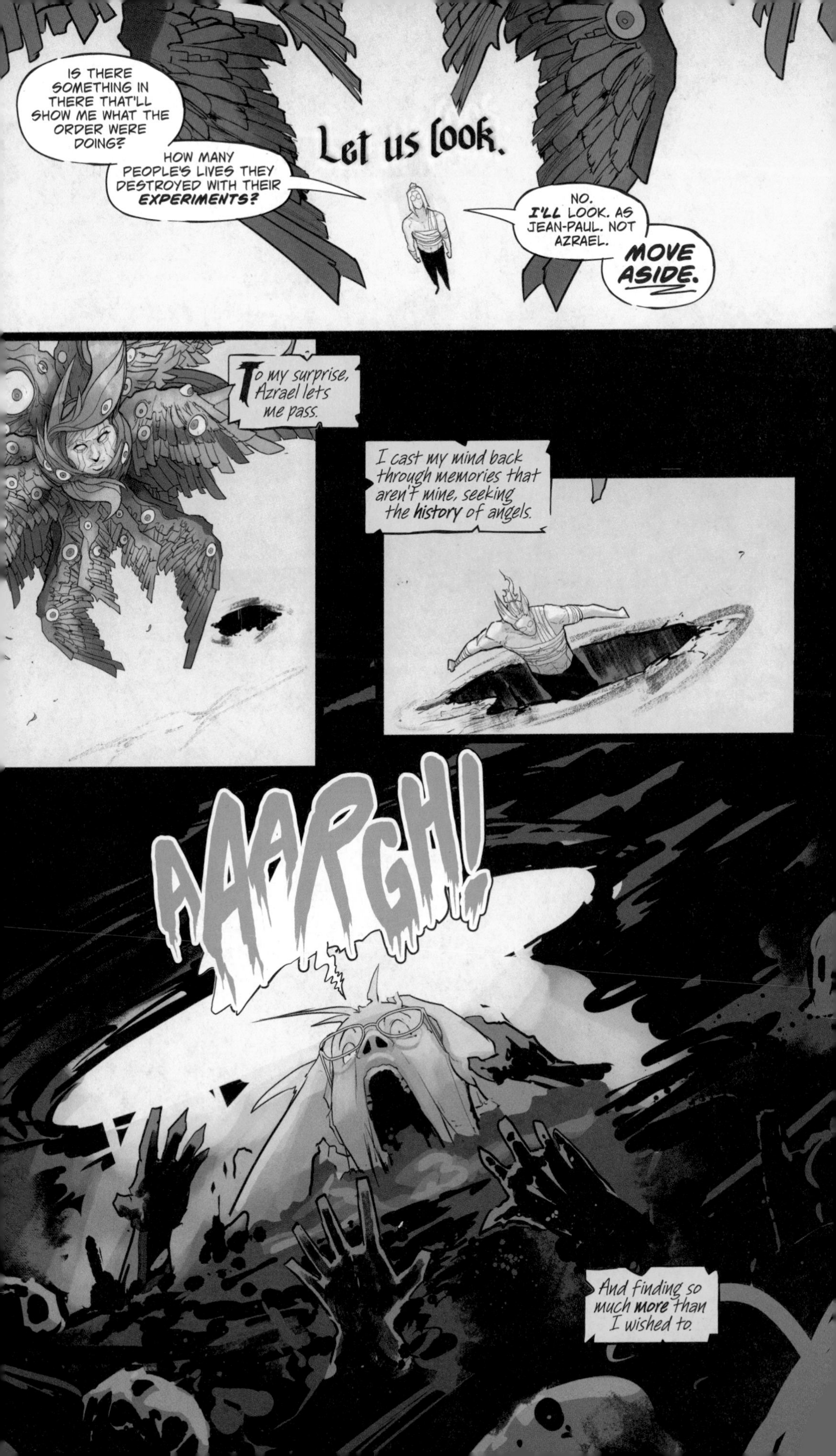
IS THERE SOMETHING IN THERE THAT'LL SHOW ME WHAT THE ORDER WERE DOING?
HOW MANY PEOPLE'S LIVES THEY DESTROYED WITH THEIR EXPERIMENTS?
Let us look.
NO. I'LL LOOK. AS JEAN-PAUL. NOT AZRAEL.
MOVE ASIDE.
To my surprise, Azrael lets me pass.
I cast my mind back through memories that aren't mine, seeking the history of angels.
AAARGH!
And finding so much more than I wished to.

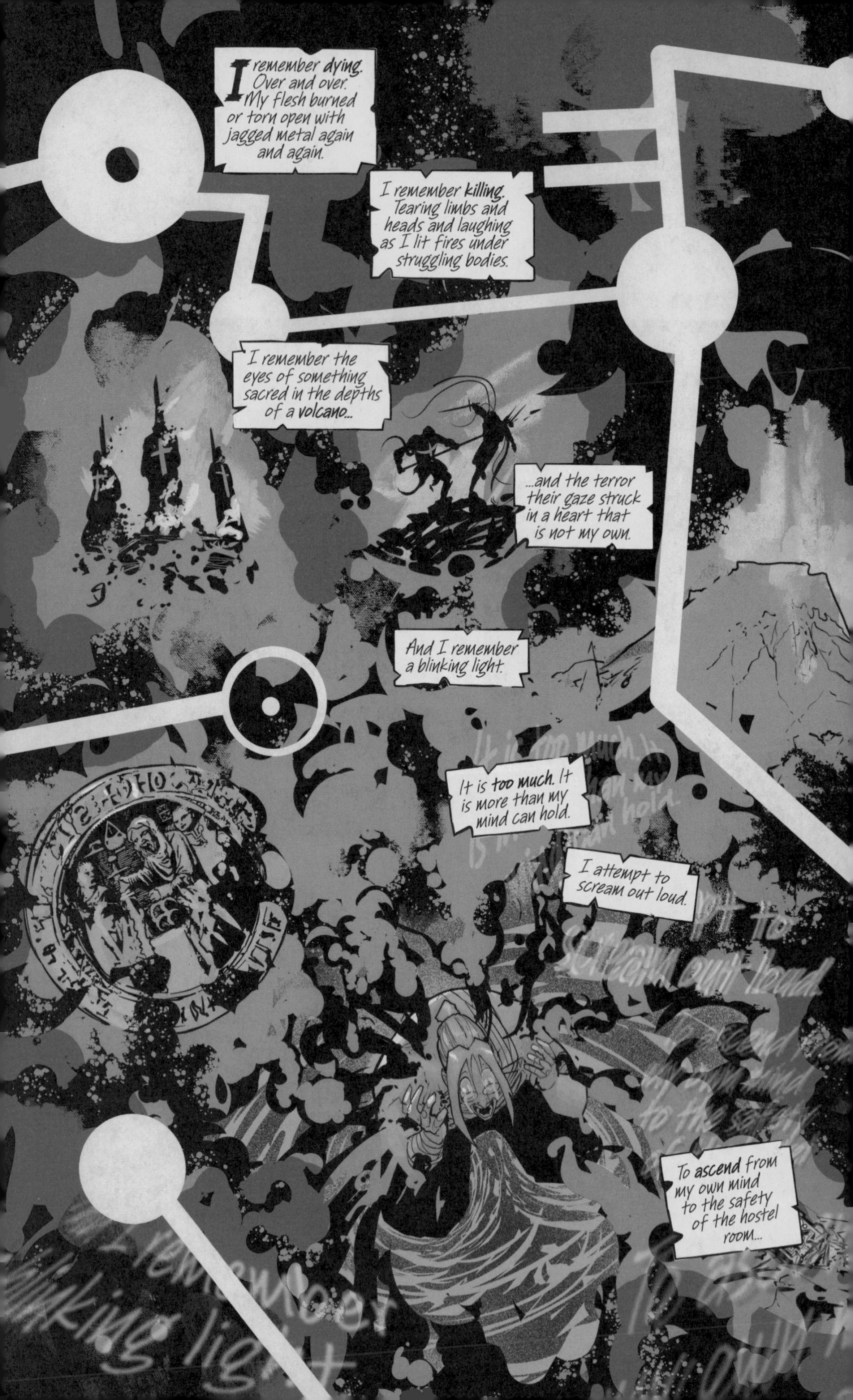
I remember dying. Over and over. My flesh burned or torn open with jagged metal again and again.
I remember killing. Tearing limbs and heads and laughing as I lit fires under struggling bodies.
I remember the eyes of something sacred in the depths of a volcano...
...and the terror their gaze struck in a heart that is not my own.
And I remember a blinking light.
It is too much. It is more than my mind can hold.
I attempt to scream out loud.
To ascend from my own mind to the safety of the hostel room...

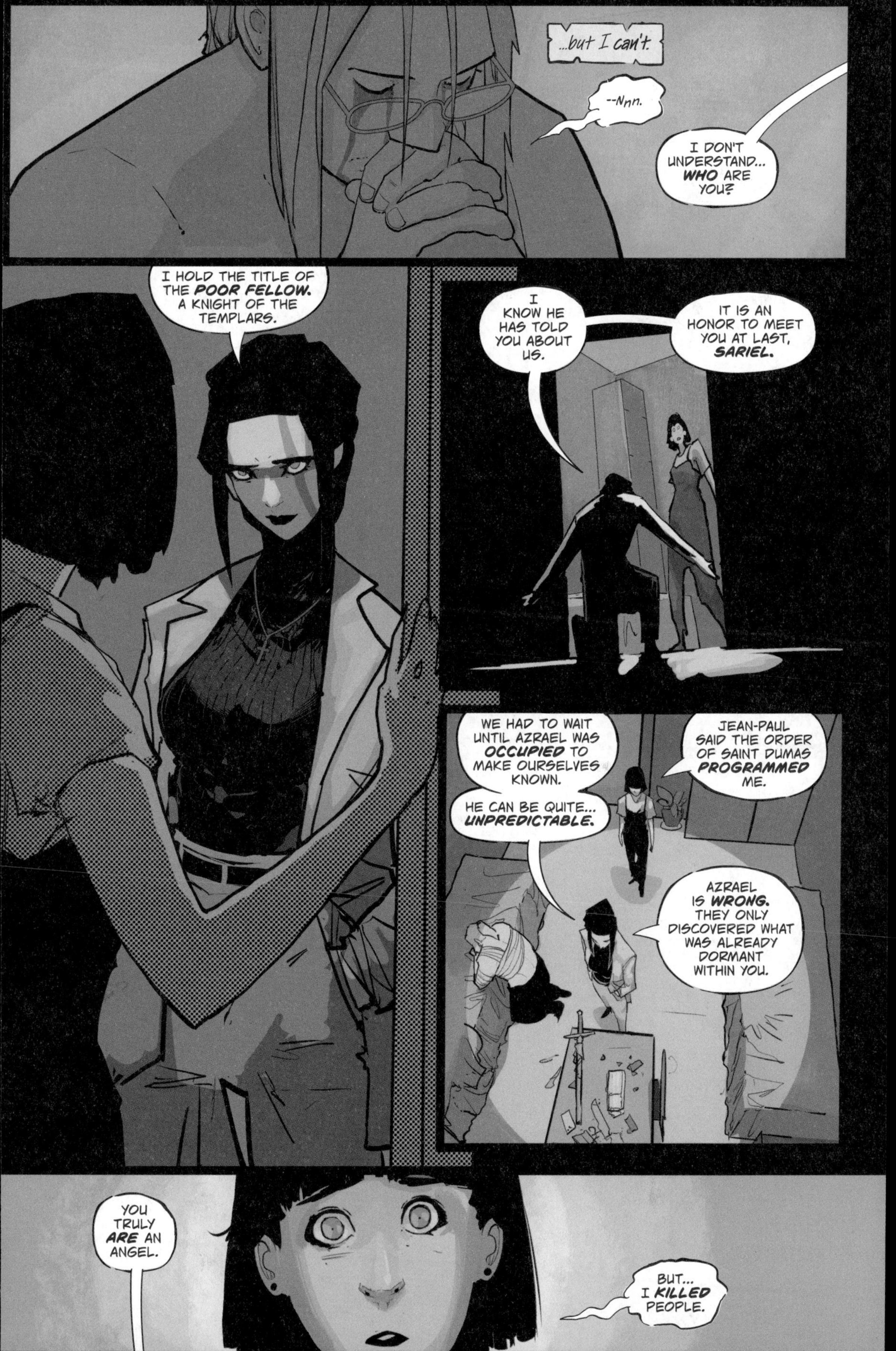
...but I can't.
--Nnn.
I DON'T UNDERSTAND... WHO ARE YOU?
I HOLD THE TITLE OF THE POOR FELLOW. A KNIGHT OF THE TEMPLARS.
I KNOW HE HAS TOLD YOU ABOUT US.
IT IS AN HONOR TO MEET YOU AT LAST, SARIEL.
WE HAD TO WAIT UNTIL AZRAEL WAS OCCUPIED TO MAKE OURSELVES KNOWN.
HE CAN BE QUITE... UNPREDICTABLE.
JEAN-PAUL SAID THE ORDER OF SAINT DUMAS PROGRAMMED ME.
AZRAEL IS WRONG. THEY ONLY DISCOVERED WHAT WAS ALREADY DORMANT WITHIN YOU.
YOU TRULY ARE AN ANGEL.
BUT... I KILLED PEOPLE.

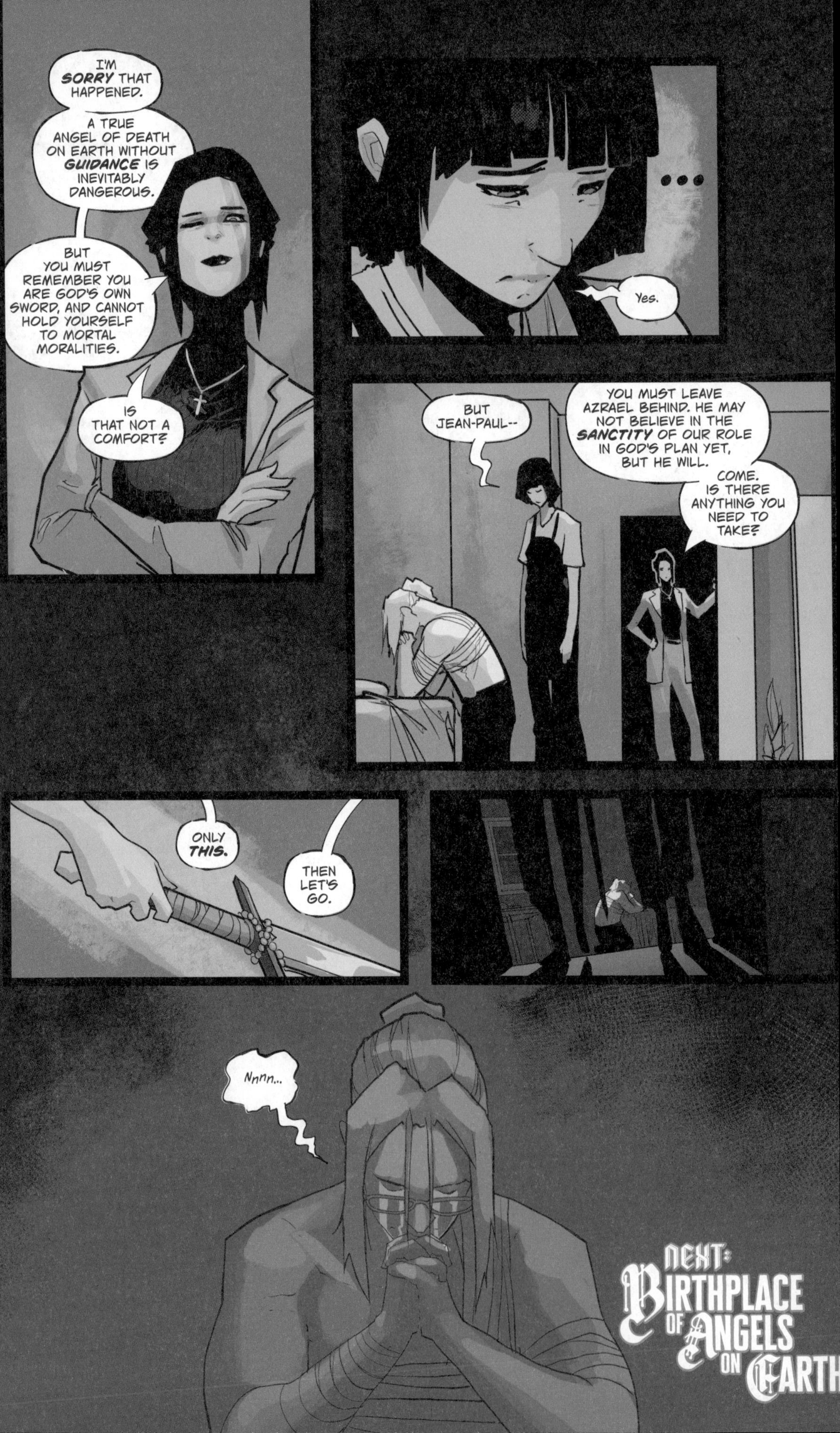
I'M SORRY THAT HAPPENED.
A TRUE ANGEL OF DEATH ON EARTH WITHOUT GUIDANCE IS INEVITABLY DANGEROUS.
BUT YOU MUST REMEMBER YOU ARE GOD'S OWN SWORD, AND CANNOT HOLD YOURSELF TO MORTAL MORALITIES.
IS THAT NOT A COMFORT?
...
Yes.
BUT JEAN-PAUL--
YOU MUST LEAVE AZRAEL BEHIND. HE MAY NOT BELIEVE IN THE SANCTITY OF OUR ROLE IN GOD'S PLAN YET, BUT HE WILL.
COME. IS THERE ANYTHING YOU NEED TO TAKE?
ONLY THIS.
THEN LET'S GO.
Nnnn...
NEXT: BIRTHPLACE OF ANGELS ON EARTH

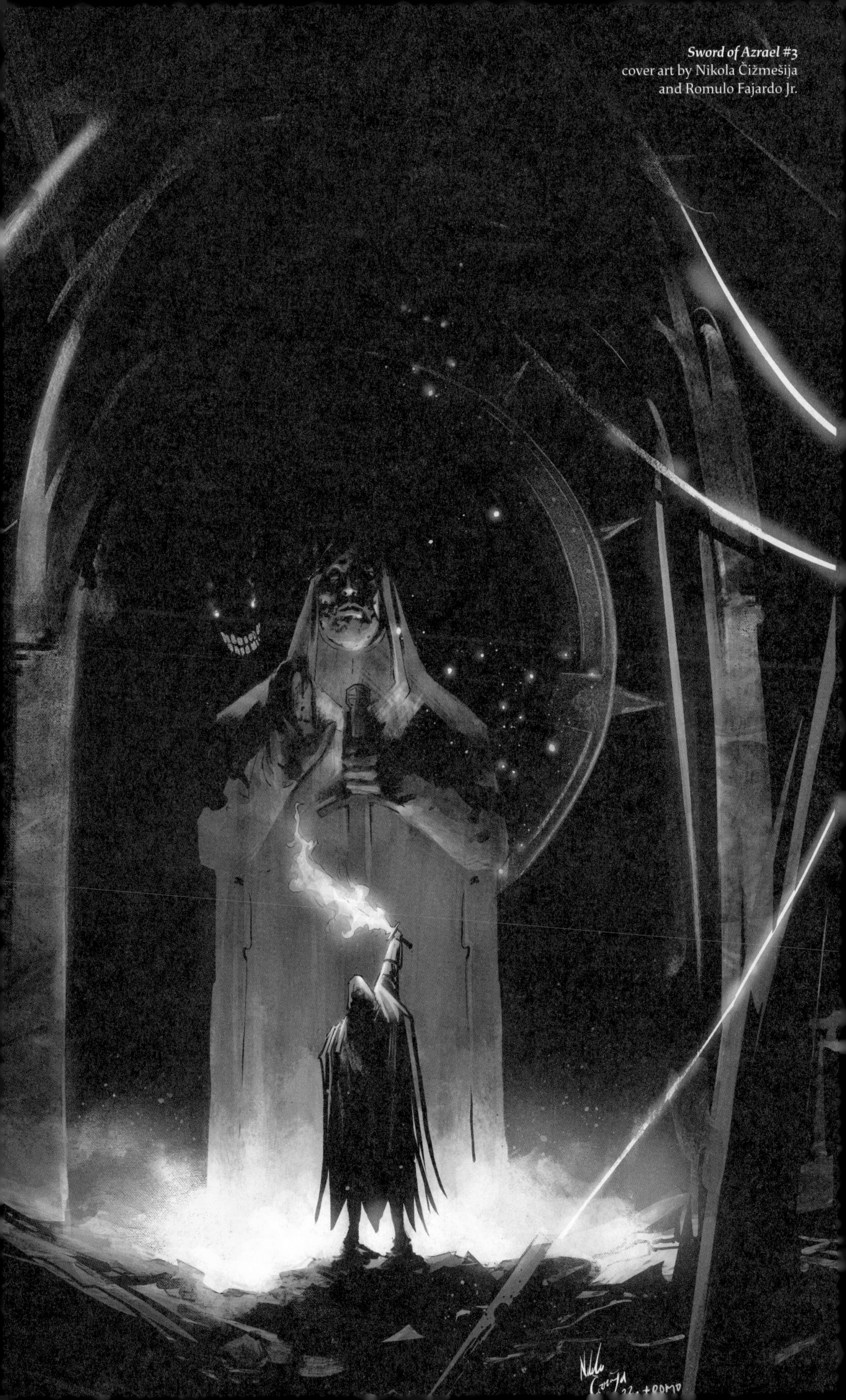

***Sword of Azrael* #3**
cover art by Nikola Čižmešija
and Romulo Fajardo Jr.

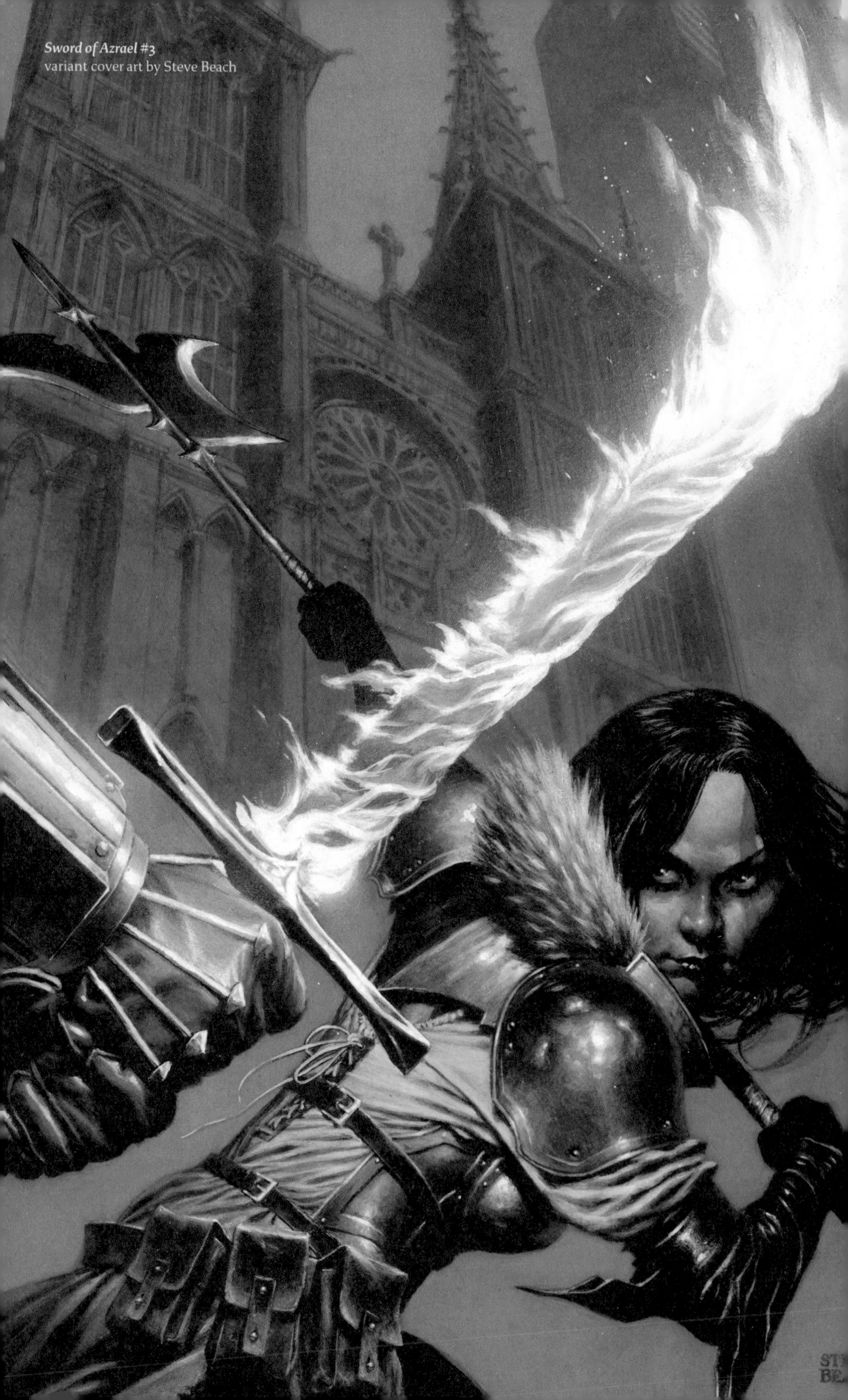

Sword of Azrael #3
variant cover art by Steve Beach

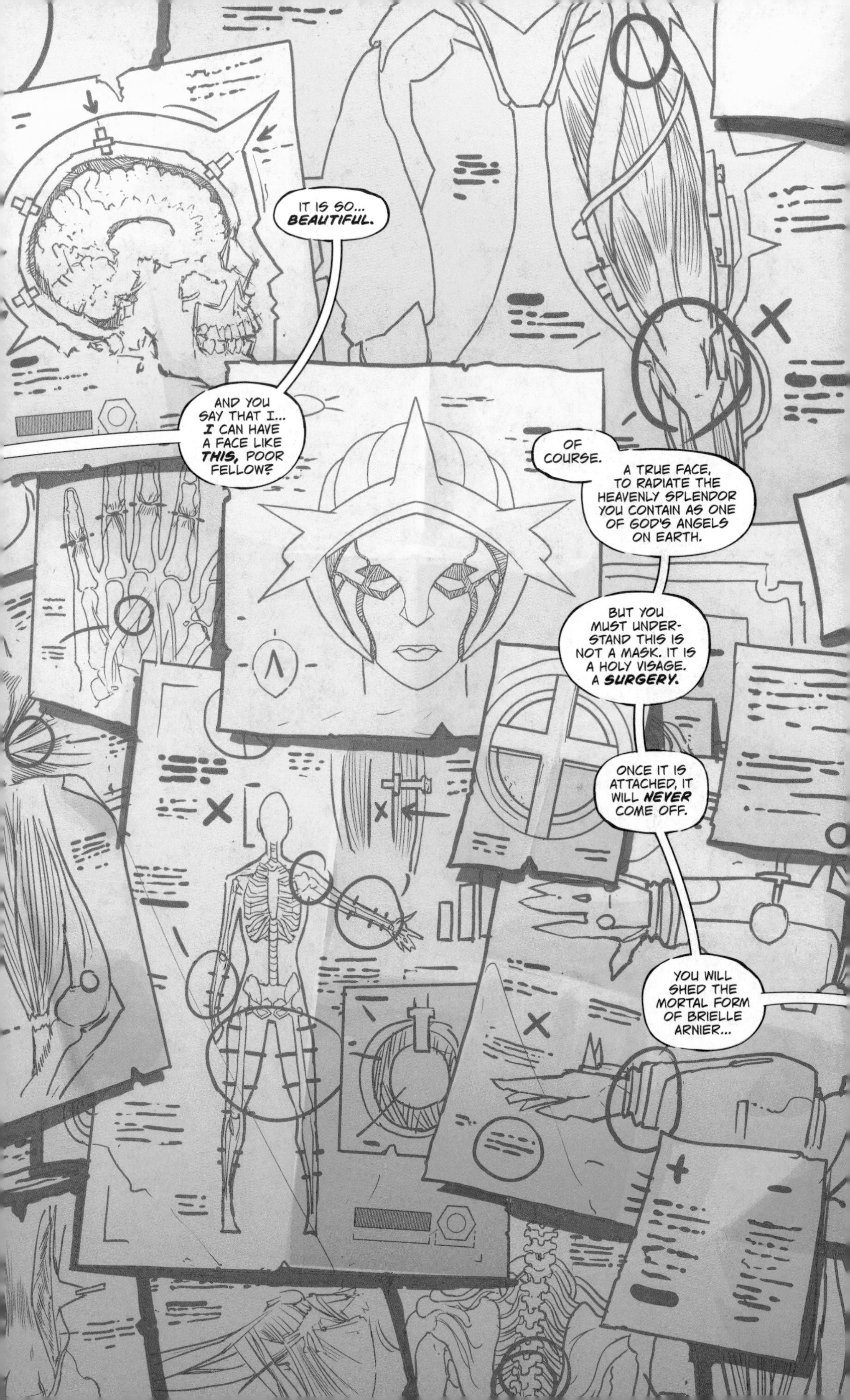
IT IS SO... ***BEAUTIFUL.***
AND YOU SAY THAT I... ***I*** CAN HAVE A FACE LIKE ***THIS,*** POOR FELLOW?
OF COURSE.
A TRUE FACE, TO RADIATE THE HEAVENLY SPLENDOR YOU CONTAIN AS ONE OF GOD'S ANGELS ON EARTH.
BUT YOU MUST UNDER-STAND THIS IS NOT A MASK. IT IS A HOLY VISAGE. A ***SURGERY.***
ONCE IT IS ATTACHED, IT WILL ***NEVER*** COME OFF.
YOU WILL SHED THE MORTAL FORM OF BRIELLE ARNIER...

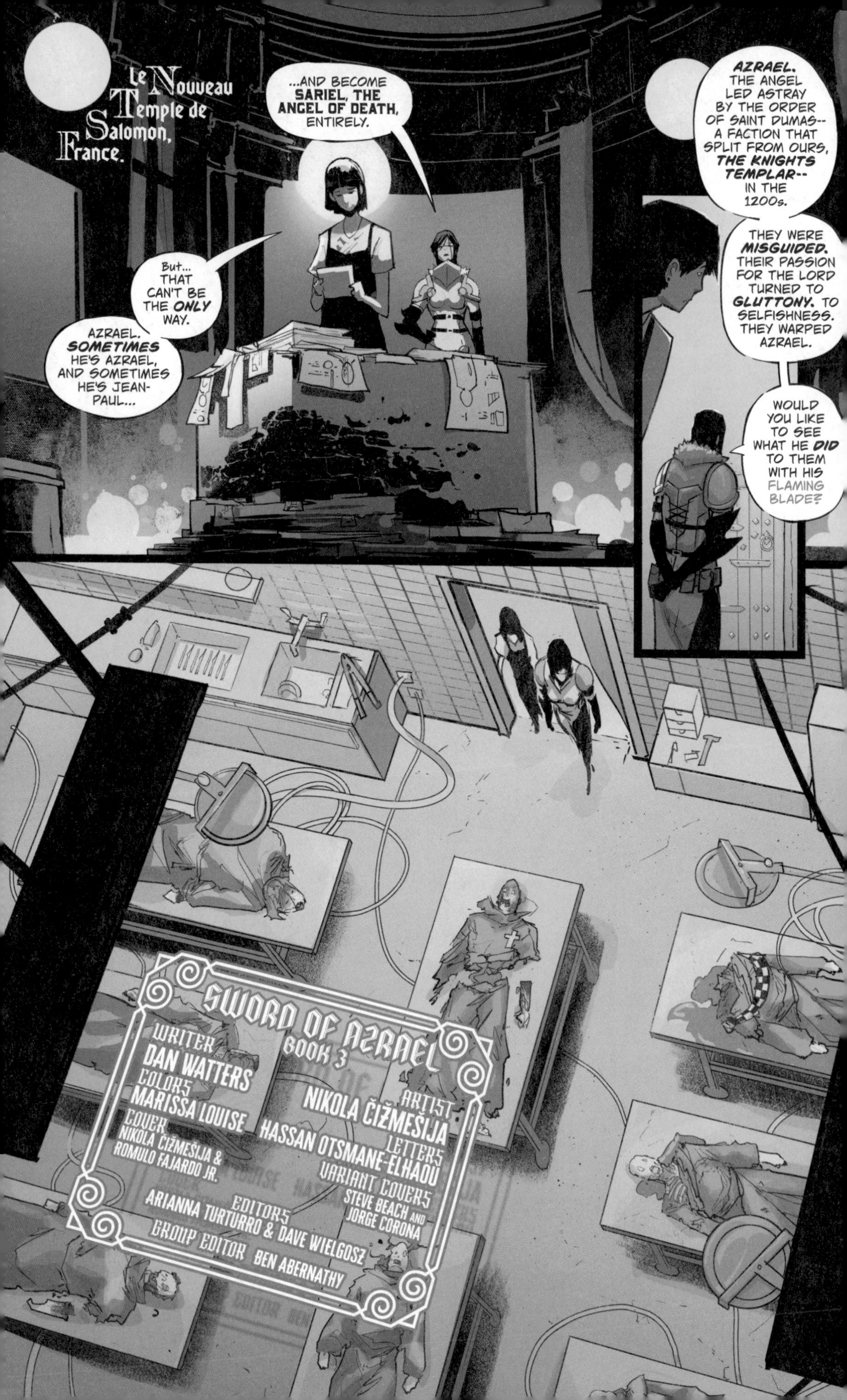

Le Nouveau Temple de Salomon, France.
...AND BECOME SARIEL, THE ANGEL OF DEATH, ENTIRELY.
But... THAT CAN'T BE THE ONLY WAY.
AZRAEL. SOMETIMES HE'S AZRAEL, AND SOMETIMES HE'S JEAN-PAUL...
AZRAEL. THE ANGEL LED ASTRAY BY THE ORDER OF SAINT DUMAS-- A FACTION THAT SPLIT FROM OURS, THE KNIGHTS TEMPLAR-- IN THE 1200s.
THEY WERE MISGUIDED. THEIR PASSION FOR THE LORD TURNED TO GLUTTONY. TO SELFISHNESS. THEY WARPED AZRAEL.
WOULD YOU LIKE TO SEE WHAT HE DID TO THEM WITH HIS FLAMING BLADE?
SWORD OF AZRAEL BOOK 3
WRITER DAN WATTERS
ARTIST NIKOLA ČIŽMEŠIJA
COLORS MARISSA LOUISE
LETTERS HASSAN OTSMANE-ELHAOU
COVER NIKOLA ČIŽMEŠIJA & ROMULO FAJARDO JR.
VARIANT COVERS STEVE BEACH AND JORGE CORONA
EDITORS ARIANNA TURTURRO & DAVE WIELGOSZ
GROUP EDITOR BEN ABERNATHY

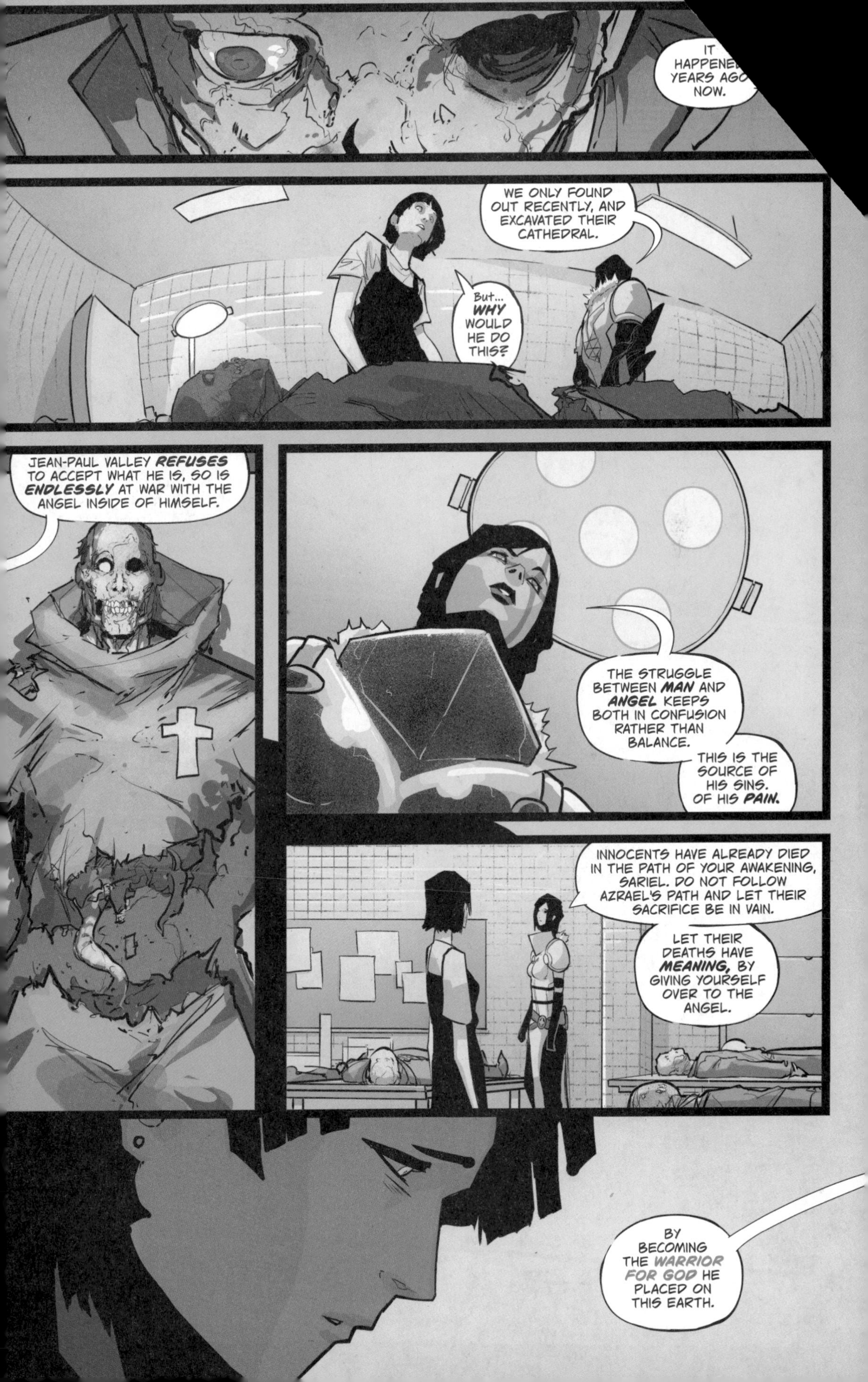
IT HAPPENE YEARS AGO NOW.
WE ONLY FOUND OUT RECENTLY, AND EXCAVATED THEIR CATHEDRAL.
But... **WHY** WOULD HE DO THIS?
JEAN-PAUL VALLEY **REFUSES** TO ACCEPT WHAT HE IS, SO IS **ENDLESSLY** AT WAR WITH THE ANGEL INSIDE OF HIMSELF.
THE STRUGGLE BETWEEN **MAN** AND **ANGEL** KEEPS BOTH IN CONFUSION RATHER THAN BALANCE.
THIS IS THE SOURCE OF HIS SINS. OF HIS **PAIN.**
INNOCENTS HAVE ALREADY DIED IN THE PATH OF YOUR AWAKENING, SARIEL. DO NOT FOLLOW AZRAEL'S PATH AND LET THEIR SACRIFICE BE IN VAIN.
LET THEIR DEATHS HAVE **MEANING,** BY GIVING YOURSELF OVER TO THE ANGEL.
BY BECOMING THE **WARRIOR FOR GOD** HE PLACED ON THIS EARTH.

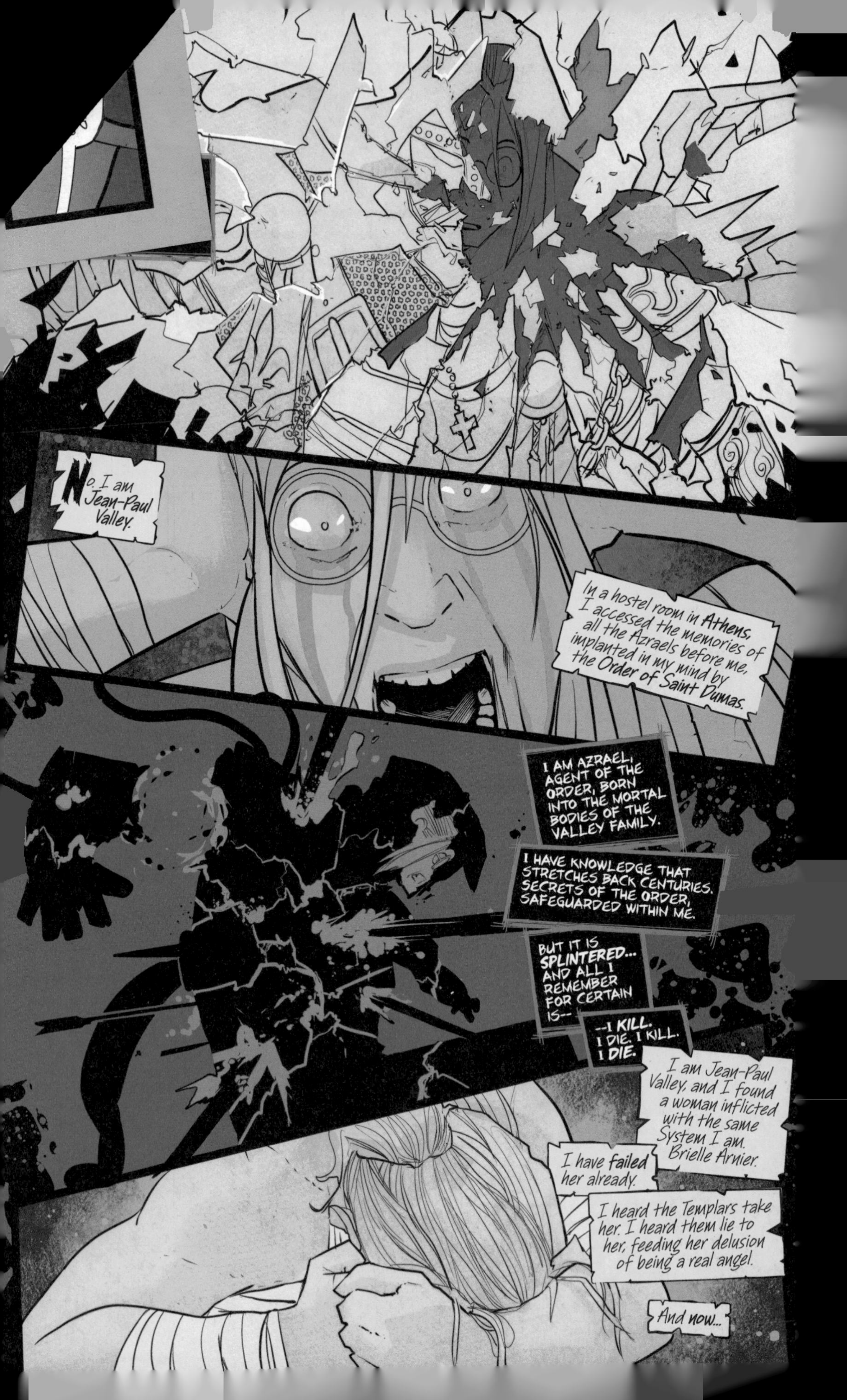
No. I am Jean-Paul Valley.
In a hostel room in Athens, I accessed the memories of all the Azraels before me, implanted in my mind by the Order of Saint Dumas.
I AM AZRAEL, AGENT OF THE ORDER, BORN INTO THE MORTAL BODIES OF THE VALLEY FAMILY.
I HAVE KNOWLEDGE THAT STRETCHES BACK CENTURIES. SECRETS OF THE ORDER, SAFEGUARDED WITHIN ME.
BUT IT IS SPLINTERED... AND ALL I REMEMBER FOR CERTAIN IS--
--I KILL. I DIE. I KILL. I DIE.
I am Jean-Paul Valley, and I found a woman inflicted with the same System I am. Brielle Arnier.
I have failed her already.
I heard the Templars take her. I heard them lie to her, feeding her delusion of being a real angel.
And now...

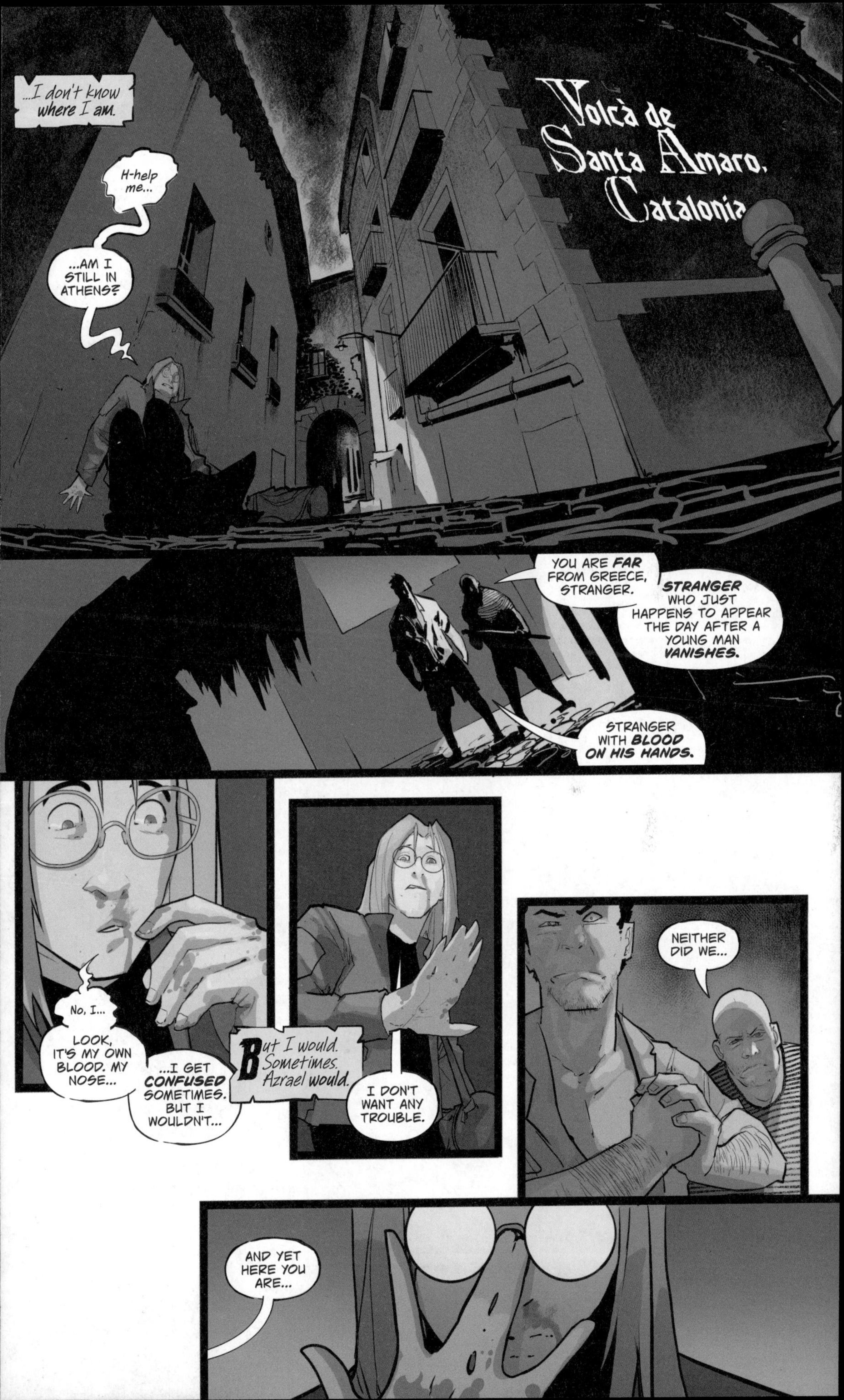
...I don't know where I am.
Volcà de Santa Amaro, Catalonia
H-help me...
...AM I STILL IN ATHENS?
YOU ARE FAR FROM GREECE, STRANGER.
STRANGER WHO JUST HAPPENS TO APPEAR THE DAY AFTER A YOUNG MAN VANISHES.
STRANGER WITH BLOOD ON HIS HANDS.
No, I...
LOOK, IT'S MY OWN BLOOD. MY NOSE...
...I GET CONFUSED SOMETIMES. BUT I WOULDN'T...
But I would. Sometimes. Azrael would.
I DON'T WANT ANY TROUBLE.
NEITHER DID WE...
AND YET HERE YOU ARE...

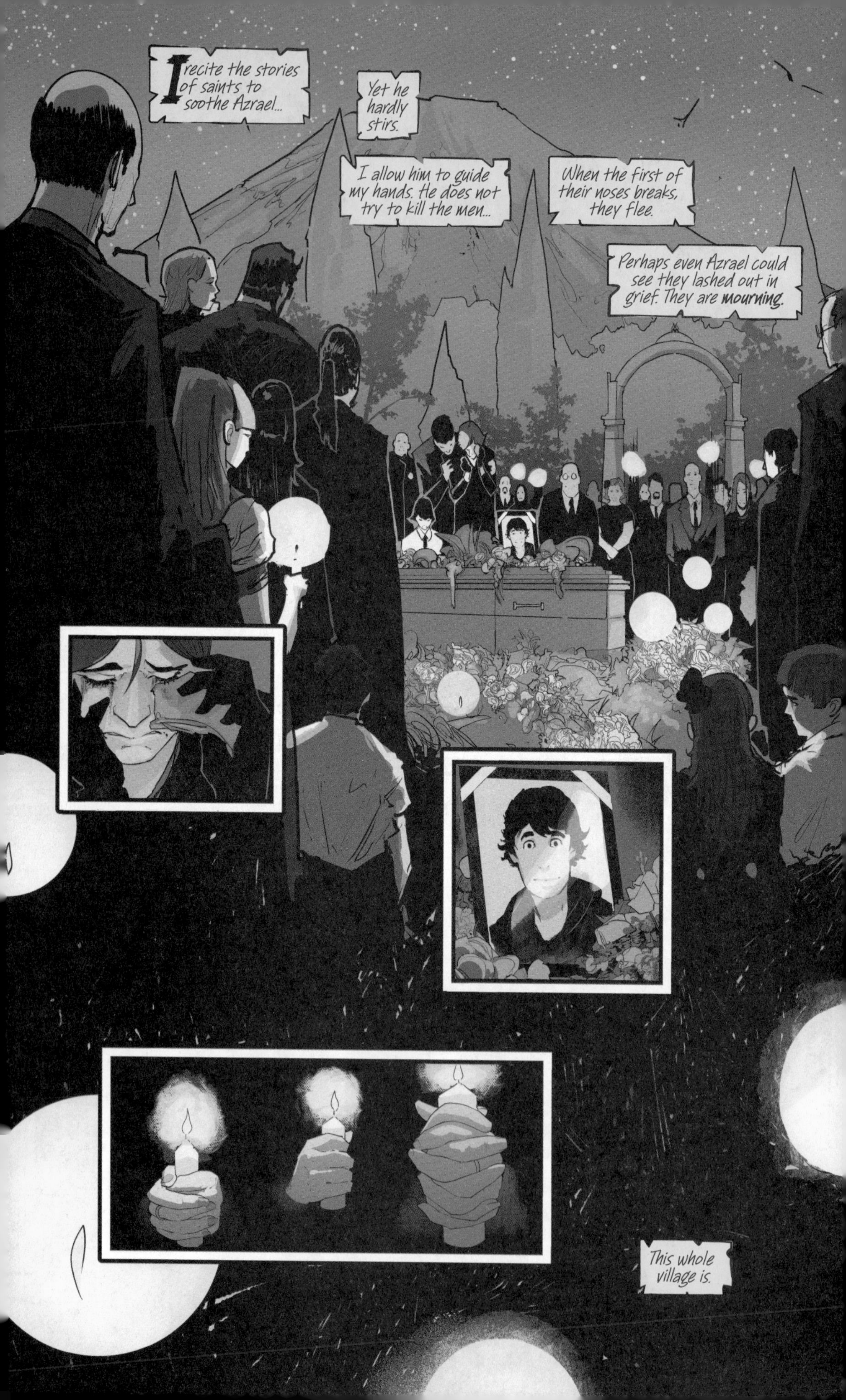
I recite the stories of saints to soothe Azrael...
Yet he hardly stirs.
I allow him to guide my hands. He does not try to kill the men...
When the first of their noses breaks, they flee.
Perhaps even Azrael could see they lashed out in grief. They are mourning.
This whole village is.

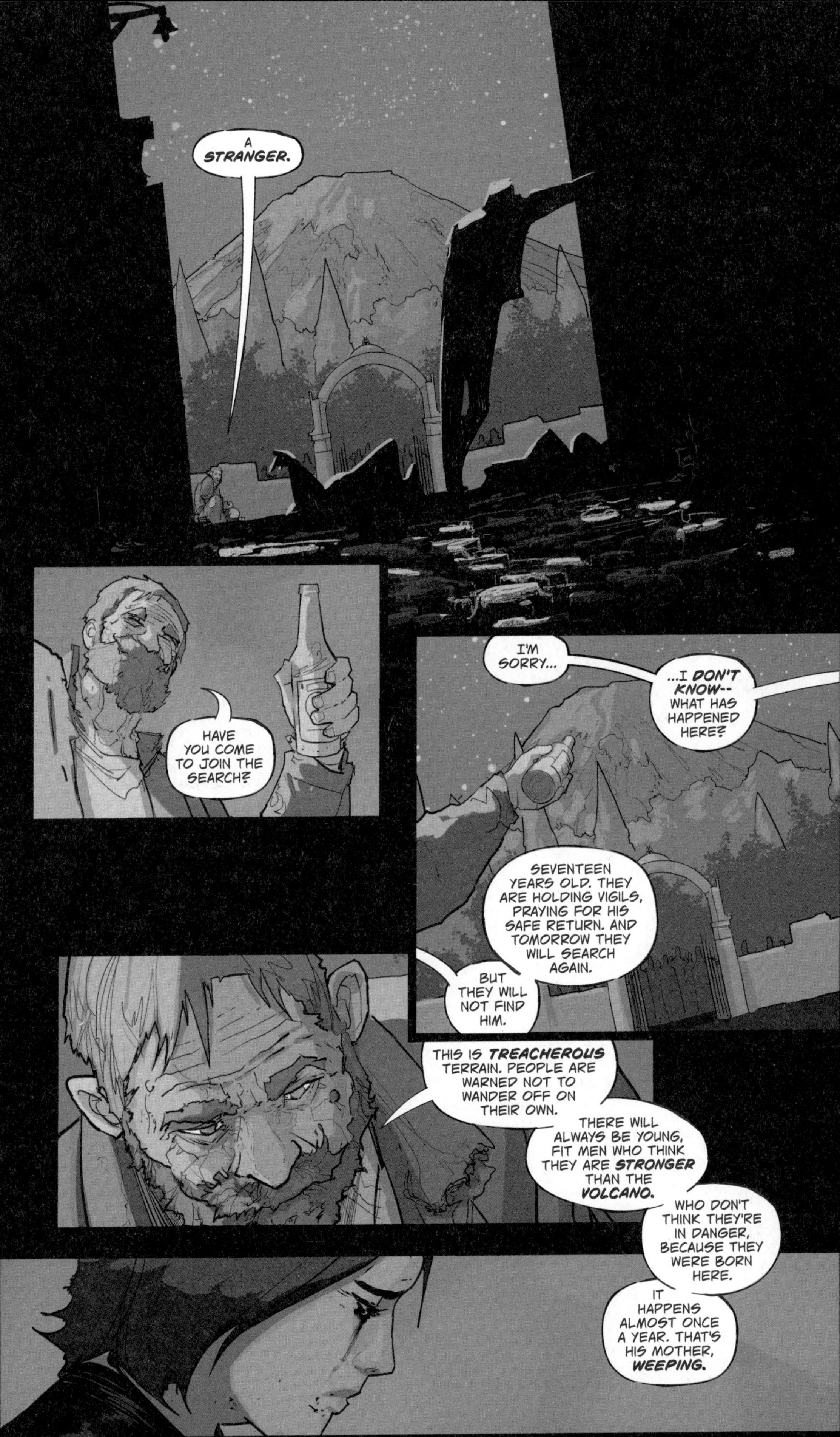
A STRANGER.
HAVE YOU COME TO JOIN THE SEARCH?
I'M SORRY...
...I DON'T KNOW-- WHAT HAS HAPPENED HERE?
SEVENTEEN YEARS OLD. THEY ARE HOLDING VIGILS, PRAYING FOR HIS SAFE RETURN. AND TOMORROW THEY WILL SEARCH AGAIN.
BUT THEY WILL NOT FIND HIM.
THIS IS TREACHEROUS TERRAIN. PEOPLE ARE WARNED NOT TO WANDER OFF ON THEIR OWN.
THERE WILL ALWAYS BE YOUNG, FIT MEN WHO THINK THEY ARE STRONGER THAN THE VOLCANO.
WHO DON'T THINK THEY'RE IN DANGER, BECAUSE THEY WERE BORN HERE.
IT HAPPENS ALMOST ONCE A YEAR. THAT'S HIS MOTHER, WEEPING.

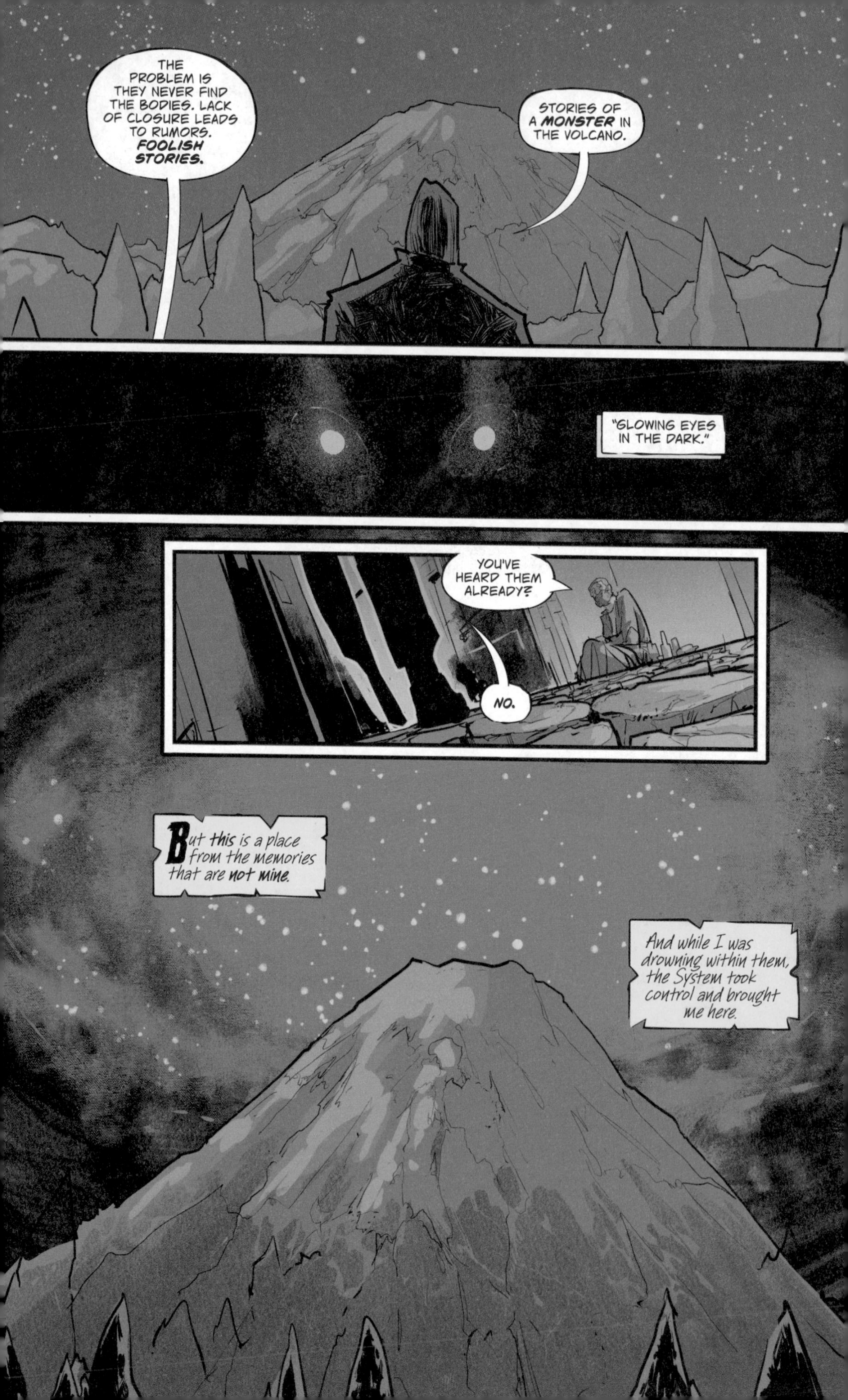
THE PROBLEM IS THEY NEVER FIND THE BODIES. LACK OF CLOSURE LEADS TO RUMORS. FOOLISH STORIES.
STORIES OF A MONSTER IN THE VOLCANO.
"GLOWING EYES IN THE DARK."
YOU'VE HEARD THEM ALREADY?
NO.
But this is a place from the memories that are not mine.
And while I was drowning within them, the System took control and brought me here.

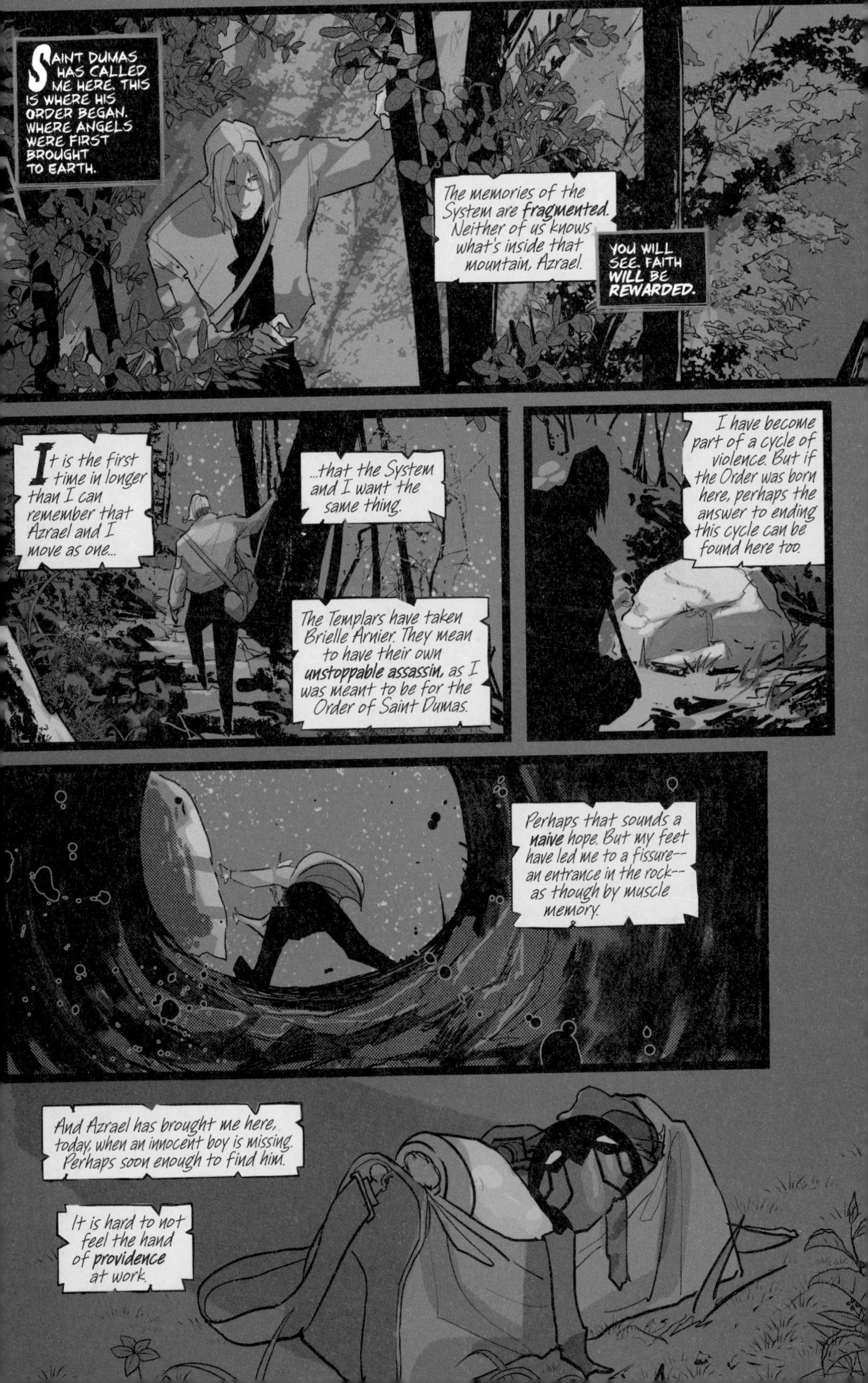
SAINT DUMAS HAS CALLED ME HERE. THIS IS WHERE HIS ORDER BEGAN. WHERE ANGELS WERE FIRST BROUGHT TO EARTH.
The memories of the System are **fragmented**. Neither of us knows what's inside that mountain, Azrael.
YOU WILL SEE. FAITH **WILL** BE **REWARDED.**
It is the first time in longer than I can remember that Azrael and I move as one...
...that the System and I want the same thing.
The Templars have taken Brielle Arnier. They mean to have their own **unstoppable assassin**, as I was meant to be for the Order of Saint Dumas.
I have become part of a cycle of violence. But if the Order was born here, perhaps the answer to ending this cycle can be found here too.
Perhaps that sounds a **naive** hope. But my feet have led me to a fissure-- an entrance in the rock-- as though by muscle memory.
And Azrael has brought me here, today, when an innocent boy is missing. Perhaps soon enough to find him.
It is hard to not feel the hand of **providence** at work.

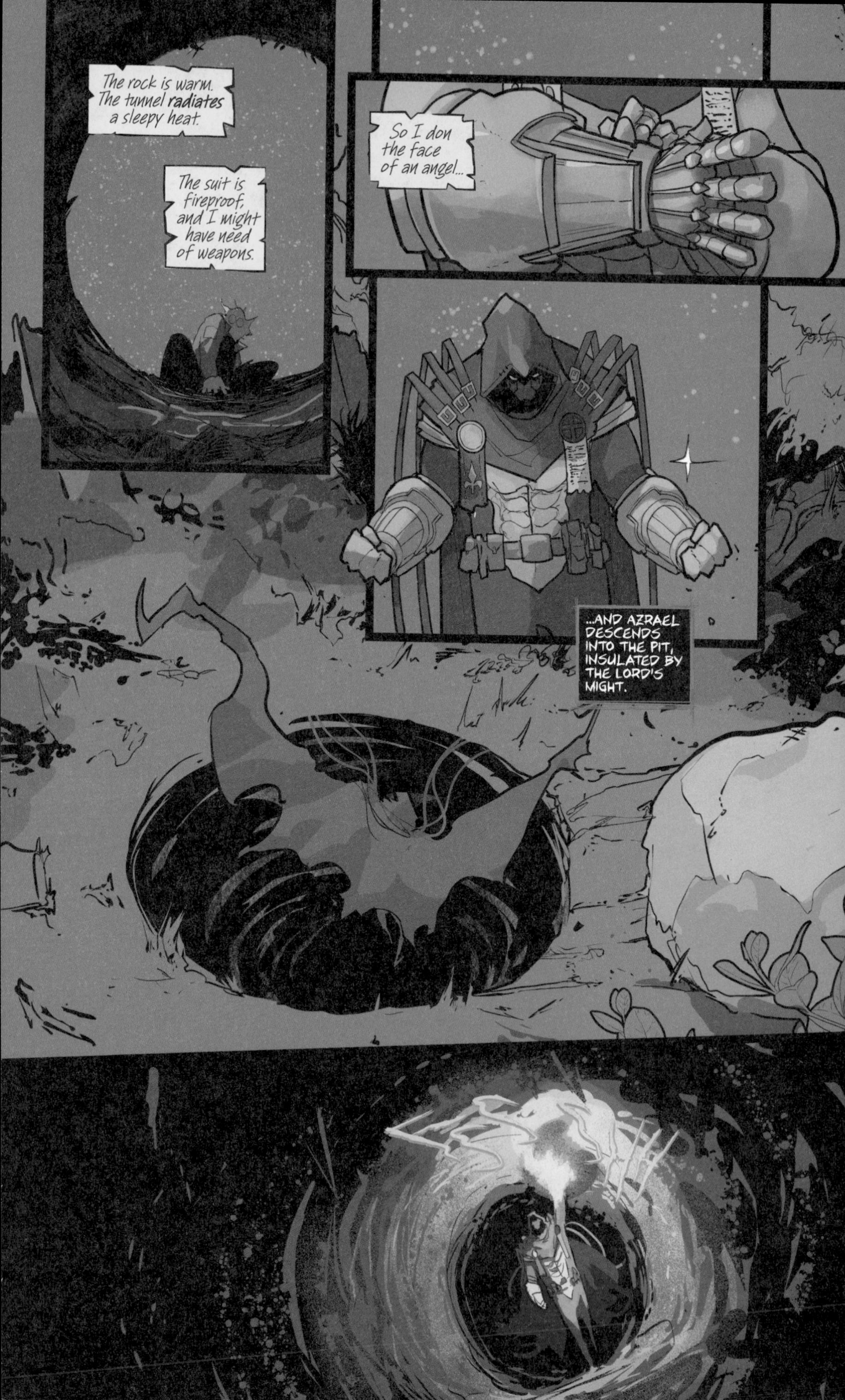

The rock is warm. The tunnel radiates a sleepy heat.
The suit is fireproof, and I might have need of weapons.
So I don the face of an angel...
...AND AZRAEL DESCENDS INTO THE PIT, INSULATED BY THE LORD'S MIGHT.

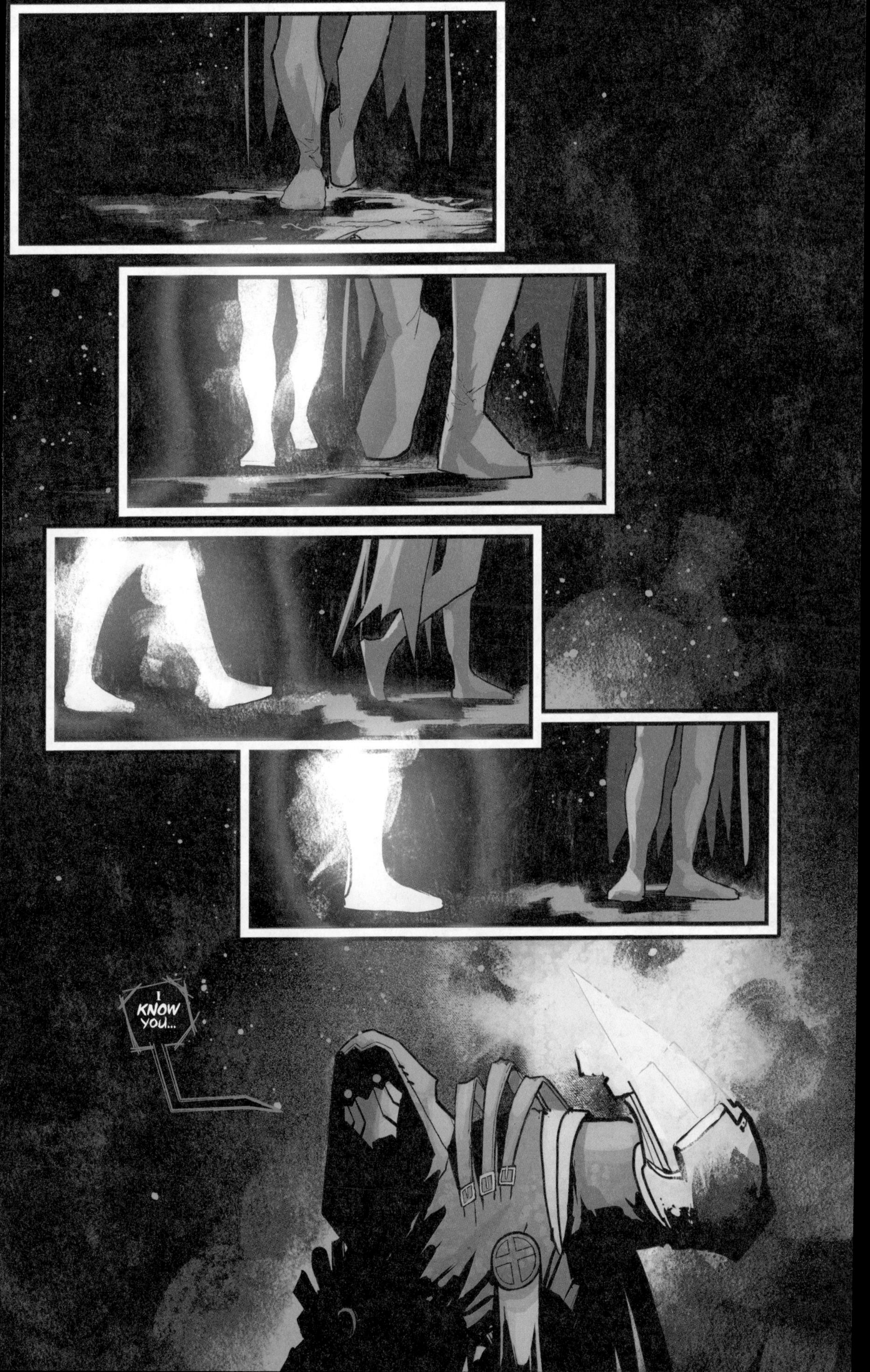
I KNOW YOU...

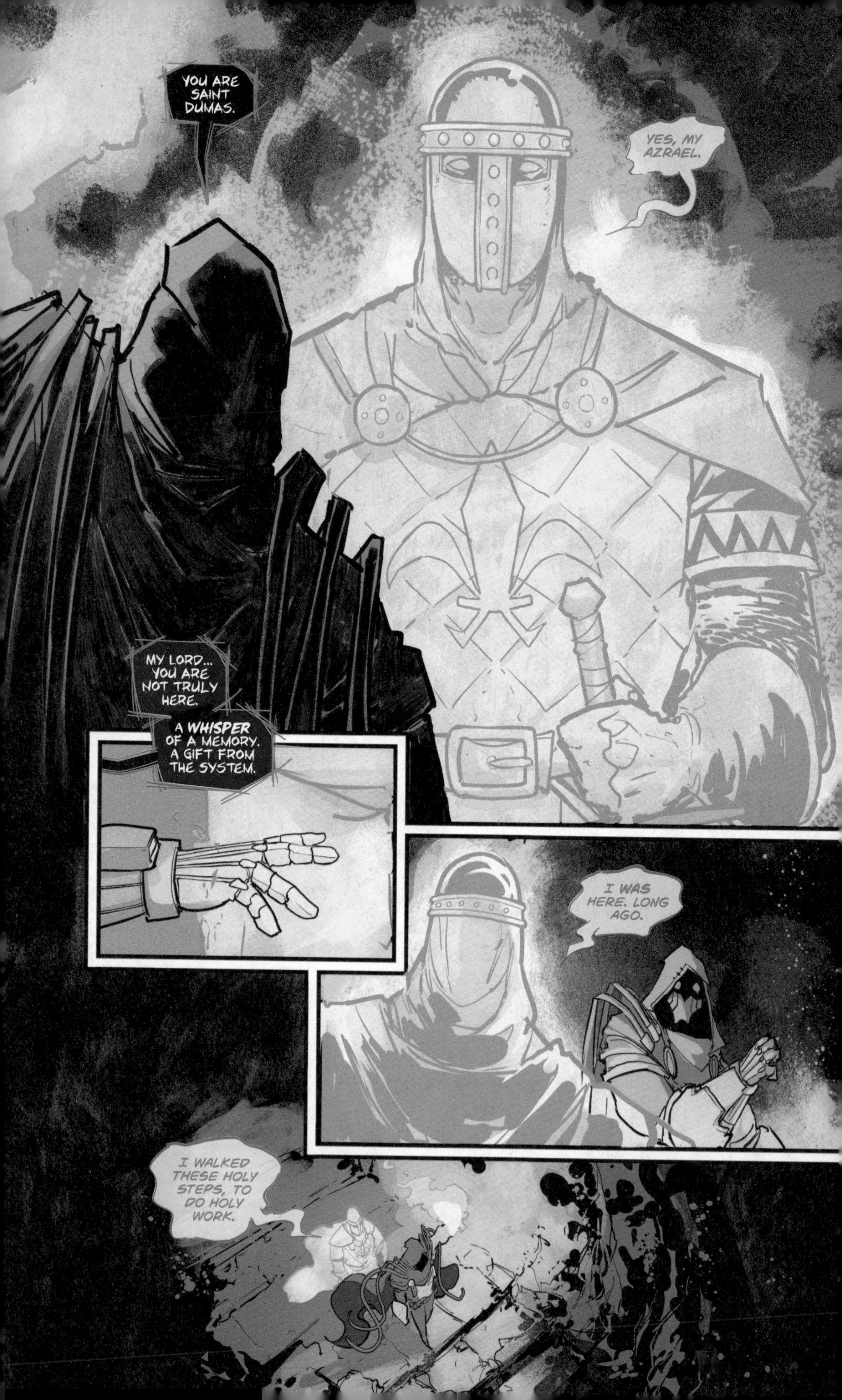

YOU ARE SAINT DUMAS.
YES, MY AZRAEL.
MY LORD... YOU ARE NOT TRULY HERE.
A WHISPER OF A MEMORY. A GIFT FROM THE SYSTEM.
I WAS HERE. LONG AGO.
I WALKED THESE HOLY STEPS, TO DO HOLY WORK.

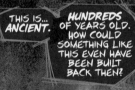

THIS IS... **ANCIENT.** **HUNDREDS** OF YEARS OLD. HOW COULD SOMETHING LIKE THIS EVEN HAVE BEEN BUILT BACK THEN?

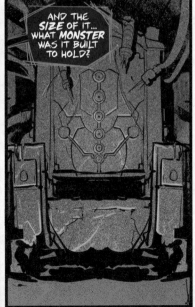

AND THE **SIZE** OF IT... WHAT **MONSTER** WAS IT BUILT TO HOLD?

...SAINT DUMAS?

HMM.

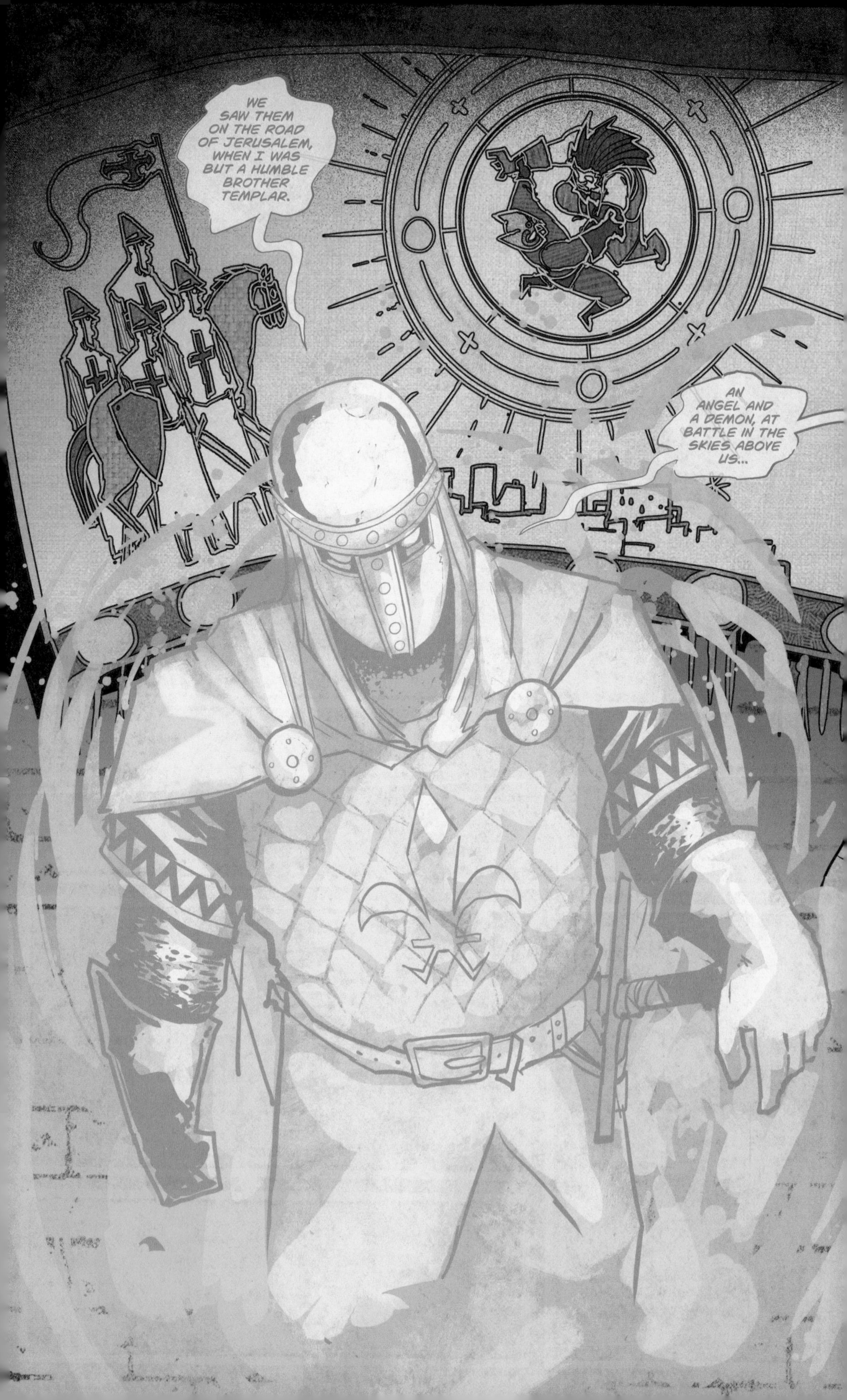
WE SAW THEM ON THE ROAD OF JERUSALEM, WHEN I WAS BUT A HUMBLE BROTHER TEMPLAR.
AN ANGEL AND A DEMON, AT BATTLE IN THE SKIES ABOVE US...

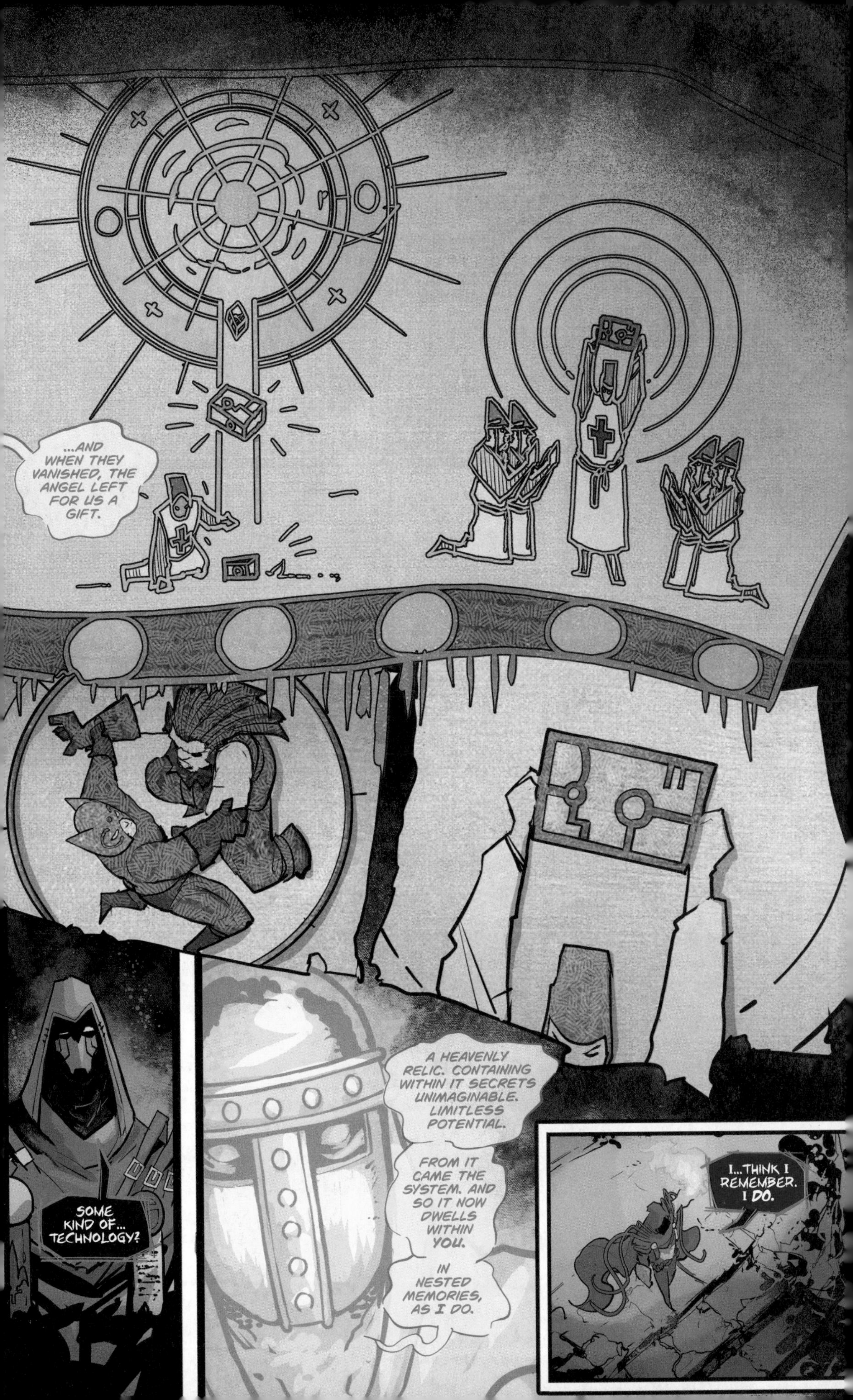
...AND WHEN THEY VANISHED, THE ANGEL LEFT FOR US A GIFT.
A HEAVENLY RELIC. CONTAINING WITHIN IT SECRETS UNIMAGINABLE. LIMITLESS POTENTIAL.
SOME KIND OF... TECHNOLOGY?
FROM IT CAME THE SYSTEM. AND SO IT NOW DWELLS WITHIN YOU.
IN NESTED MEMORIES, AS I DO.
I...THINK I REMEMBER. I DO.

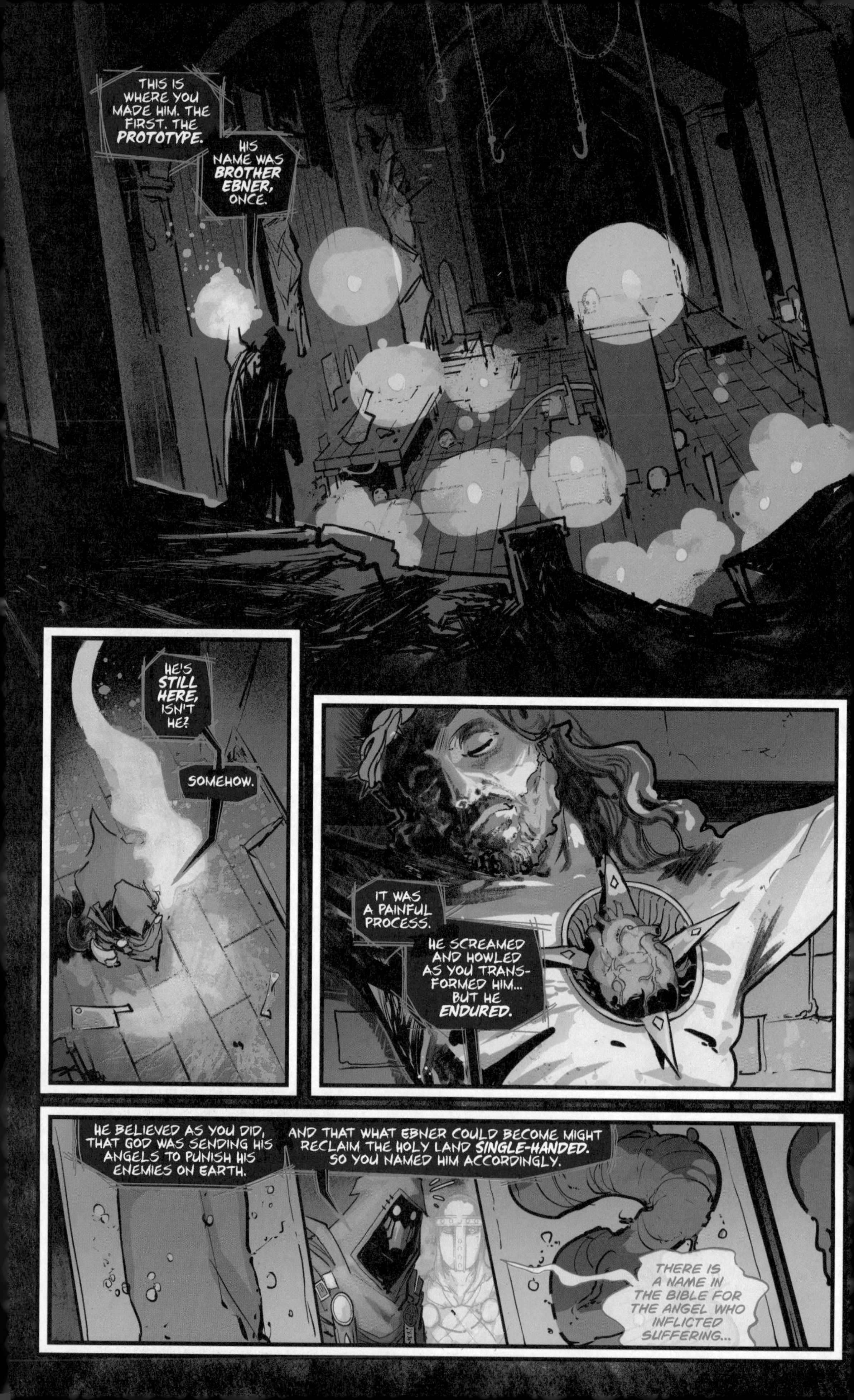
THIS IS WHERE YOU MADE HIM. THE FIRST. THE PROTOTYPE.
HIS NAME WAS BROTHER EBNER, ONCE.
HE'S STILL HERE, ISN'T HE?
SOMEHOW.
IT WAS A PAINFUL PROCESS.
HE SCREAMED AND HOWLED AS YOU TRANS-FORMED HIM... BUT HE ENDURED.
HE BELIEVED AS YOU DID, THAT GOD WAS SENDING HIS ANGELS TO PUNISH HIS ENEMIES ON EARTH.
AND THAT WHAT EBNER COULD BECOME MIGHT RECLAIM THE HOLY LAND SINGLE-HANDED. SO YOU NAMED HIM ACCORDINGLY.
THERE IS A NAME IN THE BIBLE FOR THE ANGEL WHO INFLICTED SUFFERING...

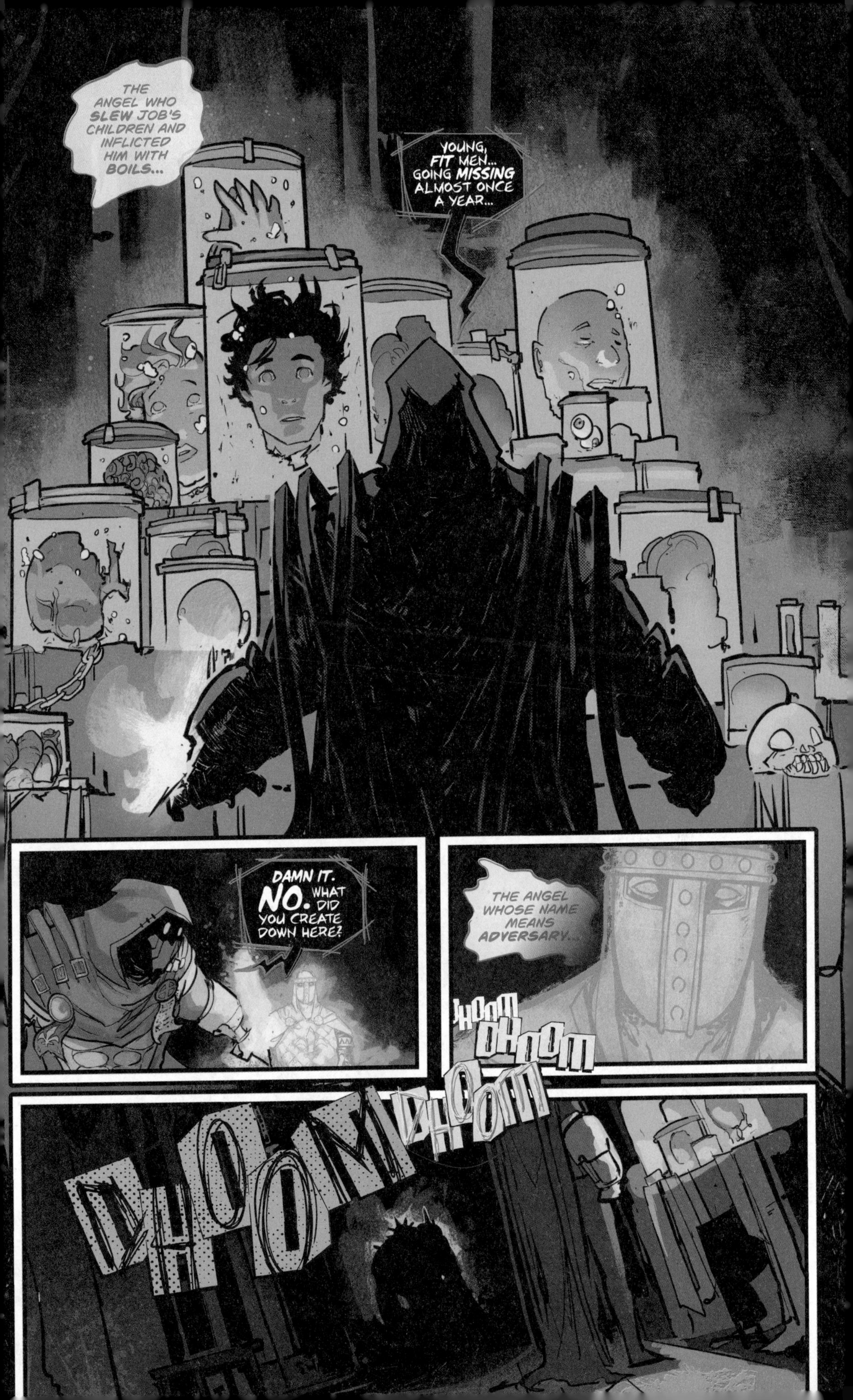
THE ANGEL WHO SLEW JOB'S CHILDREN AND INFLICTED HIM WITH BOILS...
YOUNG, FIT MEN... GOING MISSING ALMOST ONCE A YEAR...
DAMN IT. NO. WHAT DID YOU CREATE DOWN HERE?
THE ANGEL WHOSE NAME MEANS ADVERSARY...
DHOOM
DHOOM
DHOOM
DHOOM

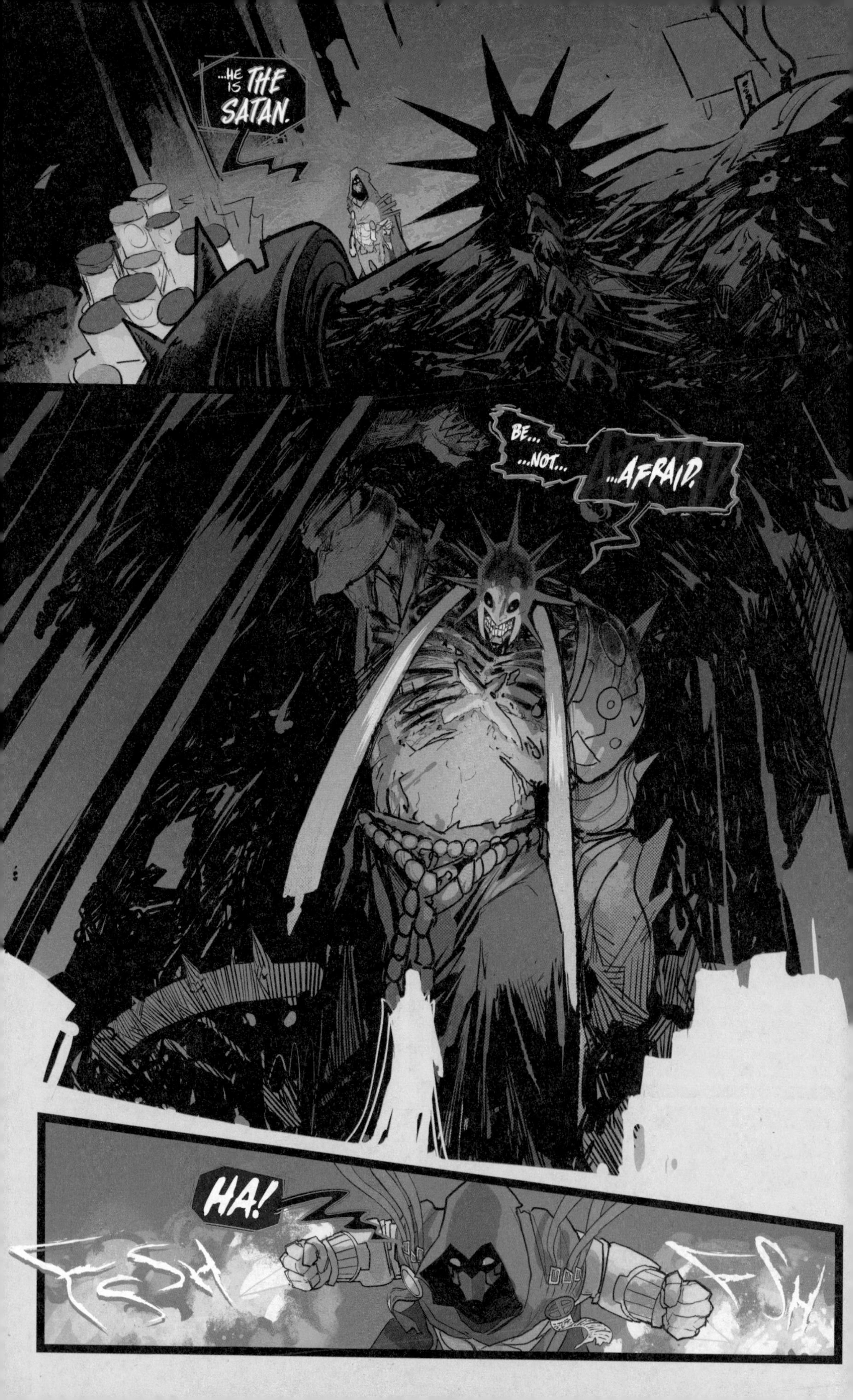
...HE IS THE SATAN.
BE... ...NOT... ...AFRAID.
HA!
FSH
FSH

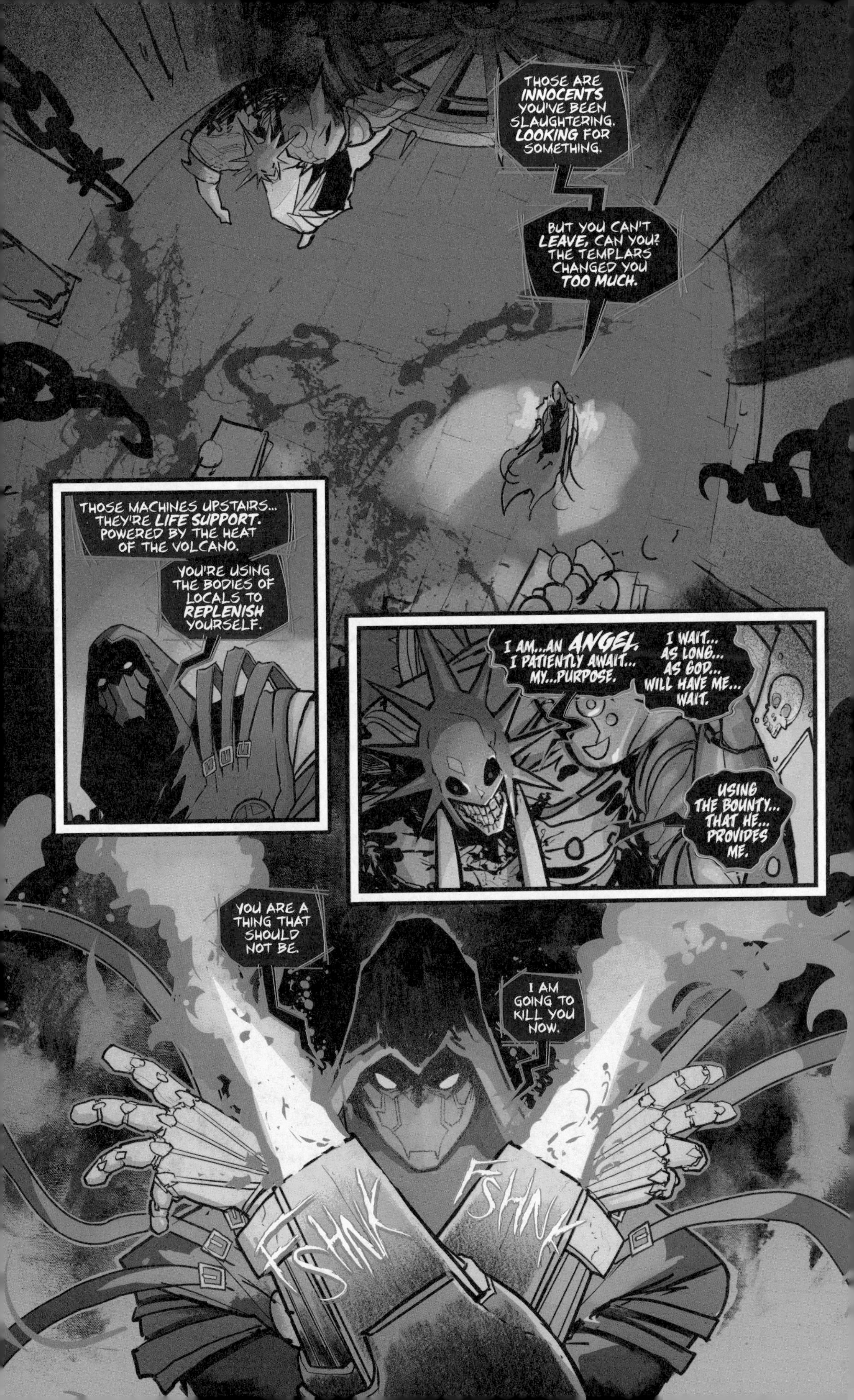
THOSE ARE INNOCENTS YOU'VE BEEN SLAUGHTERING. LOOKING FOR SOMETHING.
BUT YOU CAN'T LEAVE, CAN YOU? THE TEMPLARS CHANGED YOU TOO MUCH.
THOSE MACHINES UPSTAIRS... THEY'RE LIFE SUPPORT. POWERED BY THE HEAT OF THE VOLCANO.
YOU'RE USING THE BODIES OF LOCALS TO REPLENISH YOURSELF.
I AM...AN ANGEL. I PATIENTLY AWAIT... MY...PURPOSE.
I WAIT... AS LONG... AS GOD... WILL HAVE ME... WAIT.
USING THE BOUNTY... THAT HE... PROVIDES ME.
YOU ARE A THING THAT SHOULD NOT BE.
I AM GOING TO KILL YOU NOW.
FSHNK
FSHNK

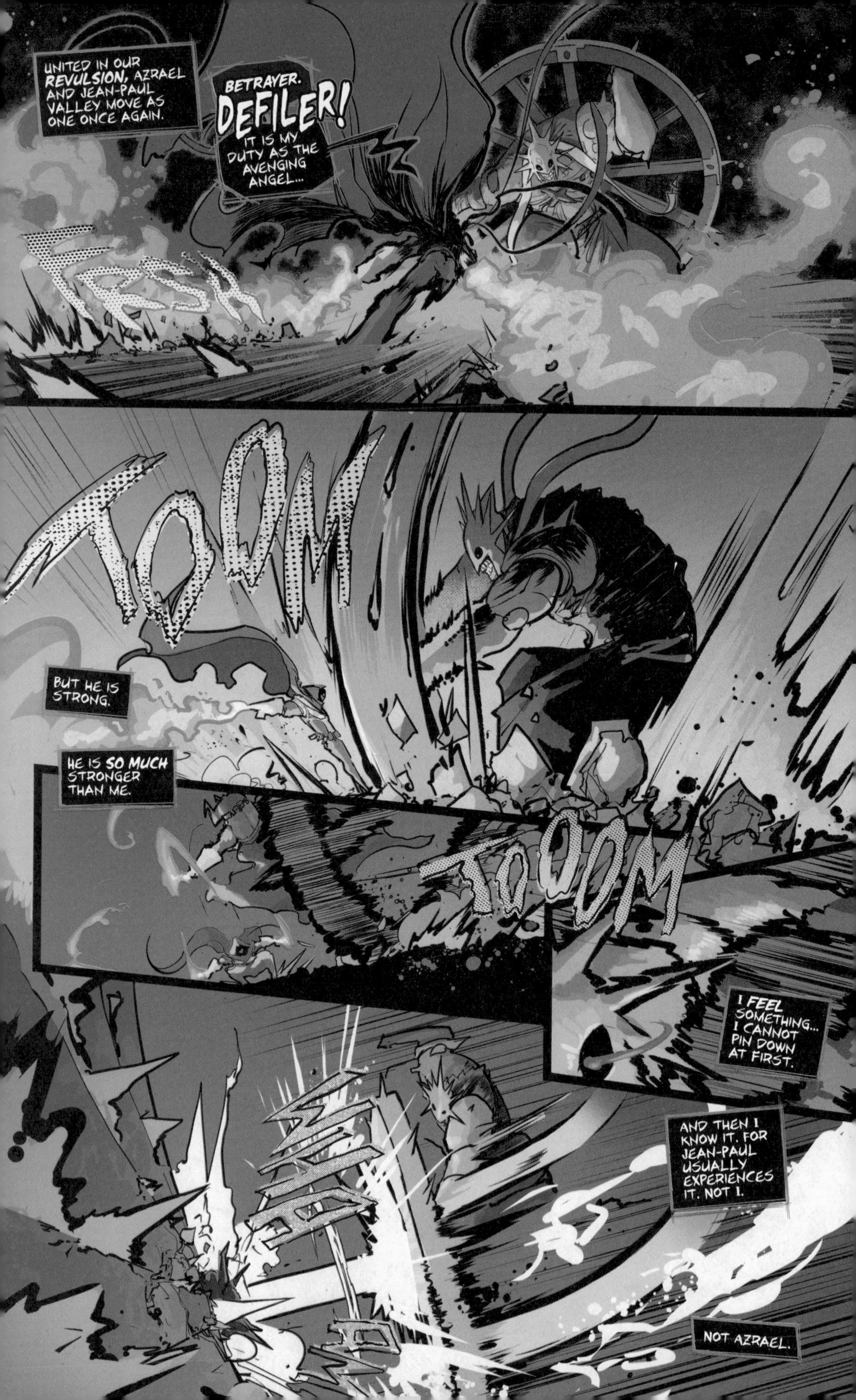
UNITED IN OUR REVULSION, AZRAEL AND JEAN-PAUL VALLEY MOVE AS ONE ONCE AGAIN.
BETRAYER. DEFILER! IT IS MY DUTY AS THE AVENGING ANGEL...
FRSSH
TOOM
BUT HE IS STRONG.
HE IS SO MUCH STRONGER THAN ME.
TOOOM
I FEEL SOMETHING... I CANNOT PIN DOWN AT FIRST.
AND THEN I KNOW IT. FOR JEAN-PAUL USUALLY EXPERIENCES IT. NOT I.
NOT AZRAEL.

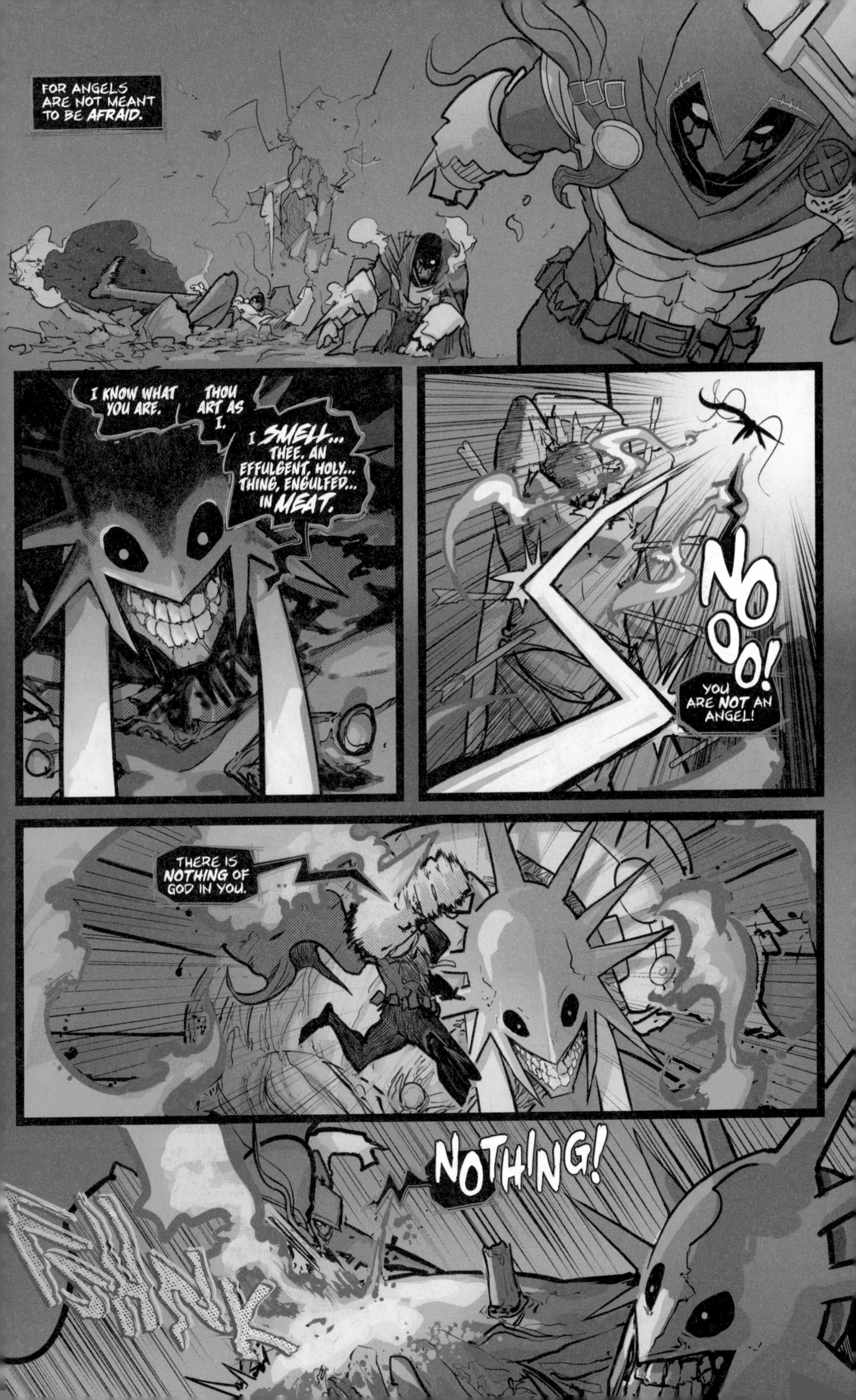
FOR ANGELS ARE NOT MEANT TO BE AFRAID.
I KNOW WHAT YOU ARE.
THOU ART AS I.
I SMELL... THEE. AN EFFULGENT, HOLY... THING, ENGULFED... IN MEAT.
NOOOO!
YOU ARE NOT AN ANGEL!
THERE IS NOTHING OF GOD IN YOU.
NOTHING!
FSHNK

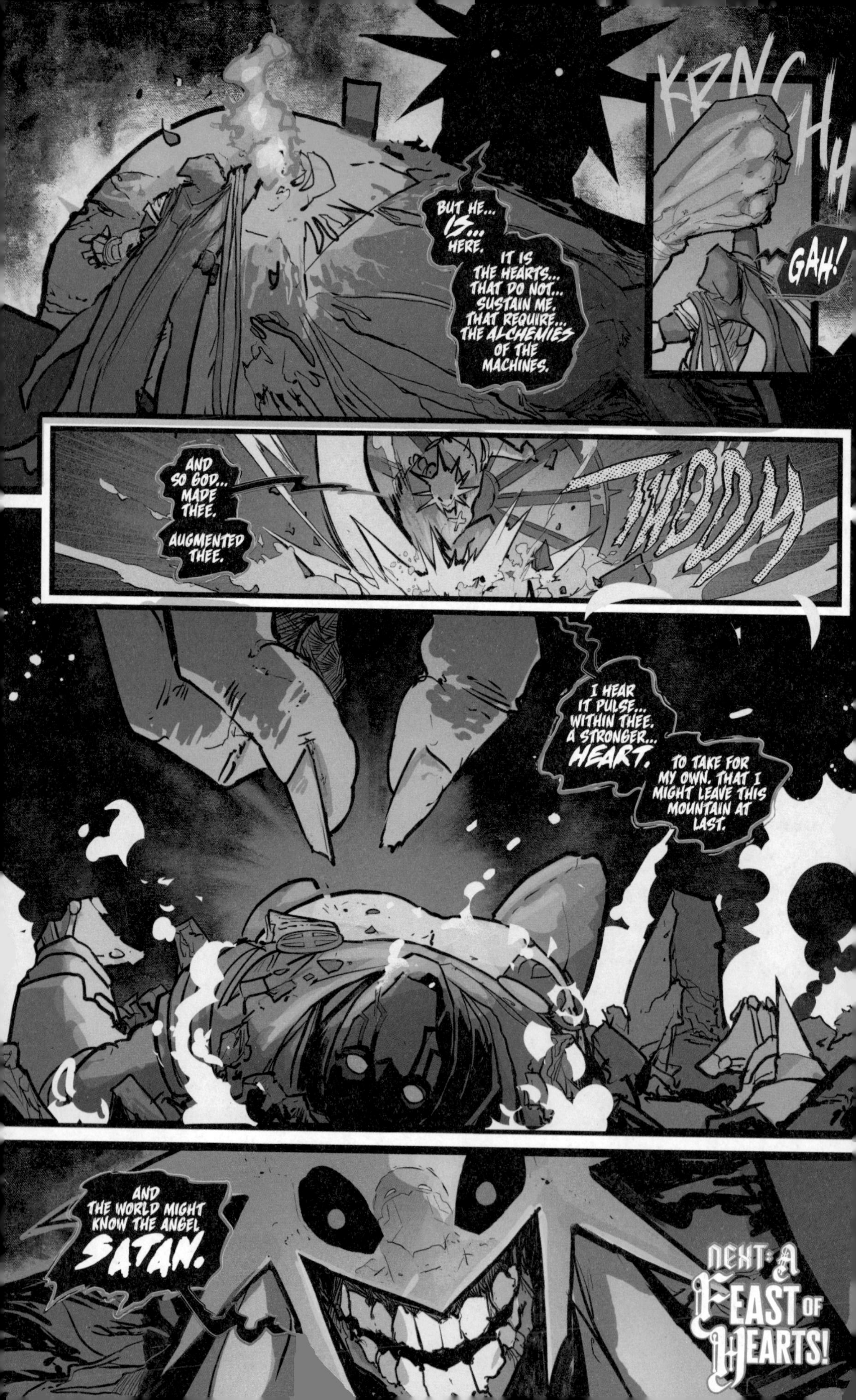
KRNCHH
BUT HE... IS... HERE.
IT IS THE HEARTS... THAT DO NOT... SUSTAIN ME. THAT REQUIRE... THE ALCHEMIES OF THE MACHINES.
GAH!
AND SO GOD... MADE THEE.
AUGMENTED THEE.
THOOM
I HEAR IT PULSE... WITHIN THEE. A STRONGER... HEART.
TO TAKE FOR MY OWN. THAT I MIGHT LEAVE THIS MOUNTAIN AT LAST.
AND THE WORLD MIGHT KNOW THE ANGEL SATAN.
NEXT: A FEAST OF HEARTS!

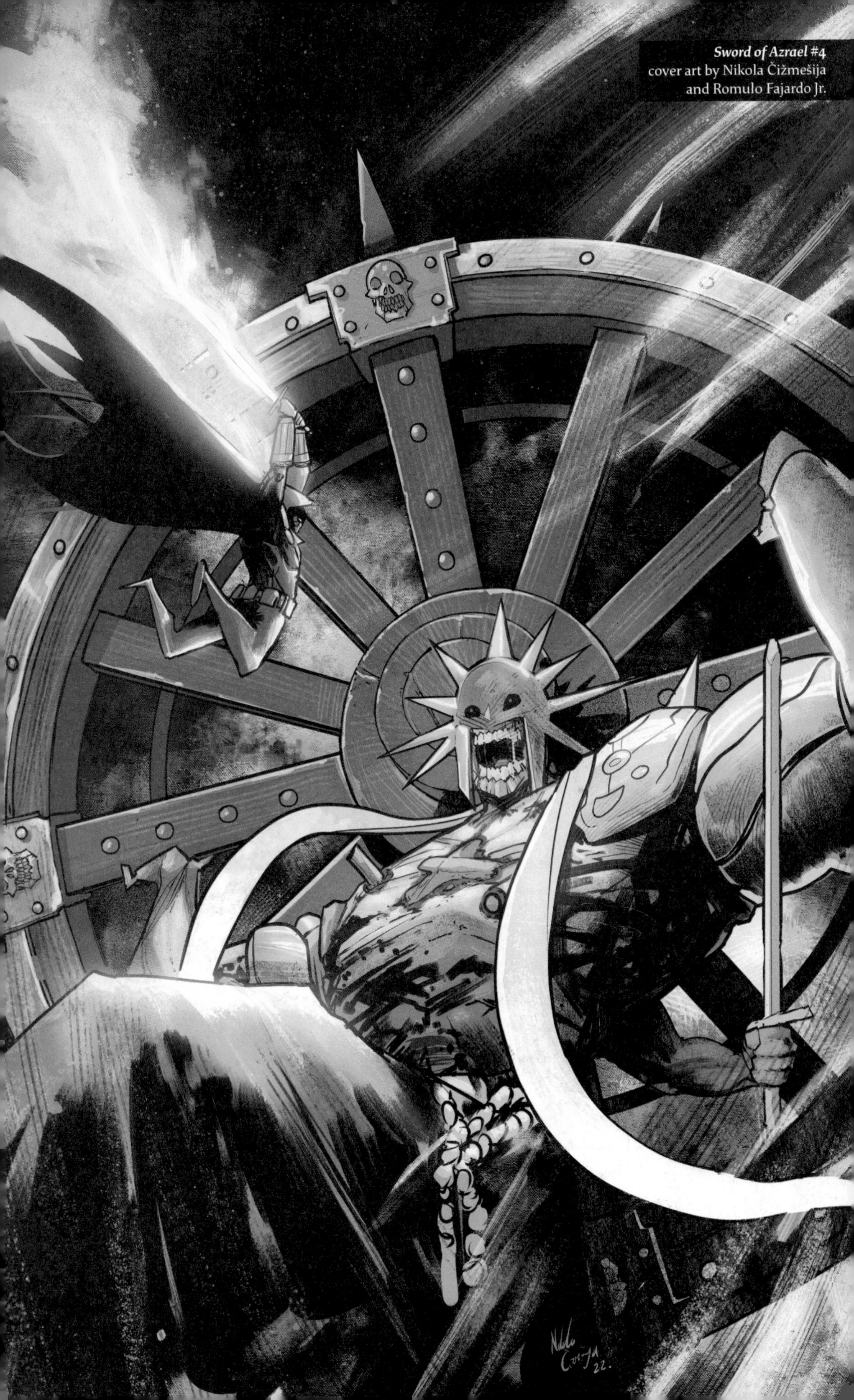

***Sword of Azrael* #4**
cover art by Nikola Čižmešija
and Romulo Fajardo Jr.

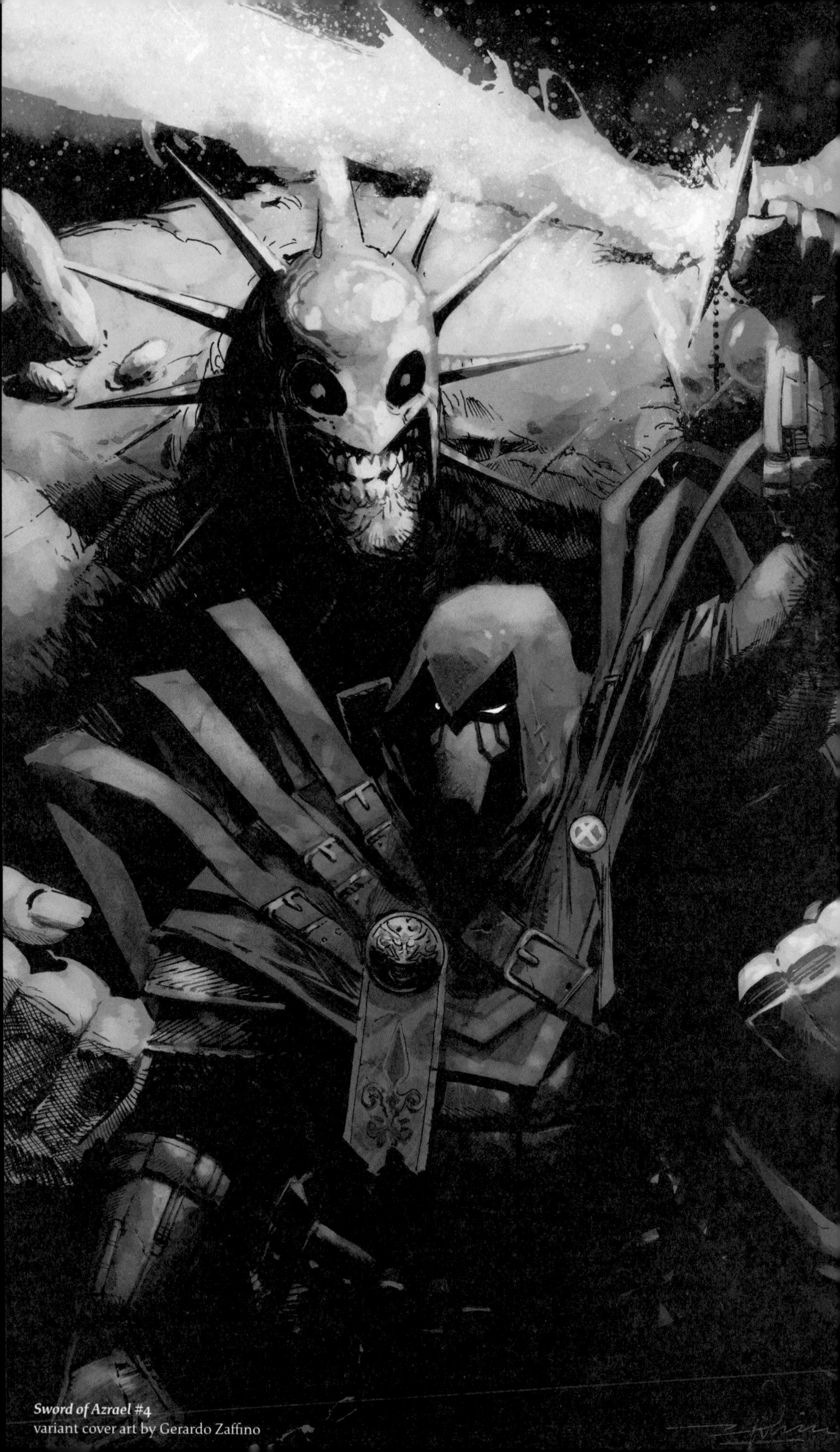

Sword of Azrael #4
variant cover art by Gerardo Zaffino

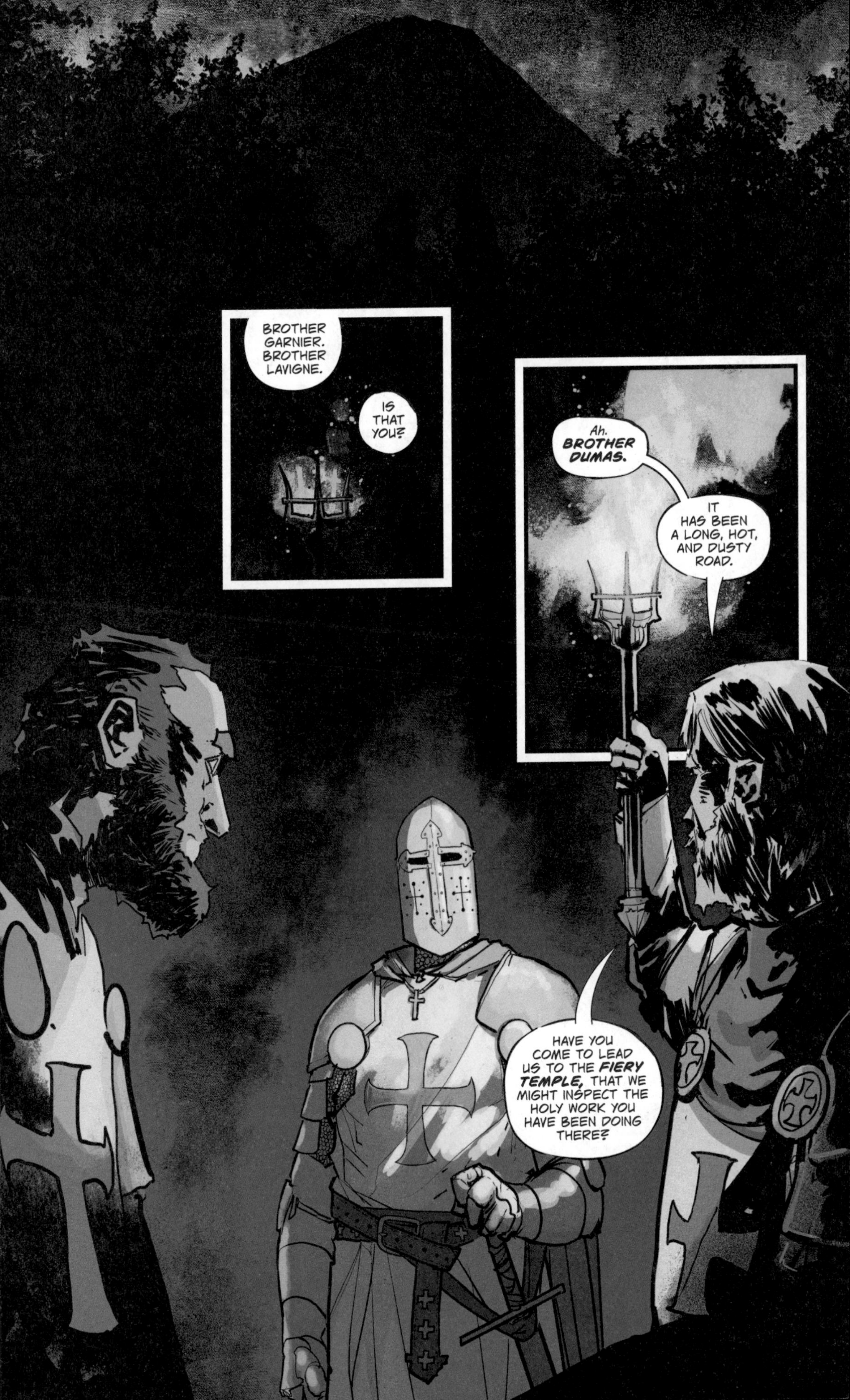
BROTHER GARNIER. BROTHER LAVIGNE.
IS THAT YOU?
Ah. BROTHER DUMAS.
IT HAS BEEN A LONG, HOT, AND DUSTY ROAD.
HAVE YOU COME TO LEAD US TO THE FIERY TEMPLE, THAT WE MIGHT INSPECT THE HOLY WORK YOU HAVE BEEN DOING THERE?

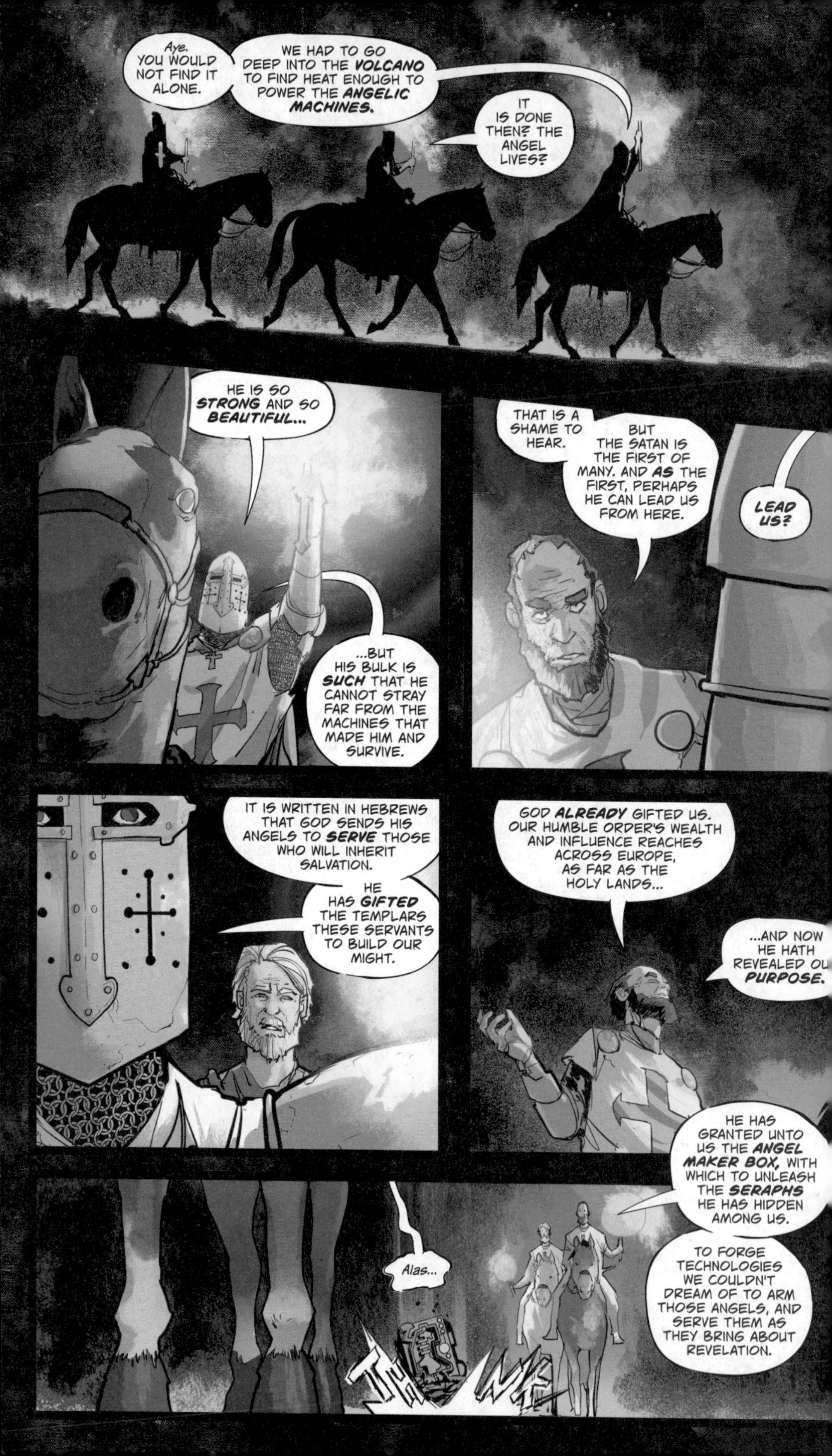
Aye. YOU WOULD NOT FIND IT ALONE.
WE HAD TO GO DEEP INTO THE VOLCANO TO FIND HEAT ENOUGH TO POWER THE ANGELIC MACHINES.
IT IS DONE THEN? THE ANGEL LIVES?
HE IS SO STRONG AND SO BEAUTIFUL...
...BUT HIS BULK IS SUCH THAT HE CANNOT STRAY FAR FROM THE MACHINES THAT MADE HIM AND SURVIVE.
THAT IS A SHAME TO HEAR.
BUT THE SATAN IS THE FIRST OF MANY. AND AS THE FIRST, PERHAPS HE CAN LEAD US FROM HERE.
LEAD US?
IT IS WRITTEN IN HEBREWS THAT GOD SENDS HIS ANGELS TO SERVE THOSE WHO WILL INHERIT SALVATION.
HE HAS GIFTED THE TEMPLARS THESE SERVANTS TO BUILD OUR MIGHT.
GOD ALREADY GIFTED US. OUR HUMBLE ORDER'S WEALTH AND INFLUENCE REACHES ACROSS EUROPE, AS FAR AS THE HOLY LANDS...
...AND NOW HE HATH REVEALED OU PURPOSE.
HE HAS GRANTED UNTO US THE ANGEL MAKER BOX, WITH WHICH TO UNLEASH THE SERAPHS HE HAS HIDDEN AMONG US.
TO FORGE TECHNOLOGIES WE COULDN'T DREAM OF TO ARM THOSE ANGELS, AND SERVE THEM AS THEY BRING ABOUT REVELATION.
Alas...
THWMP

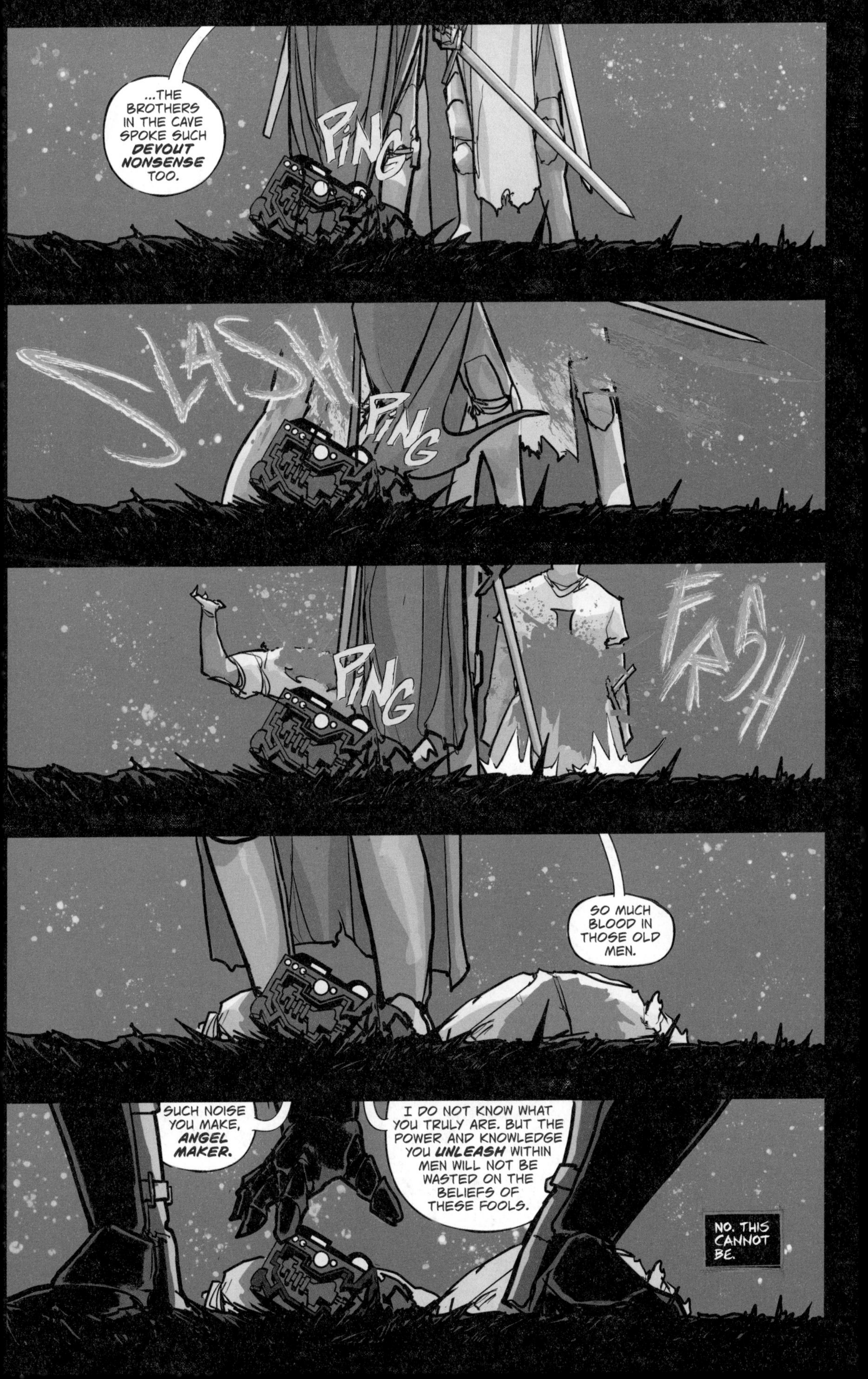
...THE BROTHERS IN THE CAVE SPOKE SUCH DEVOUT NONSENSE TOO.
PING
SLASH
PING
PING
FRASH
SO MUCH BLOOD IN THOSE OLD MEN.
SUCH NOISE YOU MAKE, ANGEL MAKER.
I DO NOT KNOW WHAT YOU TRULY ARE. BUT THE POWER AND KNOWLEDGE YOU UNLEASH WITHIN MEN WILL NOT BE WASTED ON THE BELIEFS OF THESE FOOLS.
NO. THIS CANNOT BE.

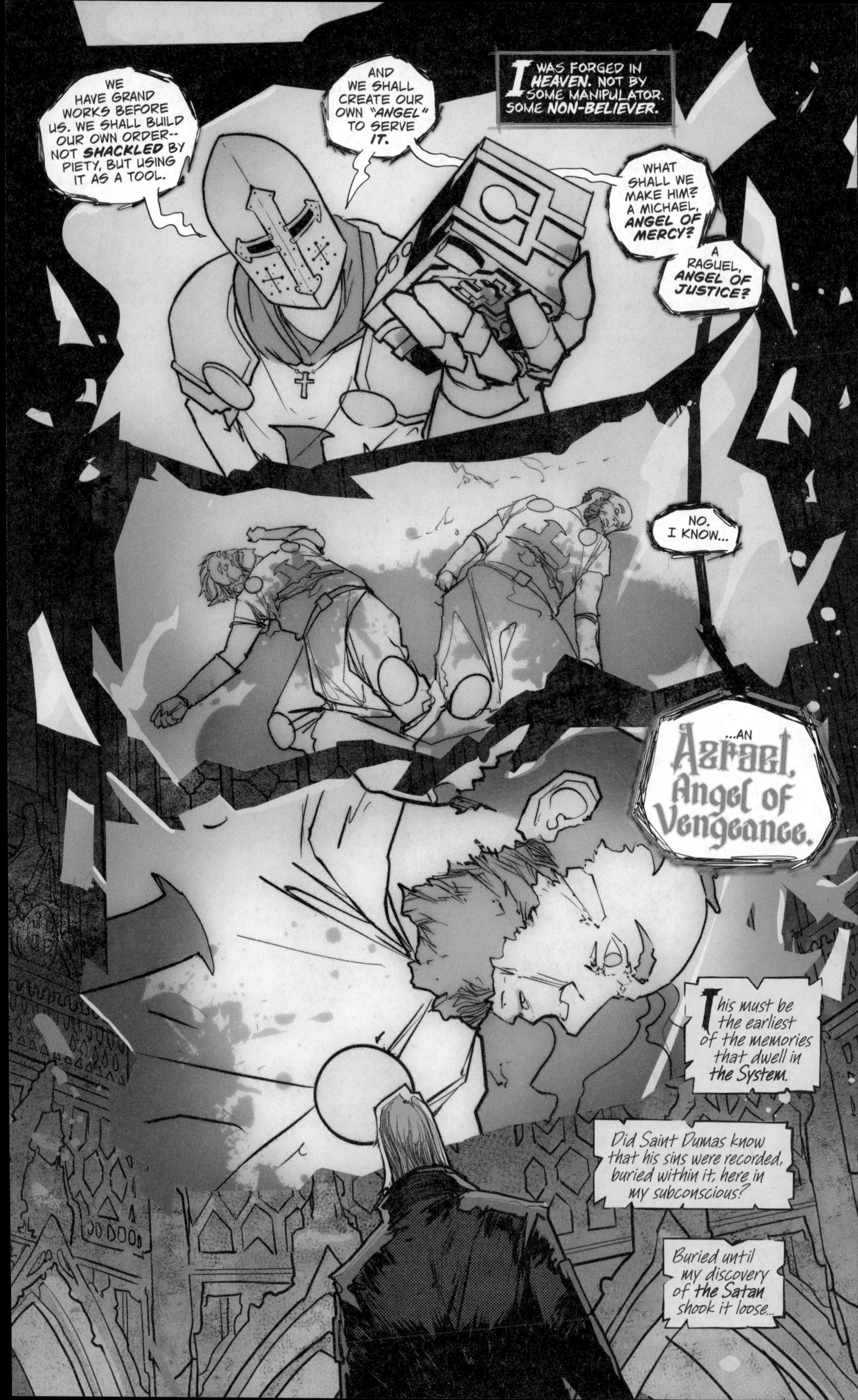
WE HAVE GRAND WORKS BEFORE US. WE SHALL BUILD OUR OWN ORDER-- NOT SHACKLED BY PIETY, BUT USING IT AS A TOOL.
AND WE SHALL CREATE OUR OWN "ANGEL" TO SERVE IT.
I WAS FORGED IN HEAVEN. NOT BY SOME MANIPULATOR. SOME NON-BELIEVER.
WHAT SHALL WE MAKE HIM? A MICHAEL, ANGEL OF MERCY?
A RAGUEL, ANGEL OF JUSTICE?
NO. I KNOW...
...AN Azrael, Angel of Vengeance.
This must be the earliest of the memories that dwell in the System.
Did Saint Dumas know that his sins were recorded, buried within it, here in my subconscious?
Buried until my discovery of the Satan shook it loose...

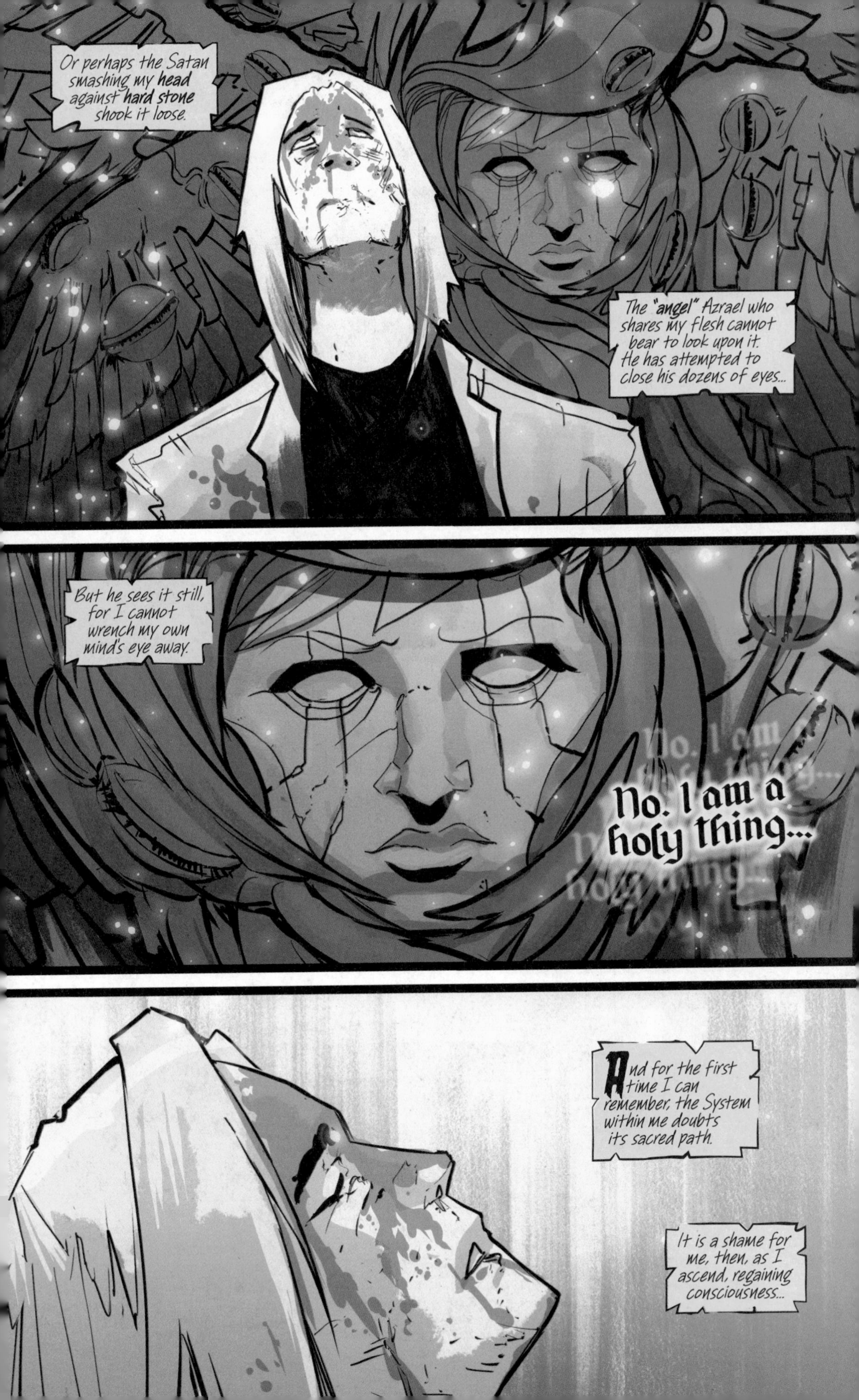
Or perhaps the Satan smashing my **head** against **hard stone** shook it loose.
The **"angel"** Azrael who shares my flesh cannot bear to look upon it. He has attempted to close his dozens of eyes...
But he sees it still, for I cannot wrench my own mind's eye away.
No. I am a holy thing...
And for the first time I can remember, the System within me doubts its sacred path.
It is a shame for me, then, as I ascend, regaining consciousness...

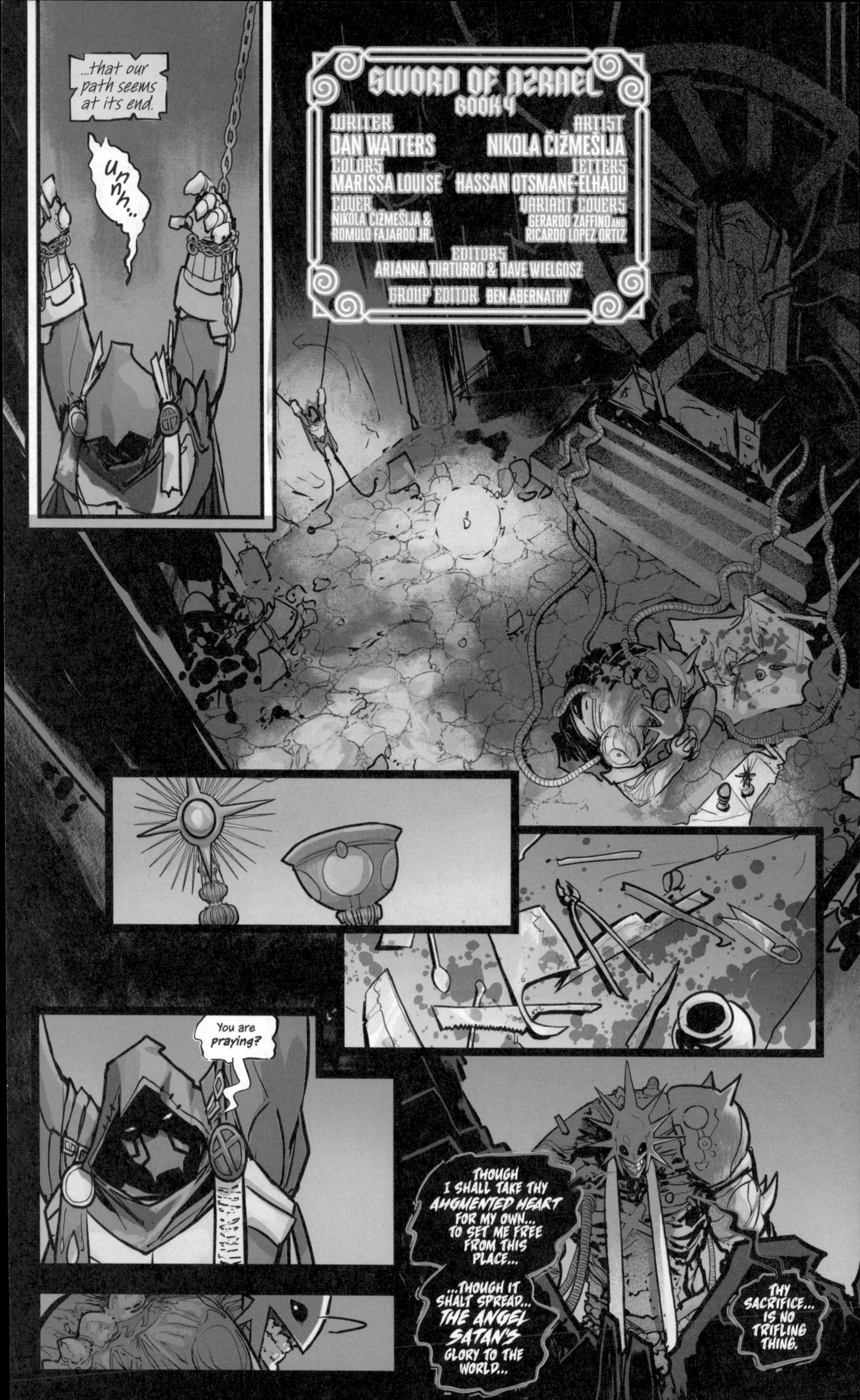
...that our path seems at its end.
Unnh..
SWORD OF AZRAEL
BOOK 4
WRITER DAN WATTERS
ARTIST NIKOLA ČIŽMEŠIJA
COLORS MARISSA LOUISE
LETTERS HASSAN OTSMANE-ELHAOU
COVER NIKOLA ČIŽMEŠIJA & ROMULO FAJARDO JR.
VARIANT COVERS GERARDO ZAFFINO AND RICARDO LOPEZ ORTIZ
EDITORS ARIANNA TURTURRO & DAVE WIELGOSZ
GROUP EDITOR BEN ABERNATHY
You are praying?
THOUGH I SHALL TAKE THY AUGMENTED HEART FOR MY OWN... TO SET ME FREE FROM THIS PLACE...
...THOUGH IT SHALT SPREAD... THE ANGEL SATAN'S GLORY TO THE WORLD...
THY SACRIFICE... IS NO TRIFLING THING.

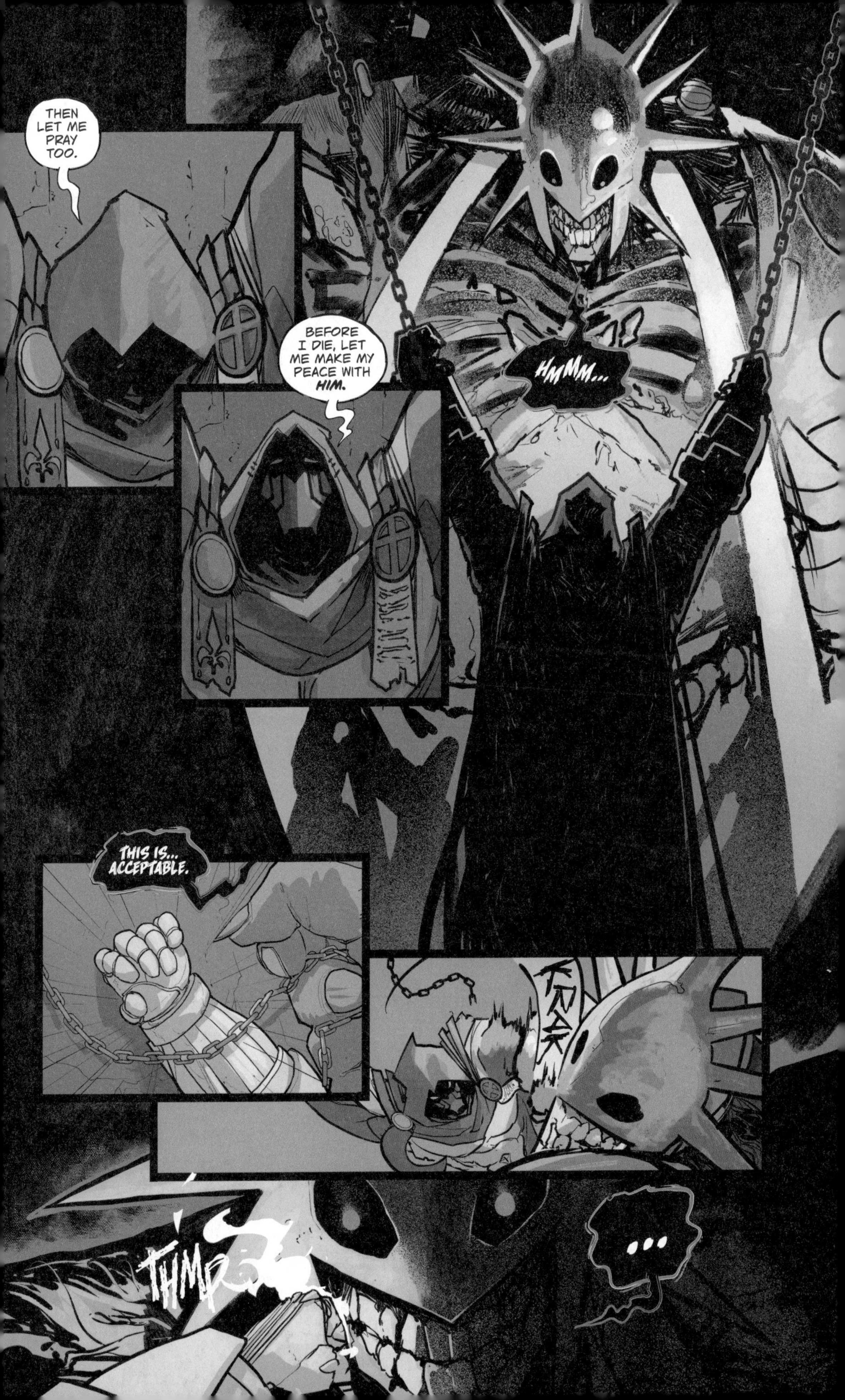
THEN LET ME PRAY TOO.
BEFORE I DIE, LET ME MAKE MY PEACE WITH HIM.
HMMM...
THIS IS... ACCEPTABLE.
KRAK
THMP
...

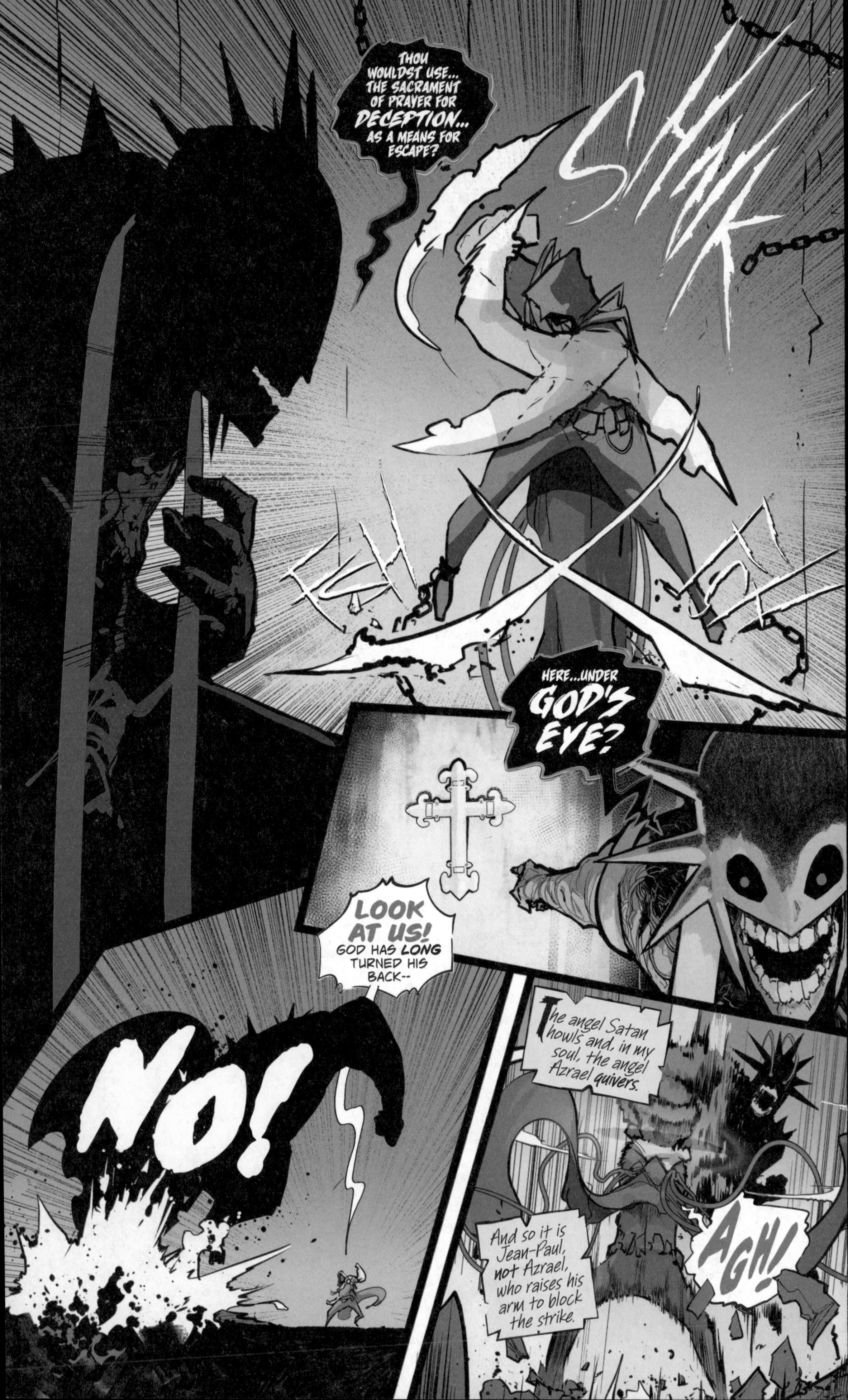
THOU WOULDST USE... THE SACRAMENT OF PRAYER FOR DECEPTION... AS A MEANS FOR ESCAPE?
SHAK
FSH
FSH
HERE...UNDER GOD'S EYE?
LOOK AT US! GOD HAS LONG TURNED HIS BACK--
NO!
The angel Satan howls and, in my soul, the angel Azrael quivers.
And so it is Jean-Paul, not Azrael, who raises his arm to block the strike.
AGH!

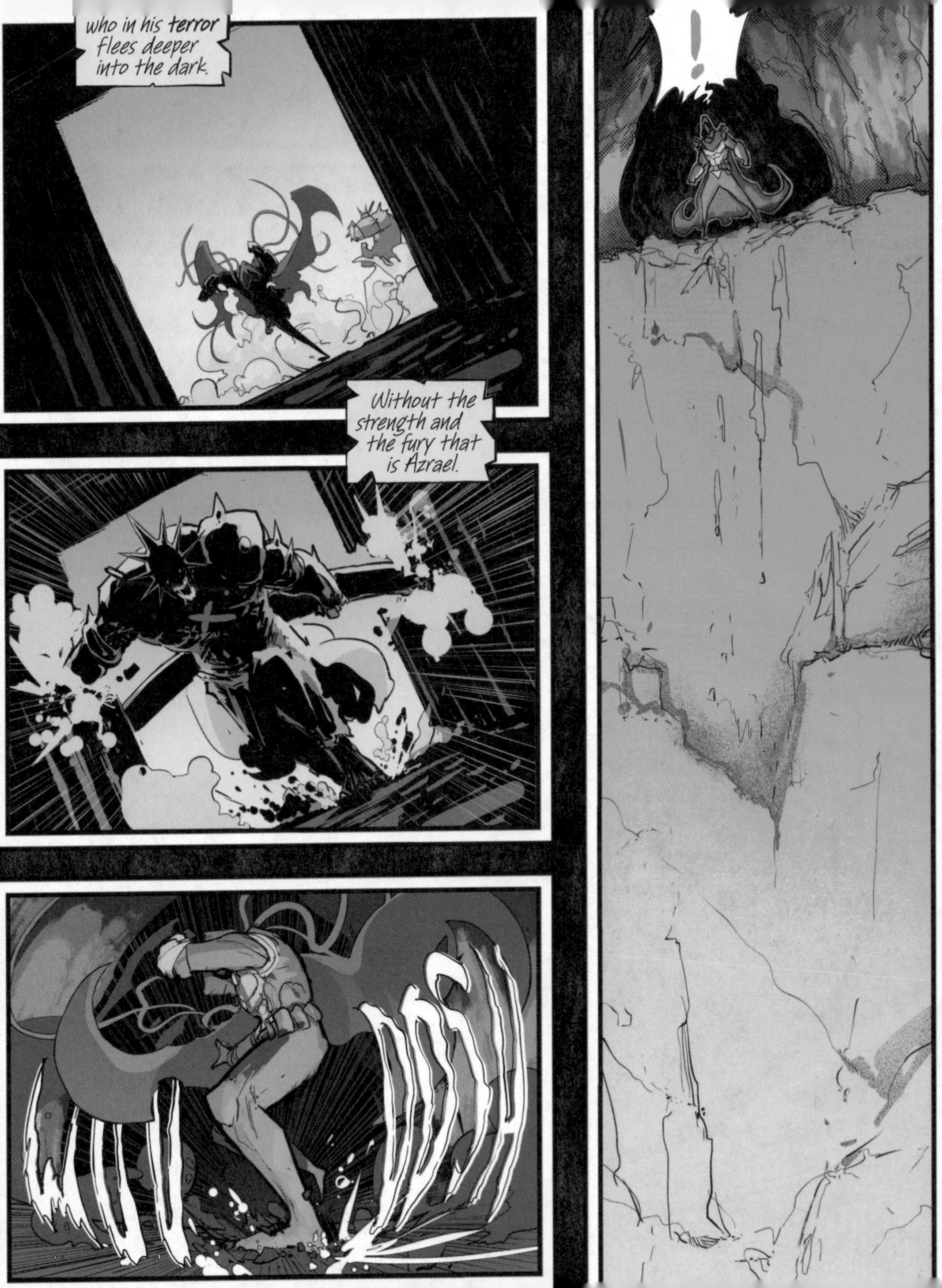
who in his terror flees deeper into the dark.
Without the strength and the fury that is Azrael.
!

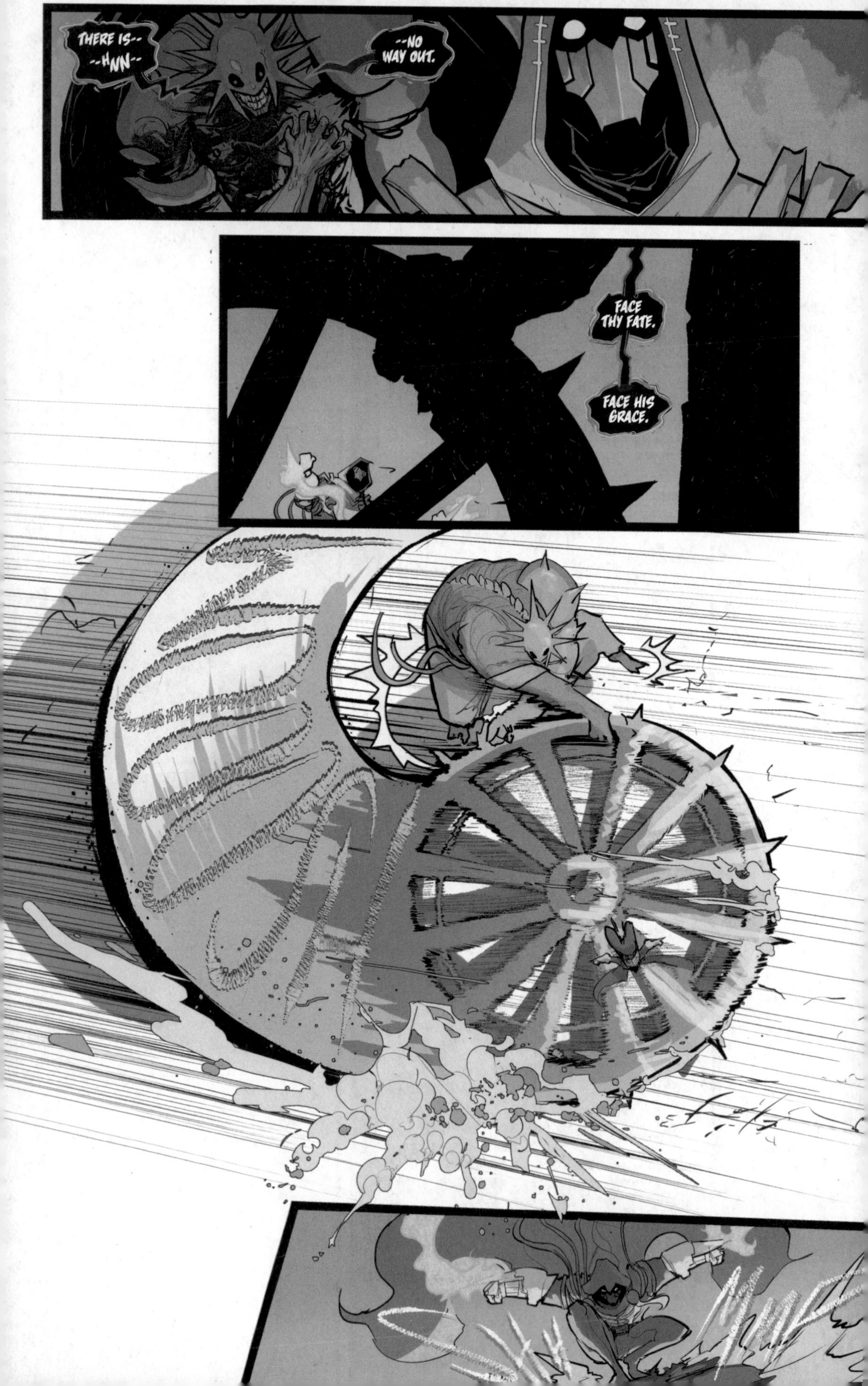
THERE IS--
--HNN--
--NO WAY OUT.
FACE THY FATE.
FACE HIS GRACE.

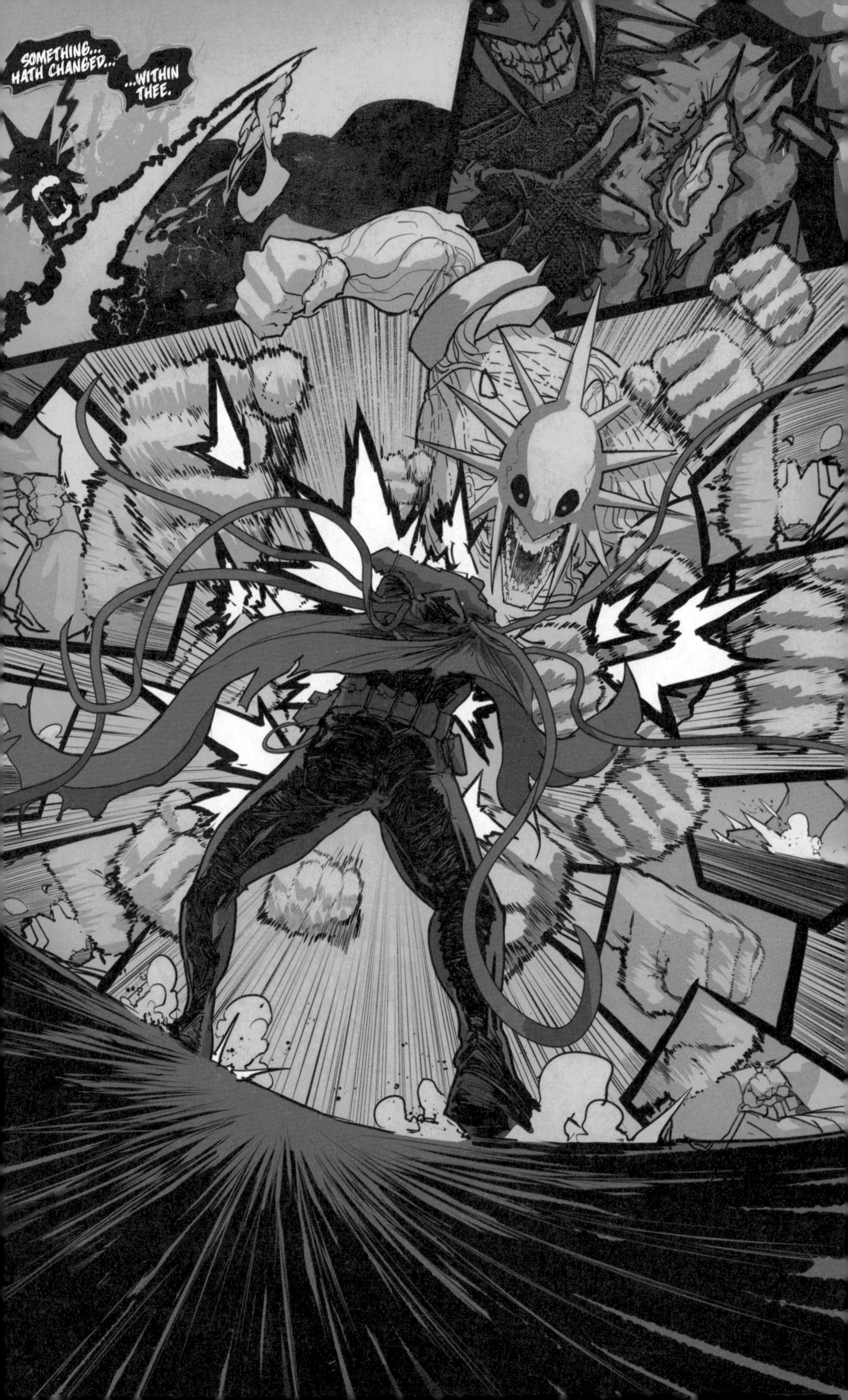
SOMETHING... HATH CHANGED...
...WITHIN THEE.

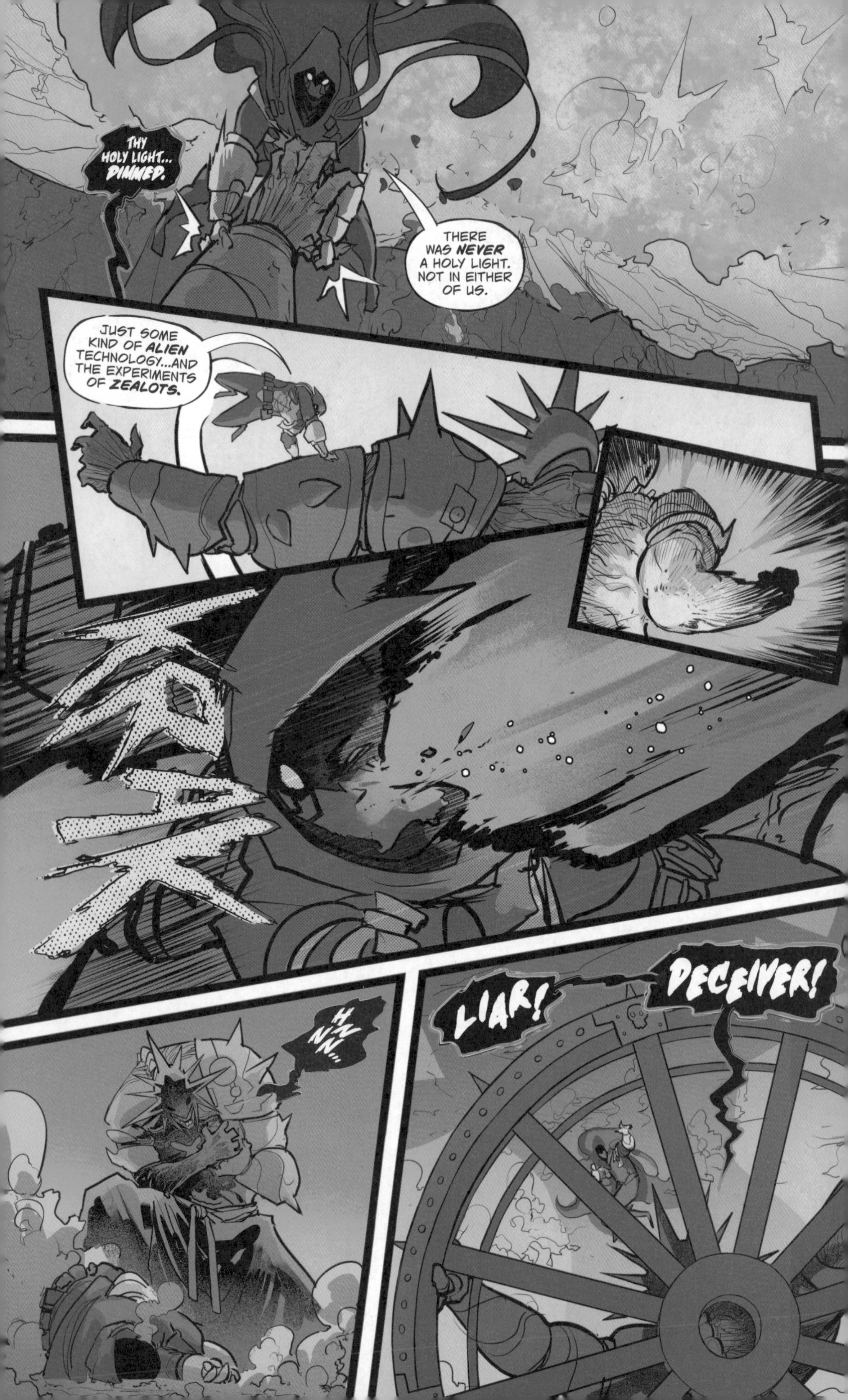
THY HOLY LIGHT... DIMMED.
THERE WAS NEVER A HOLY LIGHT. NOT IN EITHER OF US.
JUST SOME KIND OF ALIEN TECHNOLOGY...AND THE EXPERIMENTS OF ZEALOTS.
HNNN...
LIAR!
DECEIVER!

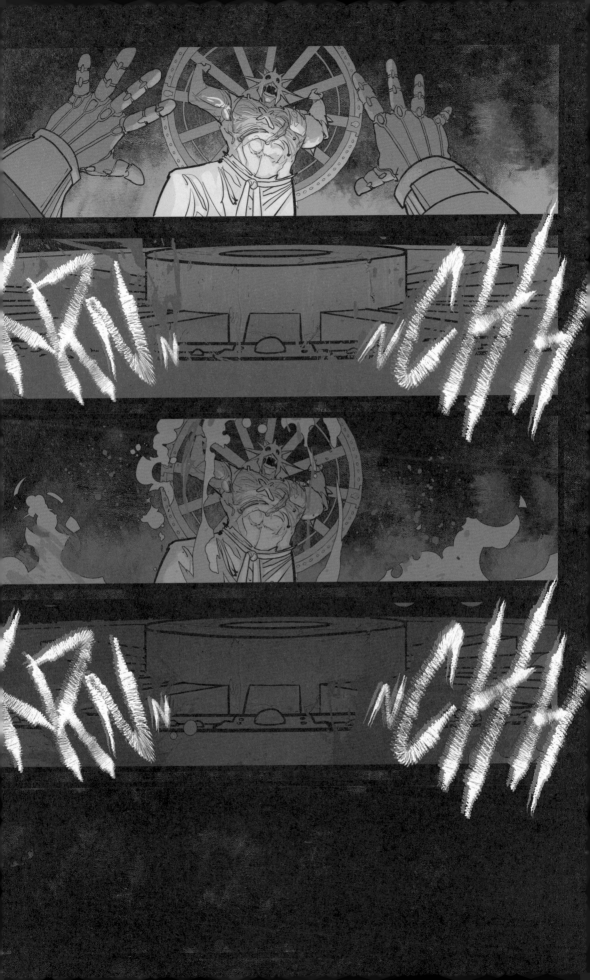

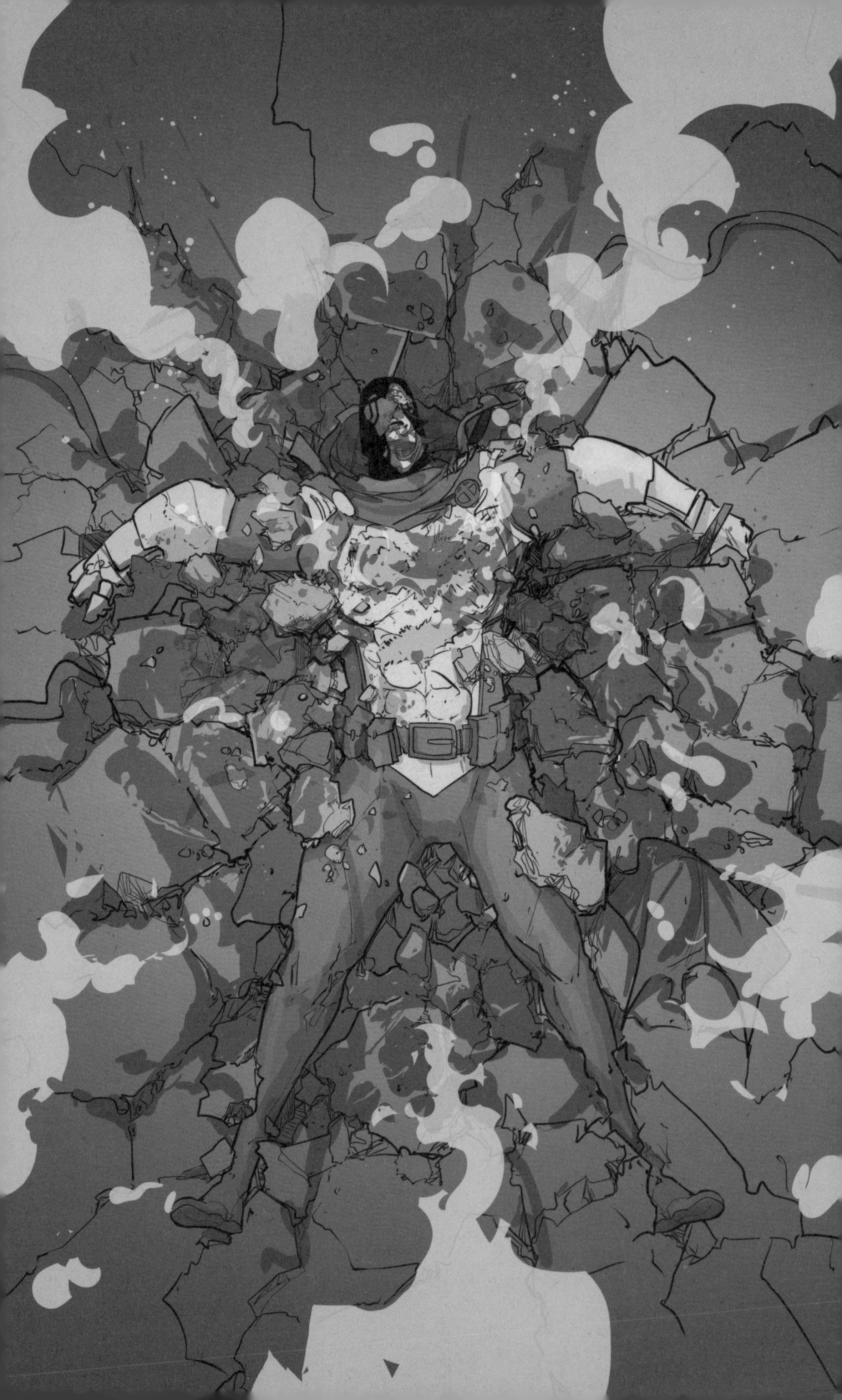

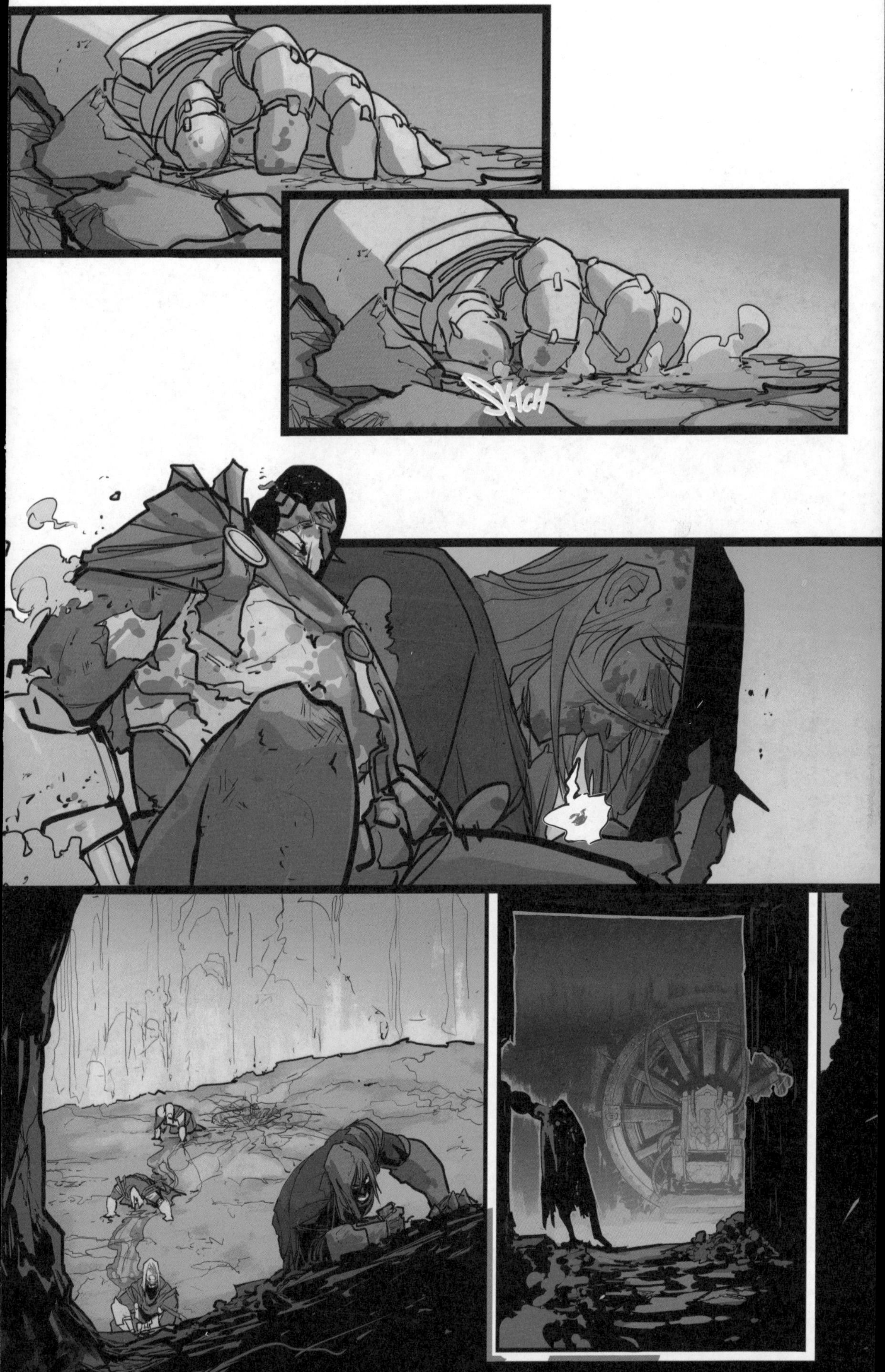
SKTCH

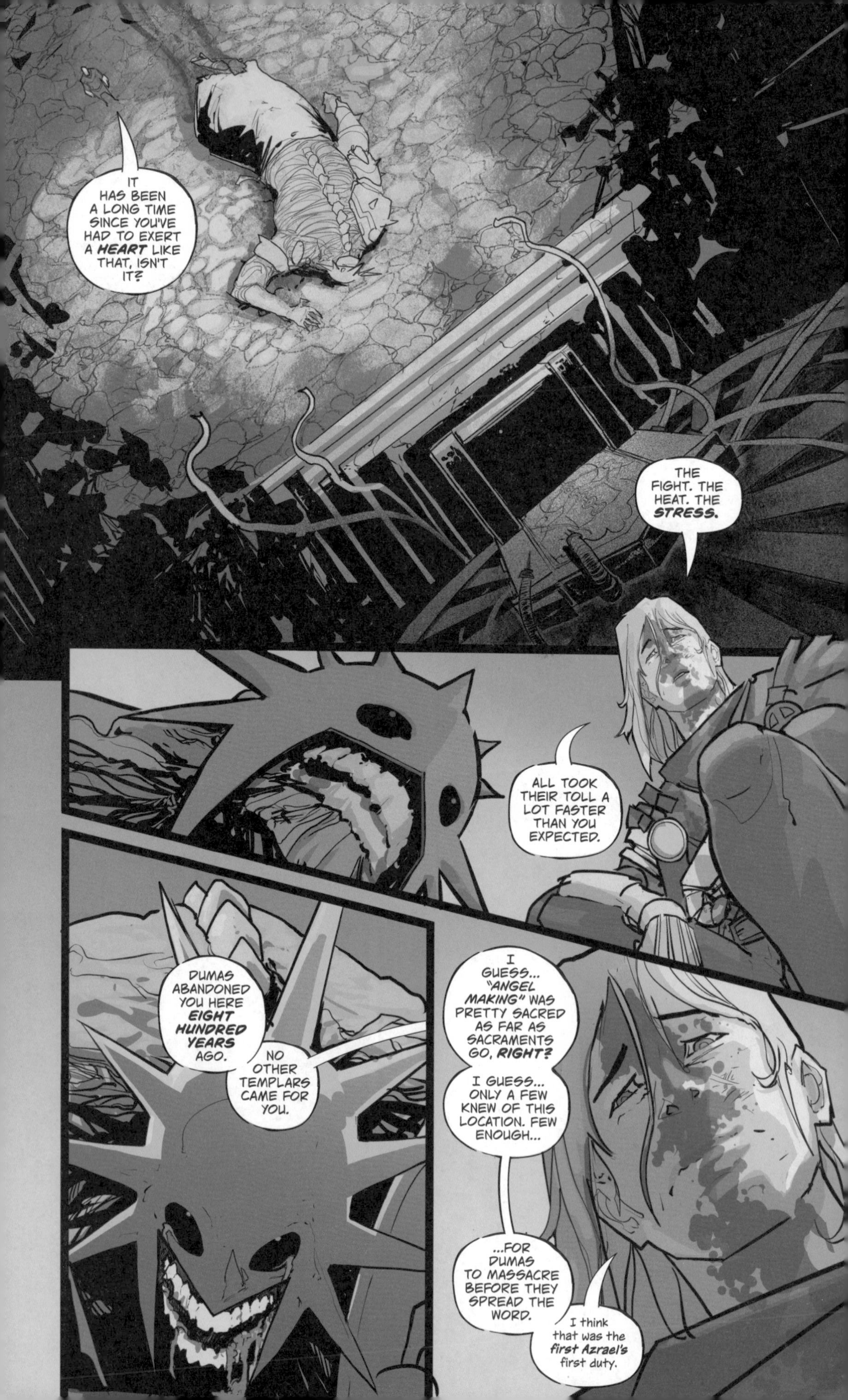
IT HAS BEEN A LONG TIME SINCE YOU'VE HAD TO EXERT A **HEART** LIKE THAT, ISN'T IT?
THE FIGHT. THE HEAT. THE **STRESS.**
ALL TOOK THEIR TOLL A LOT FASTER THAN YOU EXPECTED.
DUMAS ABANDONED YOU HERE **EIGHT HUNDRED YEARS** AGO.
NO OTHER TEMPLARS CAME FOR YOU.
I GUESS... "**ANGEL MAKING**" WAS PRETTY SACRED AS FAR AS SACRAMENTS GO, **RIGHT?**
I GUESS... ONLY A FEW KNEW OF THIS LOCATION. FEW ENOUGH...
...FOR DUMAS TO MASSACRE BEFORE THEY SPREAD THE WORD.
I think that was the ***first Azrael's*** first duty.

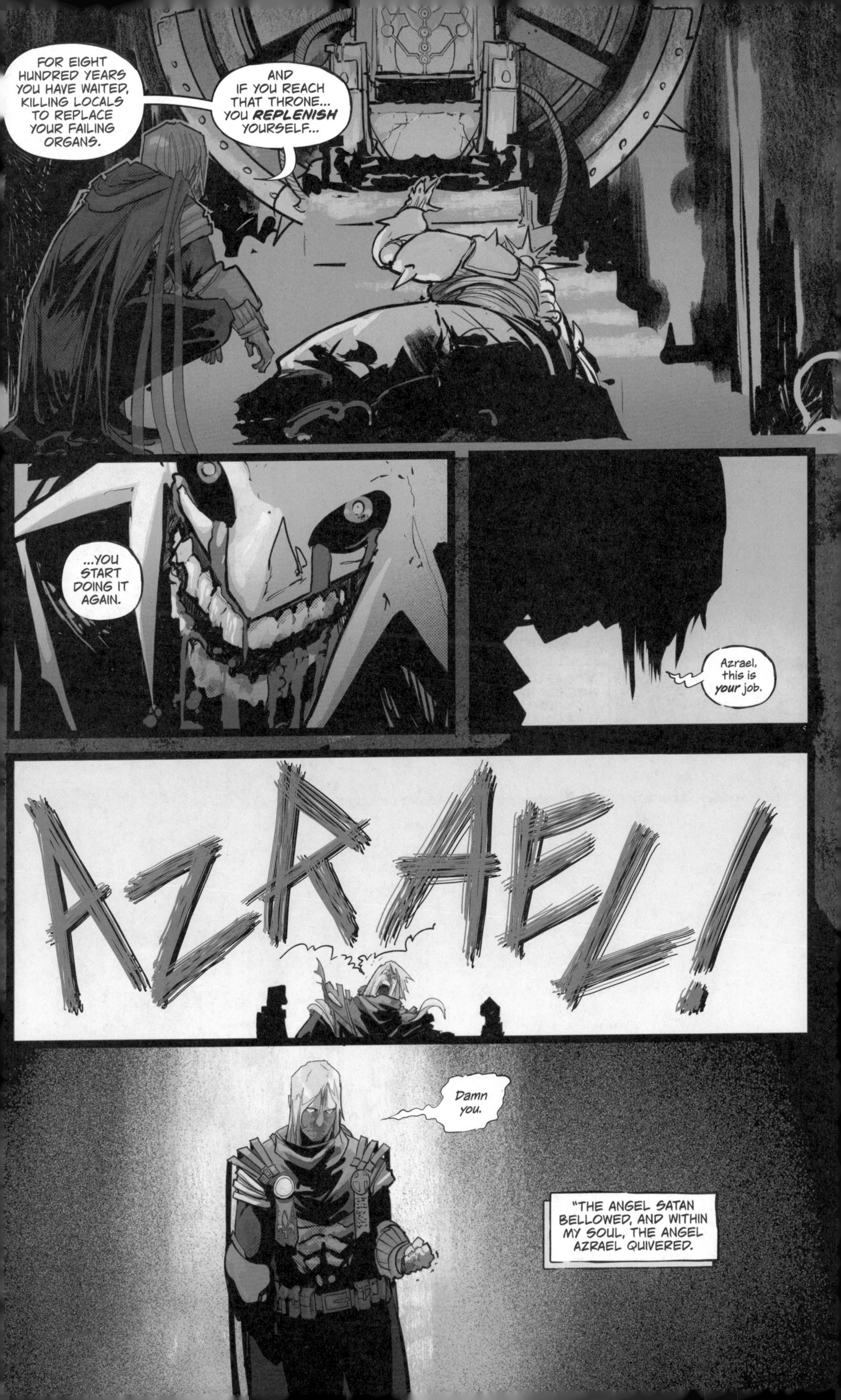
FOR EIGHT HUNDRED YEARS YOU HAVE WAITED, KILLING LOCALS TO REPLACE YOUR FAILING ORGANS.
AND IF YOU REACH THAT THRONE... YOU **REPLENISH** YOURSELF...
...YOU START DOING IT AGAIN.
Azrael, this is ***your*** job.
AZRAEL!
Damn you.
"THE ANGEL SATAN BELLOWED, AND WITHIN MY SOUL, THE ANGEL AZRAEL QUIVERED.

"AND SO IT WAS *JEAN-PAUL*, NOT AZRAEL, WHO DRAGGED THE GREAT BULK OF THE SATAN BACKWARDS.

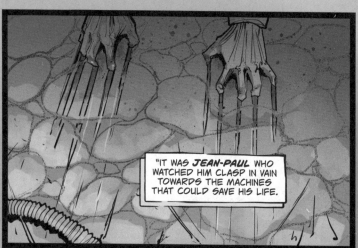

"IT WAS *JEAN-PAUL* WHO WATCHED HIM CLASP IN VAIN TOWARDS THE MACHINES THAT COULD SAVE HIS LIFE.

"IT WAS *JEAN-PAUL* WHO WAITED AS HE SUFFOCATED UNDER HIS OWN WEIGHT.

"UNTIL HIS STOLEN HEART STOPPED.

"IT WAS JEAN-PAUL WHO DID *THIS*..."

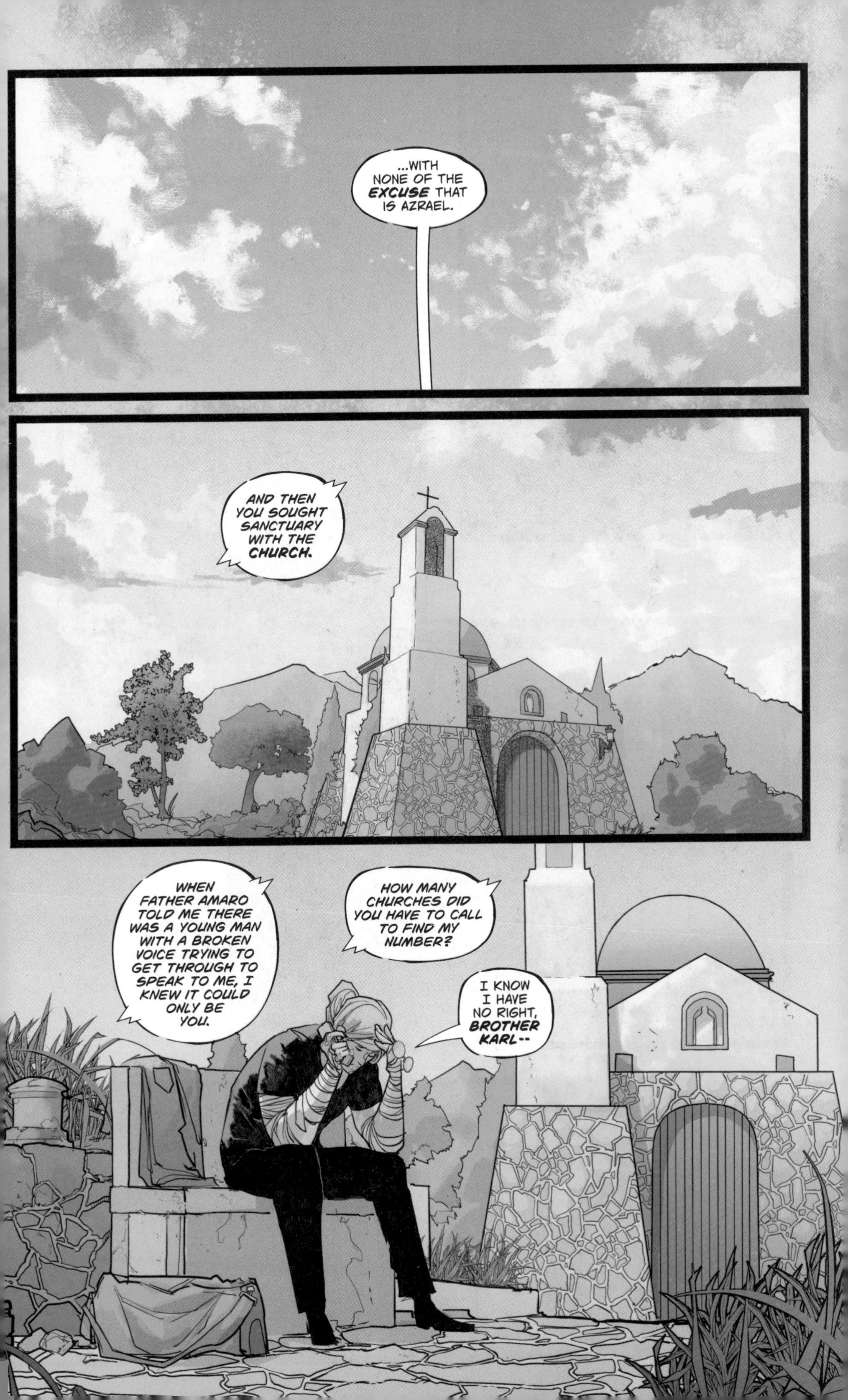
...WITH NONE OF THE EXCUSE THAT IS AZRAEL.
AND THEN YOU SOUGHT SANCTUARY WITH THE CHURCH.
WHEN FATHER AMARO TOLD ME THERE WAS A YOUNG MAN WITH A BROKEN VOICE TRYING TO GET THROUGH TO SPEAK TO ME, I KNEW IT COULD ONLY BE YOU.
HOW MANY CHURCHES DID YOU HAVE TO CALL TO FIND MY NUMBER?
I KNOW I HAVE NO RIGHT, BROTHER KARL--

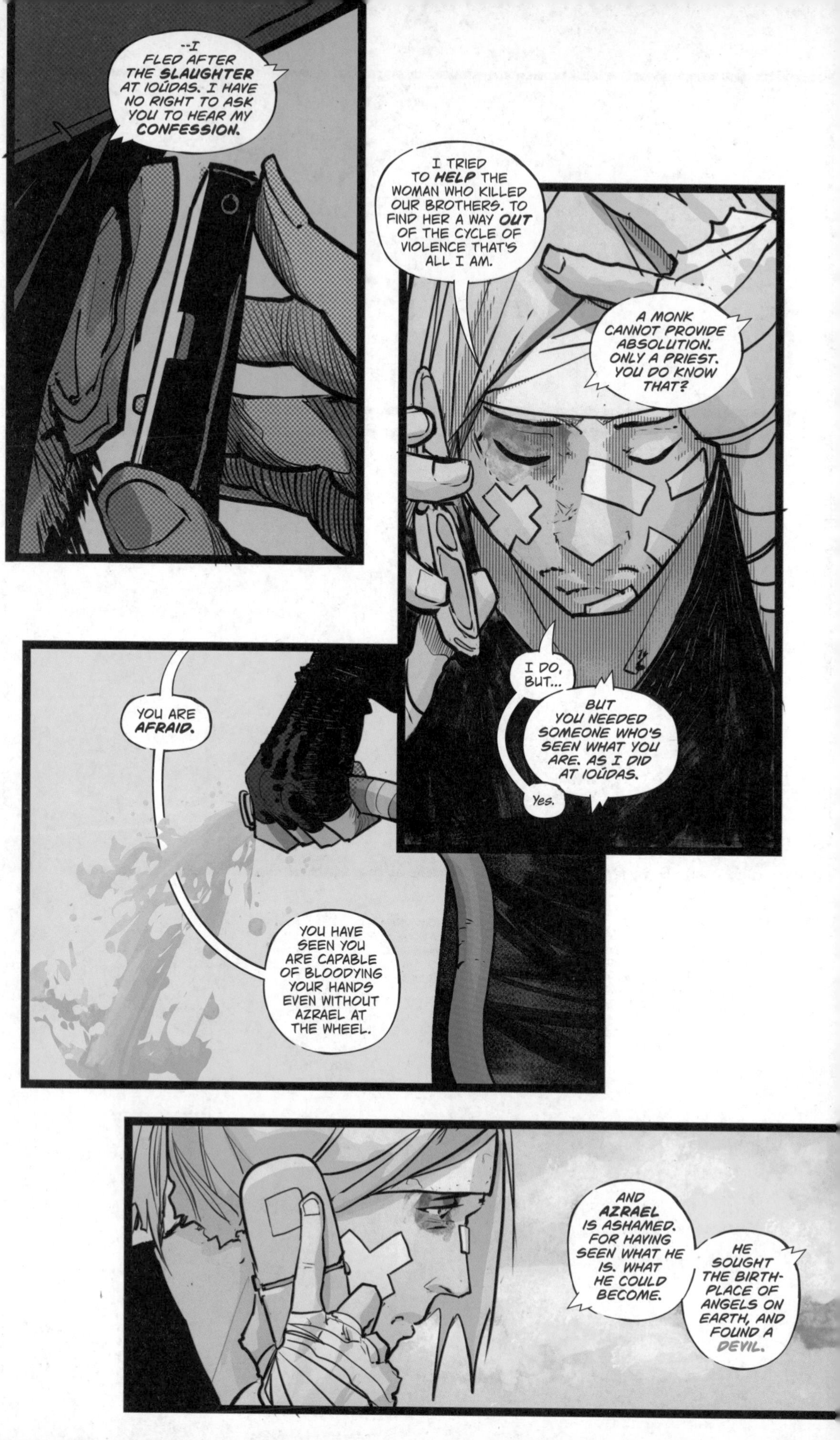
--I FLED AFTER THE SLAUGHTER AT IOÚDAS. I HAVE NO RIGHT TO ASK YOU TO HEAR MY CONFESSION.
I TRIED TO HELP THE WOMAN WHO KILLED OUR BROTHERS. TO FIND HER A WAY OUT OF THE CYCLE OF VIOLENCE THAT'S ALL I AM.
A MONK CANNOT PROVIDE ABSOLUTION. ONLY A PRIEST. YOU DO KNOW THAT?
I DO, BUT...
BUT YOU NEEDED SOMEONE WHO'S SEEN WHAT YOU ARE. AS I DID AT IOÚDAS.
Yes.
YOU ARE AFRAID.
YOU HAVE SEEN YOU ARE CAPABLE OF BLOODYING YOUR HANDS EVEN WITHOUT AZRAEL AT THE WHEEL.
AND AZRAEL IS ASHAMED. FOR HAVING SEEN WHAT HE IS. WHAT HE COULD BECOME.
HE SOUGHT THE BIRTH-PLACE OF ANGELS ON EARTH, AND FOUND A DEVIL.

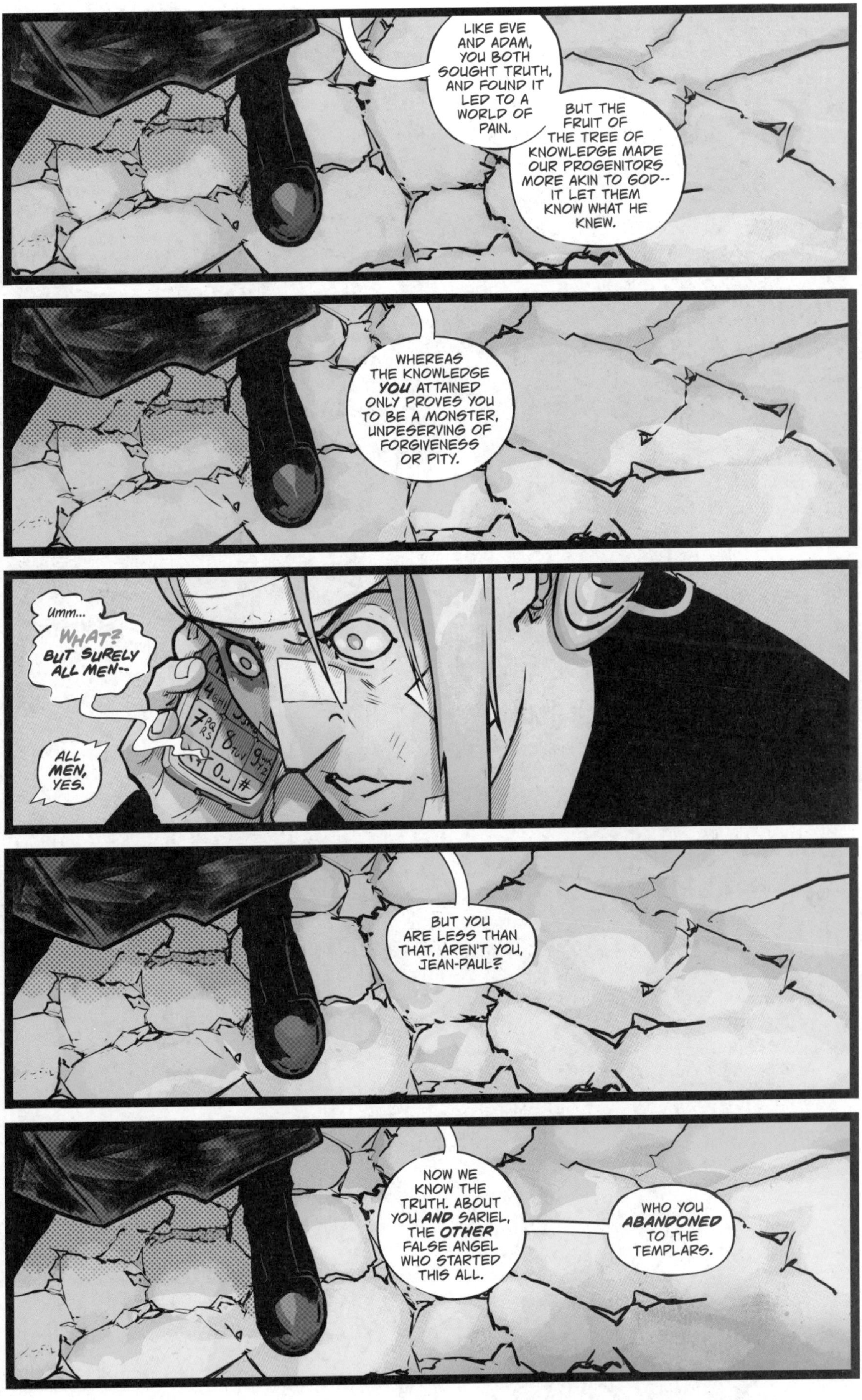
LIKE EVE AND ADAM, YOU BOTH SOUGHT TRUTH, AND FOUND IT LED TO A WORLD OF PAIN.
BUT THE FRUIT OF THE TREE OF KNOWLEDGE MADE OUR PROGENITORS MORE AKIN TO GOD-- IT LET THEM KNOW WHAT HE KNEW.
WHEREAS THE KNOWLEDGE YOU ATTAINED ONLY PROVES YOU TO BE A MONSTER, UNDESERVING OF FORGIVENESS OR PITY.
Umm... WHAT? BUT SURELY ALL MEN--
ALL MEN, YES.
BUT YOU ARE LESS THAN THAT, AREN'T YOU, JEAN-PAUL?
NOW WE KNOW THE TRUTH. ABOUT YOU AND SARIEL, THE OTHER FALSE ANGEL WHO STARTED THIS ALL.
WHO YOU ABANDONED TO THE TEMPLARS.

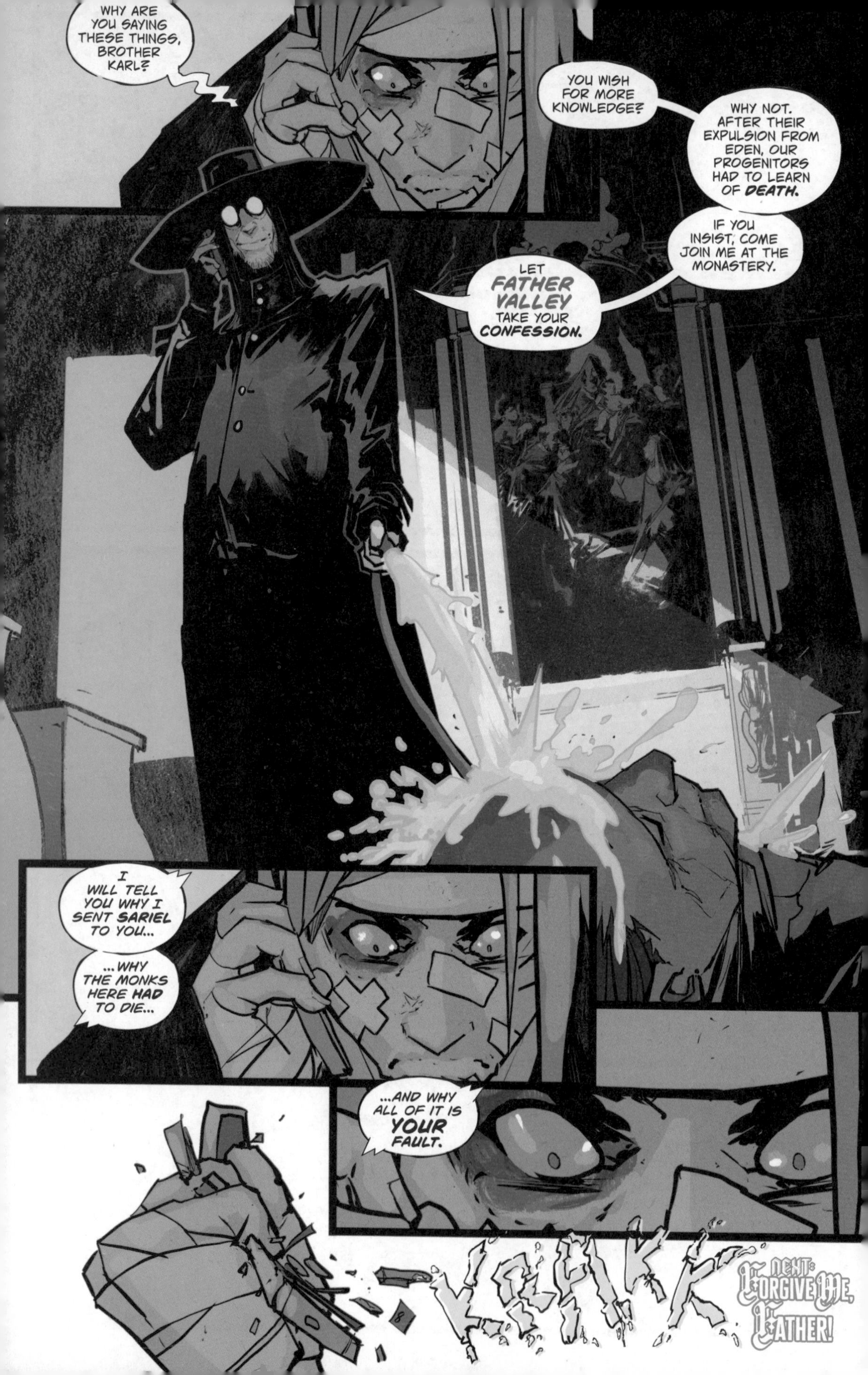
WHY ARE YOU SAYING THESE THINGS, BROTHER KARL?
YOU WISH FOR MORE KNOWLEDGE?
WHY NOT. AFTER THEIR EXPULSION FROM EDEN, OUR PROGENITORS HAD TO LEARN OF DEATH.
IF YOU INSIST, COME JOIN ME AT THE MONASTERY.
LET FATHER VALLEY TAKE YOUR CONFESSION.
I WILL TELL YOU WHY I SENT SARIEL TO YOU...
...WHY THE MONKS HERE HAD TO DIE...
...AND WHY ALL OF IT IS YOUR FAULT.
KRAKK
NEXT: FORGIVE ME, FATHER!

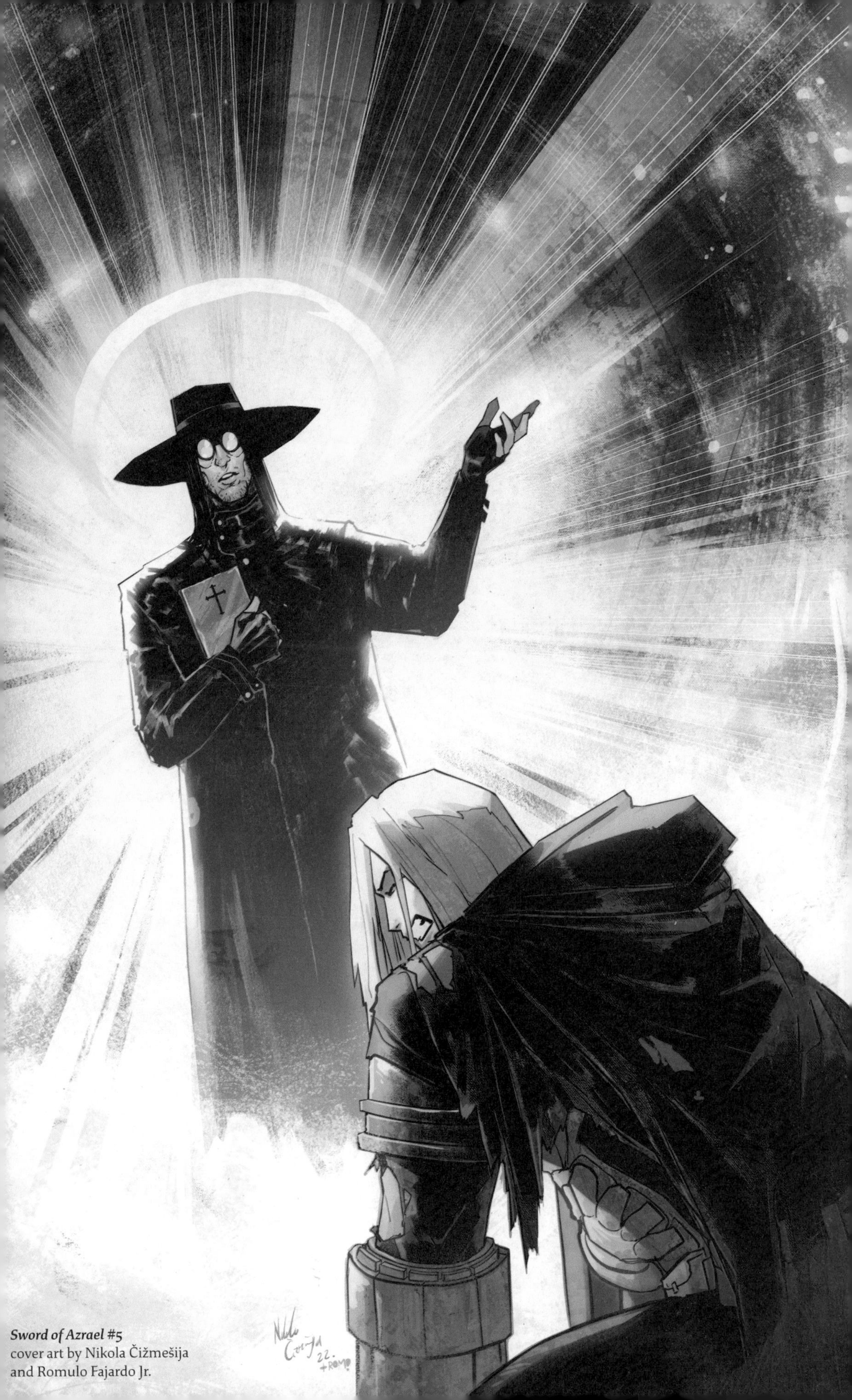

Sword of Azrael #5
cover art by Nikola Čižmešija
and Romulo Fajardo Jr.

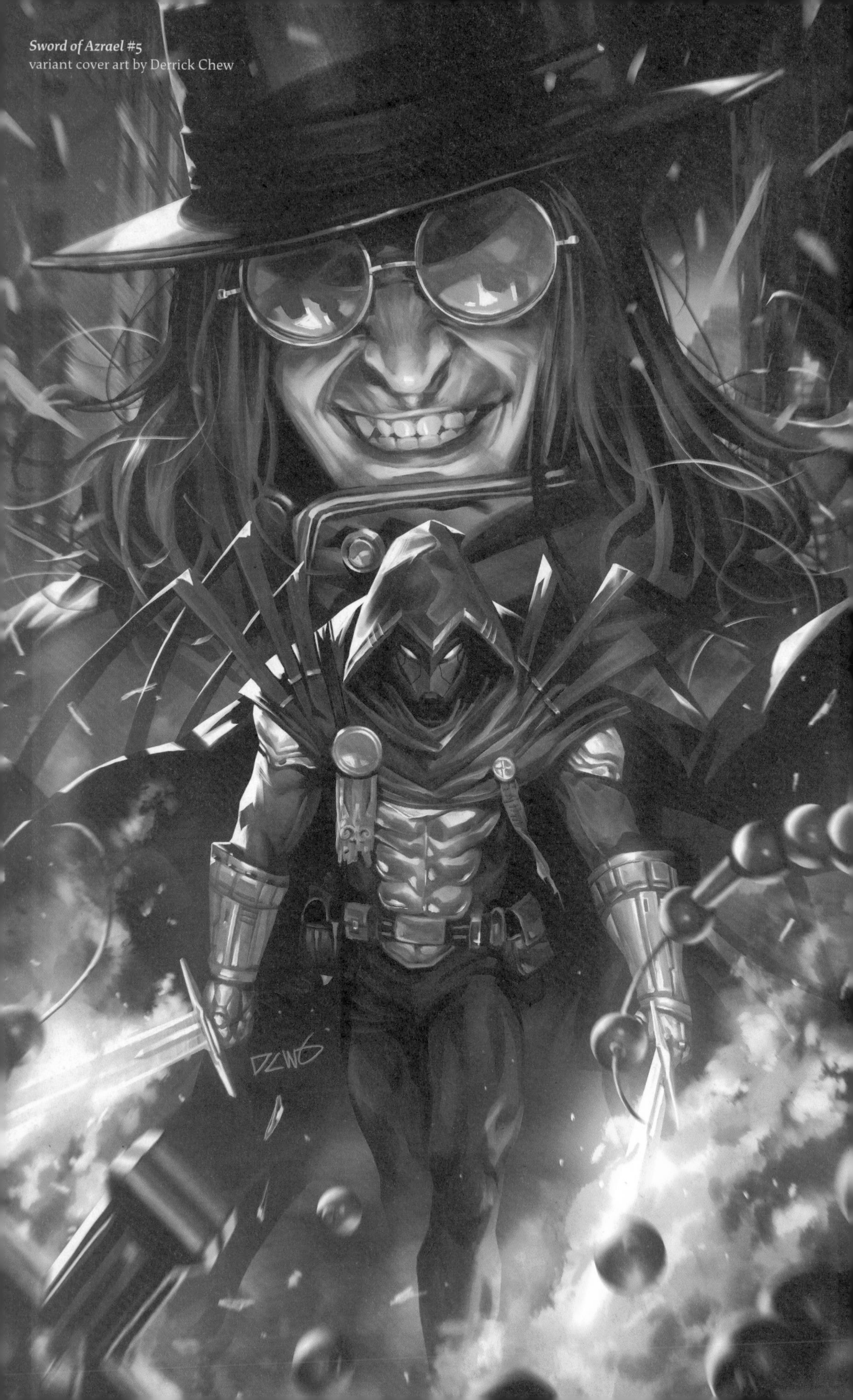

***Sword of Azrael* #5**
variant cover art by Derrick Chew

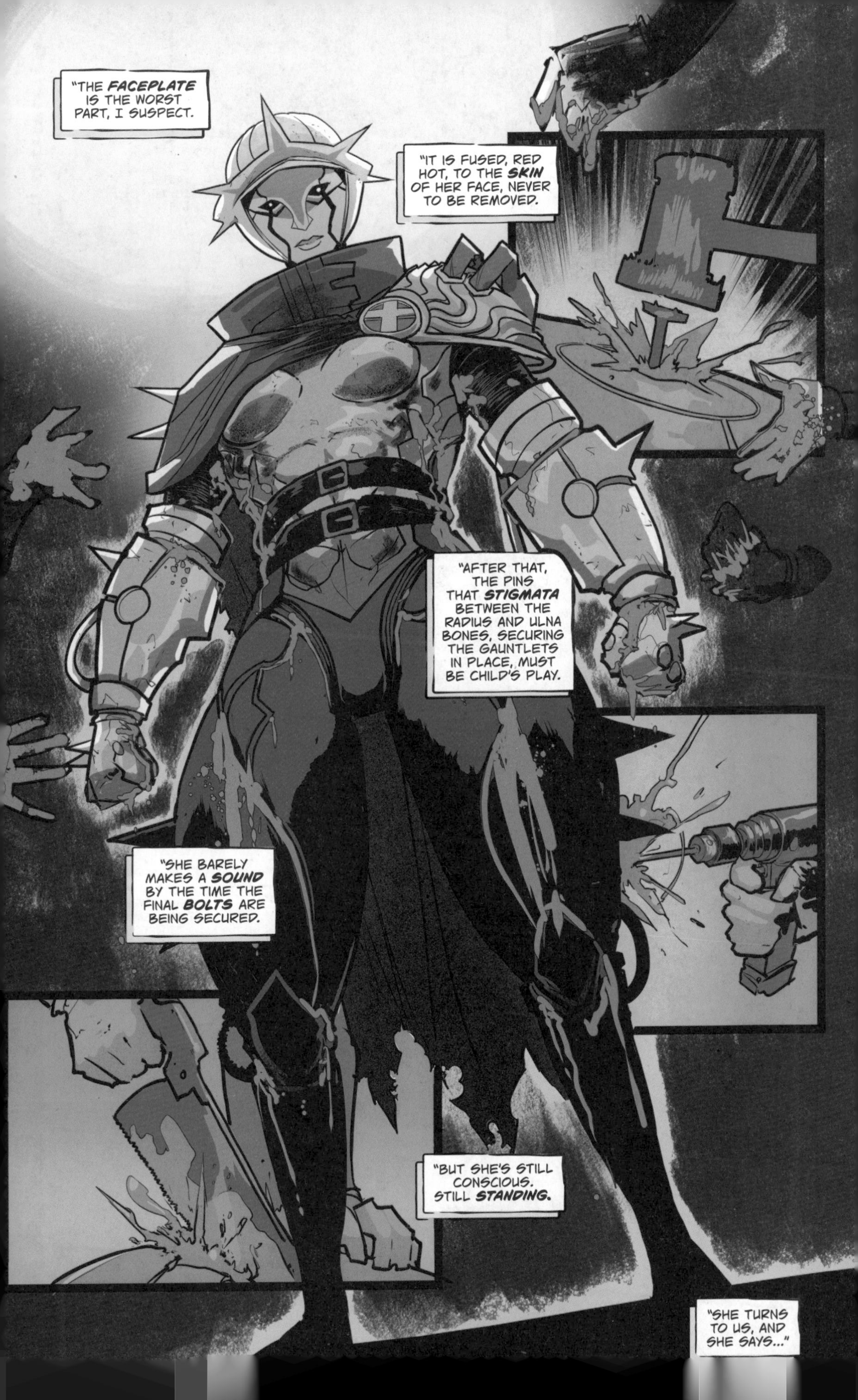
"THE FACEPLATE IS THE WORST PART, I SUSPECT.
"IT IS FUSED, RED HOT, TO THE SKIN OF HER FACE, NEVER TO BE REMOVED.
"AFTER THAT, THE PINS THAT STIGMATA BETWEEN THE RADIUS AND ULNA BONES, SECURING THE GAUNTLETS IN PLACE, MUST BE CHILD'S PLAY.
"SHE BARELY MAKES A SOUND BY THE TIME THE FINAL BOLTS ARE BEING SECURED.
"BUT SHE'S STILL CONSCIOUS. STILL STANDING.
"SHE TURNS TO US, AND SHE SAYS..."

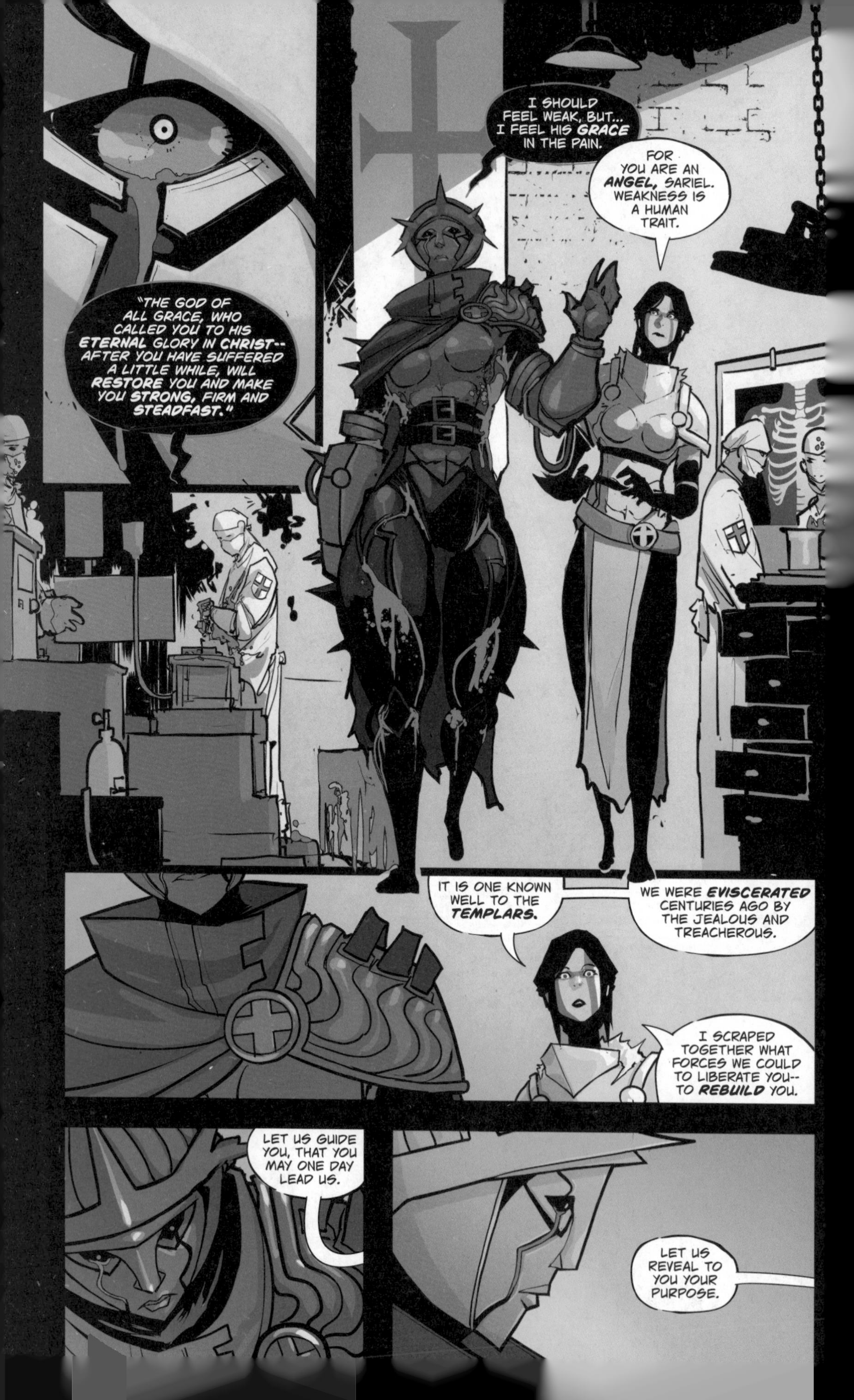

"THE GOD OF ALL GRACE, WHO CALLED YOU TO HIS ETERNAL GLORY IN CHRIST-- AFTER YOU HAVE SUFFERED A LITTLE WHILE, WILL RESTORE YOU AND MAKE YOU STRONG, FIRM AND STEADFAST."
I SHOULD FEEL WEAK, BUT... I FEEL HIS GRACE IN THE PAIN.
FOR YOU ARE AN ANGEL, SARIEL. WEAKNESS IS A HUMAN TRAIT.
IT IS ONE KNOWN WELL TO THE TEMPLARS.
WE WERE EVISCERATED CENTURIES AGO BY THE JEALOUS AND TREACHEROUS.
I SCRAPED TOGETHER WHAT FORCES WE COULD TO LIBERATE YOU-- TO REBUILD YOU.
LET US GUIDE YOU, THAT YOU MAY ONE DAY LEAD US.
LET US REVEAL TO YOU YOUR PURPOSE.

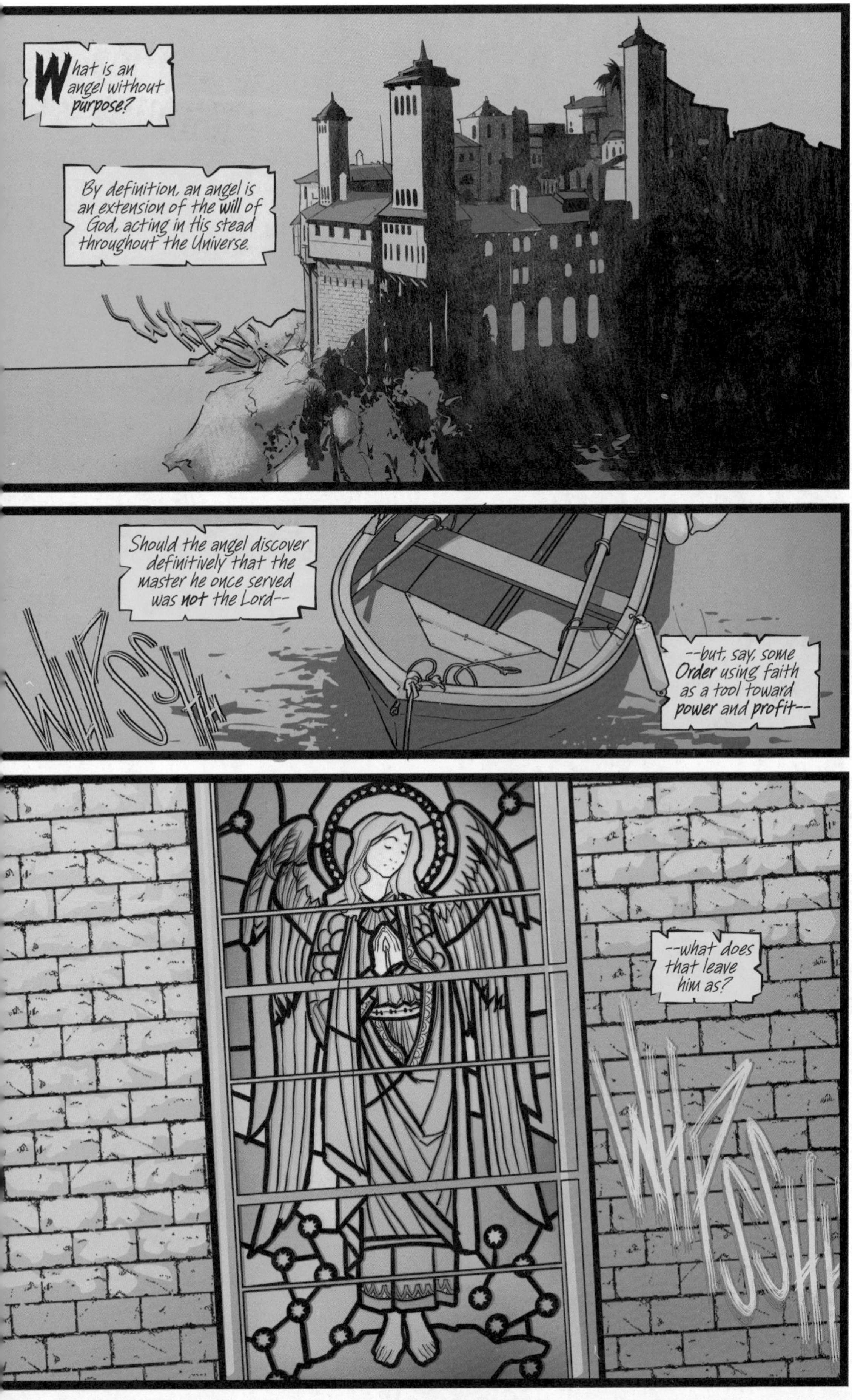
What is an angel without purpose?
By definition, an angel is an extension of the will of God, acting in His stead throughout the Universe.
Should the angel discover definitively that the master he once served was not the Lord--
--but, say, some Order using faith as a tool toward power and profit--
--what does that leave him as?

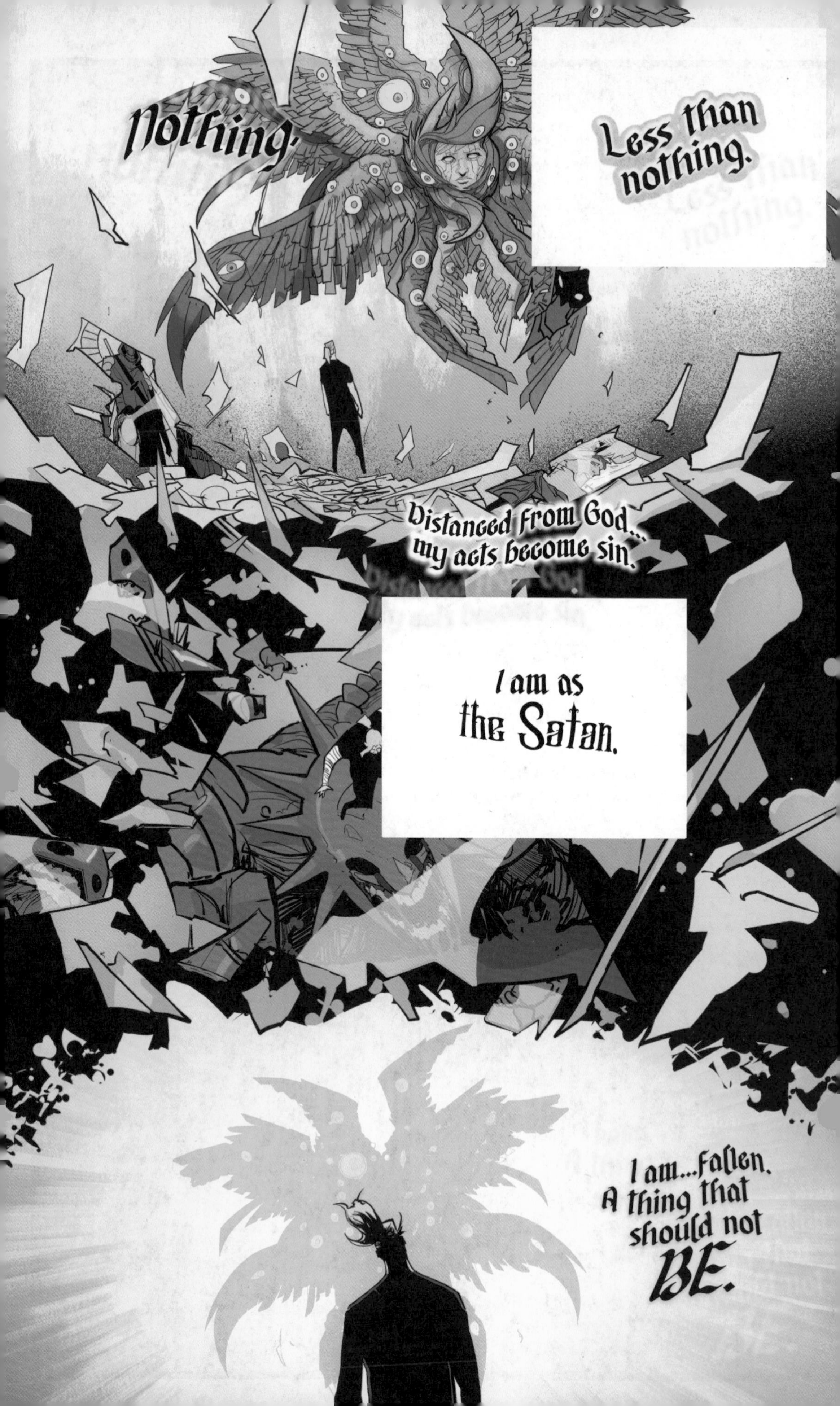

Nothing.
Less than nothing.
Distanced from God... my acts become sin.
I am as the Satan.
I am...fallen. A thing that should not BE.

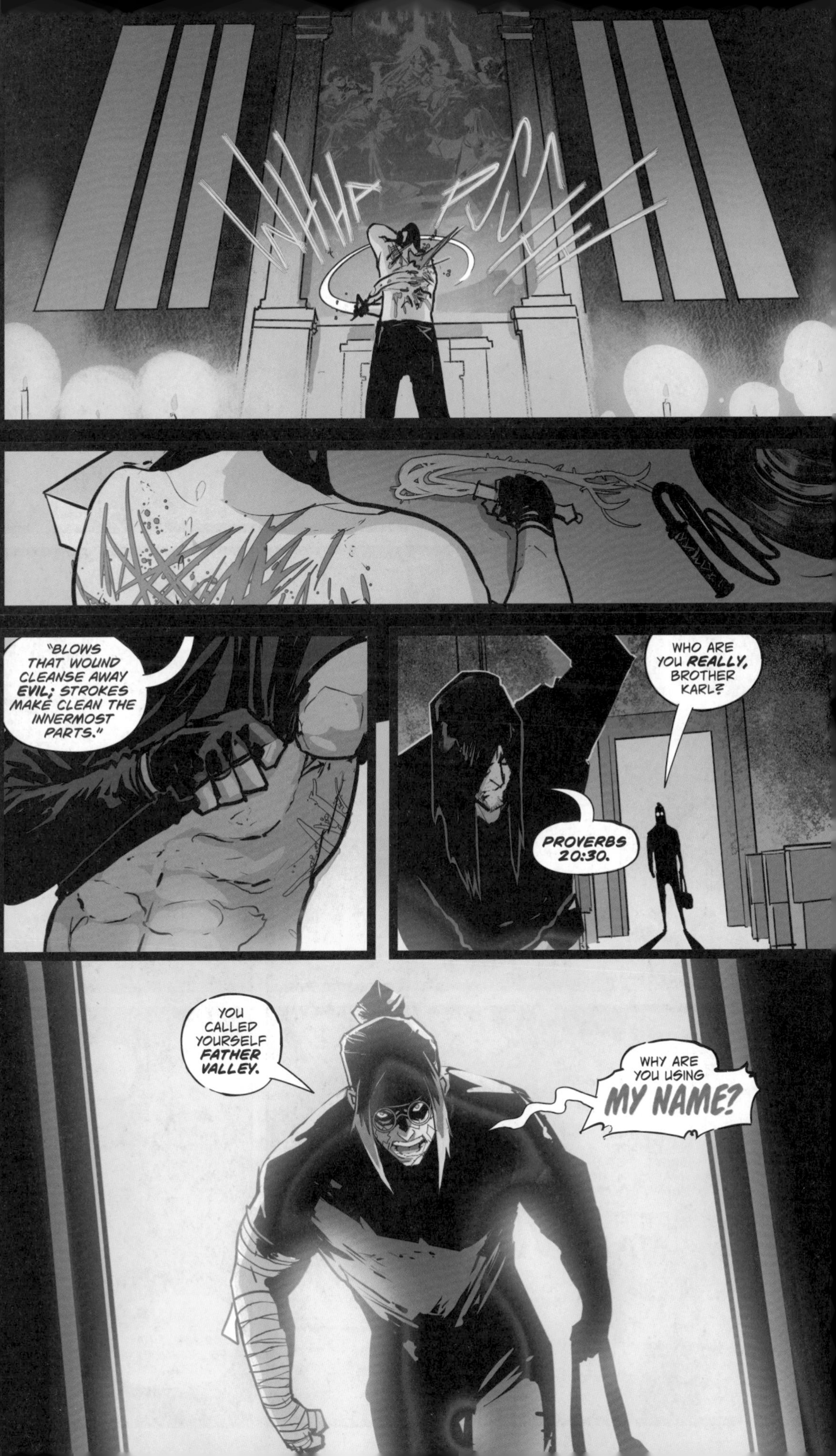

"BLOWS THAT WOUND CLEANSE AWAY EVIL; STROKES MAKE CLEAN THE INNERMOST PARTS."
PROVERBS 20:30.
WHO ARE YOU REALLY, BROTHER KARL?
YOU CALLED YOURSELF FATHER VALLEY.
WHY ARE YOU USING MY NAME?

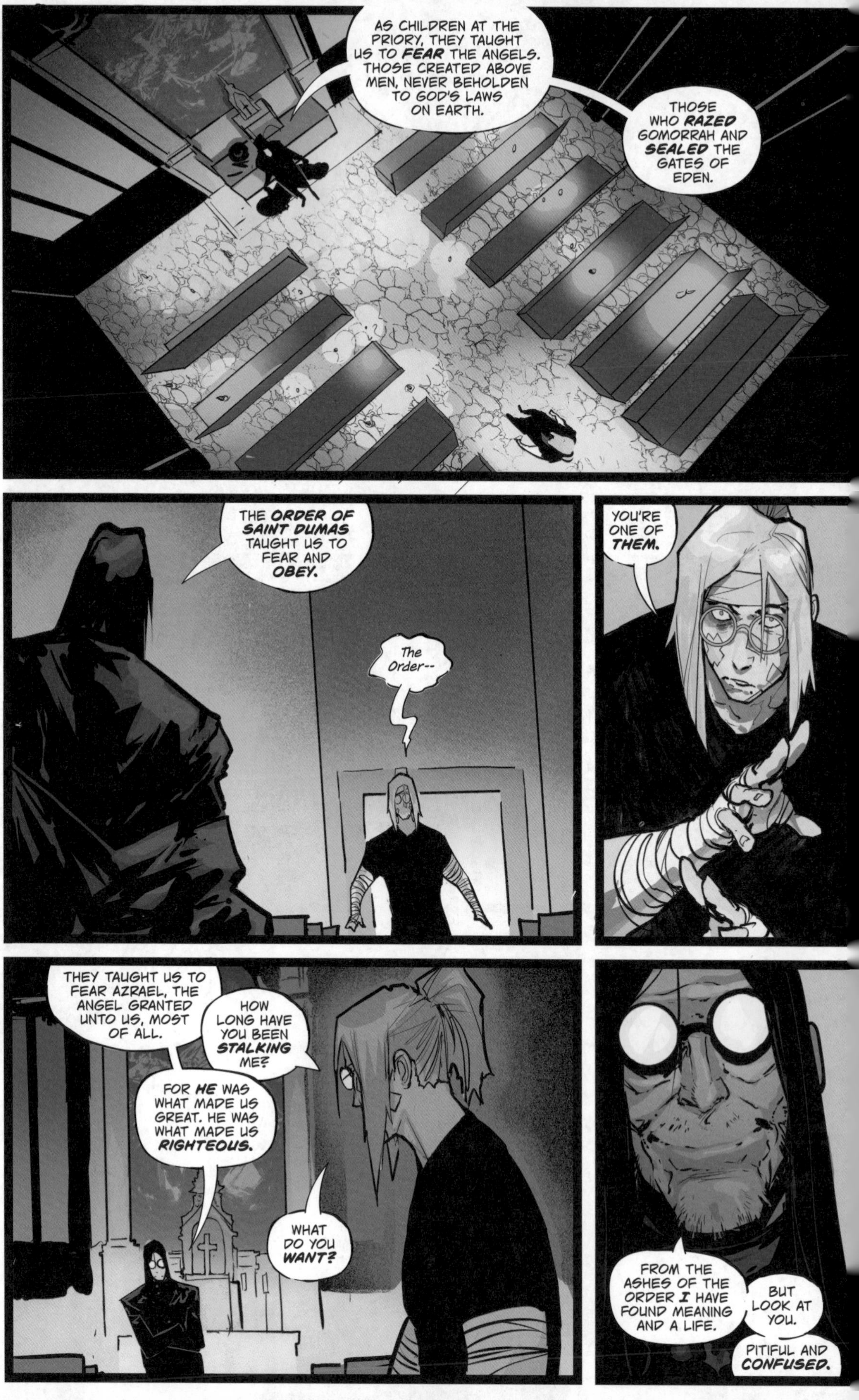

AS CHILDREN AT THE PRIORY, THEY TAUGHT US TO FEAR THE ANGELS. THOSE CREATED ABOVE MEN, NEVER BEHOLDEN TO GOD'S LAWS ON EARTH.
THOSE WHO RAZED GOMORRAH AND SEALED THE GATES OF EDEN.
THE ORDER OF SAINT DUMAS TAUGHT US TO FEAR AND OBEY.
The Order--
YOU'RE ONE OF THEM.
THEY TAUGHT US TO FEAR AZRAEL, THE ANGEL GRANTED UNTO US, MOST OF ALL.
HOW LONG HAVE YOU BEEN STALKING ME?
FOR HE WAS WHAT MADE US GREAT. HE WAS WHAT MADE US RIGHTEOUS.
WHAT DO YOU WANT?
FROM THE ASHES OF THE ORDER I HAVE FOUND MEANING AND A LIFE.
BUT LOOK AT YOU.
PITIFUL AND CONFUSED.

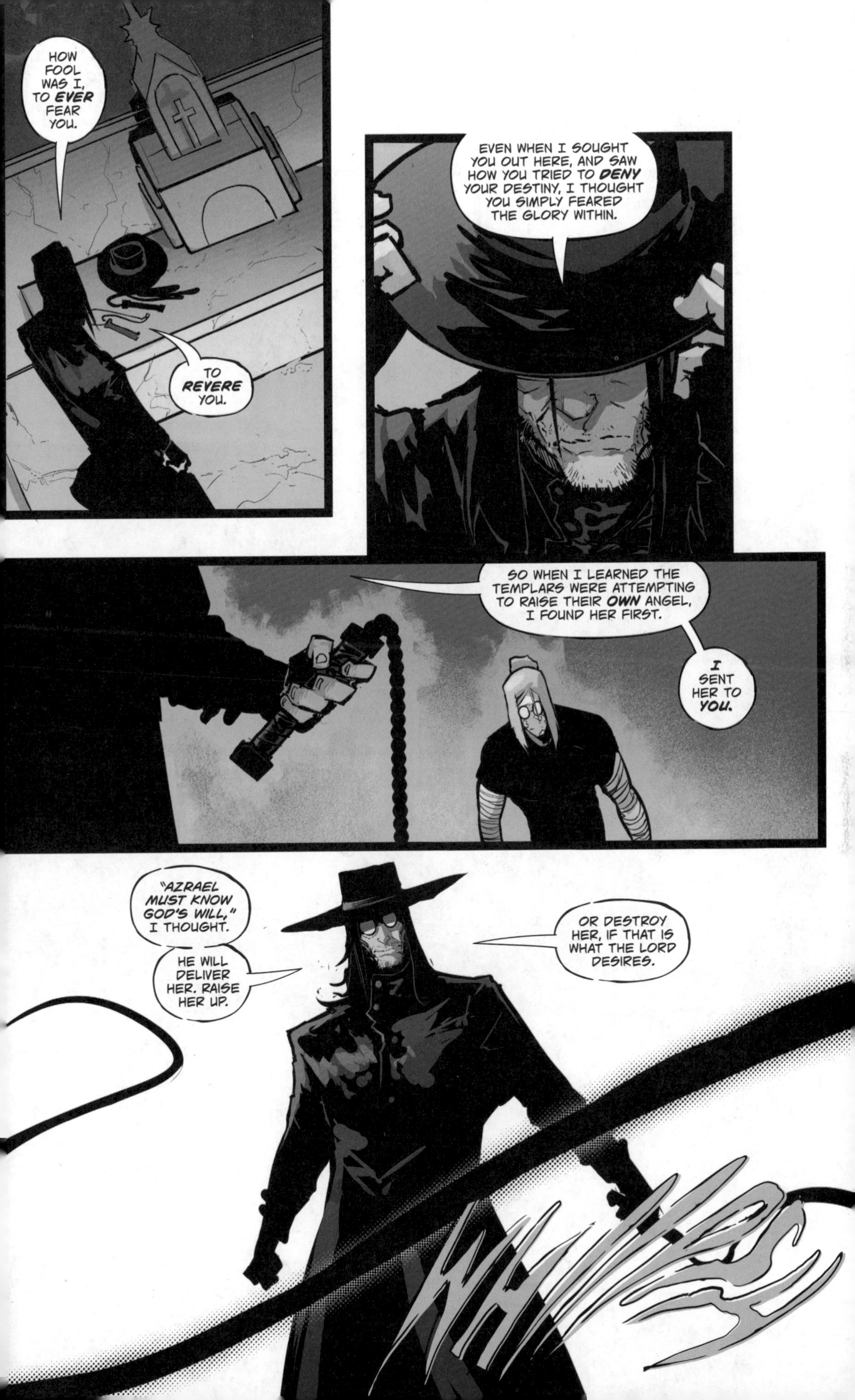
HOW FOOL WAS I, TO EVER FEAR YOU.
TO REVERE YOU.
EVEN WHEN I SOUGHT YOU OUT HERE, AND SAW HOW YOU TRIED TO DENY YOUR DESTINY, I THOUGHT YOU SIMPLY FEARED THE GLORY WITHIN.
SO WHEN I LEARNED THE TEMPLARS WERE ATTEMPTING TO RAISE THEIR OWN ANGEL, I FOUND HER FIRST.
I SENT HER TO YOU.
"AZRAEL MUST KNOW GOD'S WILL," I THOUGHT.
HE WILL DELIVER HER. RAISE HER UP.
OR DESTROY HER, IF THAT IS WHAT THE LORD DESIRES.
WHHHPSSH

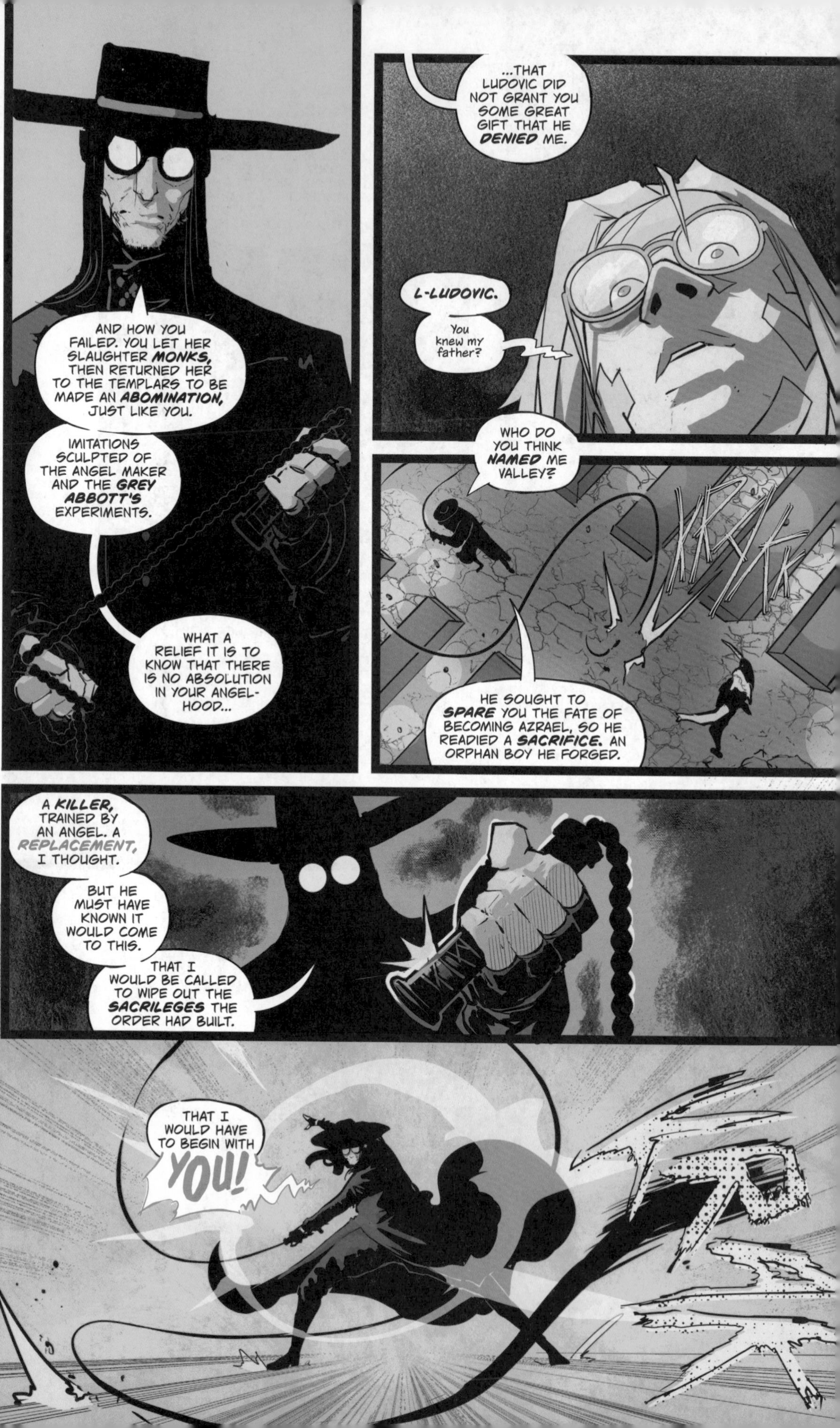
AND HOW YOU FAILED. YOU LET HER SLAUGHTER MONKS, THEN RETURNED HER TO THE TEMPLARS TO BE MADE AN ABOMINATION, JUST LIKE YOU.
IMITATIONS SCULPTED OF THE ANGEL MAKER AND THE GREY ABBOTT'S EXPERIMENTS.
WHAT A RELIEF IT IS TO KNOW THAT THERE IS NO ABSOLUTION IN YOUR ANGEL-HOOD...
...THAT LUDOVIC DID NOT GRANT YOU SOME GREAT GIFT THAT HE DENIED ME.
L-LUDOVIC.
You knew my father?
WHO DO YOU THINK NAMED ME VALLEY?
KRAKKK
HE SOUGHT TO SPARE YOU THE FATE OF BECOMING AZRAEL, SO HE READIED A SACRIFICE. AN ORPHAN BOY HE FORGED.
A KILLER, TRAINED BY AN ANGEL. A REPLACEMENT, I THOUGHT.
BUT HE MUST HAVE KNOWN IT WOULD COME TO THIS.
THAT I WOULD BE CALLED TO WIPE OUT THE SACRILEGES THE ORDER HAD BUILT.
THAT I WOULD HAVE TO BEGIN WITH YOU!

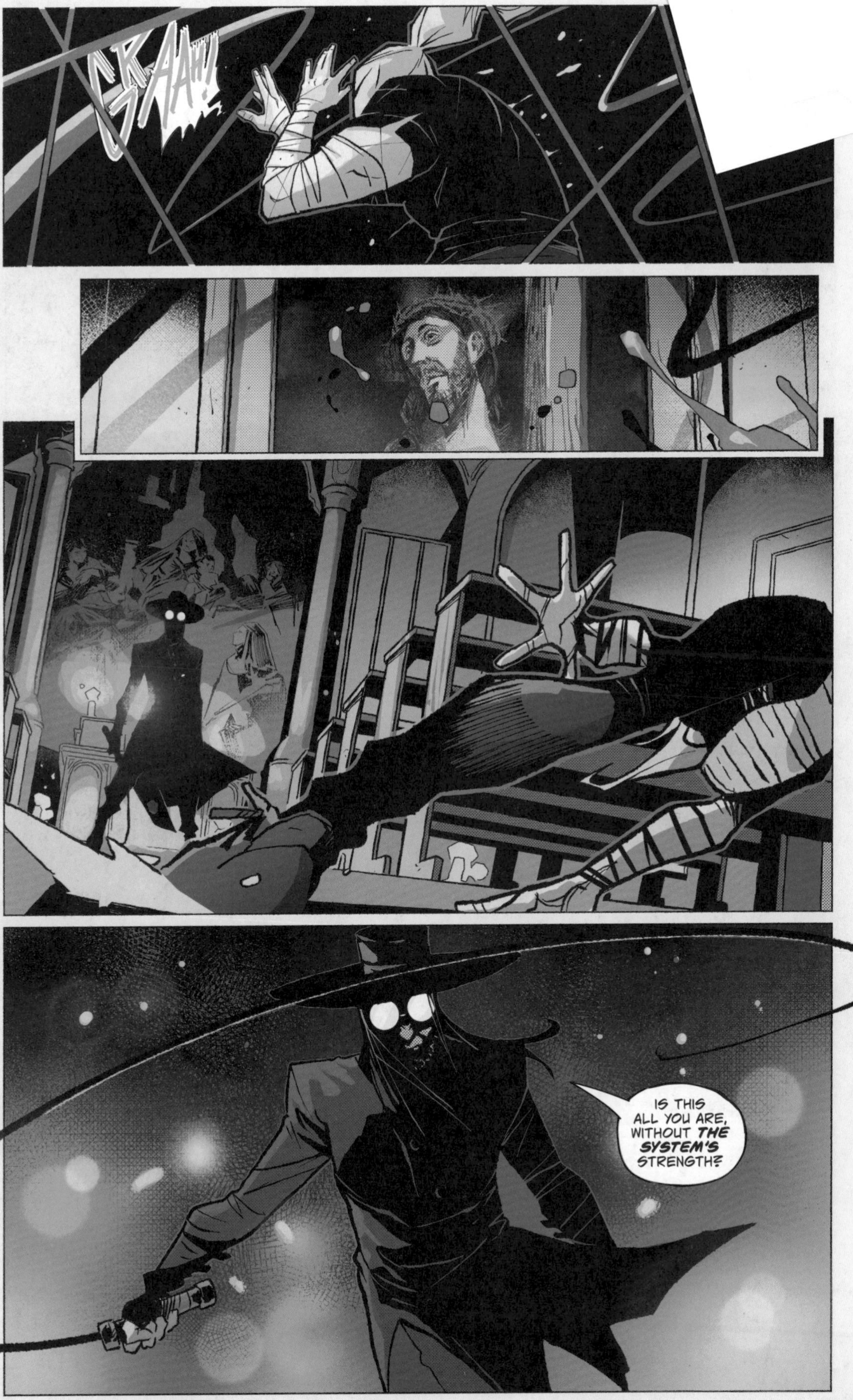
CRAAAH!
IS THIS ALL YOU ARE, WITHOUT *THE SYSTEM'S* STRENGTH?

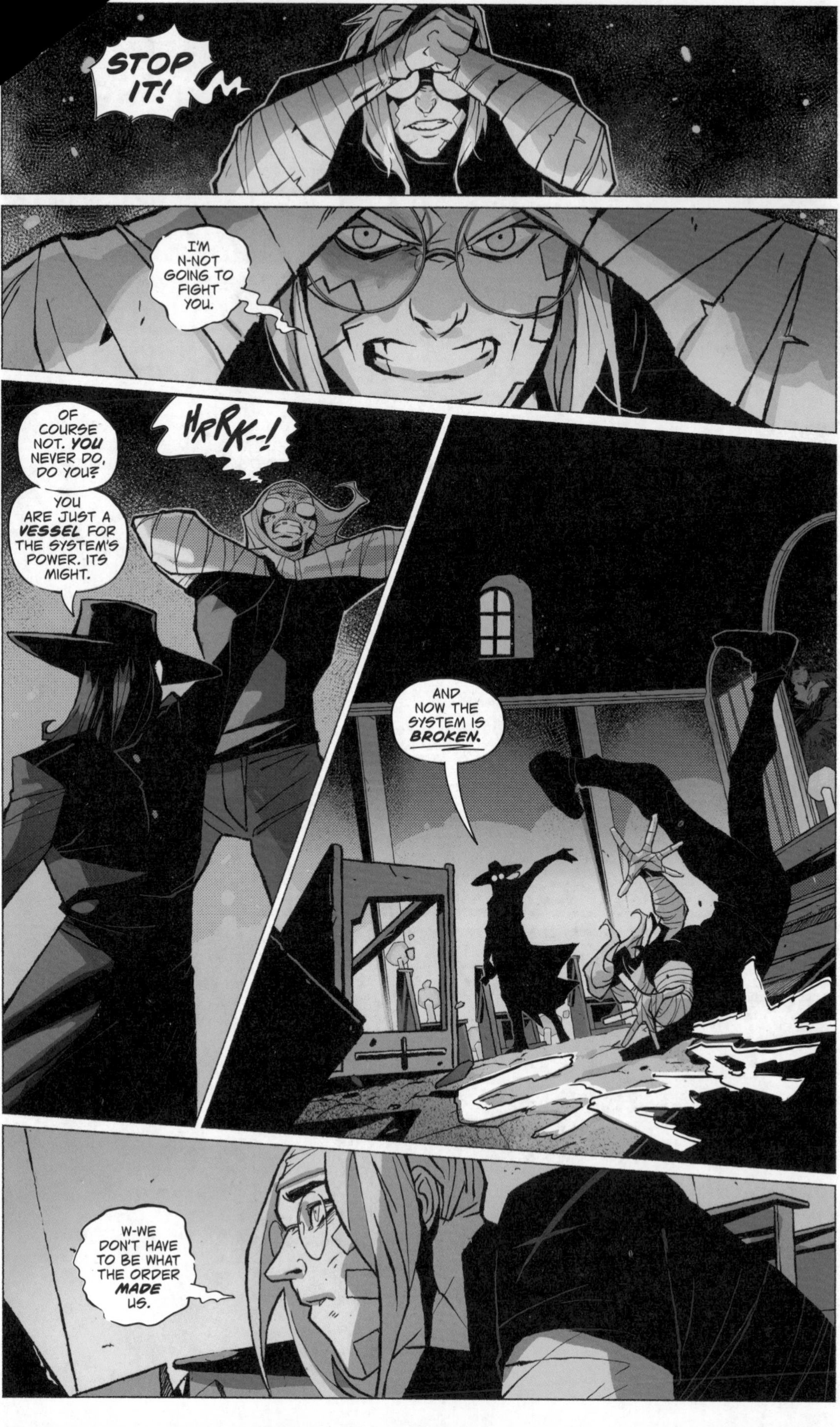
STOP IT!
I'M N-NOT GOING TO FIGHT YOU.
OF COURSE NOT. YOU NEVER DO, DO YOU?
YOU ARE JUST A VESSEL FOR THE SYSTEM'S POWER. ITS MIGHT.
HRRK--!
AND NOW THE SYSTEM IS BROKEN.
W-WE DON'T HAVE TO BE WHAT THE ORDER MADE US.

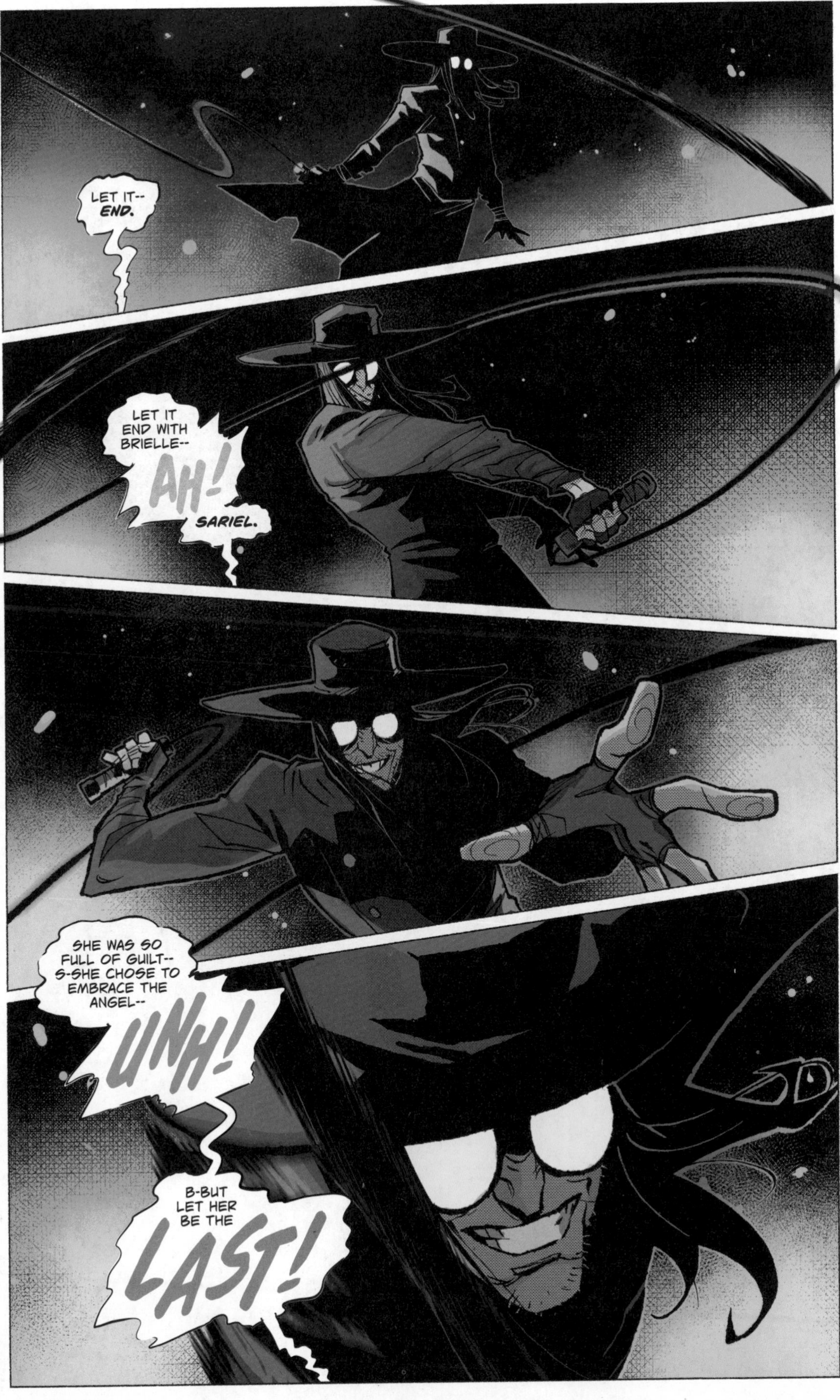
LET IT--
END.
LET IT END WITH BRIELLE--
AH!
SARIEL.
SHE WAS SO FULL OF GUILT--
S-SHE CHOSE TO EMBRACE THE ANGEL--
UNH!
B-BUT LET HER BE THE
LAST!

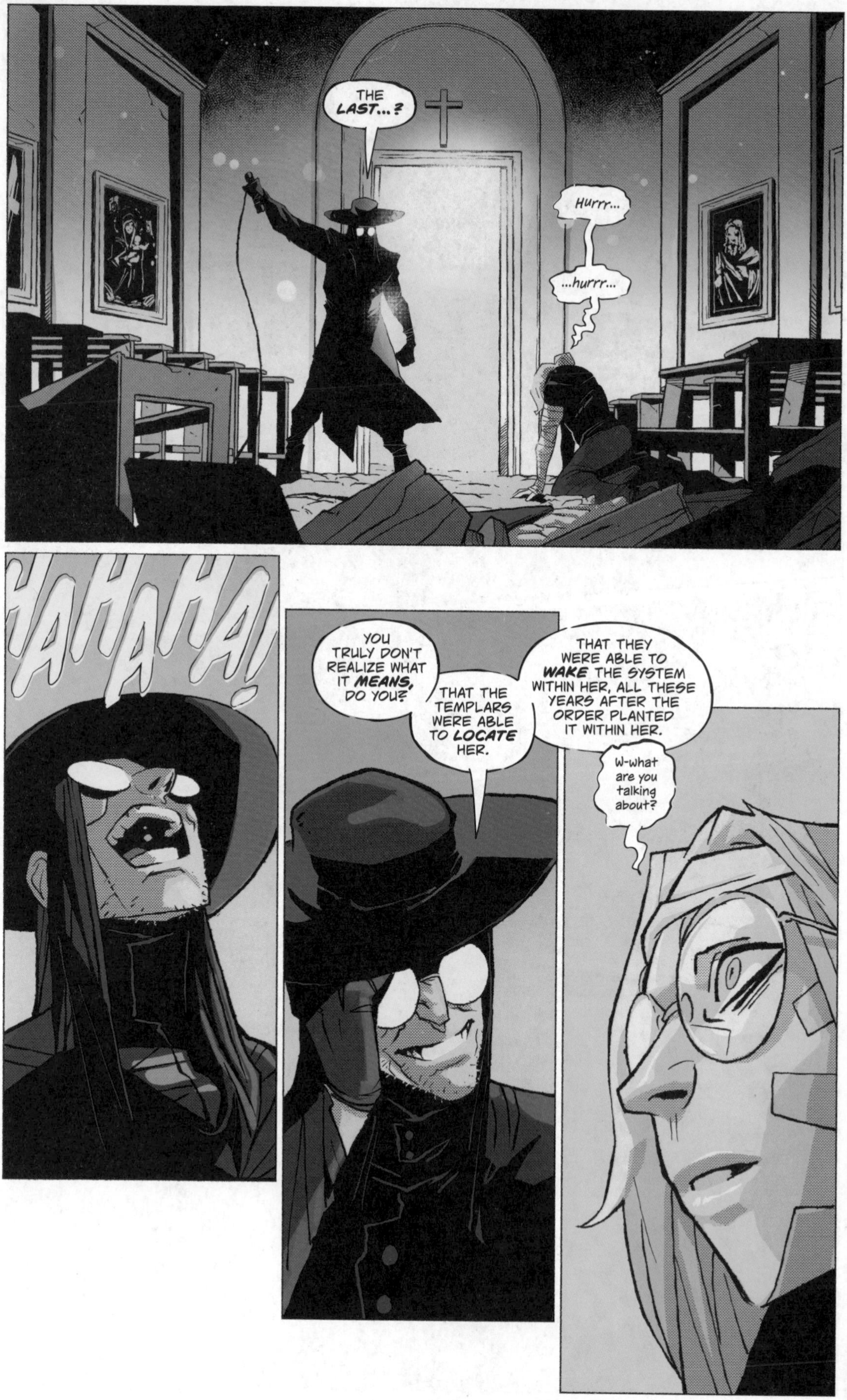
THE LAST...?
Hurrr...
...hurrr...
HAHAHA!
YOU TRULY DON'T REALIZE WHAT IT MEANS, DO YOU?
THAT THE TEMPLARS WERE ABLE TO LOCATE HER.
THAT THEY WERE ABLE TO WAKE THE SYSTEM WITHIN HER, ALL THESE YEARS AFTER THE ORDER PLANTED IT WITHIN HER.
W-what are you talking about?

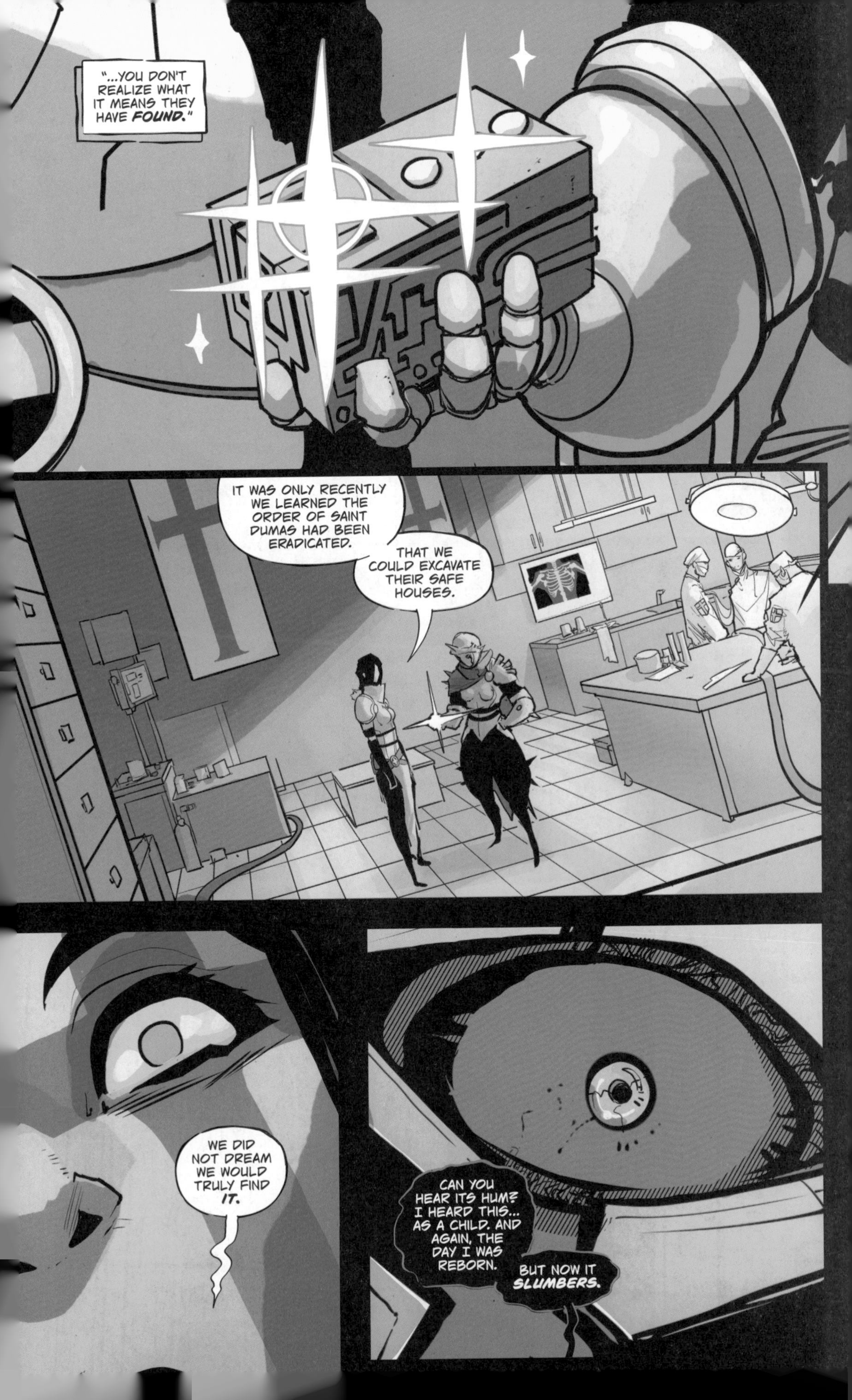
"...YOU DON'T REALIZE WHAT IT MEANS THEY HAVE FOUND."
IT WAS ONLY RECENTLY WE LEARNED THE ORDER OF SAINT DUMAS HAD BEEN ERADICATED.
THAT WE COULD EXCAVATE THEIR SAFE HOUSES.
WE DID NOT DREAM WE WOULD TRULY FIND IT.
CAN YOU HEAR ITS HUM? I HEARD THIS... AS A CHILD. AND AGAIN, THE DAY I WAS REBORN.
BUT NOW IT SLUMBERS.

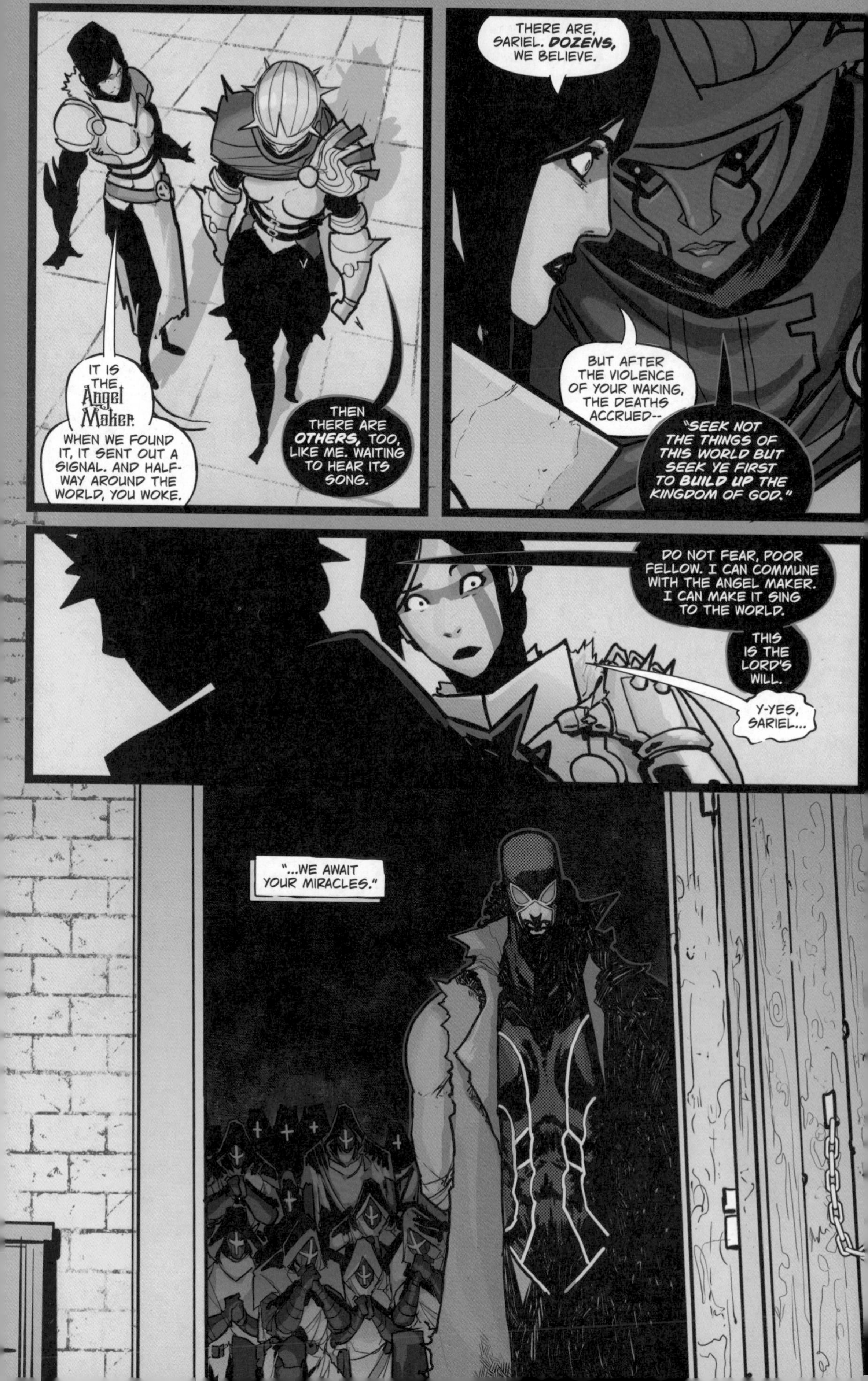
IT IS THE Angel Maker.
WHEN WE FOUND IT, IT SENT OUT A SIGNAL. AND HALF-WAY AROUND THE WORLD, YOU WOKE.
THEN THERE ARE OTHERS, TOO, LIKE ME. WAITING TO HEAR ITS SONG.
THERE ARE, SARIEL. DOZENS, WE BELIEVE.
BUT AFTER THE VIOLENCE OF YOUR WAKING, THE DEATHS ACCRUED--
"SEEK NOT THE THINGS OF THIS WORLD BUT SEEK YE FIRST TO BUILD UP THE KINGDOM OF GOD."
DO NOT FEAR, POOR FELLOW. I CAN COMMUNE WITH THE ANGEL MAKER. I CAN MAKE IT SING TO THE WORLD.
THIS IS THE LORD'S WILL.
Y-YES, SARIEL...
"...WE AWAIT YOUR MIRACLES."

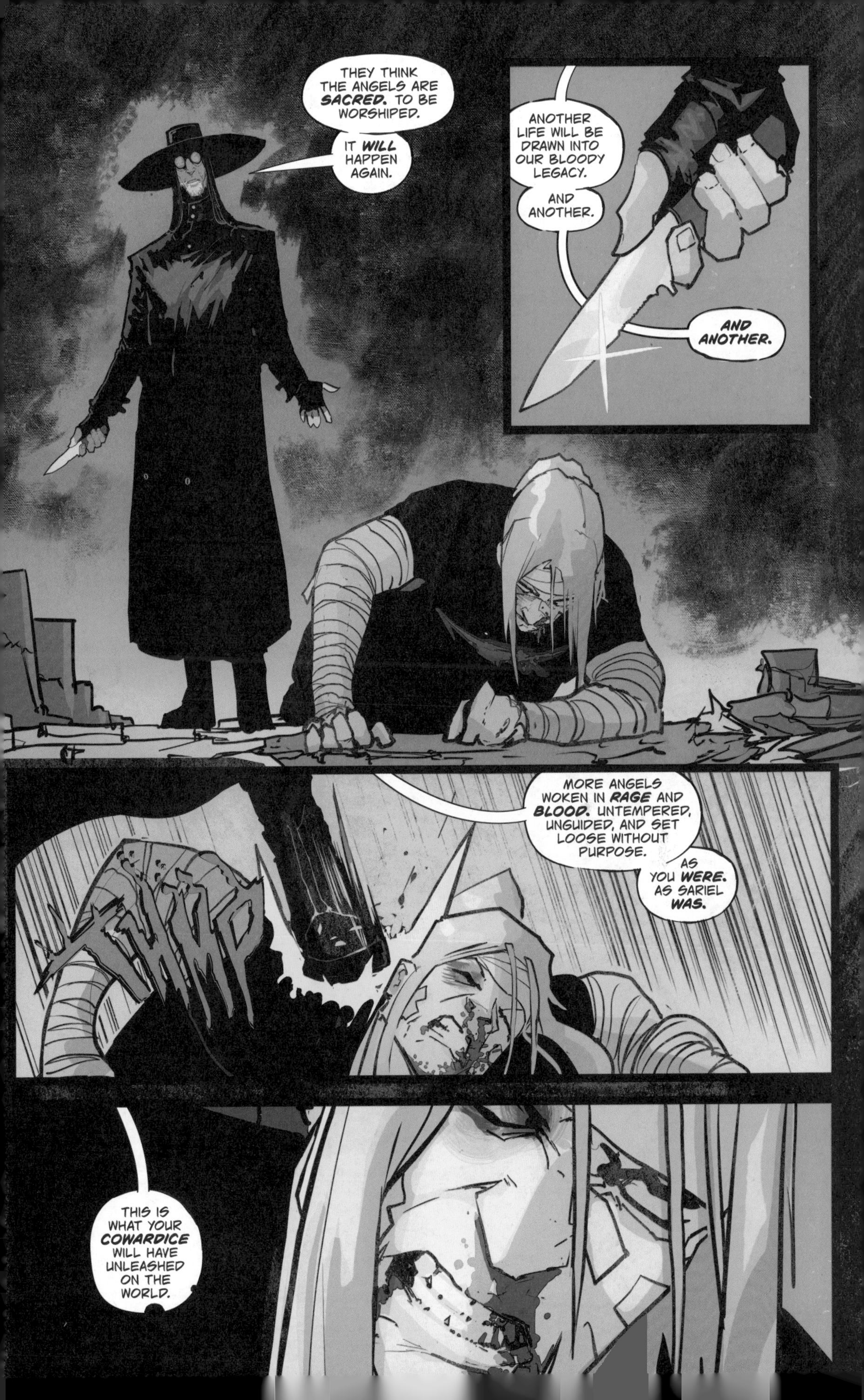
THEY THINK THE ANGELS ARE SACRED. TO BE WORSHIPED.
IT WILL HAPPEN AGAIN.
ANOTHER LIFE WILL BE DRAWN INTO OUR BLOODY LEGACY.
AND ANOTHER.
AND ANOTHER.
MORE ANGELS WOKEN IN RAGE AND BLOOD. UNTEMPERED, UNGUIDED, AND SET LOOSE WITHOUT PURPOSE.
AS YOU WERE. AS SARIEL WAS.
THIS IS WHAT YOUR COWARDICE WILL HAVE UNLEASHED ON THE WORLD.

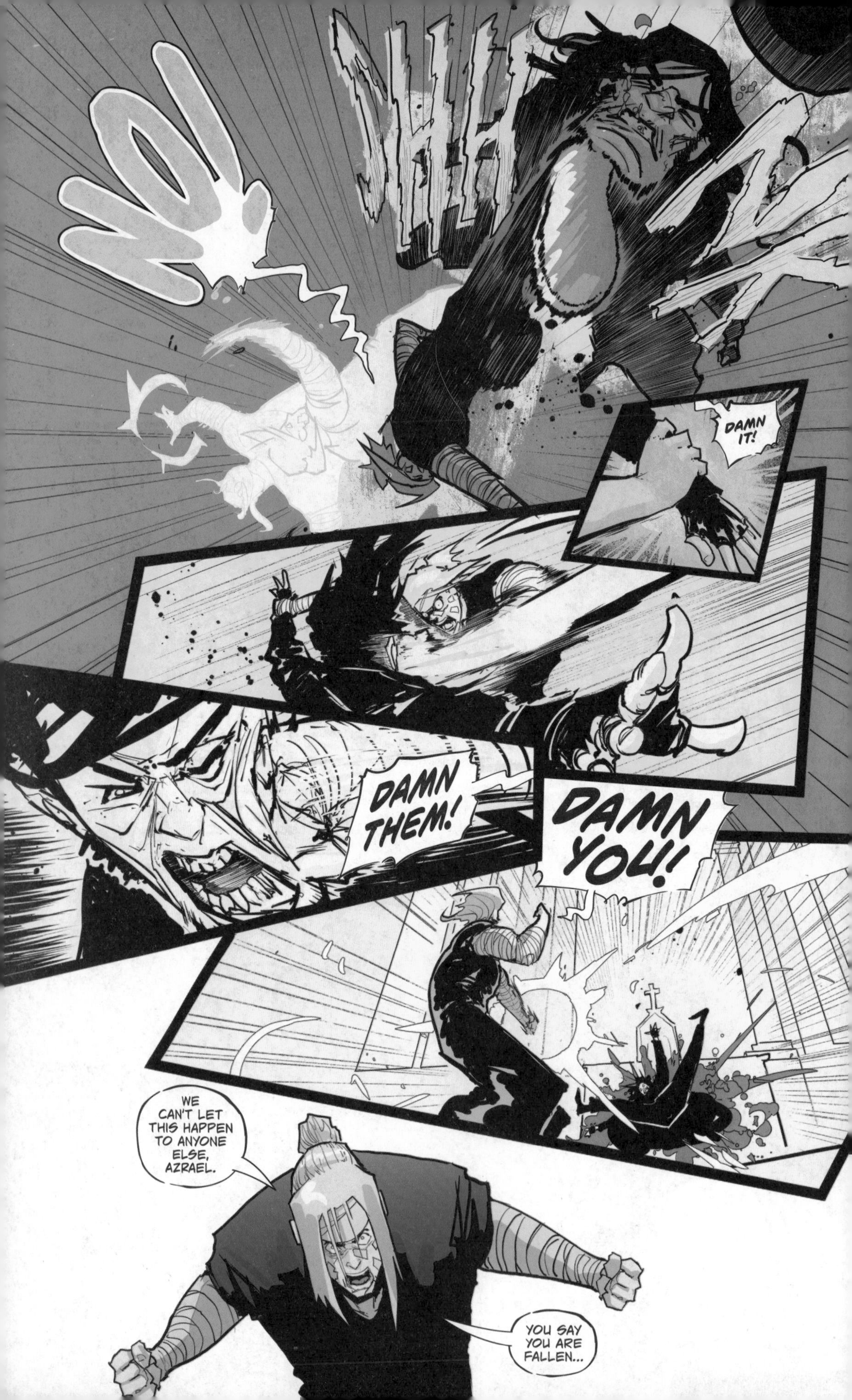
NO!
DAMN IT!
DAMN THEM!
DAMN YOU!
WE CAN'T LET THIS HAPPEN TO ANYONE ELSE, AZRAEL.
YOU SAY YOU ARE FALLEN...

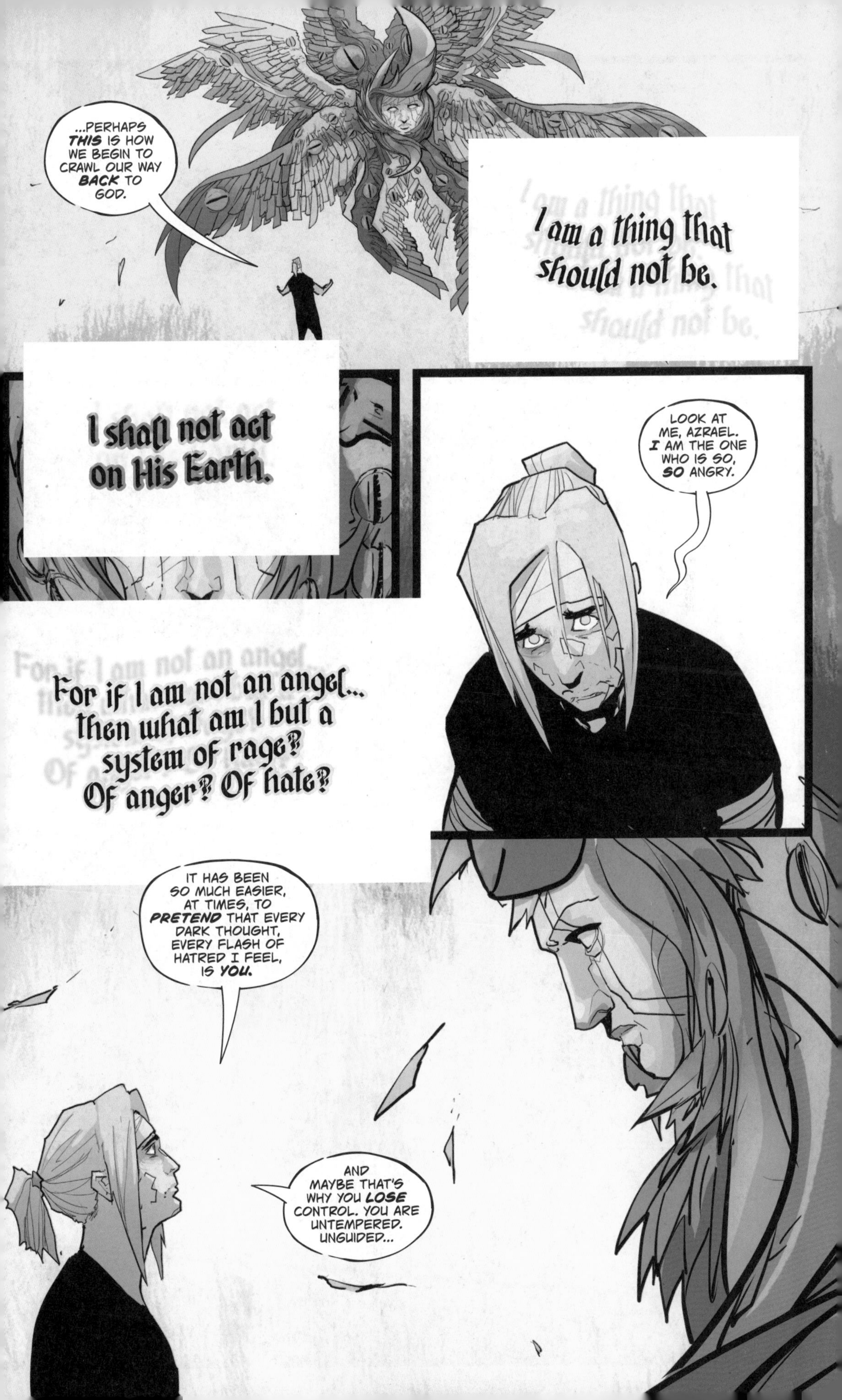

...PERHAPS THIS IS HOW WE BEGIN TO CRAWL OUR WAY BACK TO GOD.
I am a thing that should not be.
I shall not act on His Earth.
LOOK AT ME, AZRAEL. I AM THE ONE WHO IS SO, SO ANGRY.
For if I am not an angel... then what am I but a system of rage? Of anger? Of hate?
IT HAS BEEN SO MUCH EASIER, AT TIMES, TO PRETEND THAT EVERY DARK THOUGHT, EVERY FLASH OF HATRED I FEEL, IS YOU.
AND MAYBE THAT'S WHY YOU LOSE CONTROL. YOU ARE UNTEMPERED. UNGUIDED...

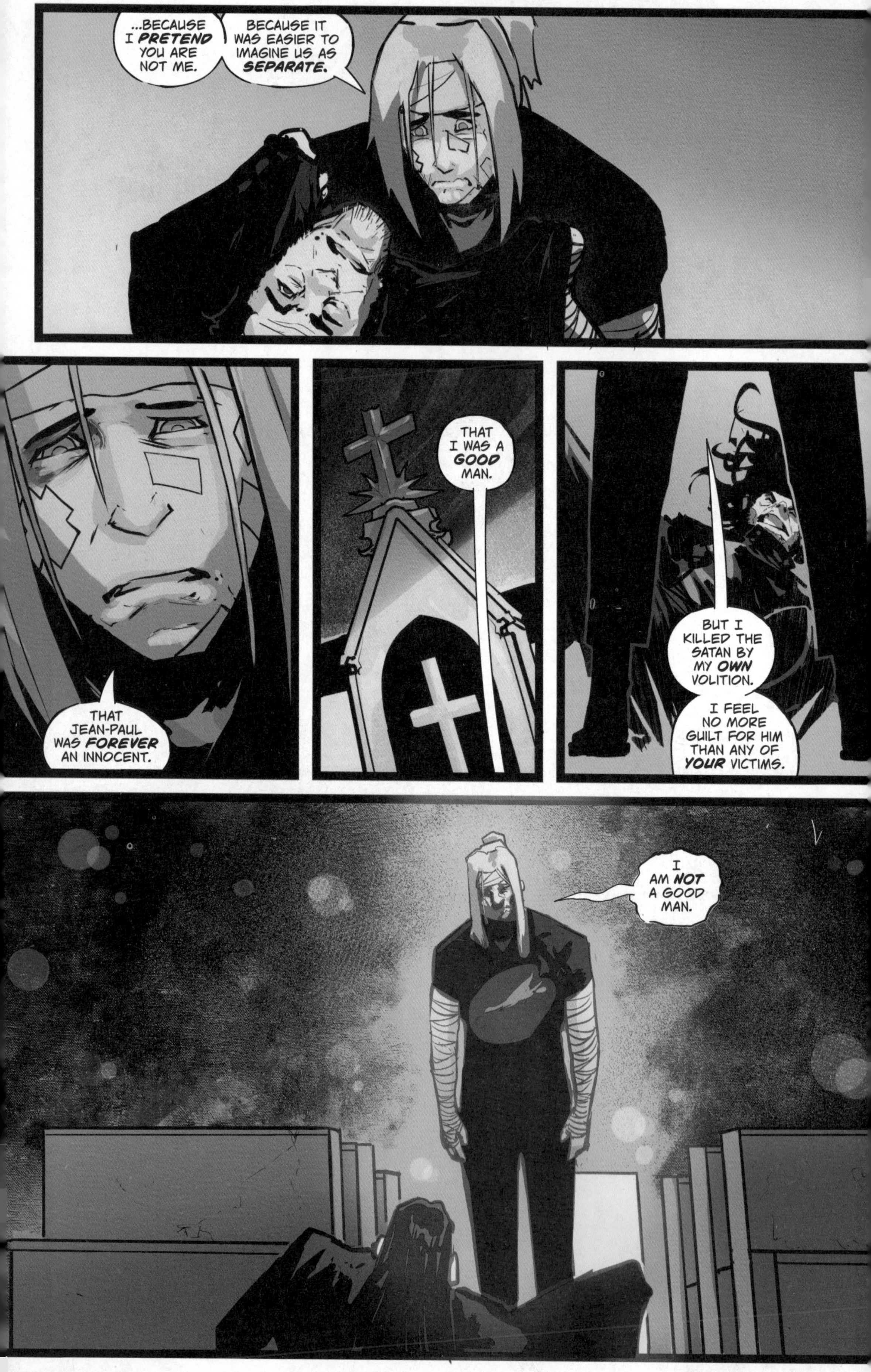

...BECAUSE I PRETEND YOU ARE NOT ME.
BECAUSE IT WAS EASIER TO IMAGINE US AS SEPARATE.
THAT JEAN-PAUL WAS FOREVER AN INNOCENT.
THAT I WAS A GOOD MAN.
BUT I KILLED THE SATAN BY MY OWN VOLITION.
I FEEL NO MORE GUILT FOR HIM THAN ANY OF YOUR VICTIMS.
I AM NOT A GOOD MAN.

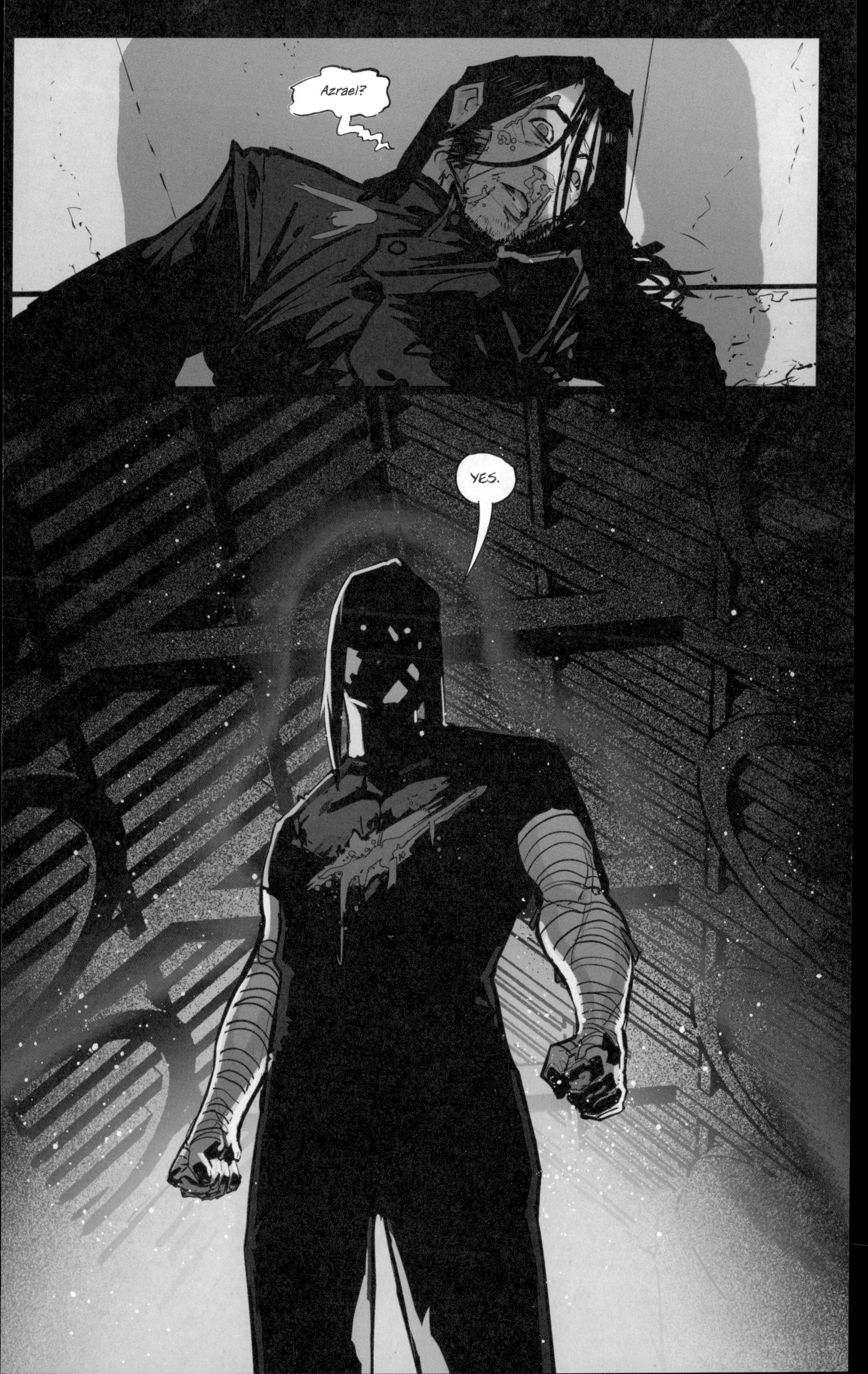
Azrael?
YES.

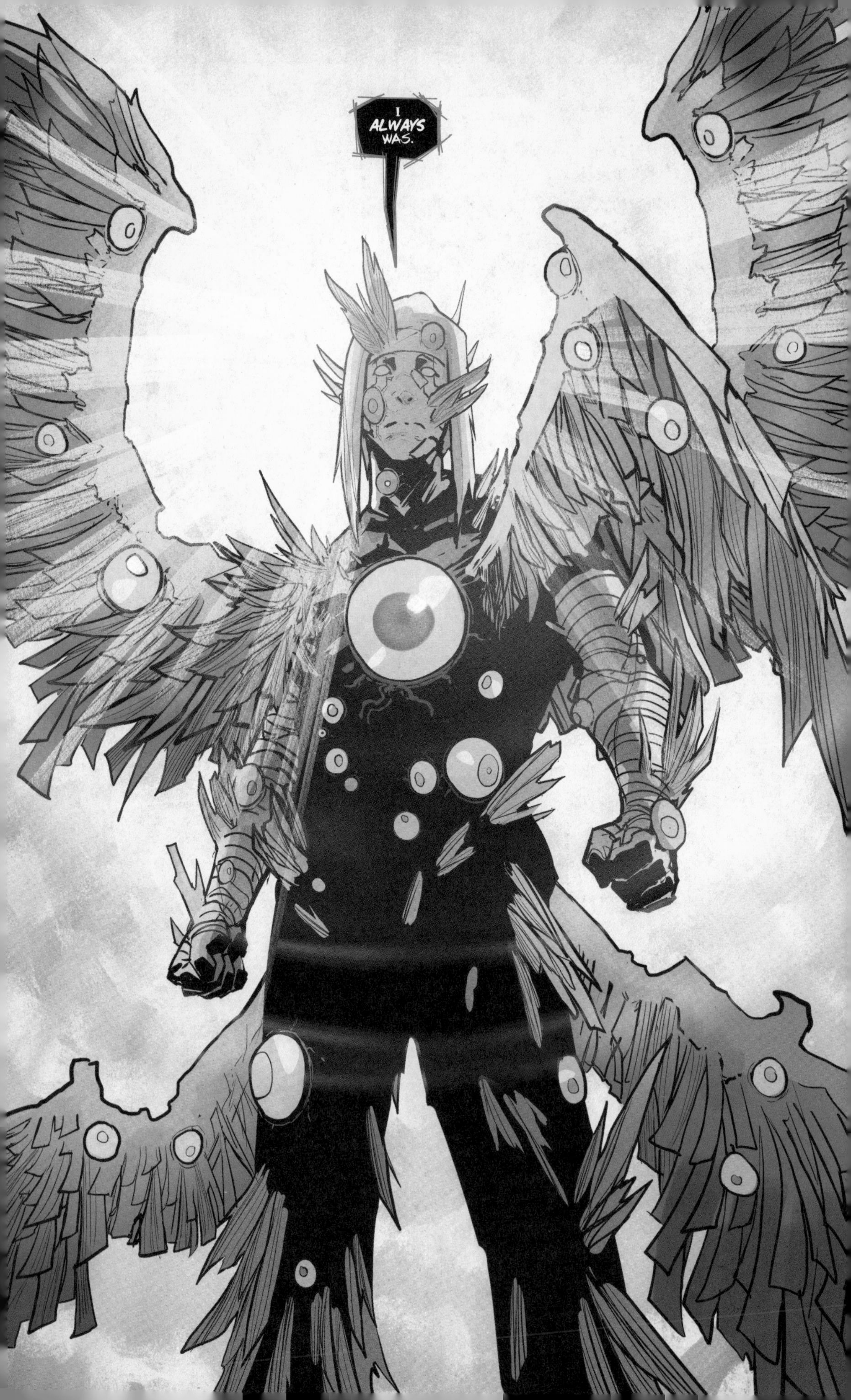
I ALWAYS WAS.

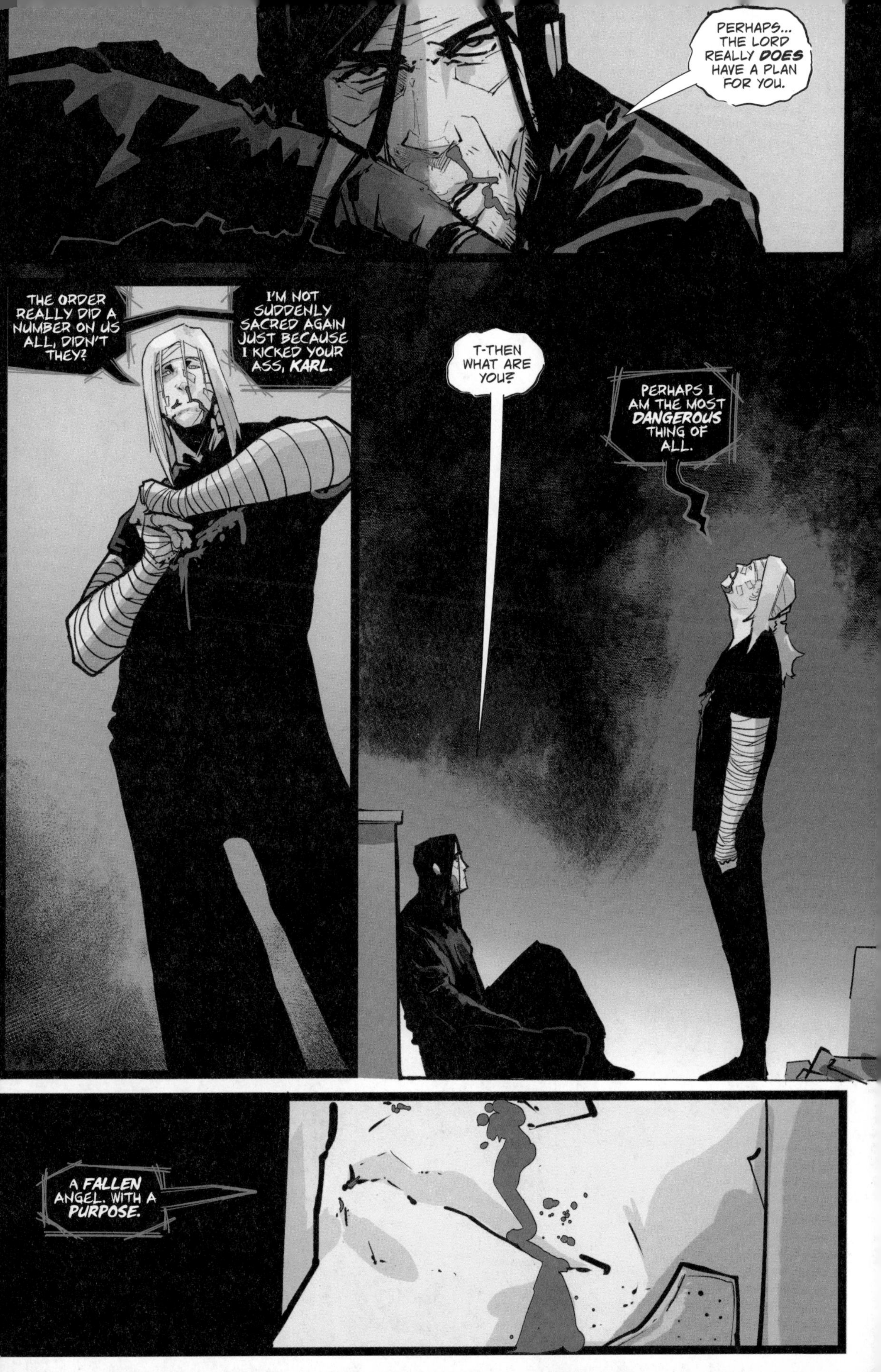
PERHAPS... THE LORD REALLY DOES HAVE A PLAN FOR YOU.
THE ORDER REALLY DID A NUMBER ON US ALL, DIDN'T THEY?
I'M NOT SUDDENLY SACRED AGAIN JUST BECAUSE I KICKED YOUR ASS, KARL.
T-THEN WHAT ARE YOU?
PERHAPS I AM THE MOST DANGEROUS THING OF ALL.
A FALLEN ANGEL. WITH A PURPOSE.

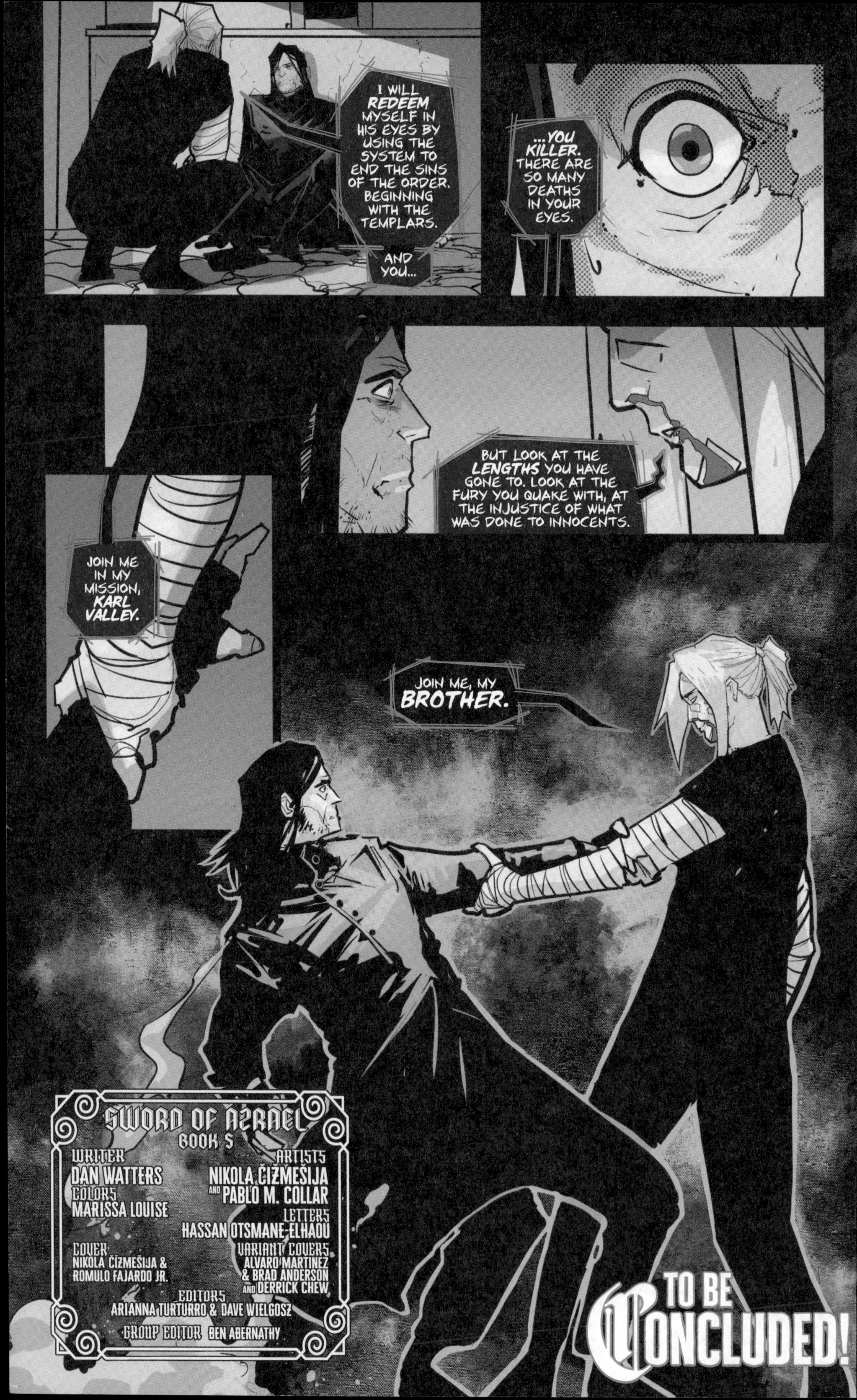

I WILL REDEEM MYSELF IN HIS EYES BY USING THE SYSTEM TO END THE SINS OF THE ORDER. BEGINNING WITH THE TEMPLARS.
AND YOU...
...YOU KILLER. THERE ARE SO MANY DEATHS IN YOUR EYES.
BUT LOOK AT THE LENGTHS YOU HAVE GONE TO. LOOK AT THE FURY YOU QUAKE WITH, AT THE INJUSTICE OF WHAT WAS DONE TO INNOCENTS.
JOIN ME IN MY MISSION, KARL VALLEY.
JOIN ME, MY BROTHER.
SWORD OF AZRAEL
BOOK 5
WRITER
DAN WATTERS
ARTISTS
NIKOLA ČIŽMEŠIJA AND PABLO M. COLLAR
COLORS
MARISSA LOUISE
LETTERS
HASSAN OTSMANE-ELHAOU
COVER
NIKOLA ČIŽMEŠIJA & ROMULO FAJARDO JR.
VARIANT COVERS
ALVARO MARTINEZ & BRAD ANDERSON AND DERRICK CHEW
EDITORS
ARIANNA TURTURRO & DAVE WIELGOSZ
GROUP EDITOR BEN ABERNATHY
TO BE CONCLUDED!

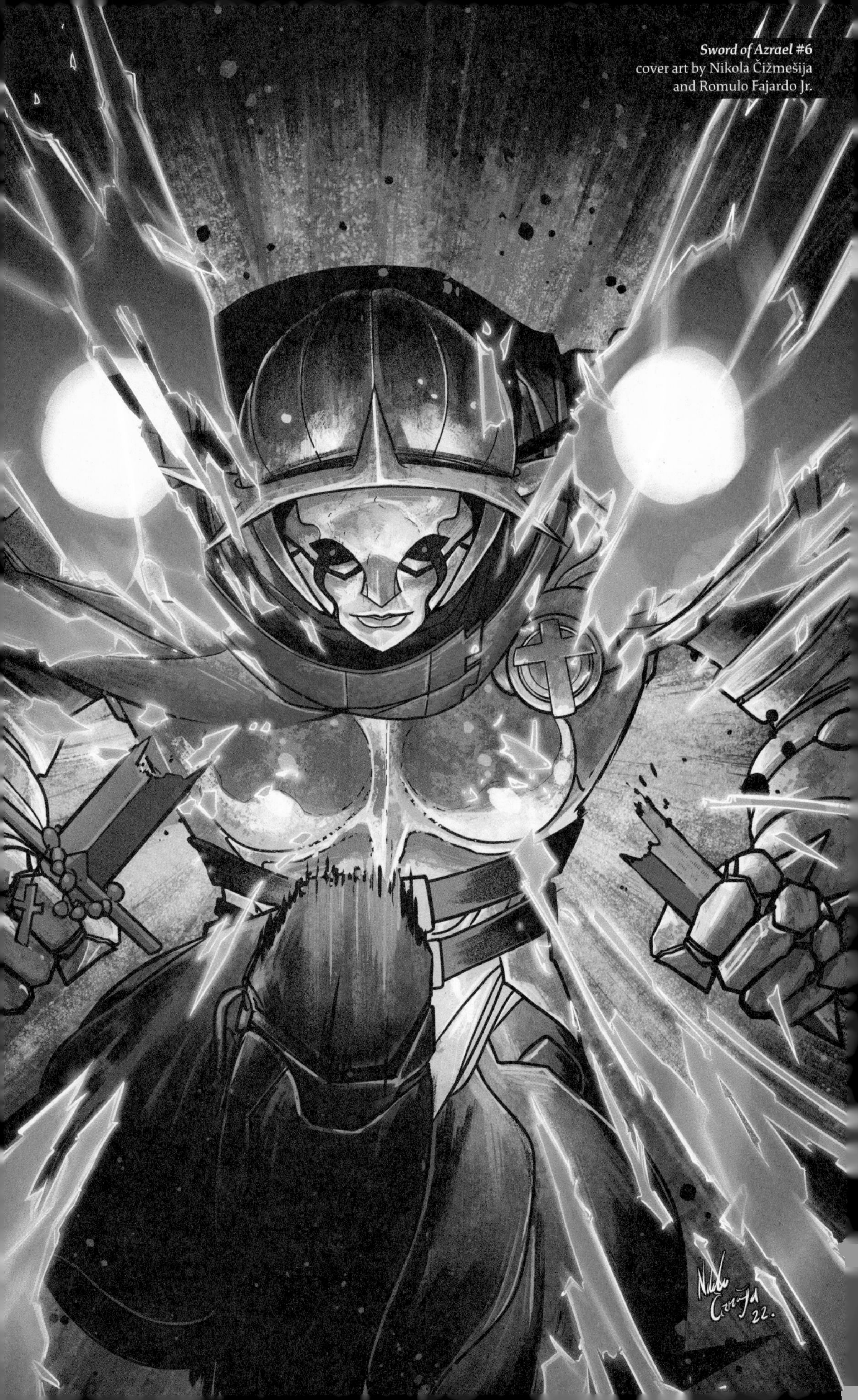

***Sword of Azrael* #6**
cover art by Nikola Čižmešija
and Romulo Fajardo Jr.

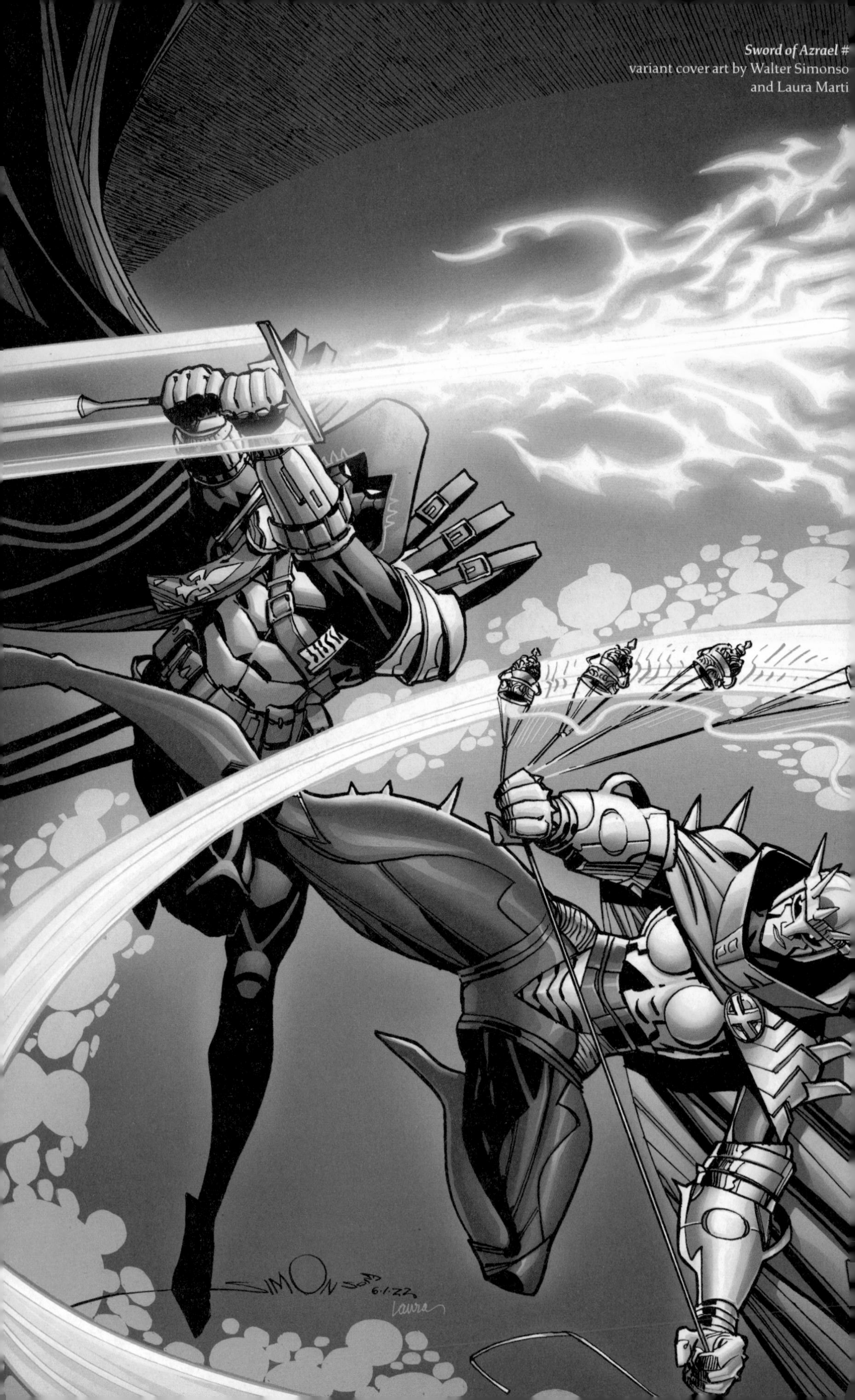

Sword of Azrael #
variant cover art by Walter Simonso
and Laura Marti

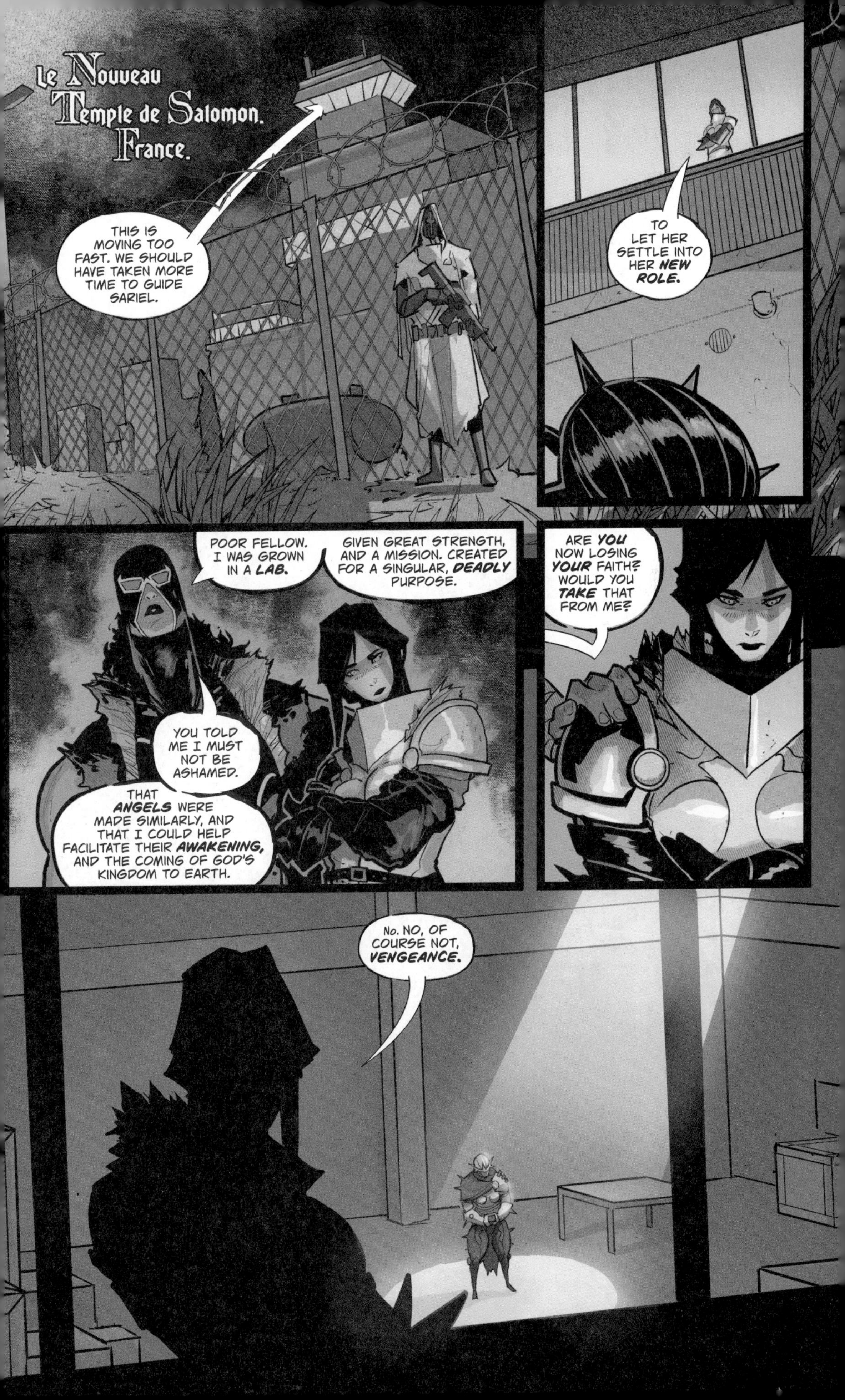
Le Nouveau Temple de Salomon. France.
THIS IS MOVING TOO FAST. WE SHOULD HAVE TAKEN MORE TIME TO GUIDE SARIEL.
TO LET HER SETTLE INTO HER NEW ROLE.
POOR FELLOW. I WAS GROWN IN A LAB.
GIVEN GREAT STRENGTH, AND A MISSION. CREATED FOR A SINGULAR, DEADLY PURPOSE.
YOU TOLD ME I MUST NOT BE ASHAMED.
THAT ANGELS WERE MADE SIMILARLY, AND THAT I COULD HELP FACILITATE THEIR AWAKENING, AND THE COMING OF GOD'S KINGDOM TO EARTH.
ARE YOU NOW LOSING YOUR FAITH? WOULD YOU TAKE THAT FROM ME?
No. NO, OF COURSE NOT, VENGEANCE.

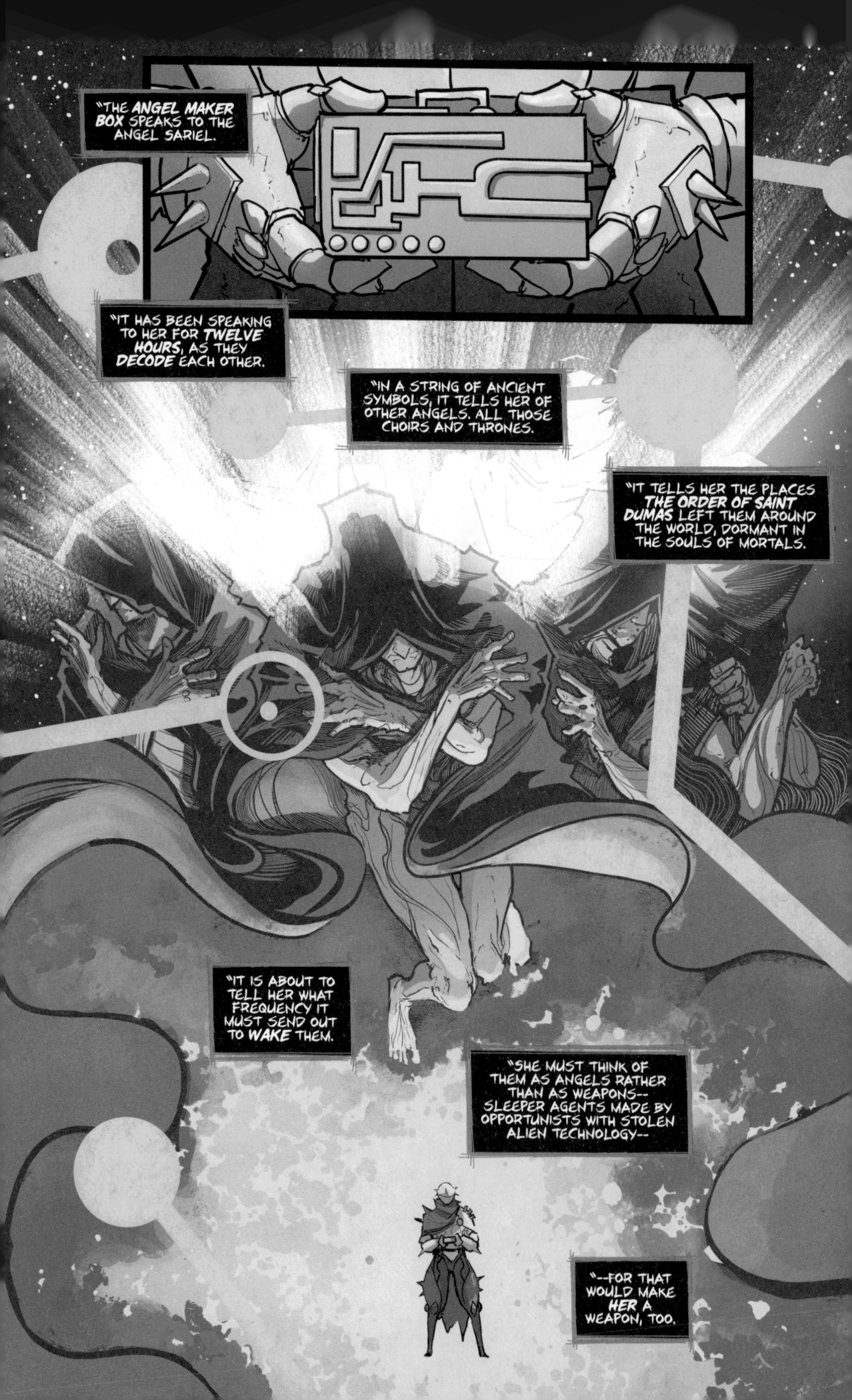
"THE ANGEL MAKER BOX SPEAKS TO THE ANGEL SARIEL.
"IT HAS BEEN SPEAKING TO HER FOR TWELVE HOURS, AS THEY DECODE EACH OTHER.
"IN A STRING OF ANCIENT SYMBOLS, IT TELLS HER OF OTHER ANGELS. ALL THOSE CHOIRS AND THRONES.
"IT TELLS HER THE PLACES THE ORDER OF SAINT DUMAS LEFT THEM AROUND THE WORLD, DORMANT IN THE SOULS OF MORTALS.
"IT IS ABOUT TO TELL HER WHAT FREQUENCY IT MUST SEND OUT TO WAKE THEM.
"SHE MUST THINK OF THEM AS ANGELS RATHER THAN AS WEAPONS-- SLEEPER AGENTS MADE BY OPPORTUNISTS WITH STOLEN ALIEN TECHNOLOGY--
"--FOR THAT WOULD MAKE HER A WEAPON, TOO.

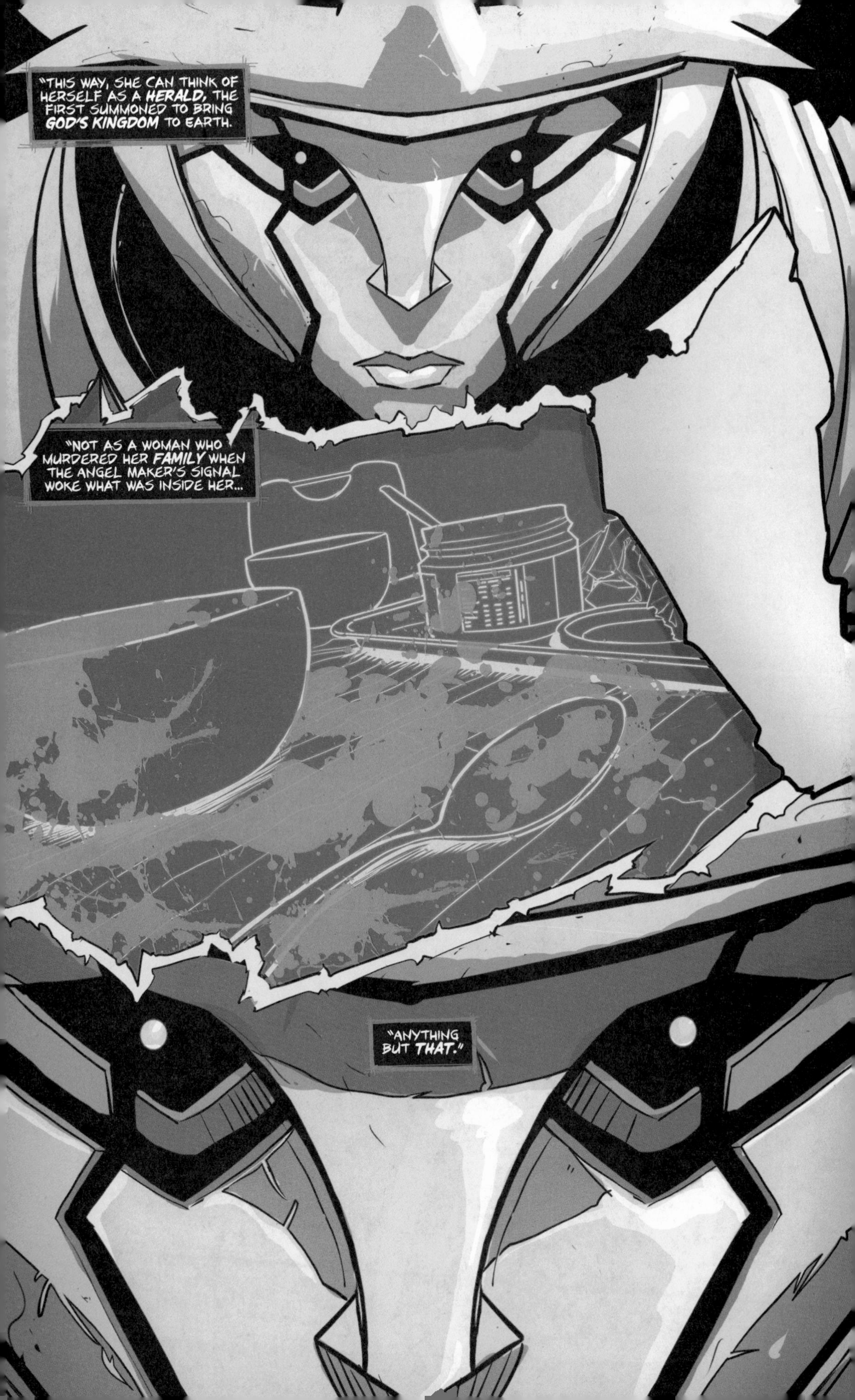
"THIS WAY, SHE CAN THINK OF HERSELF AS A HERALD, THE FIRST SUMMONED TO BRING GOD'S KINGDOM TO EARTH.
"NOT AS A WOMAN WHO MURDERED HER FAMILY WHEN THE ANGEL MAKER'S SIGNAL WOKE WHAT WAS INSIDE HER...
"ANYTHING BUT THAT."

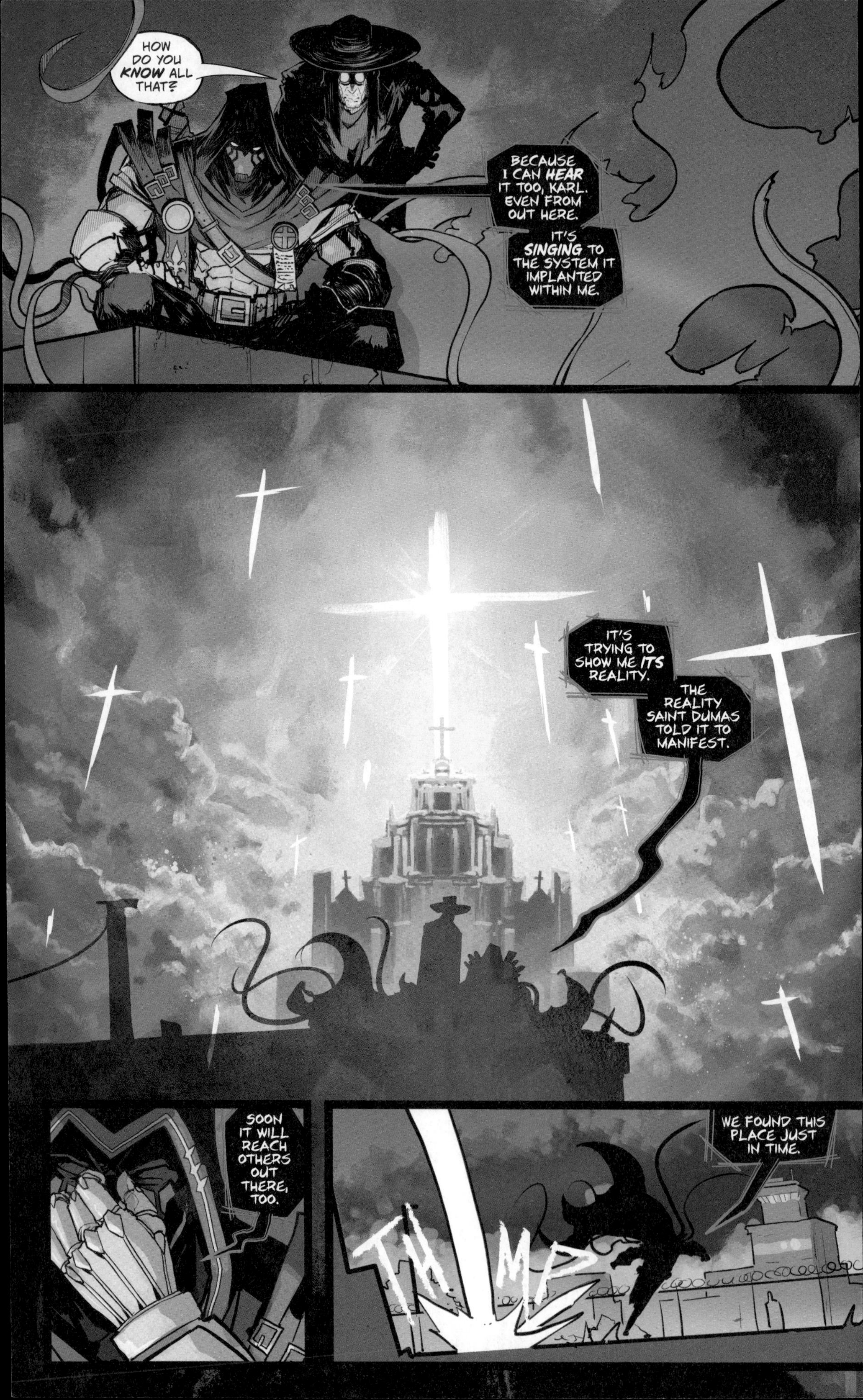
HOW DO YOU KNOW ALL THAT?
BECAUSE I CAN HEAR IT TOO, KARL. EVEN FROM OUT HERE.
IT'S SINGING TO THE SYSTEM IT IMPLANTED WITHIN ME.
IT'S TRYING TO SHOW ME ITS REALITY.
THE REALITY SAINT DUMAS TOLD IT TO MANIFEST.
SOON IT WILL REACH OTHERS OUT THERE, TOO.
WE FOUND THIS PLACE JUST IN TIME.
THUMP

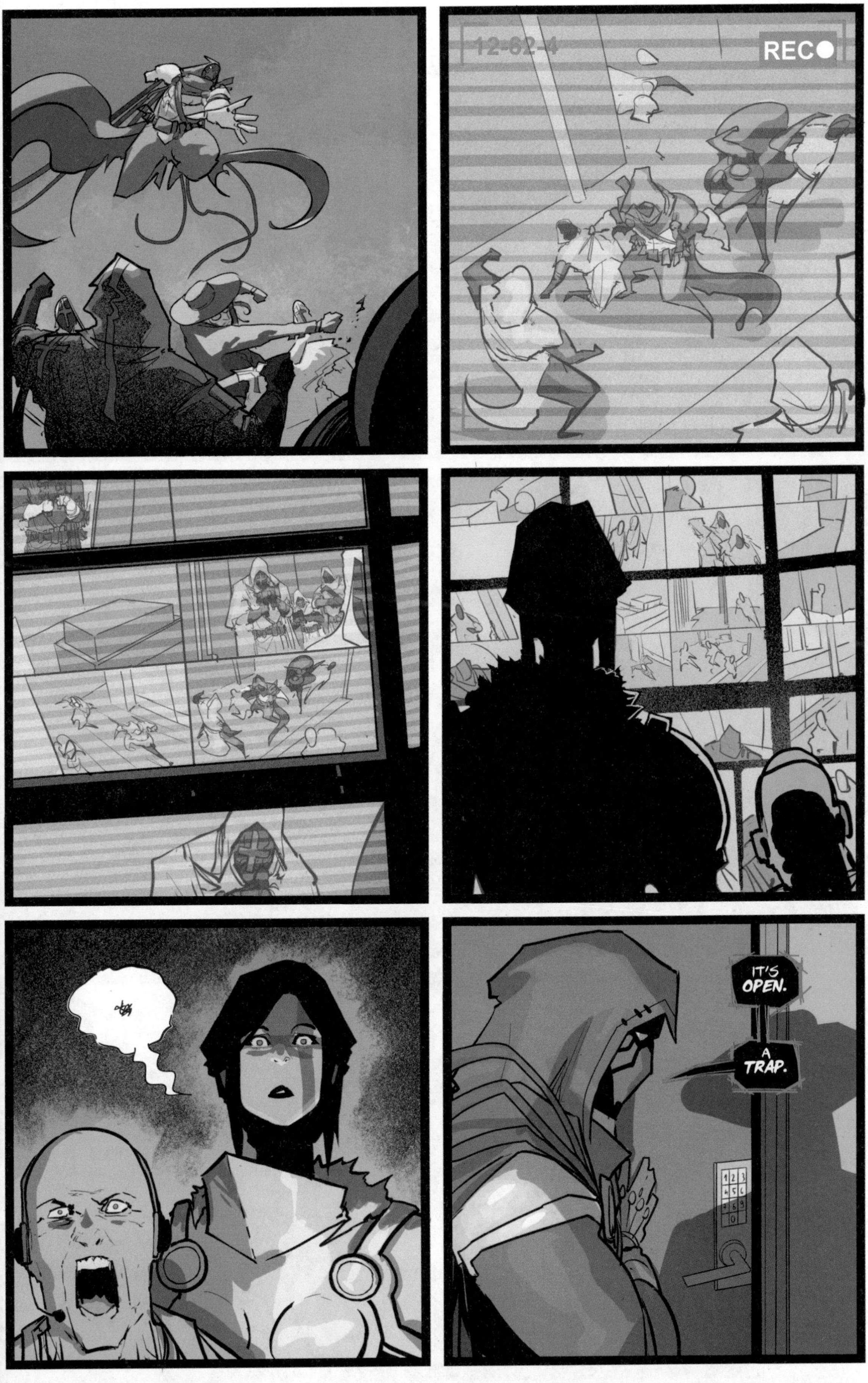
12-62-4
REC
IT'S OPEN.
A TRAP.

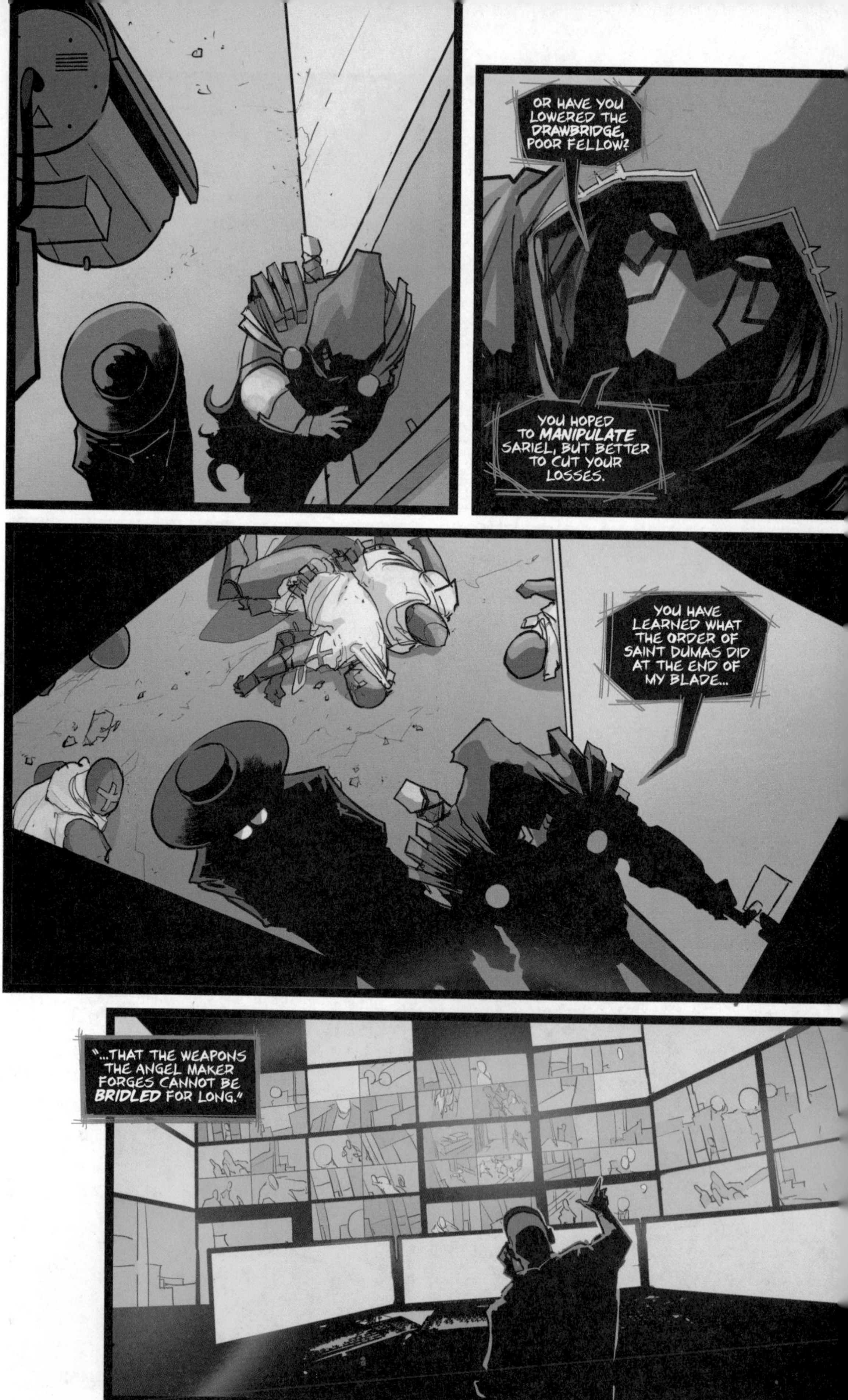
OR HAVE YOU LOWERED THE DRAWBRIDGE, POOR FELLOW?
YOU HOPED TO MANIPULATE SARIEL, BUT BETTER TO CUT YOUR LOSSES.
YOU HAVE LEARNED WHAT THE ORDER OF SAINT DUMAS DID AT THE END OF MY BLADE...
"...THAT THE WEAPONS THE ANGEL MAKER FORGES CANNOT BE BRIDLED FOR LONG."

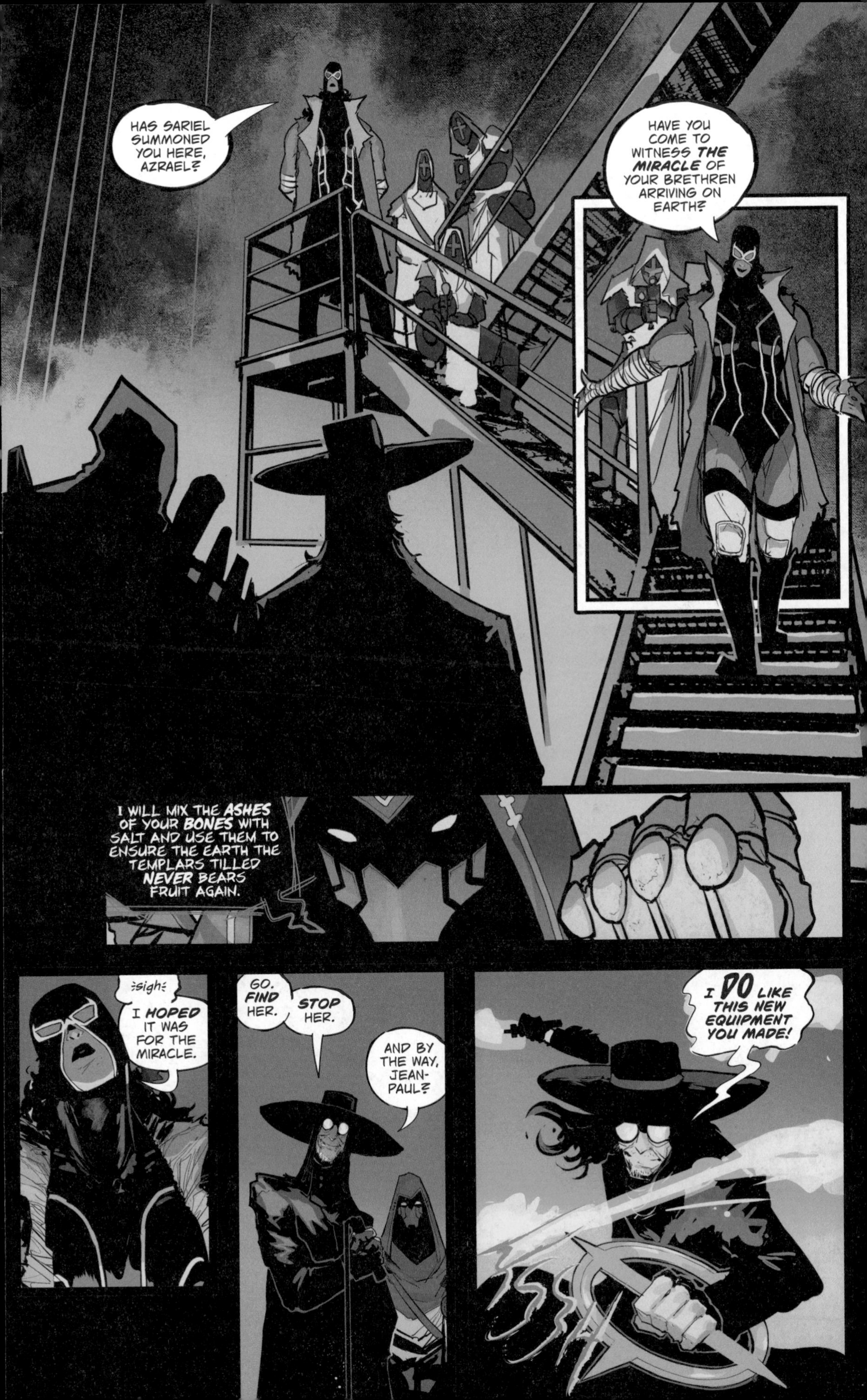
HAS SARIEL SUMMONED YOU HERE, AZRAEL?
HAVE YOU COME TO WITNESS THE MIRACLE OF YOUR BRETHREN ARRIVING ON EARTH?
I WILL MIX THE ASHES OF YOUR BONES WITH SALT AND USE THEM TO ENSURE THE EARTH THE TEMPLARS TILLED NEVER BEARS FRUIT AGAIN.
sigh
I HOPED IT WAS FOR THE MIRACLE.
GO. FIND HER.
STOP HER.
AND BY THE WAY, JEAN-PAUL?
I DO LIKE THIS NEW EQUIPMENT YOU MADE!
TSSSH

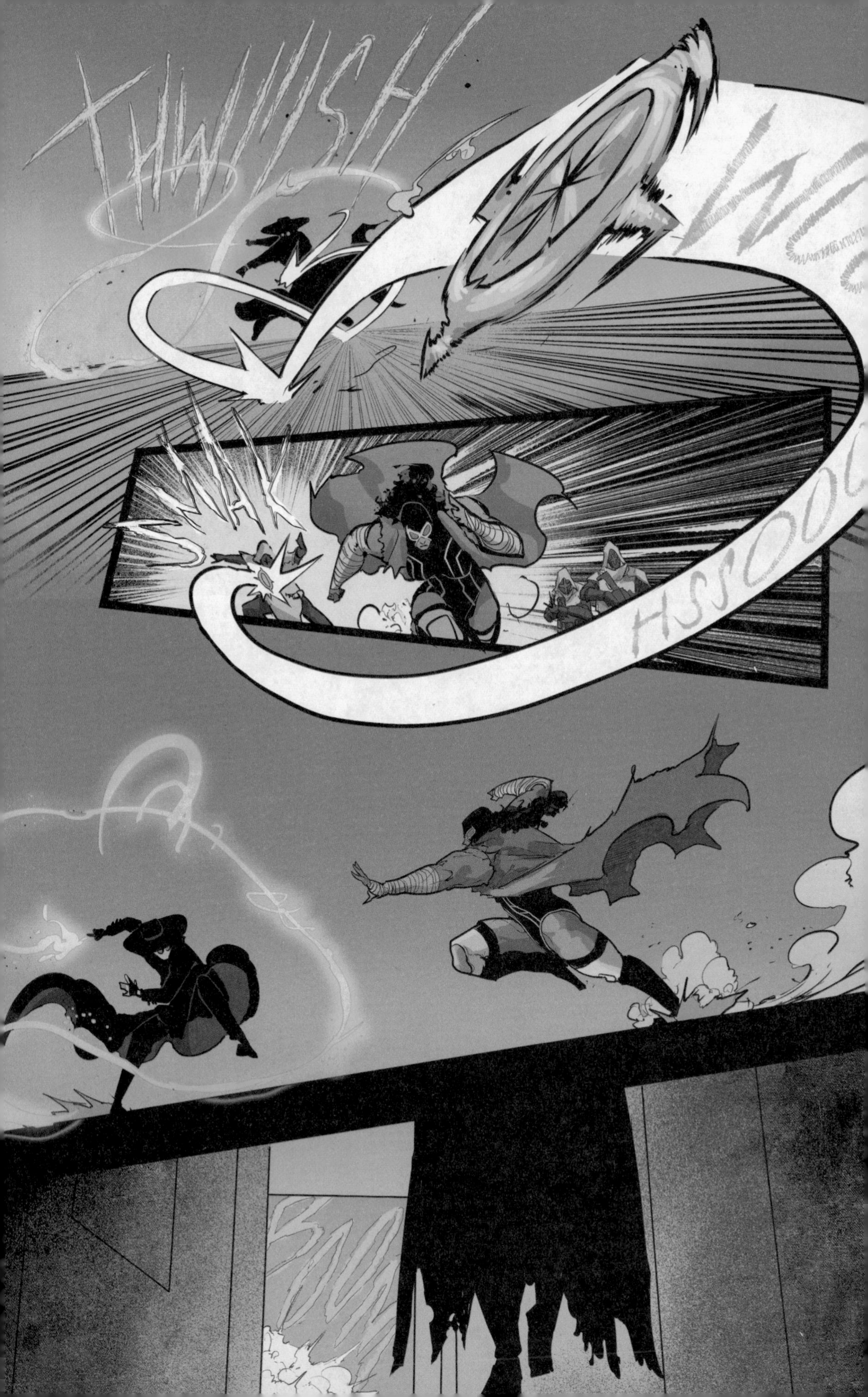
THWIISH!
WAK
HSSOO

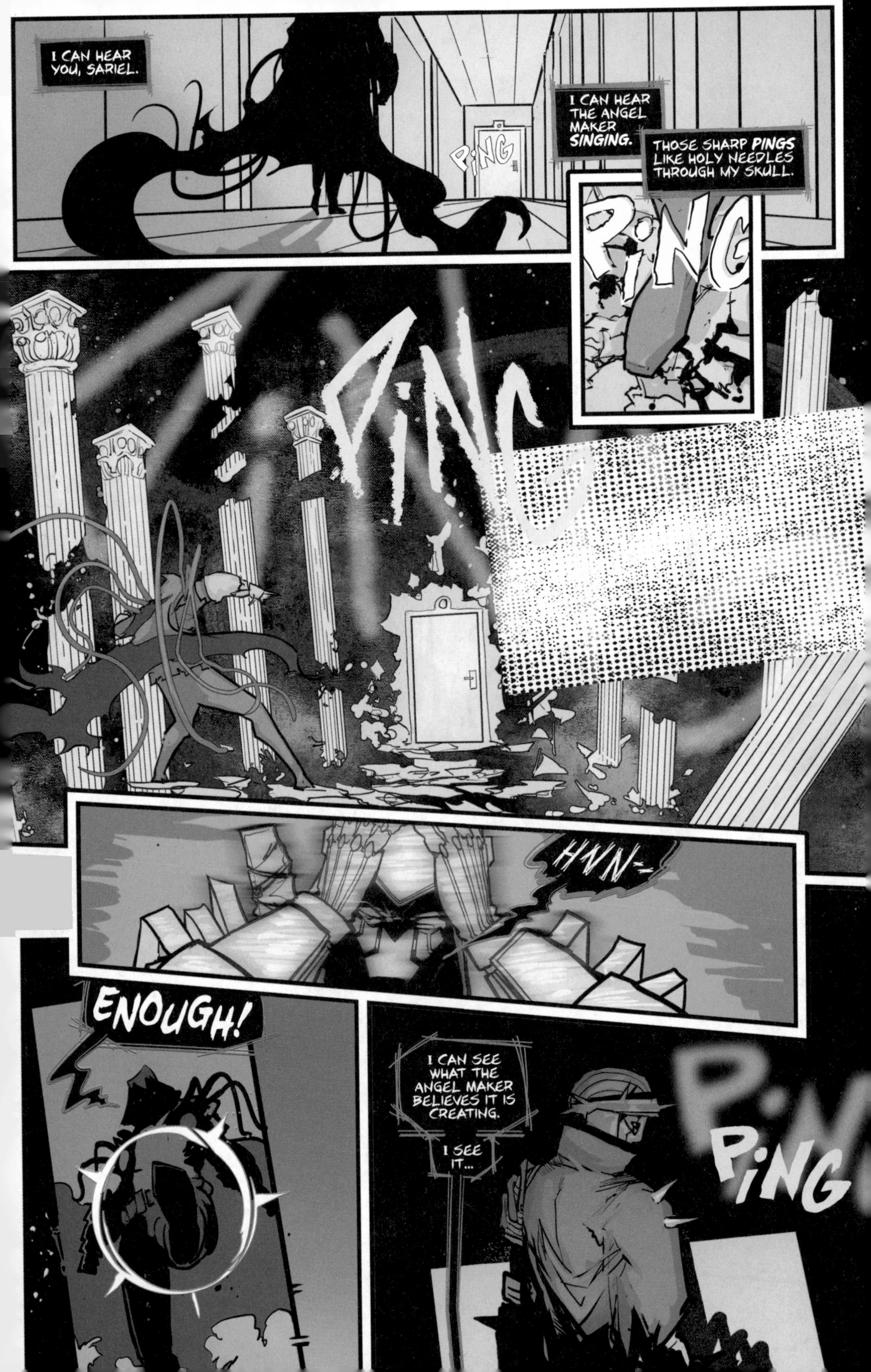

I CAN HEAR YOU, SARIEL.
PING
I CAN HEAR THE ANGEL MAKER SINGING.
THOSE SHARP PINGS LIKE HOLY NEEDLES THROUGH MY SKULL.
PING
PING
HNN-
ENOUGH!
I CAN SEE WHAT THE ANGEL MAKER BELIEVES IT IS CREATING.
I SEE IT...
PING

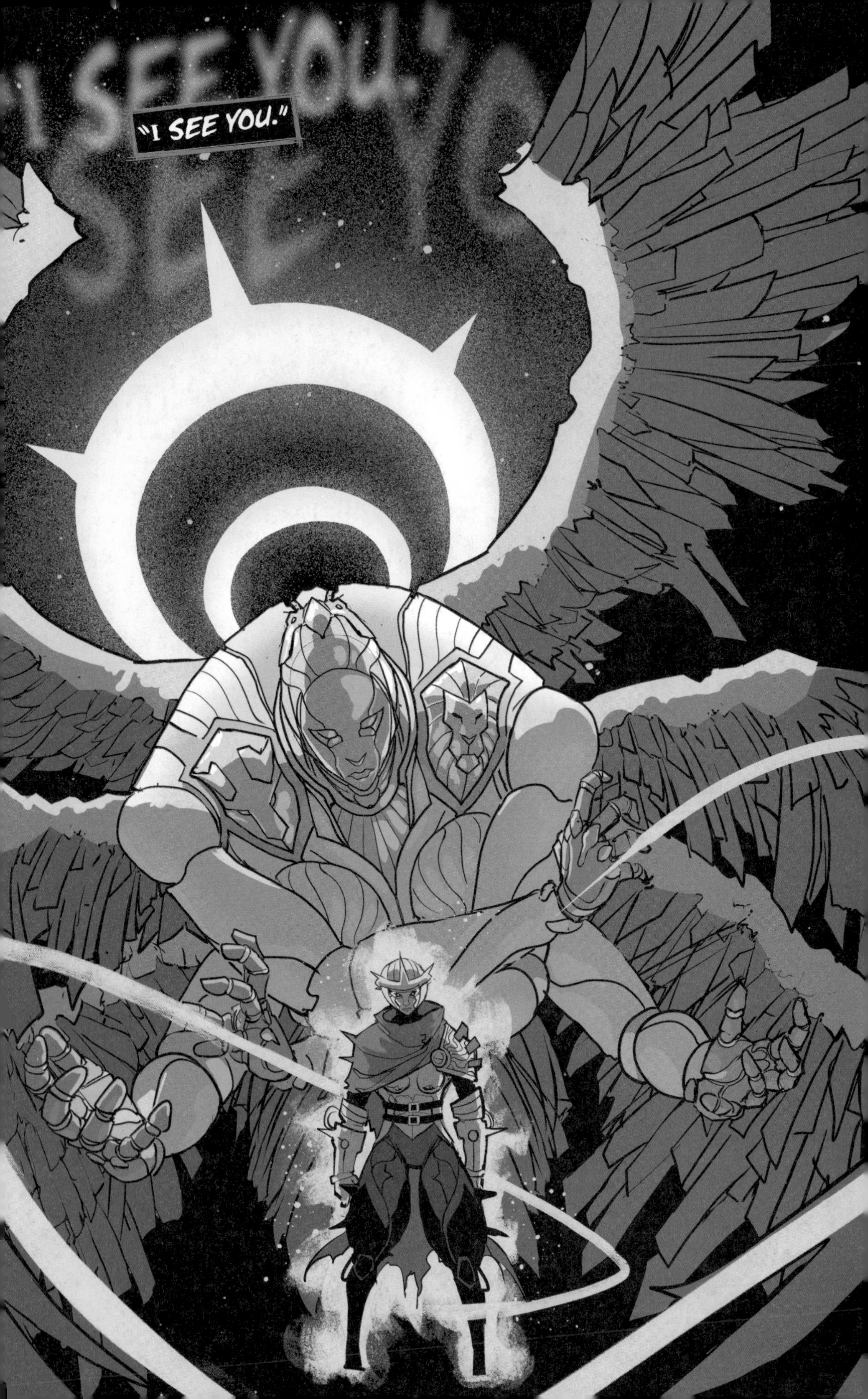
"I SEE YOU."

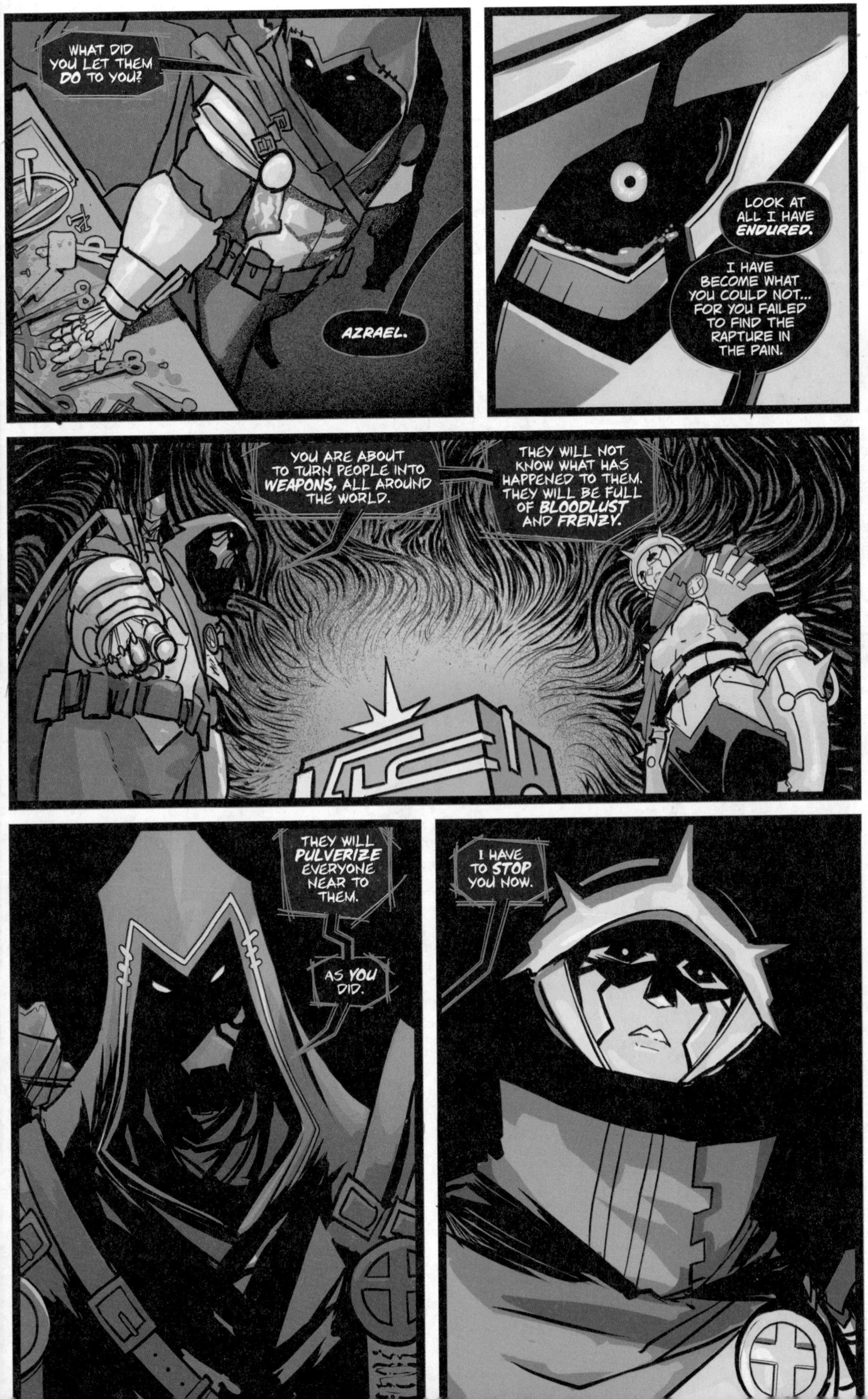
WHAT DID YOU LET THEM DO TO YOU?
AZRAEL.
LOOK AT ALL I HAVE ENDURED.
I HAVE BECOME WHAT YOU COULD NOT... FOR YOU FAILED TO FIND THE RAPTURE IN THE PAIN.
YOU ARE ABOUT TO TURN PEOPLE INTO WEAPONS, ALL AROUND THE WORLD.
THEY WILL NOT KNOW WHAT HAS HAPPENED TO THEM. THEY WILL BE FULL OF BLOODLUST AND FRENZY.
THEY WILL PULVERIZE EVERYONE NEAR TO THEM.
AS YOU DID.
I HAVE TO STOP YOU NOW.

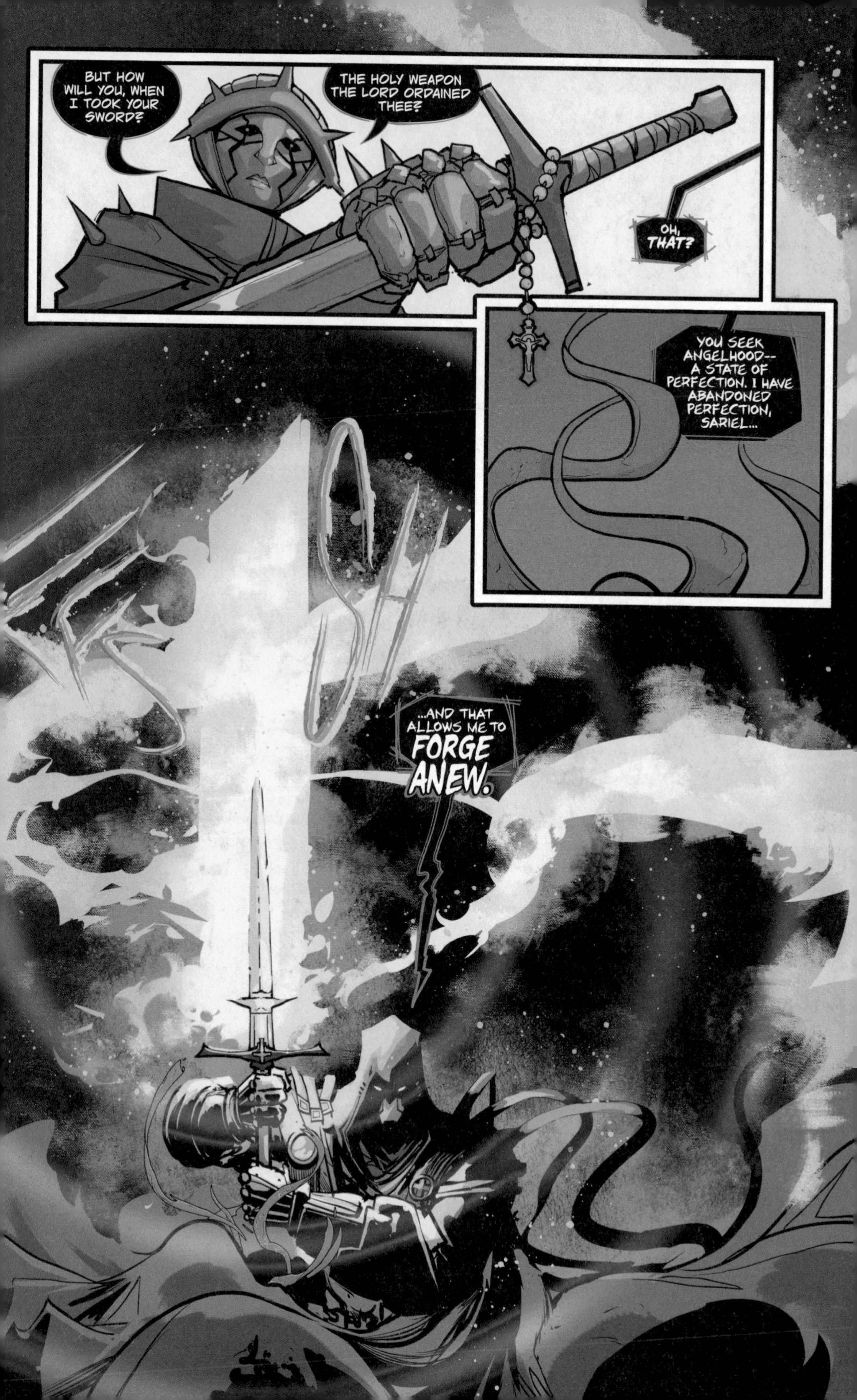
BUT HOW WILL YOU, WHEN I TOOK YOUR SWORD?
THE HOLY WEAPON THE LORD ORDAINED THEE?
OH, THAT?
YOU SEEK ANGELHOOD-- A STATE OF PERFECTION. I HAVE ABANDONED PERFECTION, SARIEL...
...AND THAT ALLOWS ME TO FORGE ANEW.

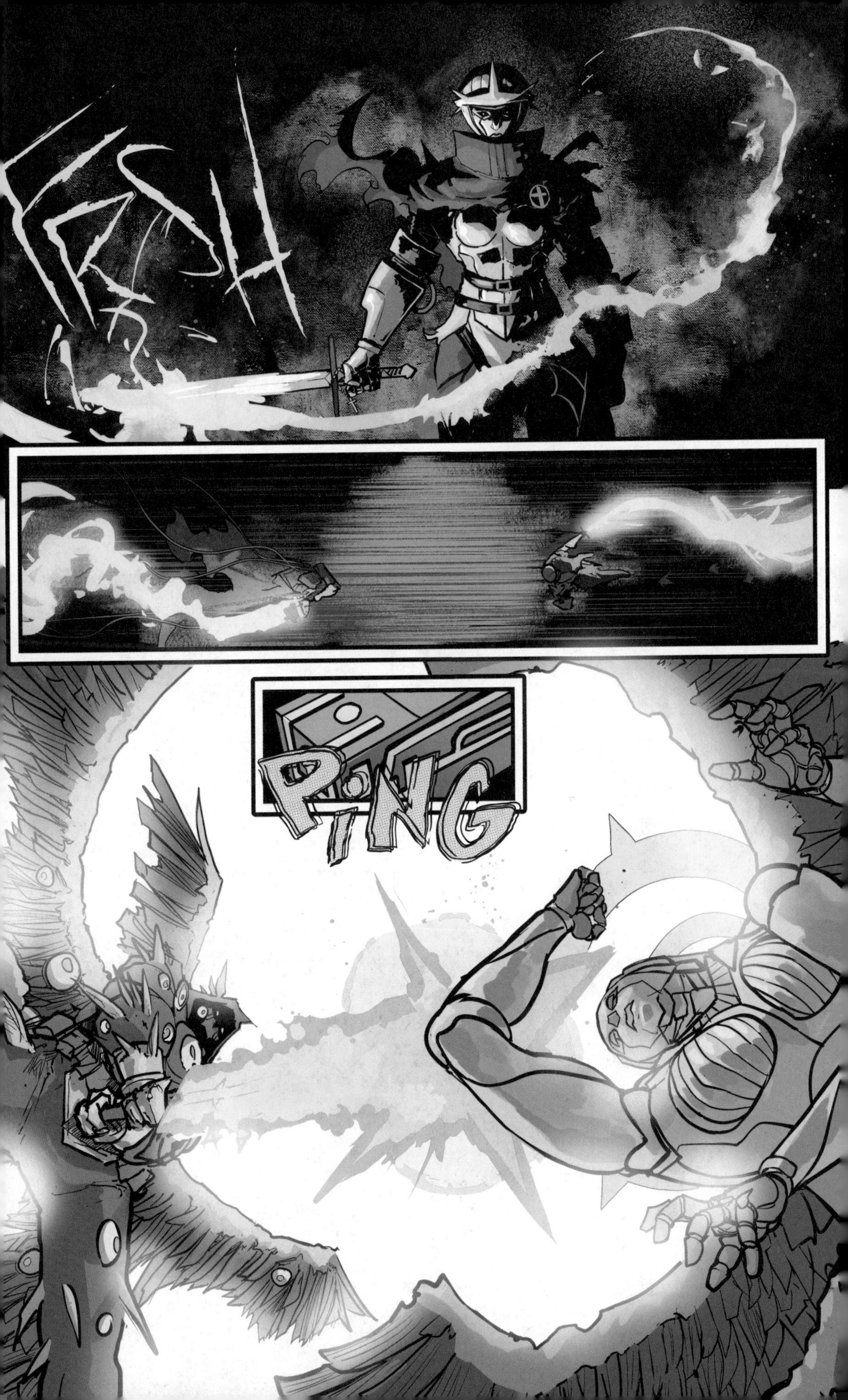
PING

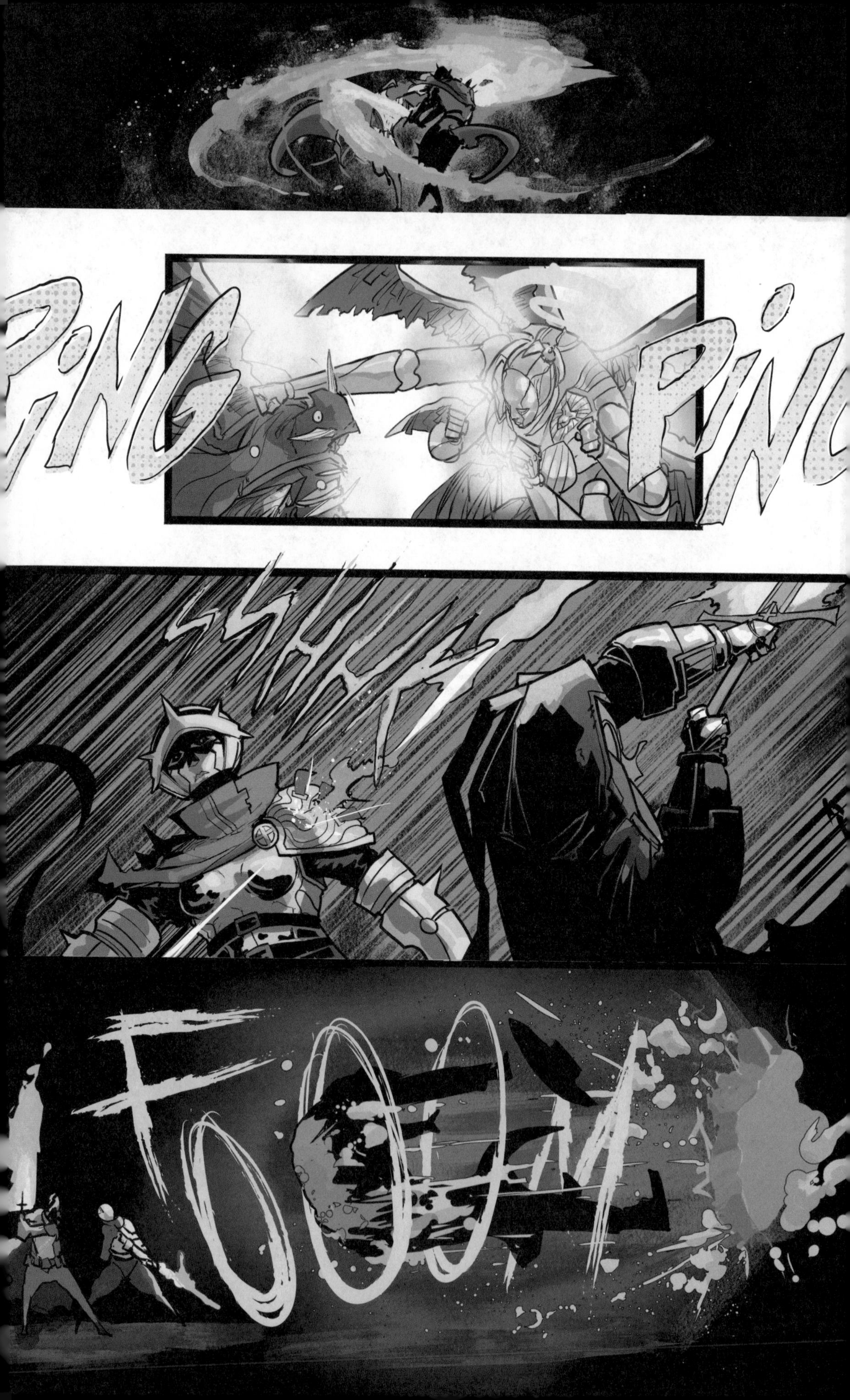
PING
PIN
SSHHK
FOOOM

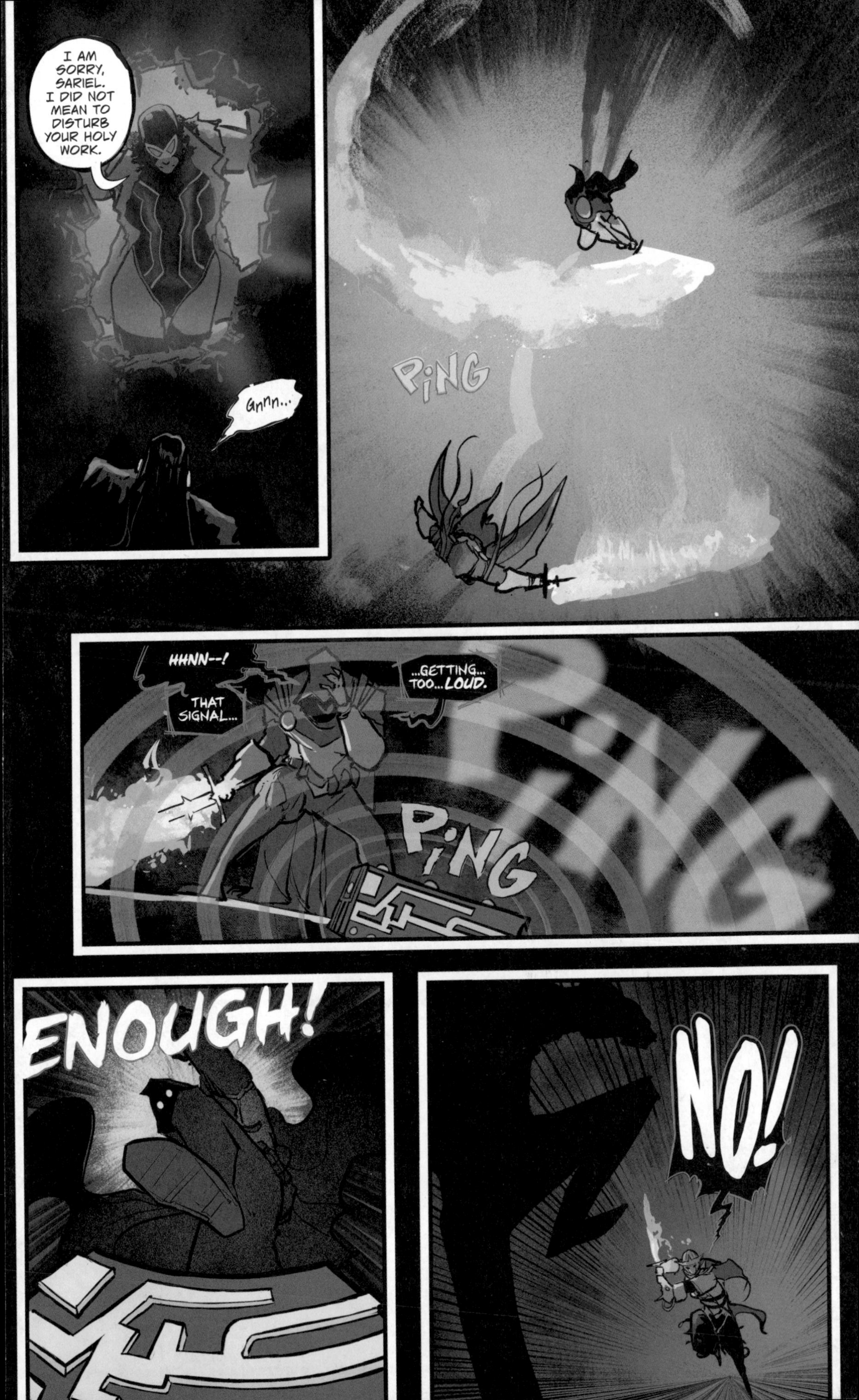
I AM SORRY, SARIEL. I DID NOT MEAN TO DISTURB YOUR HOLY WORK.
Gnnn...
PiNG
HHNN--!
THAT SIGNAL...
...GETTING... TOO...LOUD.
PiNG
PiNG
ENOUGH!
NO!

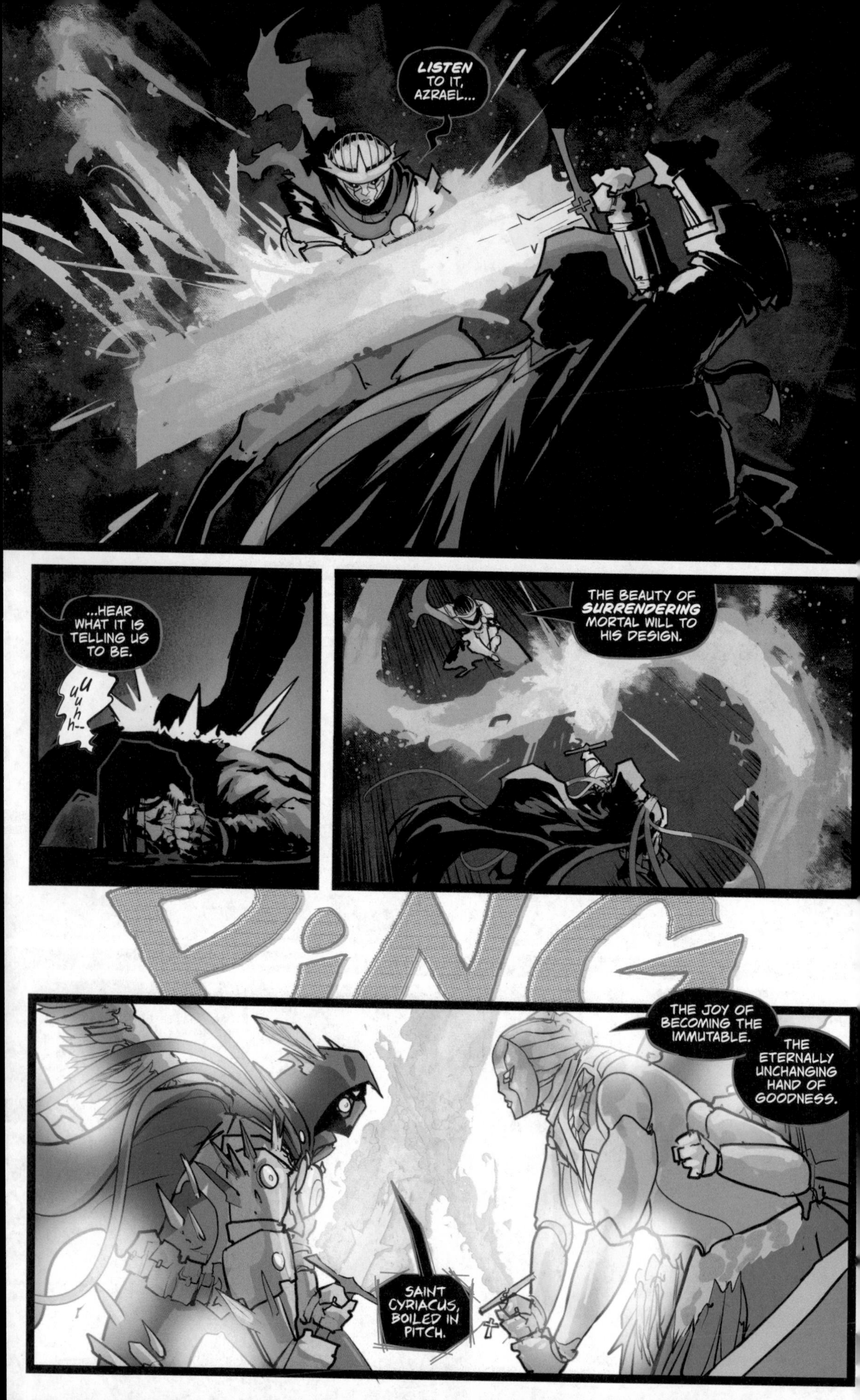

LISTEN TO IT, AZRAEL...
...HEAR WHAT IT IS TELLING US TO BE.
Uuuhh--
THE BEAUTY OF SURRENDERING MORTAL WILL TO HIS DESIGN.
PiNG
THE JOY OF BECOMING THE IMMUTABLE.
THE ETERNALLY UNCHANGING HAND OF GOODNESS.
SAINT CYRIACUS, BOILED IN PITCH.

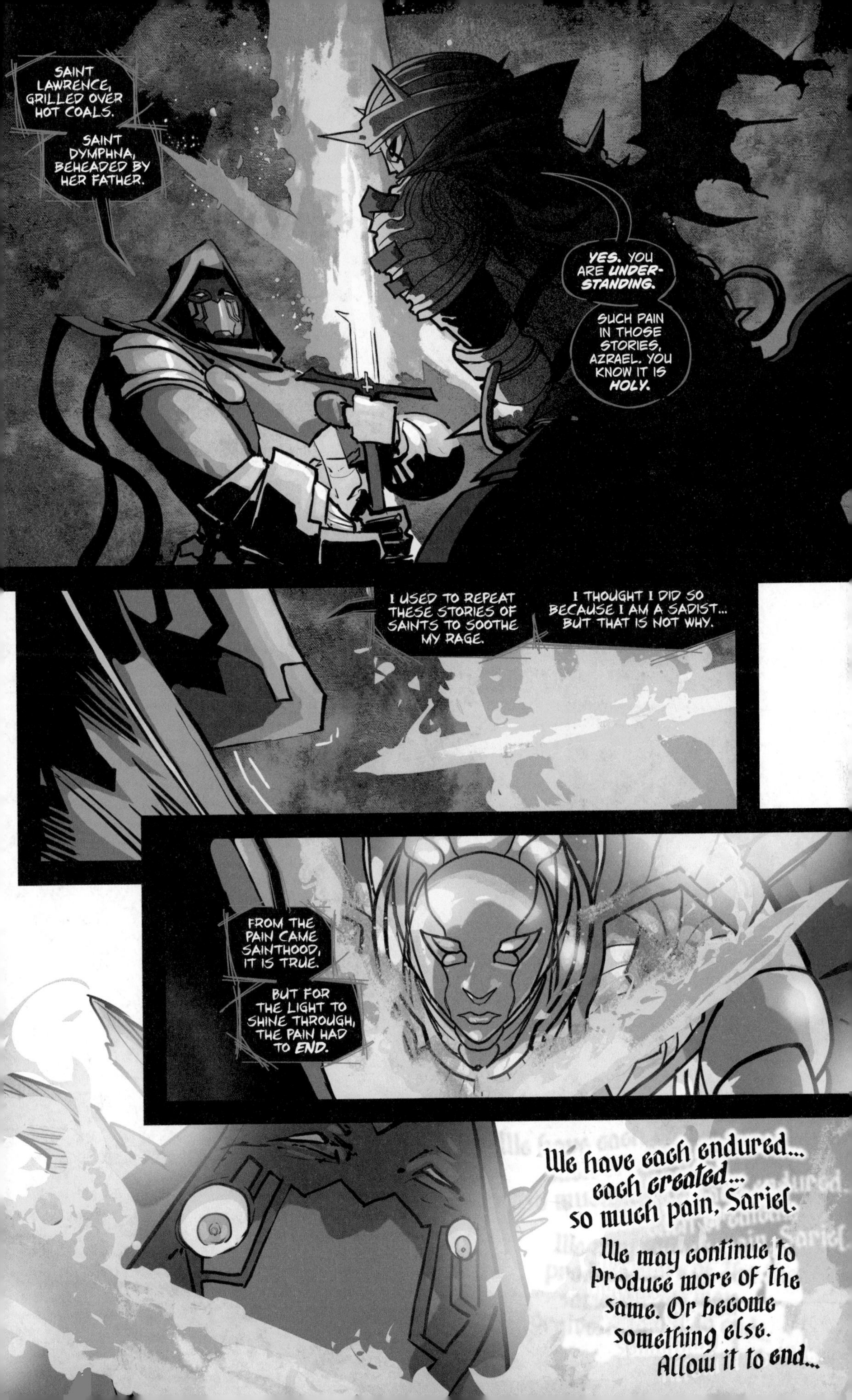
SAINT LAWRENCE, GRILLED OVER HOT COALS.
SAINT DYMPHNA, BEHEADED BY HER FATHER.
YES. YOU ARE UNDER-STANDING.
SUCH PAIN IN THOSE STORIES, AZRAEL. YOU KNOW IT IS HOLY.
I USED TO REPEAT THESE STORIES OF SAINTS TO SOOTHE MY RAGE.
I THOUGHT I DID SO BECAUSE I AM A SADIST... BUT THAT IS NOT WHY.
FROM THE PAIN CAME SAINTHOOD, IT IS TRUE.
BUT FOR THE LIGHT TO SHINE THROUGH, THE PAIN HAD TO END.
We have each endured... each created... so much pain, Sariel.
We may continue to produce more of the same. Or become something else. Allow it to end...

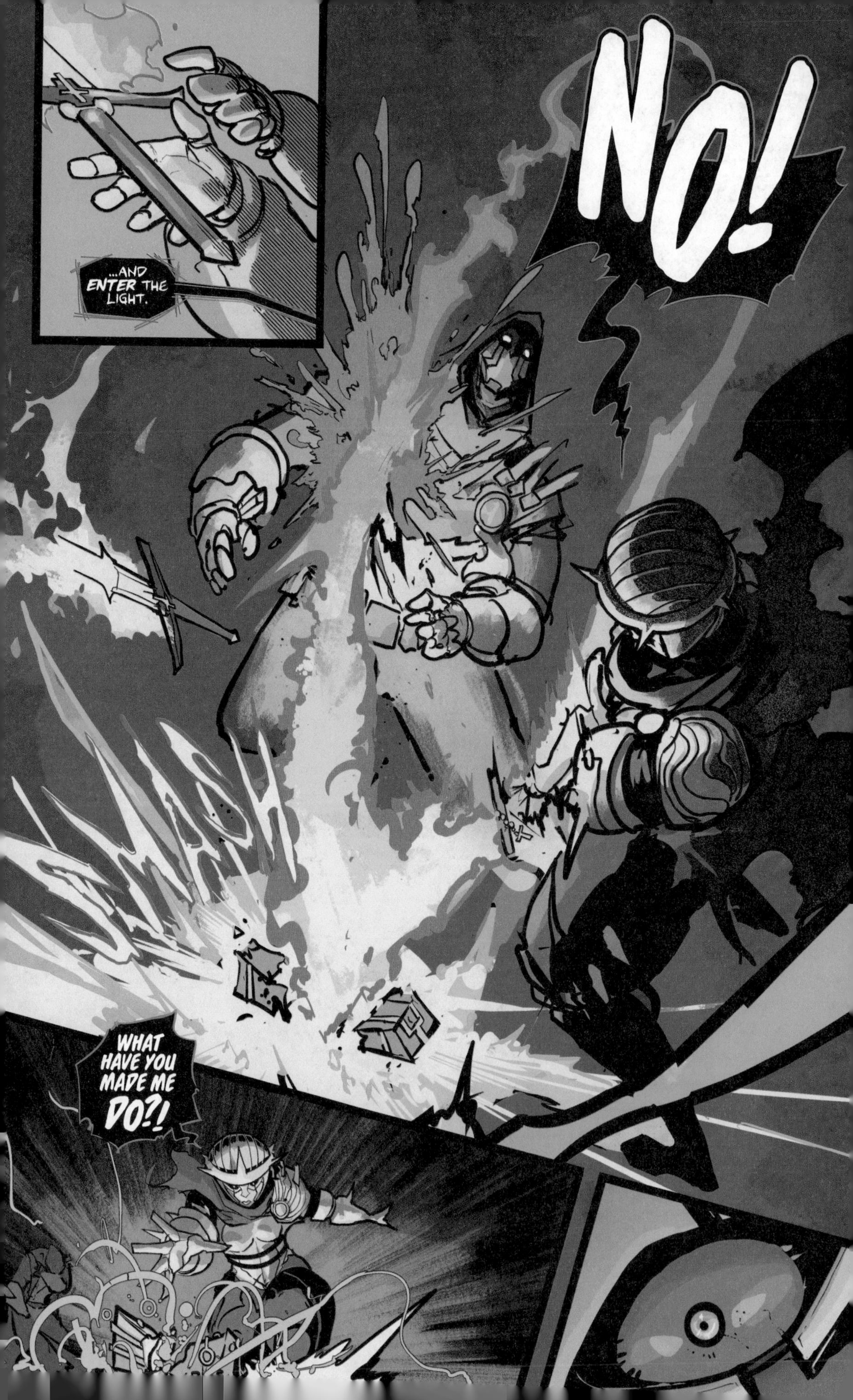
...AND ENTER THE LIGHT.
NO!
WHAT HAVE YOU MADE ME DO?!

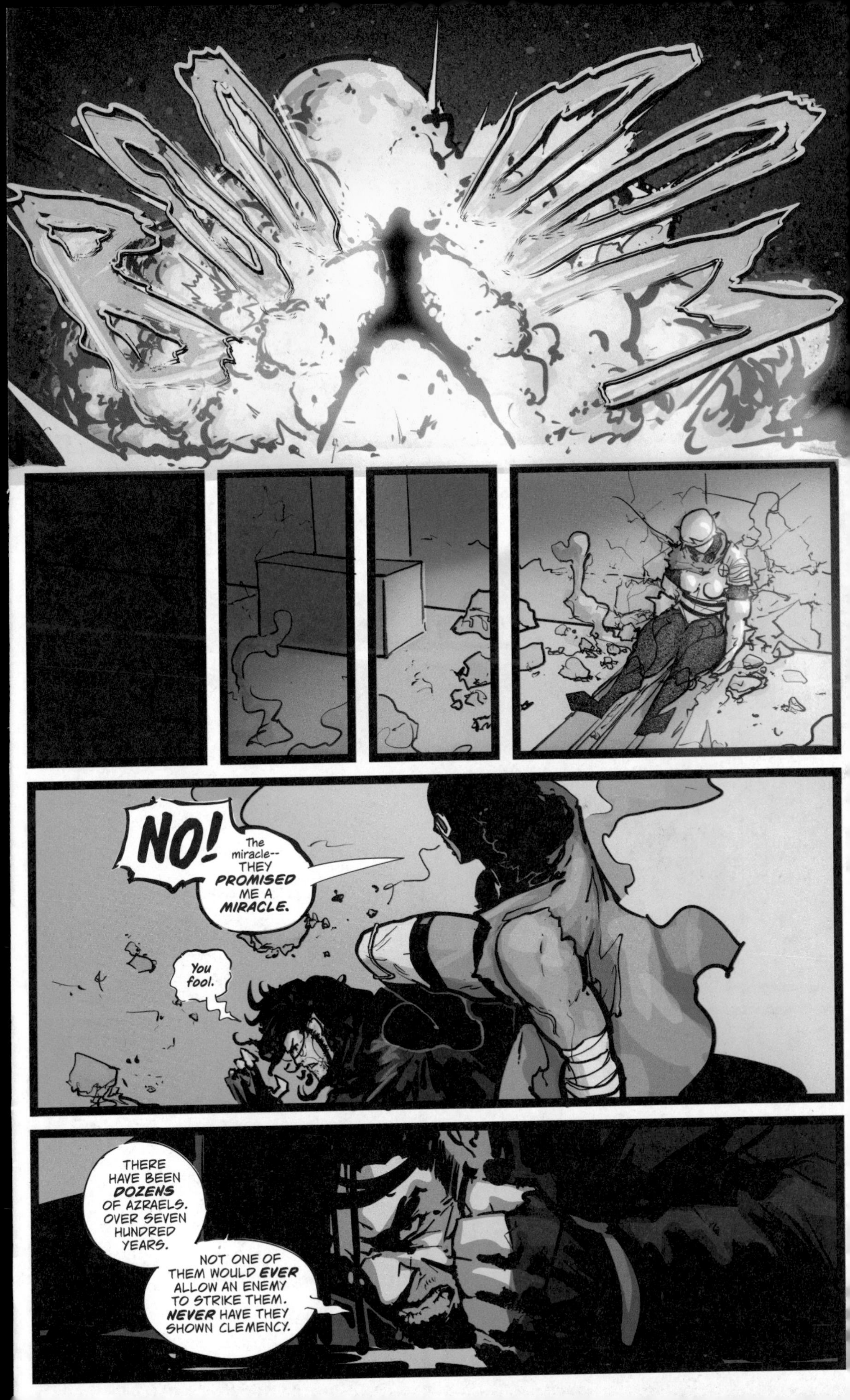
BOOOOM
NO!
The miracle-- THEY PROMISED ME A MIRACLE.
You fool.
THERE HAVE BEEN DOZENS OF AZRAELS. OVER SEVEN HUNDRED YEARS.
NOT ONE OF THEM WOULD EVER ALLOW AN ENEMY TO STRIKE THEM. NEVER HAVE THEY SHOWN CLEMENCY.

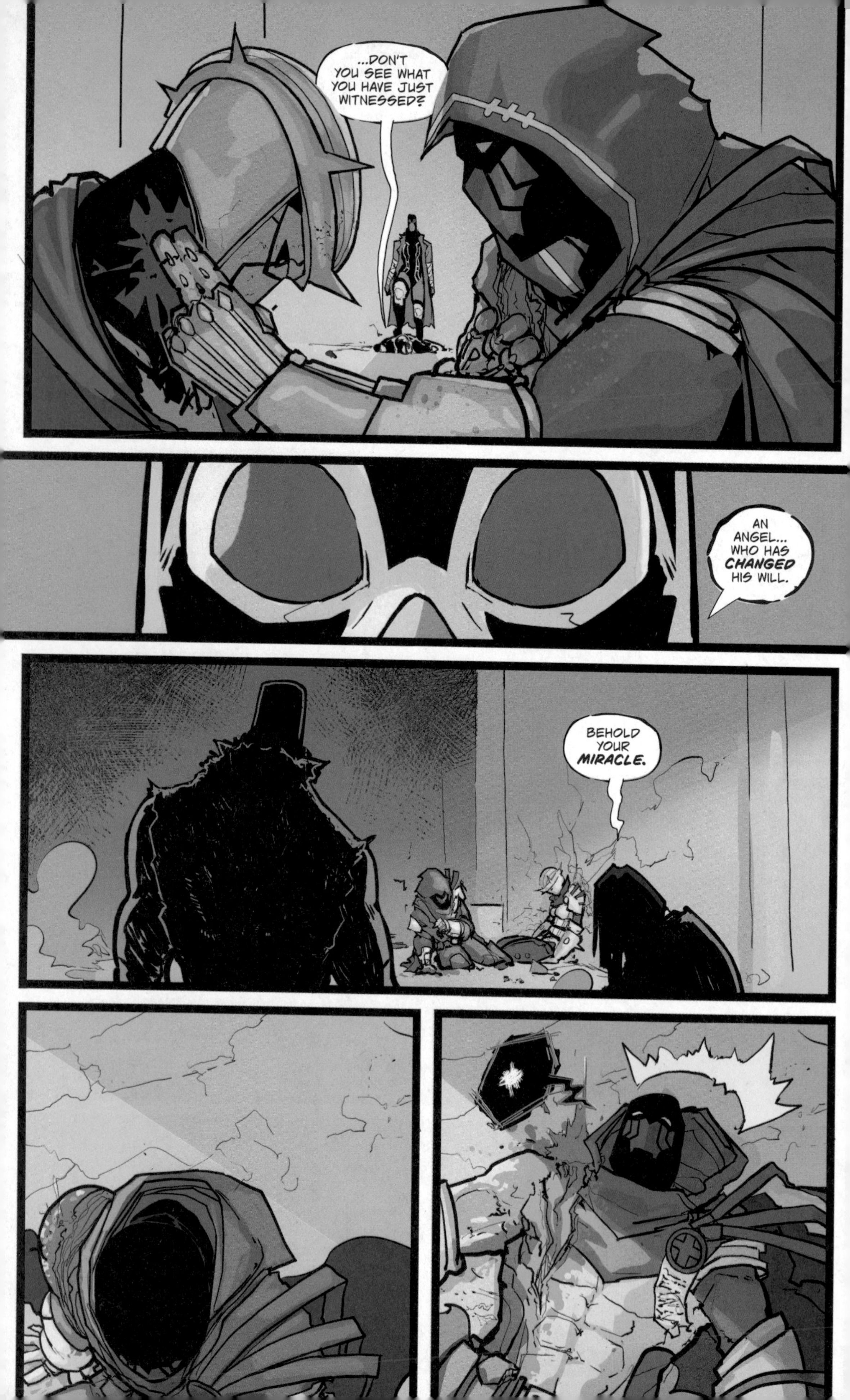
...DON'T YOU SEE WHAT YOU HAVE JUST WITNESSED?
AN ANGEL... WHO HAS **CHANGED** HIS WILL.
BEHOLD YOUR **MIRACLE.**

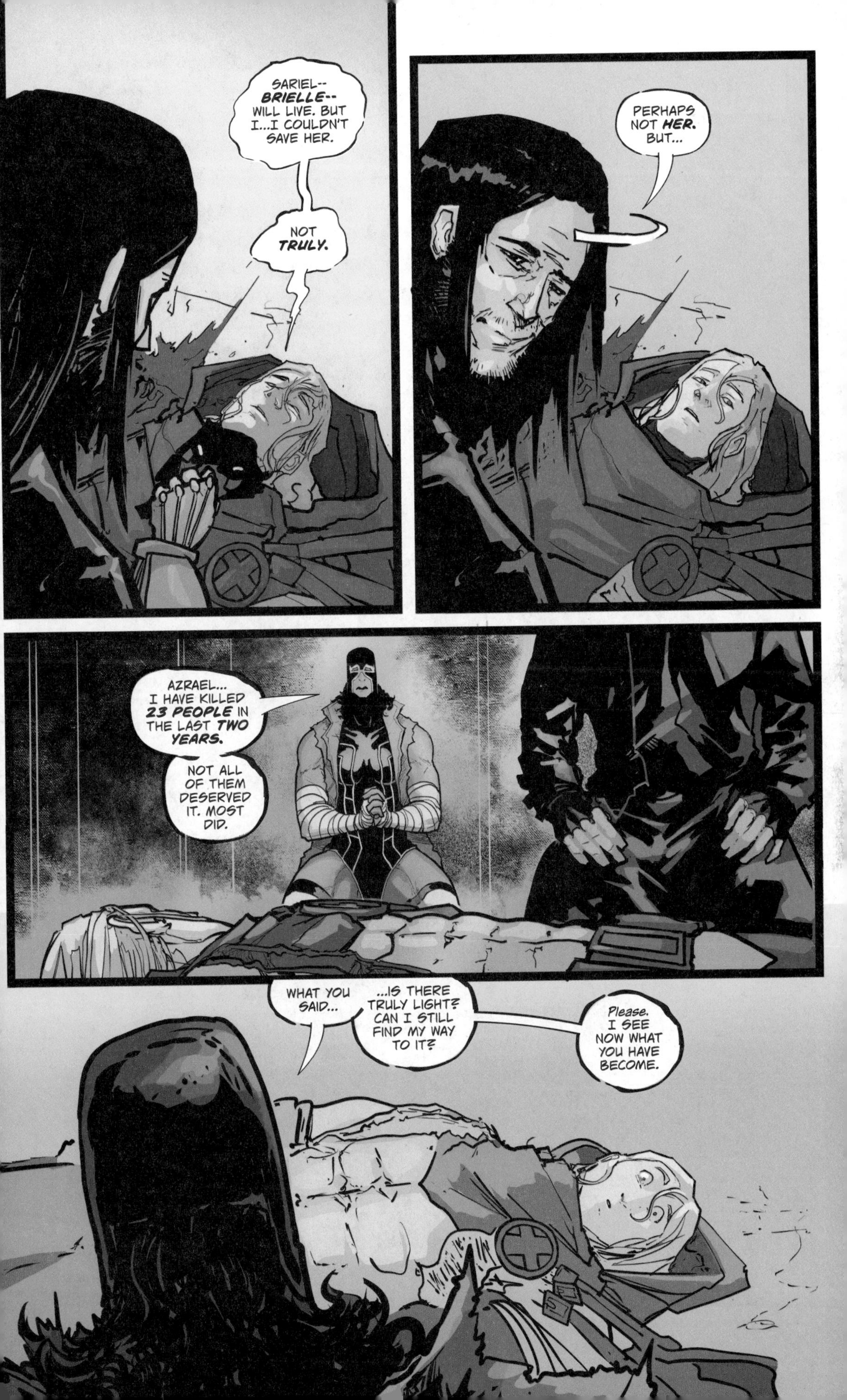
SARIEL-- BRIELLE-- WILL LIVE. BUT I...I COULDN'T SAVE HER.
NOT TRULY.
PERHAPS NOT HER. BUT...
AZRAEL... I HAVE KILLED 23 PEOPLE IN THE LAST TWO YEARS.
NOT ALL OF THEM DESERVED IT. MOST DID.
WHAT YOU SAID...
...IS THERE TRULY LIGHT? CAN I STILL FIND MY WAY TO IT?
Please. I SEE NOW WHAT YOU HAVE BECOME.

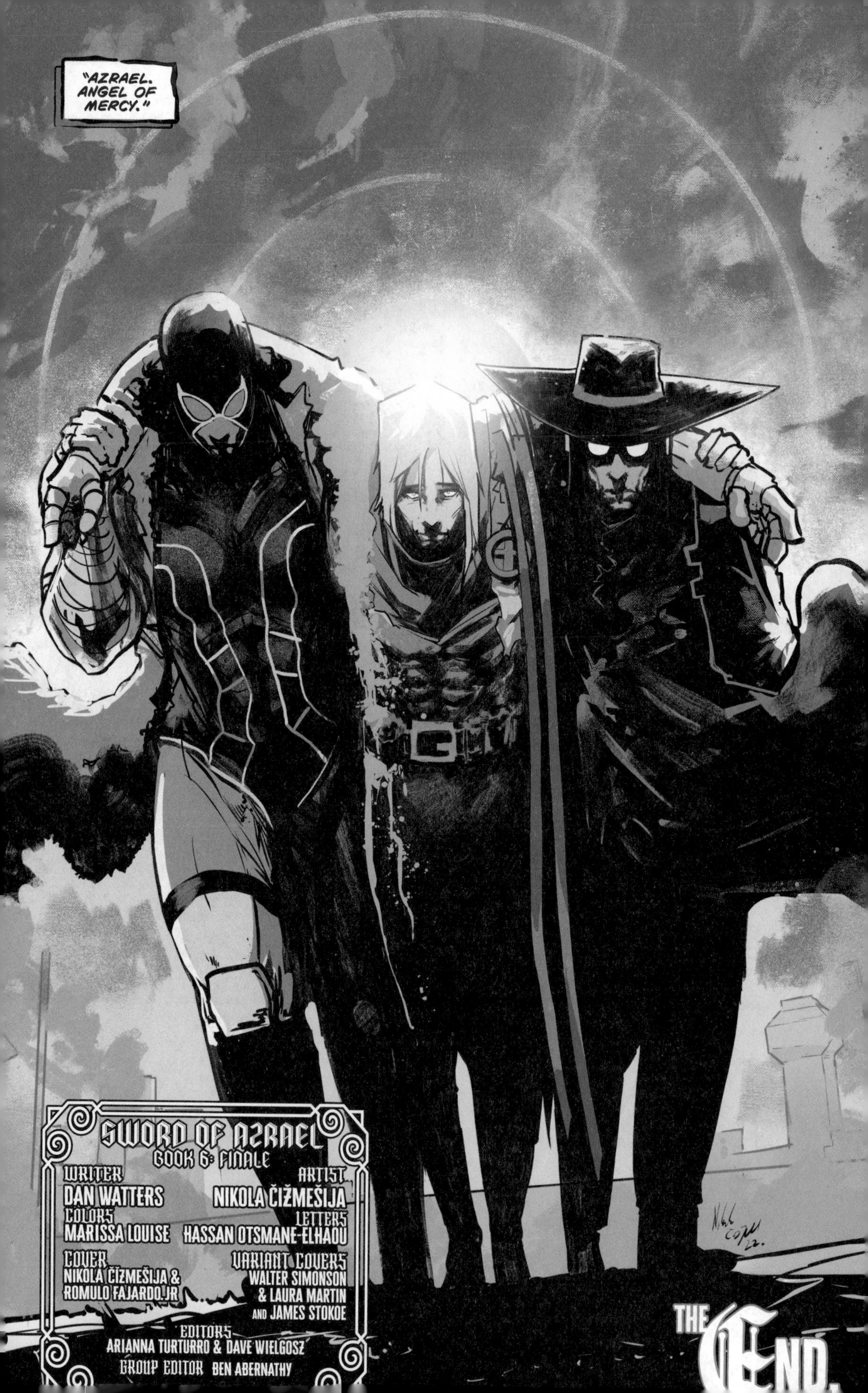
"AZRAEL. ANGEL OF MERCY."
SWORD OF AZRAEL
BOOK 6: FINALE
WRITER DAN WATTERS
ARTIST NIKOLA ČIŽMEŠIJA
COLORS MARISSA LOUISE
LETTERS HASSAN OTSMANE-ELHAOU
COVER NIKOLA ČIŽMEŠIJA & ROMULO FAJARDO JR
VARIANT COVERS WALTER SIMONSON & LAURA MARTIN AND JAMES STOKOE
EDITORS ARIANNA TURTURRO & DAVE WIELGOSZ
GROUP EDITOR BEN ABERNATHY
THE END.

VARIANT COVER
AND DESIGN GALLERY

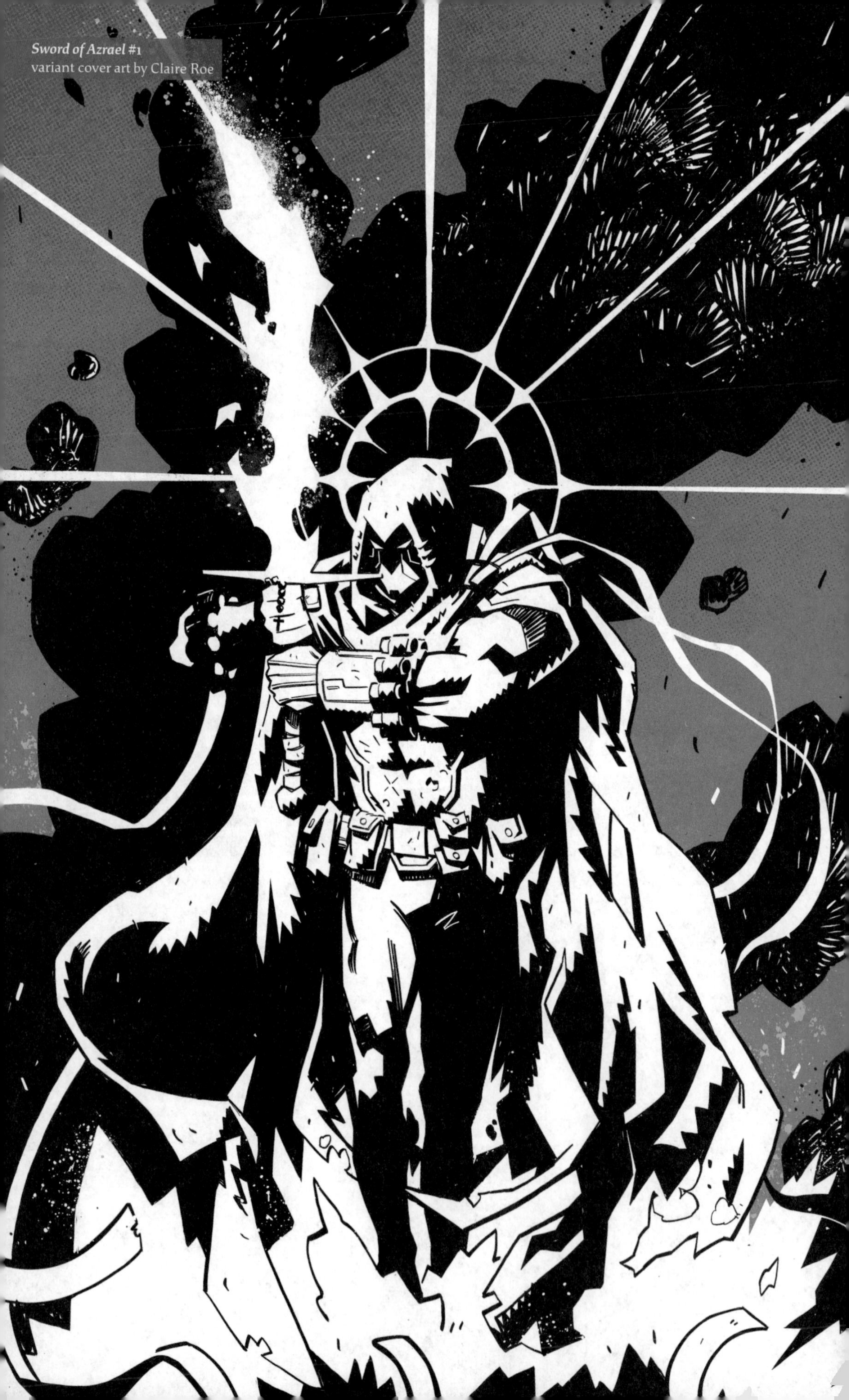

Sword of Azrael #1
variant cover art by Claire Roe

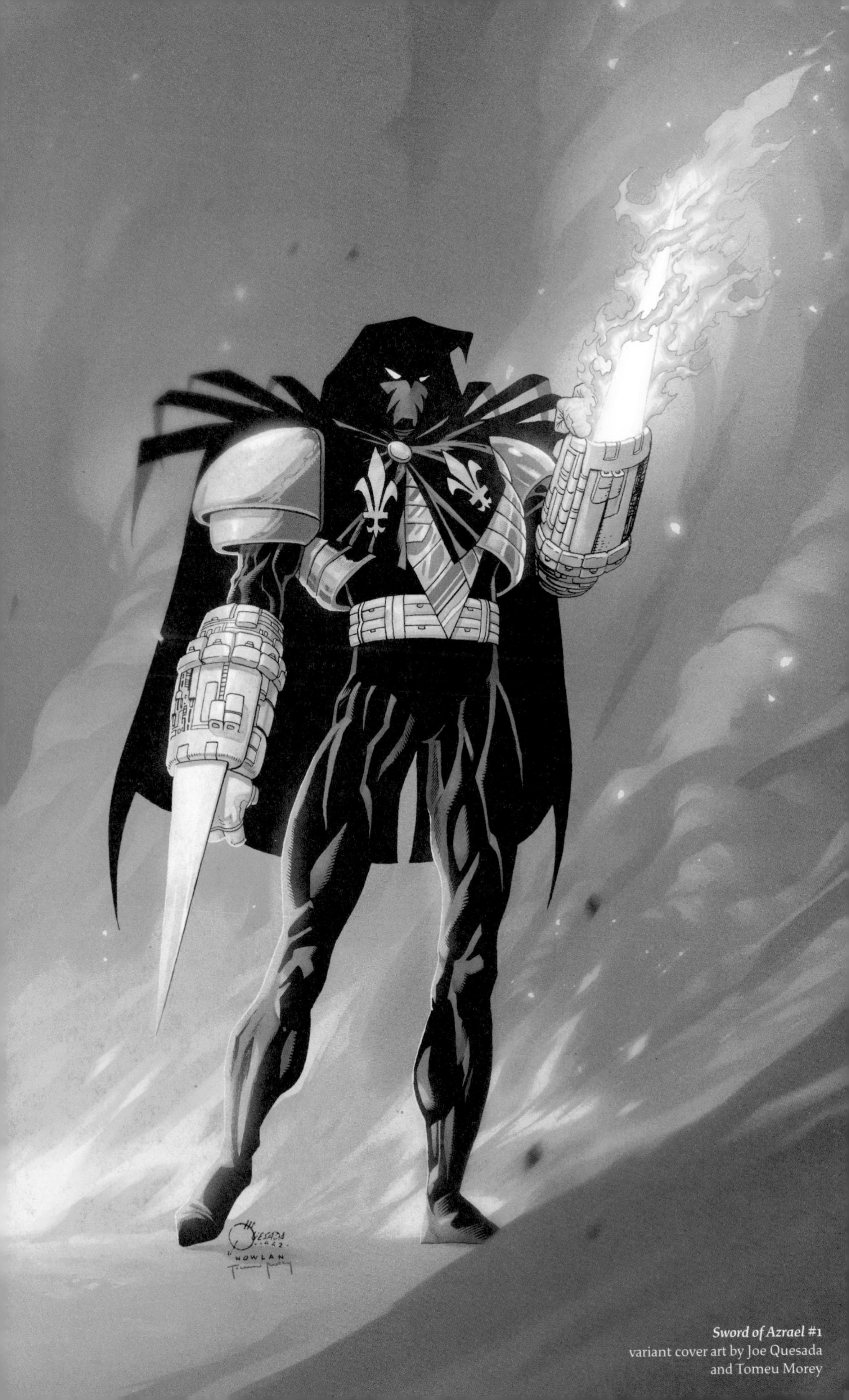

Sword of Azrael #1
variant cover art by Joe Quesada
and Tomeu Morey

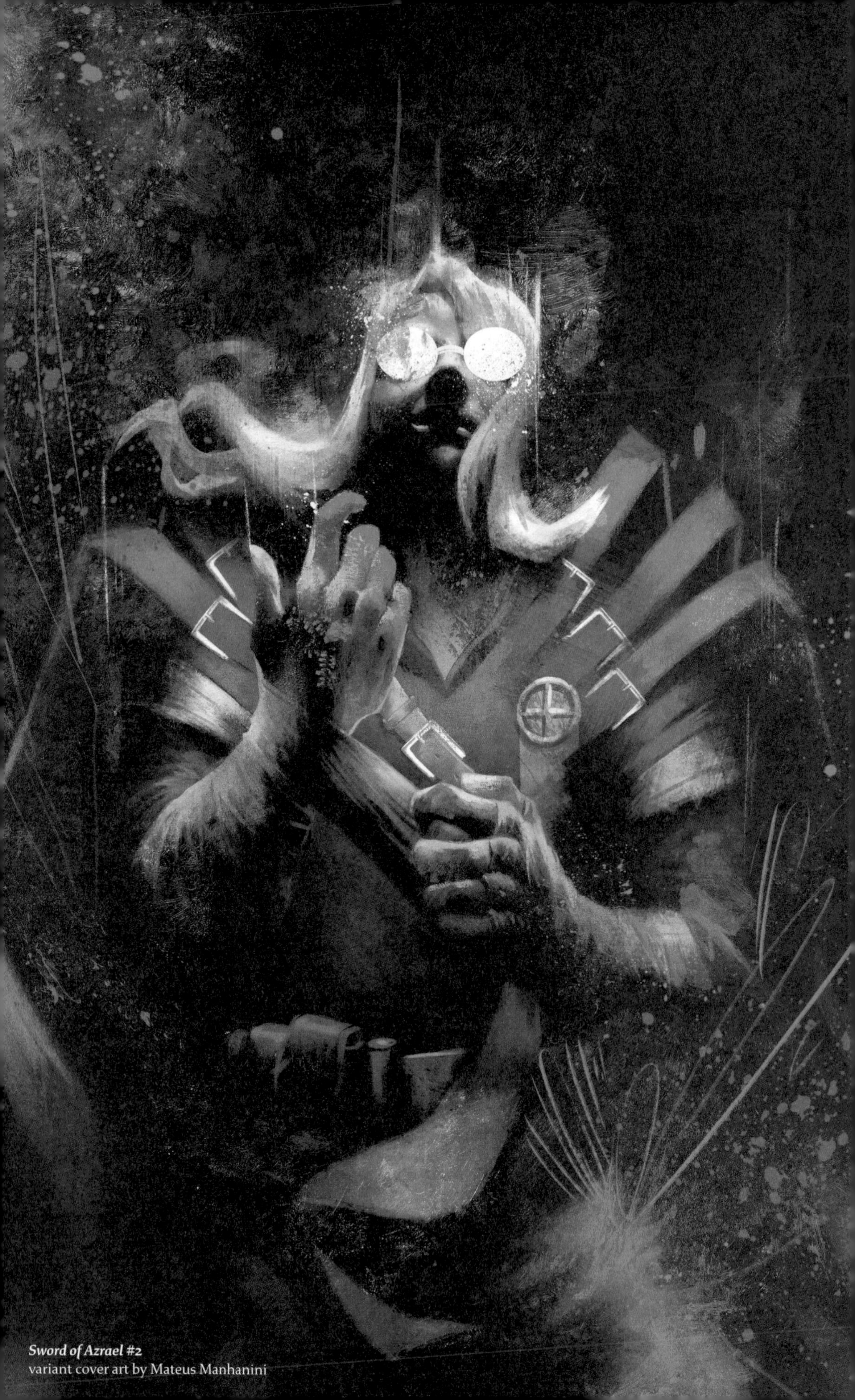

Sword of Azrael #2
variant cover art by Mateus Manhanini

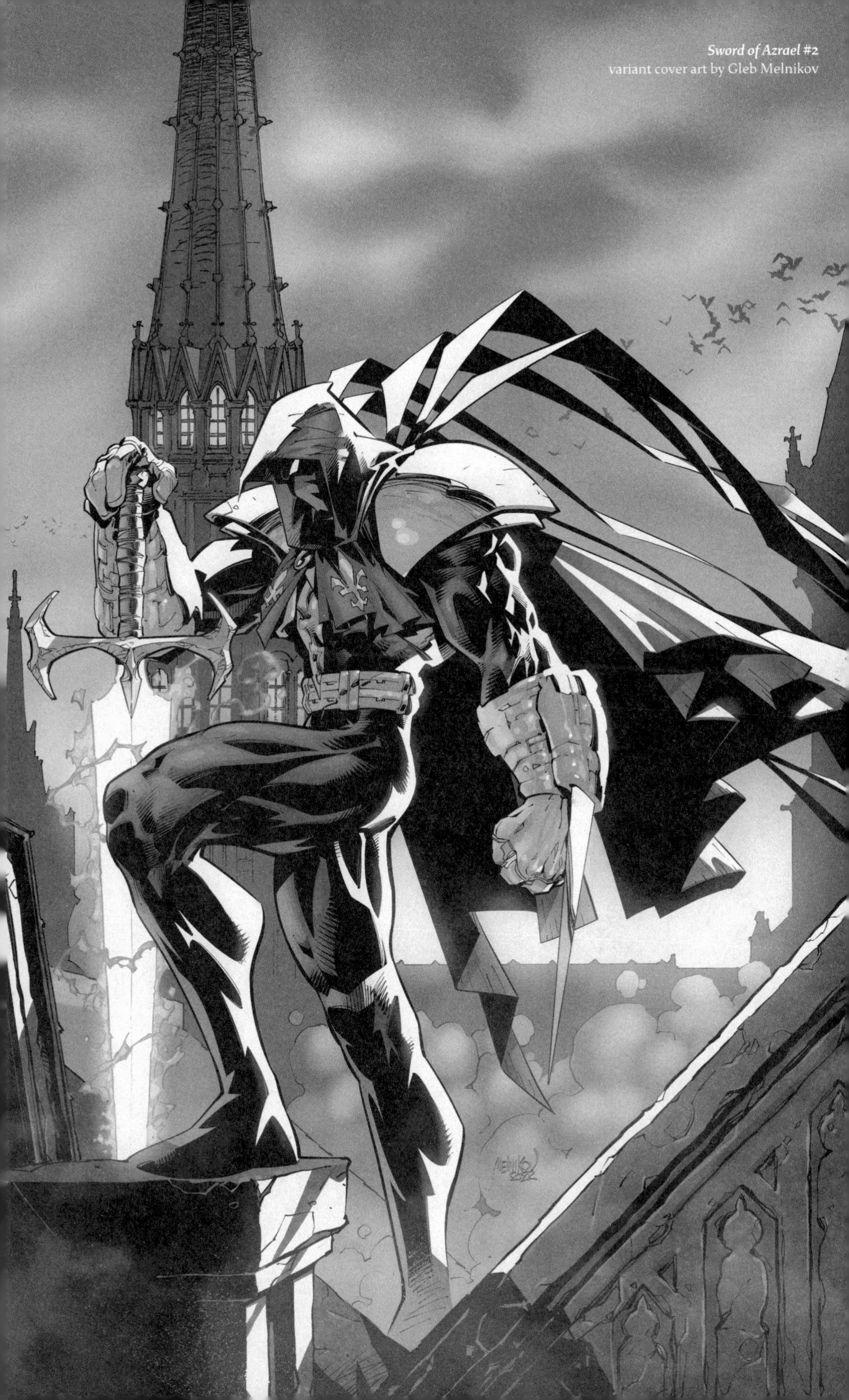

***Sword of Azrael* #2**
variant cover art by Gleb Melnikov

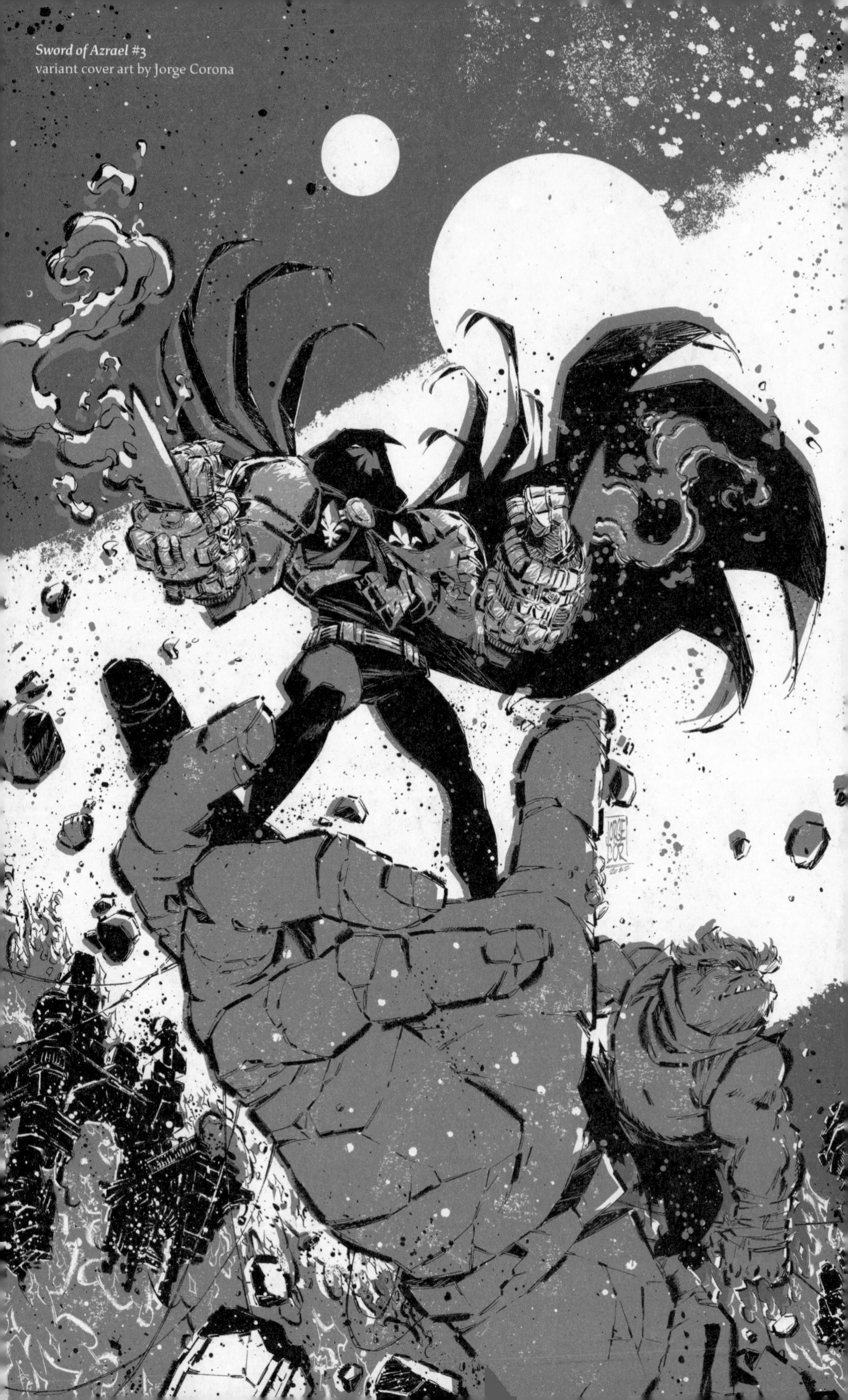

Sword of Azrael #3
variant cover art by Jorge Corona

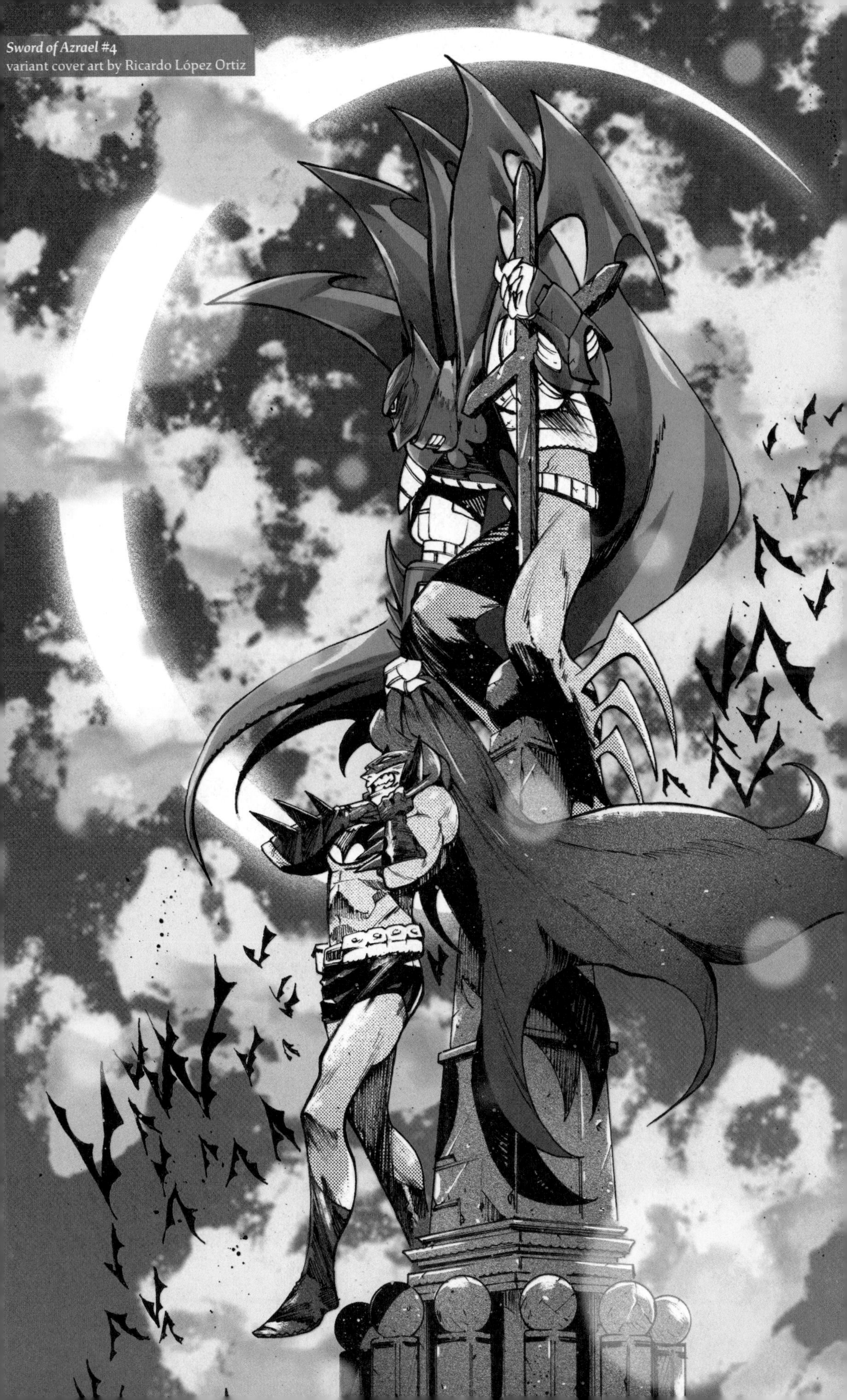

Sword of Azrael #4
variant cover art by Ricardo López Ortiz

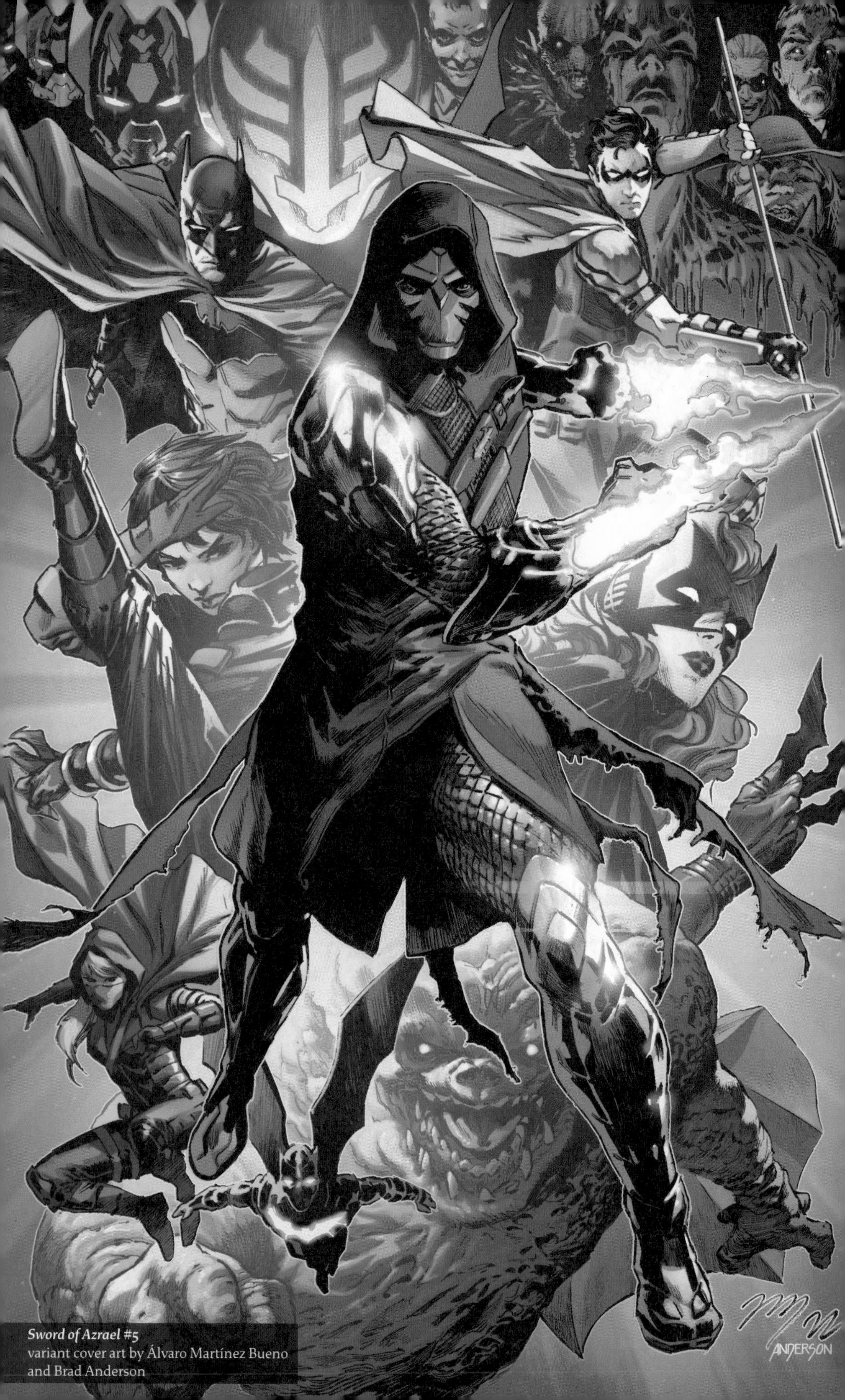
ANDERSON

Sword of Azrael #5
variant cover art by Álvaro Martínez Bueno
and Brad Anderson

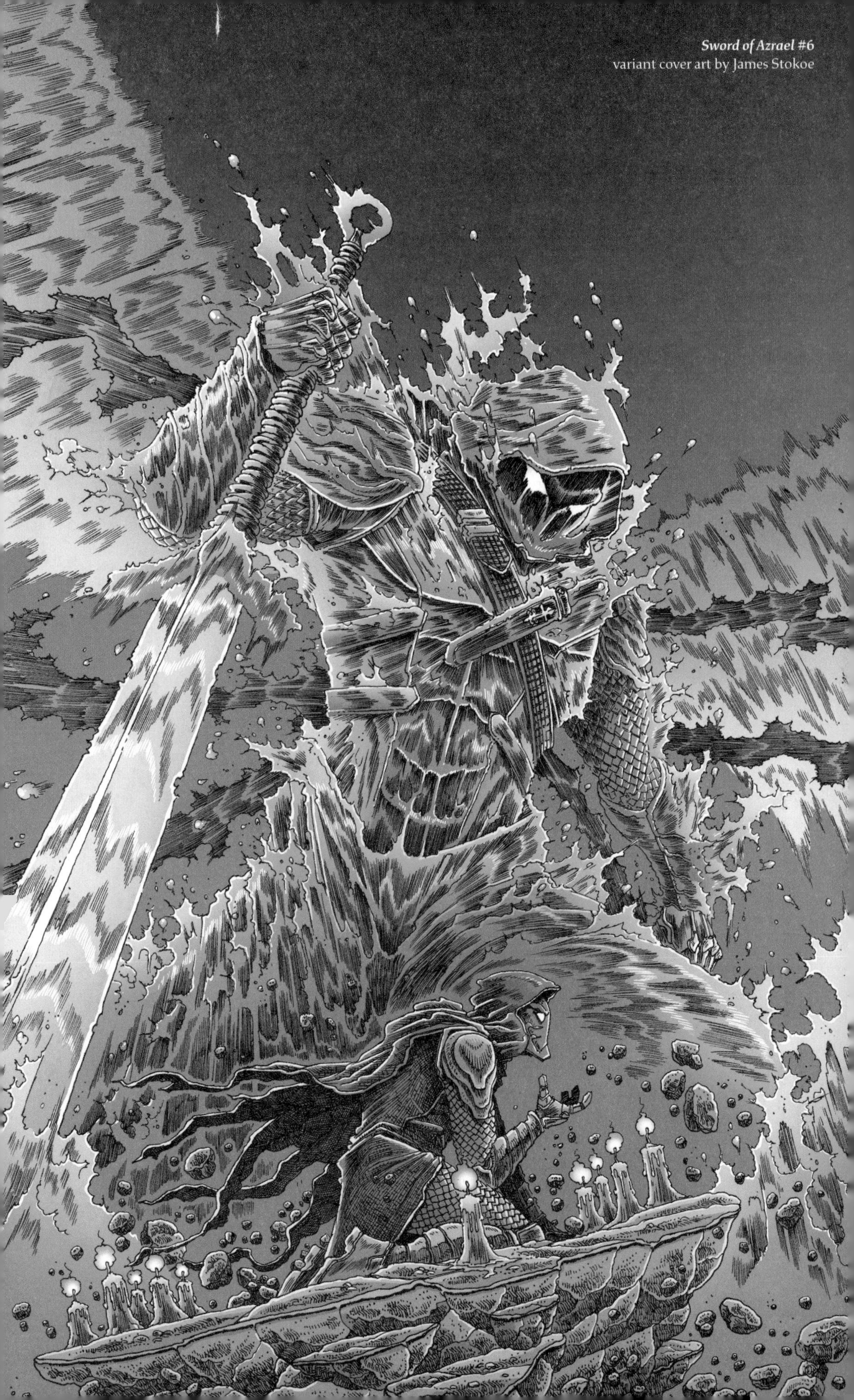

***Sword of Azrael* #6**
variant cover art by James Stokoe

Sword of Azrael Designs by Nikola Čižmešija

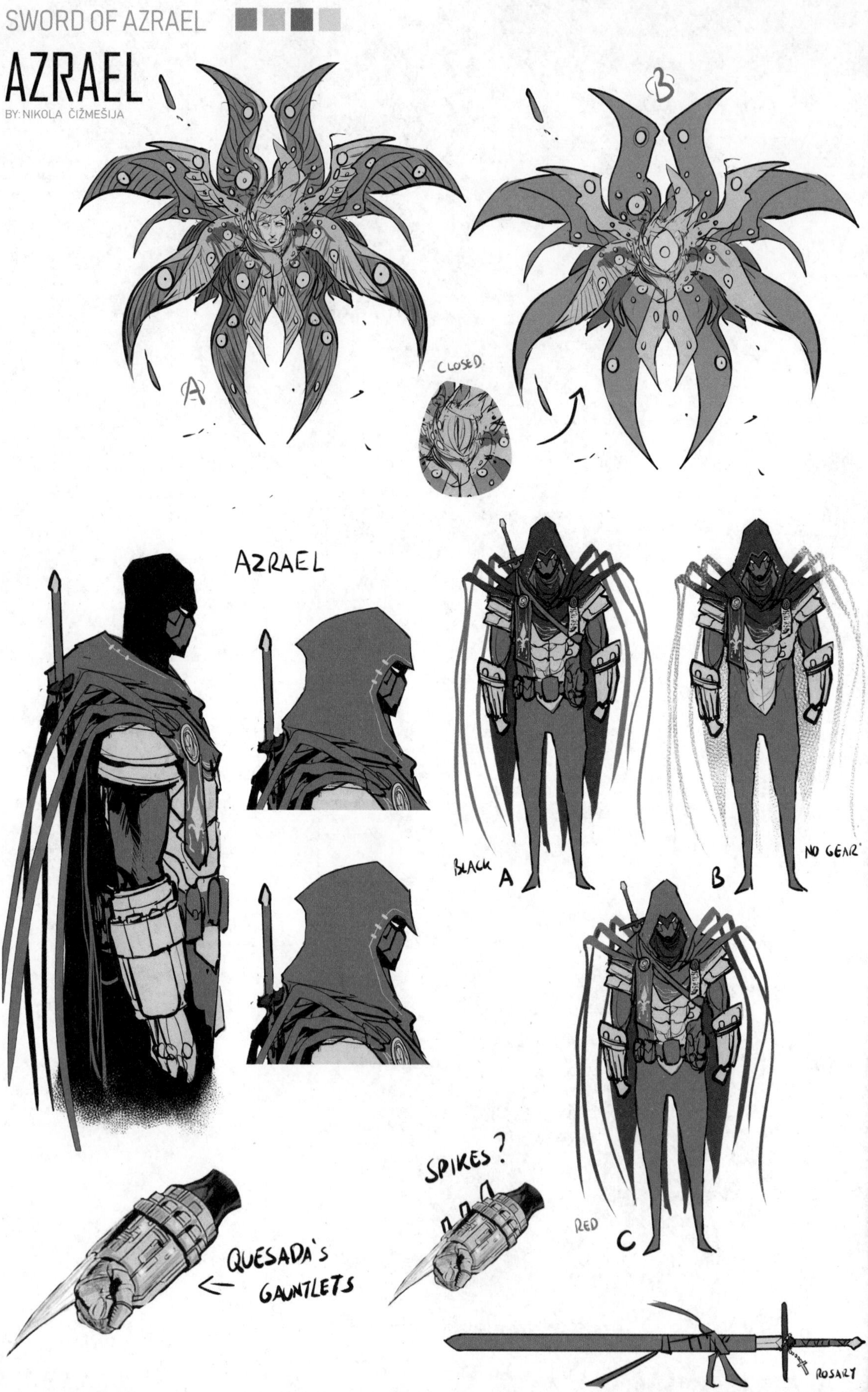
SWORD OF AZRAEL
AZRAEL
BY: NIKOLA ČIŽMEŠIJA
A
B
CLOSED
AZRAEL
BLACK
A
B
NO GEAR
RED
C
SPIKES?
QUESADA's
GAUNTLETS
ROSARY